Asia East by South

A series published under the auspices of
the Southeast Asia Program, Cornell University

Southeast Asia in the Early Modern Era: Trade, Power, and Belief
   edited by Anthony Reid

The papers in this volume grew out of a conference sponsored by the Joint Committee on Southeast Asia of the Social Science Research Council and the American Council of Learned Societies.

Southeast Asia in the Early Modern Era

Trade, Power, and Belief

Edited by ANTHONY REID

CORNELL UNIVERSITY PRESS

Ithaca and London

First published 1993 by Cornell University Press.
First printing, Cornell Paperbacks, 1993.

International Standard Book Number 0-8014-2848-3 (cloth)
International Standard Book Number 0-8014-8093-0 (paper)
Library of Congress Catalog Card Number 92-54969

Printed in the United States of America

Librarians: Library of Congress cataloging information appears on the last page of the book.

♾The paper in this book meets the minimum requirements of the American National Standard for Information Sciences—Permanence of Paper for Printed Library Materials, ANSI Z39.48-1984.

Cloth printing   10   9   8   7   6   5   4   3   2   1

Paperback printing   10   9   8   7   6   5   4   3   2

This book is gratefully dedicated to

JOHN SMAIL

Contents

Illustrations and Maps

MAPS

Preface

This volume arose from the sense that the period from the fifteenth century to the eighteenth was one of intense change in Southeast Asia, the implications of which for the region as a whole have not been understood. Having worked to free the period from the role assigned it earlier, as a precursor of European imperialism (D. G. E. Hall's "earlier phase of European expansion"), historians have not known what to do with it. The great debate about Indianization provided a focus for the preceding period, which had animated several important books.[1] In the most recent two centuries, sources become more accessible and common themes of imperialism and nationalism easy to discern. The early modern era seemed a period of awkward transition and divergent tendencies, yet it demanded attention as the source of many of the states, faiths, and preoccupations that have dominated the modern period.

The region is diverse in language, culture, and historiographic tradition, so common themes are difficult for a single scholar to disentangle. The Joint Committee on Southeast Asia of the Social Science Research Council and the American Council of Learned Societies therefore resolved to organize a conference that would bring together a variety of specialists. A key figure in this decision was John Smail, always keenly interested in the structure of Southeast Asian history, and then chairman of the Joint Committee. With his cooperation, a call to a conference went out in 1987. John was subsequently obliged by illness to

---

[1]The most recent, *Southeast Asia in the 9th to 14th Centuries*, ed. David Marr and A. C. Milner (Singapore, 1986), shared a common parentage with this volume as an SSRC/ACLS initiative.

retire, and this book is offered to him in gratitude not only for his role in starting this enterprise but also for a life as teacher and guide.

Through the good offices of Luis Filipe Thomaz, the Institute for Overseas History of the New University of Lisbon agreed to host a conference at Belem in Lisbon on 4–7 December 1989. We are most grateful to Professor Thomaz, to the local committee under Maria Fernanda Correia, and to the Fondação Oriente for making this most stimulating conference possible.

Several scholars contributed to the success of that conference in addition to those represented in this volume. We thank Leonard Blussé, Vicente Rafael, Jorge Alvez, Maria de Conceicão Flores, and M. João Figueiroa Rego for the stimulus they provided. Mme Dang Bich Ha also contributed a paper but was at the last minute prevented by communications difficulties from attending.

In Canberra, Kristine Alilunas-Rodgers has had the primary burden of editing the papers to a uniform and satisfactory format. The fact that it has been possible to have this book published in reasonable time is chiefly to her credit. Keith Mitchell and his colleagues at the Australian National University Cartography Unit drew the maps.

ANTHONY REID

Canberra, Australia

Abbreviations

ANTT	Arquivo Nacional da Torre do Tombo
BKI	*Bijdragen tot de Taal-, Land-, en Volkenkunde van de Koninklijk Instituut*
JAAS	*Journal of Asian and African Studies*
JAH	*Journal of Asian History*
JAS	*Journal of Asian Studies*
JBRS	*Journal of the Burma Research Society*
JESHO	*Journal of the Economic and Social History of the Orient*
JMBRAS	*Journal of the Malayan Branch of the Royal Asiatic Society*
JRAS	*Journal of the Royal Asiatic Society*
JSEAH	*Journal of Southeast Asian History*
JSEAS	*Journal of Southeast Asian Studies*
JSS	*Journal of the Siam Society*
MAS	*Modern Asian Studies*
PQCS	*Philippine Quarterly of Culture and Society*
RUL	Rangoon University Library
VKI	*Verhandelingen van de Koninklijk Instituut voor Taal-, Land-, en Volkenkunde*
VOC	Vereenigde Oost-Indische Compagnie. When used in references, this refers to VOC records held in the Koloniaal Archief of the Algemene Rijksarchief, The Hague.

*Southeast Asia
in the Early
Modern Era*

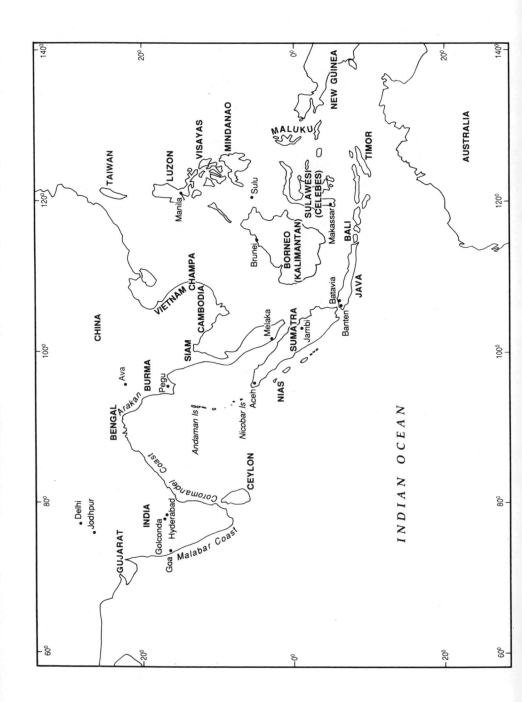

Introduction: A Time and a Place

Anthony Reid

The early modern period is increasingly recognized as a watershed in human history. For the first time the world was physically united by the opening of direct trade routes between Europe and every other corner of the globe. Yet at least by the second half of the seventeenth century, it is now clear, northwestern Europe and Japan parted company with the other Eurasian civilizations to pursue their capitalist transformations. The relations between the countries of Europe's Atlantic seaboard and the rest of the world became ever more weighted with inequality, not only in military effectiveness (the first sign to appear), but in productivity, technology, scientific method, and eventually self-esteem.

Whereas Europe's "miracle" is difficult to disentangle from its military and economic domination of more populous quarters of the world, Japan followed a very different route. Isolating itself from all foreign contact save that provided by tightly controlled Dutch and Chinese trade at Nagasaki, the Tokugawa shogunate unified the country, banned the use of firearms, and developed a flourishing urban economy that laid the basis for Japan's twentieth-century rise. By holding its population constant while substantially increasing productivity and welfare, Japan achieved economic advances in the seventeenth and eighteenth centuries which matched those of the most advanced European countries.[1]

---

[1]Thomas C. Smith, *Native Sources of Japanese Industrialization, 1750–1920* (Berkeley, Calif., 1988), pp. 15–49. Akira Hayami and Yoshiro Tsubouchi, eds., *Economic and Demographic Development in Rice Growing Societies: Some Aspects of East Asian Economic History (1500–1900)*. Proceedings, Tenth International Economic History Conference (Leuven, 1990), pp. 1–5.

The Japanese case in particular and the globalization of the issues in general by many of the most influential modern historians (Fernand Braudel, Carlo Cipolla, Geoffrey Parker, Immanuel Wallerstein, Barrington Moore) have made it clear that the early modern period is critical for every part of the world. If the capitalist "miracle" was not limited to Europe, then each case needs to be studied with care to examine what happened and why. We can no longer think in simplistic terms of winners and losers, of capitalist Europe and a third world doomed to stagnation and poverty; rather, we must examine a variety of ways of coping with the explosive forces at work during the period.

Japan belatedly forced itself on the attention of economic historians by its spectacular twentieth-century performance, undermining attempts to identify unique sociocultural features of Europe which made capitalism possible. Although Japan was the first Asian country to complete the transition to industrial capitalism, it is certainly not the last. Southeast Asian economies too, led by Singapore, Malaysia, and Thailand, have recently grown as rapidly as any known to history. There too economic confidence gives rise to intellectual confidence. Instead of the question what was wrong with Asian cultures, frequently asked only a few decades ago, attention is now directed to what is right about them. Neither question is helpful, but it is no longer possible to assume that the place of Asia was ordained by environment or culture to be part of a static or declining third world.

In the extraordinary period between the fifteenth and seventeenth centuries, Southeast Asia played a critical role. As a maritime region athwart vital trade routes it was immediately and profoundly influenced by the global commercial expansion of the "long sixteenth century" (so called because its features began to appear in the fifteenth century and collapsed in the early seventeenth). It was the region most affected by the explosion of Chinese maritime activity at the beginning of the fifteenth century and the source of the spices and much of the pepper that drew the Spanish to America and eventually the Philippines and the Portuguese to India and Southeast Asia. Some of the elements that formed part of a capitalist transition elsewhere—the quickening of commerce, the monetization of transactions, the growth of cities, the accumulation of capital, and the specialization of function—can also be observed in Southeast Asia during this period. The changes in belief and cultural systems were even more profound. Islam and Christianity became the dominant religions of the Island world and pockets of the Mainland, while Buddhism was transformed by its alliance with centralizing states in Burma, Siam, Laos, and Cambodia.

At the same time, no part of Asia suffered more quickly or profoundly the effects of European intrusion. Through warfare, impregnable fortifications, and monopoly commerce, Europeans had by 1650 gained control of the vital ports and products that had previously linked the region to the expanding world economy. Although they remained only peripheral players in the ongoing life of the region, they had changed the delicate balance between commerce and kingship. Like Japan, and even more abruptly, Southeast Asian countries all discovered the negative side of the expansion of global commerce and the rapid advance of military technology. Unlike Japan, they were unable to insulate themselves from it without fundamental change to their political systems.

A Place

As a region, Southeast Asia is crucial to the resolution of the dilemmas of early modern history. But is it a region at all? Unlike Western Europe, India, the Arab world, China, or even "sinicized" eastern Asia as a whole, it has no common high religion, language, or classical culture (except those it loosely shares with India) and has never been part of a single polity. Its very name is an externally imposed geographic convenience, which has only recently replaced even less satisfactory terms such as Further India or Indo-China.

Yet those who travel to Southeast Asia, from China, India, or anywhere else know at once that they are in a different place. In part this is a matter of environment. Physically marked by its warm climate, high and dependable rainfall, and ubiquitous waterways, Southeast Asia developed lifestyles dominated by the forest, the rice-growing river valleys, and fishing. Its people grew the same crops by the same methods, ate the same food in the same manner, and lived in similar houses elevated on poles against the perils of flood or forest animals. Its geography militated against unified empires arising from great rivers or vast plains. It generated instead a multiplicity of political forms interlinked by the ease of waterborne transport.

Paradoxically, the diversity of Southeast Asia and its openness to outside influences were among its defining characteristics. Every state in the region was built on cultural trade-offs both internal and external. Overall population density was low, probably averaging no more than six inhabitants per square kilometer in the seventeenth century. Pockets of dense settlement around trading cities and permanent rice fields were surrounded by forests thinly peopled by shifting cultivators. This

Map 2. Political centers in Southeast Asia

sort of distribution created a fundamental dualism of hill and valley, upstream and downstream, interior and coast. In coastal waters boat-dwelling sea nomads had similar relations with rulers ashore. No state incorporated such dependents fully; they remained a stateless penumbra of the state, often indispensable providers of forest or sea products, messengers, warriors and slaves—tributary but distinct, and perceived as uncivilized but also as free.

Despite their dependence on such hinterland peoples, rulers were more preoccupied by their relations with rival powers controlling other rivers and ports. Even if the stronger rulers claimed through their titles and the architecture of their capitals to be *cakravartin*, world rulers embodying on earth the Indic gods in heaven, they were all intensely conscious of inhabiting a pluralistic world. Political life was an endless struggle for people, for trade and for status between rival centers. The exchanging of envoys and letters was one of the finer political arts, and words and gestures were studied for the slightest hint of superiority or inferiority. Success in this competitive world was measured by the number of ships in the harbor; of men, boats, and elephants in royal processions; of tributaries from nearby and equals from afar who paid their respects to the king.

Between about 1400 and 1700, universalist faiths based on sacred scripture took hold throughout the region. Eventually they created profound divisions between an Islamic arc in the south, a Confucian political orthodoxy in Vietnam, a Theravada Buddhist bastion in the rest of the Mainland, and a Christian outrider in the Philippines. Yet even in the process of religious change there was a common openness to outside ideas, a common need for allies from farther afield to help subordinate rivals closer to hand.

Probably crucial to the perception of Southeast Asia as a region was the fact that the barriers of sea and mountain separating it from China and India were more significant than any internal boundaries. The majority of outsiders who came to the region did so by means of long sea voyages. Malay-speakers (who in this period included maritime traders of every ethnolinguistic group) identified their region as "below the winds," in distinction to the world of outsiders (especially Indians, Arabs, and Europeans) who came from "above the winds" by taking advantage of the prevailing Indian Ocean monsoon. For the Chinese and Japanese, Southeast Asia was the "south seas," also reached by sea. Even adoption of outside faiths did not eliminate the distinctiveness of a region uniquely defined by nature. The mountain barriers across the north of the region, and the sea elsewhere, ensured that, while Southeast Asians were endlessly involved in exchanges of territory, people, and ideas with each other, invasions were few and migrations gradual from the rest of the Asian landmass.

Vietnam's relation with China might appear to give the lie to this generalization. Ruled by the Middle Kingdom for most of the first Christian millennium, Vietnam acquired its writing system and consequently much of its literary culture from China. Yet alone of the southern regions conquered by the Han and T'ang dynasties, the people of the Red River delta retained a sufficiently distinct identity to claim their independence in 939 and reclaim it after each subsequent Chinese invasion. The last serious invasion was that of the Ming, who reoccupied Vietnam from 1407 to 1428 but were driven out by Le Loi, founder of the most brilliant of Vietnamese dynasties. Under the Le rulers, Vietnamese political institutions were rebuilt in a more Confucian mold than ever, but the resulting centralized mandarinate was used to ensure that Vietnam remained permanently independent of China.

Vietnam thus became a barrier to any further Chinese southward expansion by land. Although the hills forming its northern border were by no means impassable, they were sufficient to serve as a stable frontier for a thousand years. By contrast, Vietnam's southern border was constantly changing, as Vietnamese armies had the better of their ceaseless wars first with Champa and later with Cambodia. It is therefore impossible to draw a line around early modern Southeast Asia which excludes Vietnam. Despite its cultural and commercial links with China, Vietnam was Southeast Asian. Particularly so was the southern Vietnamese kingdom established by Nguyen Hoang on former Cham territory. Not only through its intermingling of Vietnamese and Austronesian (Chamic) peoples, but also through its physical environment, its place in Asian trade, and the timing of its rise to prominence, this kingdom was characteristic of early modern Southeast Asia. It is therefore appropriate that this volume represent some of the scholarly attention at last being paid to this kingdom.

A Time

For the generation of Southeast Asianists represented in this volume, it goes without saying that Southeast Asia is at the center of their story, and they therefore seek to develop categories of analysis that make sense there rather than in Europe or somewhere else. The fact that no essays are included specifically on the roles of Europeans or Chinese, despite their profound effects on the economic history of the region, might be held to suggest that we have not yet escaped the period of reaction against the Europocentric excesses of a previous generation.

Nevertheless "early modern" is yet another periodization imposed on Southeast Asia by outsiders. Even they have only recently begun to apply the term to the region, and it would be unfamiliar to all but a few insiders.[2] It functions here as a link between regional history and global history. As against such older terms as Renaissance, Reformation, or Age of Discovery, it has the advantage of being less culture bound to a European schema, less laden with triumphalist values.[3] Its implication that this period sees the emergence of the forces that would shape the modern world is plausible for Southeast Asia, provided that modernity is understood in a broad and pluralistic sense.

Periodization itself is by no means a recent or Western idea. At least for the political and religious elite who composed texts and inscriptions, the rise and fall of dynasties has long been a familiar theme in Asia. Chronicles were typically written to add to the legitimacy of a new dynasty by demonstrating both continuity and discontinuity with its predecessor. Continuity was necessary to associate the new regime with remembered past grandeur, through a genealogical link in most cases but also through the possession of the historic citadel (in Vietnam and Laos), of the regalia (in the Malay Archipelago), or of a sacred image (in the Theravada states).

But new dynasties and their chroniclers also sought to distance themselves from past failures by emphasizing that a new period had begun. Typically an auspicious site was carefully chosen for a new capital. Vietnam is the exception, changing dynasties relatively frequently but maintaining its capital at Hanoi. In Siam, dynasties were relatively stable, and modern history records only two major capitals and dynasties—Ayutthaya in 1351–1767 (punctuated by the Burmese conquest of 1569) and Bangkok from 1782, with the one-reign Thonburi period in between. In Java and Burma capitals changed even more frequently than dynasties as kings sought more auspicious locations after each setback.

It has been argued for these two culture areas in particular that a

[2]The first use of which I am aware is a University of Michigan dissertation by James Pfister in 1972 ("Compulsions to Engage in War . . . in an Early Modern Period of Mainland Southeast Asian History"), referring to 1500–39. More recently, Victor Lieberman has taken it up: "Wallerstein's System and the International Context of Early Modern Southeast Asian History," *JAH* 24 (1990), 70–90.

[3]The Center for Early Modern History at the University of Minnesota makes the point that comparative study is particularly fruitful in this period and that "early modern history requires equal attention to very different cultures as they come into contact with each other."

"law of impermanence" created a cyclical interaction of creation and destruction, of concentration and diffusion of power.[4] The evil deeds of the king, prophecies, astrological conjunctions, and (in Java) the turning of a century in the Javanese era foreordained that a dynasty would lose its legitimacy as a link between the supernatural and the natural. The regime collapsed into disorder, and a new conquering king was needed.

Interacting with this cyclical pattern of dynasties were other types of periodization. Both Islam and Buddhism introduced a sacred history of much greater length than the dynastic cycle. At one level men lived in the interval between divine revelation and messianic deliverance. In the Theravada case the Buddhist religion would last five thousand years, but after eighty thousand another Buddha, Metteya, would commence a new religion. This was not necessarily an upward progression; indeed, inexorable decay of human devotion and morality was more marked a theme, particularly as the moment of ultimate deliverance approached.[5] On a more immediate level, these religions were known to have arrived relatively recently and to have increased in influence and splendor through the pious acts of rulers and saints. Temples, shrines, and mosques were often dated precisely as markers of this progression. Many religious narratives, therefore, did in practice assume a linear quality.

Finally, the rapid technological and economic change that marked the sixteenth and seventeenth centuries may have added a further pattern closer in character to a "modern" linear view of history. At least one seventeenth-century chronicle, the history of Goa, identified each reign of the ruling house of Makassar not only with battles and royal marriages but also with the innovations in technology and statecraft that marked it.[6] The two seventeenth-century chronicle traditions of Siam, van Vliet and Luang Prasoet, also have some of this sense of linear progress.[7] Such developments at the height of the early modern

---

[4]Victor Lieberman, *Burmese Administrative Cycles: Anarchy and Conquest, c. 1580–1760* (Princeton, N.J., 1984), pp. 3–5; M. C. Ricklefs, *Jogjakarta under Sultan Mangkubumi, 1749–1792: A History of the Division of Java* (London, 1974), pp. 176–90; S. Supomo, "The Image of Majapahit in Later Javanese and Indonesian Writing," in *Perceptions of the Past in Southeast Asia*, ed. Anthony Reid and David Marr (Singapore, 1979), pp. 174–77; Benedict Anderson, "A Time of Darkness and a Time of Light," in ibid., p. 231.

[5]Charnvit Kasetsiri, "Thai Historiography from Ancient Times to the Modern Period," in ibid., pp. 156–58; Michael Aung-Thwin, *Pagan: The Origins of Modern Burma* (Honolulu, 1985), pp. 40–43.

[6]*Sedjarah Goa*, ed. G. J. Wolhoff and Abdurrahim (Makassar, n.d.), e.g., pp. 49–51, 55, 64, 69.

[7]English translations are Jeremias van Vliet, *The Short History of the Kings of Siam*, trans. (from Dutch) Leonard Andaya, ed. David Wyatt (Bangkok, 1975), esp. pp. 68–69, 77–78, 88–89; O. Frankfurter, trans., "Events in Ayudhya from Chulasakaraj 686–966," *JSS* 6, no. 3 (1909), esp. 8, 11, 18.

period impose a need for great caution in delineating a "traditional" mode of historical discourse on the basis of eighteenth- and nineteenth-century chronicles.

Along with the dominance of nationalist perspectives in the twentieth century came the modern notion that history ought to be periodized in relation to the dominant features of each age. Each nationalism has had its own categories. In general, those historians who claimed continuity with specific precolonial states (Vietnam, Thailand, Burma, Cambodia, and to some extent Malaysia) tended to maintain a periodization in dynastic terms while debating how this might interact with Marxist categories. Indonesians and Filipinos did not have this option. Despite their desire to stand colonial historiography on its head, the early nationalist historians tended to replicate its categories, with the arrival of the Europeans soon after 1500, the beginning of systematic colonialism around 1800, and its end in 1945 being their major turning points. Teodoro Agoncillo in the Philippines or Tan Malaka in Indonesia might have considered the colonial period "a lost history," but they did not develop an alternative periodization.[8]

More recently, however, there has been a tendency to see the period that is the subject of this book as having its own logic apart from the advent of Europeans. The third of a six-volume national history of Indonesia is devoted to "the period of the rise and development of Islamic states in Indonesia" and covers roughly 1500–1700, though going well back into the fifteenth century.[9] The doyen of contemporary Indonesian historians, Sartono Kartodirdjo, though beginning his "modern history" in 1500, also treats the European factor as only one among many contending forces until the nineteenth century.[10]

Before leaving the question of indigenous perceptions of period, we should note the tendency within particular ethnolinguistic traditions to locate a kind of "golden age" in the early modern period, before the slow decline into colonial domination. This is particularly the case for Malays, Acehnese, Makassarese, Balinese,[11] and Laotians, whose great states all reached their political peak between 1470 and 1650. Though the record is more mixed for the larger states, there is an understandable fascination with the brief pinnacles of personal power achieved in

[8]Teodoro Agoncillo and Oscar Alfonso, *A Short History of the Filipino People* (Manila, 1960), p. iii. Tan Malaka as cited in R. Moh. Ali, *Pengantar Ilmu Sedjarah Indonesia* (Jakarta, 1953), p. 145.

[9]Uka Tjandrasasmita, ed., *Jaman Pertumbuhan dan Perkembangan Kerajaan-Kerajaan Islam di Indonesia*, vol. 3 of *Sejarah Nasional Indonesia* (Jakarta, 1977).

[10]Sartono Kartodirdjo, *Pengantar Sejarah Indonesia Baru, 1500–1900: Dari Emporium Sampai Imperium* (Jakarta, 1987).

[11]Most recently, Ide Anak Agung Gde Agung, *Bali in the Nineteenth Century* (Jakarta, 1991), p. 6.

Burma by Bayin-naung (r. 1551–81), in Java by Sultan Agung (r. 1613–46), and in Siam by Narai (r. 1656–88).

This volume grew out of a conviction that the early modern period marks a watershed for Southeast Asia in various respects yet has remained curiously blurred in the historiography. Agreement was less easy to reach on the boundaries or dominant features of the period, or whether it is helpful to attempt to delineate them for a whole diverse region. Nevertheless, the reader is entitled to some explanation of what we mean by "early modern."

All those who use the term include in it the sixteenth and seventeenth centuries, with more or less extension backward into the fifteenth and forward into the eighteenth.[12] Two contributors to this collection debate whether the seventeenth century marks a major break that might constitute the end of a period, but none discusses its beginning. The reader may be inclined to infer from the overwhelming focus on the sixteenth and seventeenth centuries that European intervention did indeed inaugurate the early modern era in Southeast Asia. Only in one respect can this be accepted without qualification: the sources available to the historian change in nature and increase greatly in quantity with the opening of the sixteenth century. The Portuguese and still more their successors, the Spanish and Dutch, chronicled and described Southeast Asia in far greater detail than the Arabs and Chinese before them. The bronze plate inscriptions that had been the major indigenous sources were already becoming scarce in the fourteenth century. They were replaced by royal and religious chronicles, poetry, and edifying texts written on ephemeral materials, increasingly paper. Virtually no such texts have survived from before 1500. The earliest surviving substantial works are copies from the eighteenth and nineteenth centuries, with only a handful of sixteenth- and seventeenth-century texts preserved by chance in European libraries.

When we look with care at the factors critical to the early modern era in Southeast Asia, however, most of them begin before the arrival of European fleets. I review these factors below under four heads: a commercial upturn; new military technology; the growth of new, more centralized states; and the spread of externally validated scriptural orthodoxies in religion. Though the essays of Leonard Andaya and Luis Filipe Thomaz show how sixteenth-century materials can be read to reconstruct the fifteenth, it must be admitted that the evidence available to document these trends before 1500 remains unsatisfactory. I

[12]The University of Minnesota Center for Early Modern History definition is more expansive, taking in 1350 to 1750.

have argued elsewhere that 1400 is a more satisfactory beginning for this critical period of change than 1500, but the fragmentary nature of the evidence makes any such precision highly problematic.[13]

Commercial Upturn

The determination of the Portuguese and Spanish to find the sources of pepper, clove, and nutmeg was a consequence of the growing importance of these spices in European life. In the 1390s about six metric tons of cloves and one and a half of nutmeg reached Europe each year from Maluku in eastern Indonesia. A century later, 52 tons of cloves and 26 of nutmeg arrived. The spices were carried across the Indian Ocean by Muslim traders of various nationalities to markets in Egypt and Beirut, where they were purchased by Italian merchants, predominantly Venetians. This was only a small branch of Southeast Asia's trade, and its rapid expansion in the fifteenth century was probably replicated elsewhere. The fifteenth century was a time of expansion in population and international commerce not only in the Mediterranean but also in Southeast Asia's largest external market, China. The reign of the second Ming emperor, Yung Lo (r. 1403–24), was a period of exceptional Chinese involvement with the region, which appears to have stimulated the pepper and clove trade, increased the circulation of silver and other metals, and given rise to several new port cities.

Whereas the economic history of the fifteenth century must remain speculative, the subsequent rise in Southeast Asian commercial activity to a peak in the early seventeenth century is clearer. England and Holland joined the Chinese, Japanese, Spanish, Portuguese, and Indians in competing to buy the products of the region—pepper, cloves, nutmeg, cinnamon, sandalwood, lacquer, silk, and deer hides. Prices were kept high by a massive inflow of silver from Japan and the New World. Indian cloth of all kinds was imported to the region in exchange for these exports. The evidence suggests that both the silver influx and imports of Indian cloth were at a peak from 1600 to 1640 which was not again reached until the eighteenth century.[14]

This international competition narrowed to a few players in the second half of the seventeenth century. The Japanese withdrew by Tokugawa decree in 1635; the Gujaratis, Arabs, and Persians found the European pressure too great; the Portuguese lost their stronghold of

---

[13]Anthony Reid, "An 'Age of Commerce' in Southeast Asia," *MAS* 24, no. 1 (1990), 5–6.
[14]Ibid., pp. 4–21.

Melaka to the Dutch in 1641. The Dutch East India Company (VOC) established a monopoly of nutmeg in 1621 and one of cloves during the 1650s. Some degree of competition remained in other products, but the VOC's ability to dominate Southeast Asian supplies made these exports, too, less attractive in world markets. In her essay, Barbara Andaya explains the effects on Jambi of falling international pepper prices, and similar observations could be made for much of Southeast Asia.

New products were exported from Southeast Asia in the eighteenth century on a larger scale than ever before—notably sugar, coffee, and tobacco. These, however, were plantation crops largely managed by Europeans and Chinese. The now dominant Dutch and English companies found opium more suitable than Indian cloth as an import to Southeast Asia, since they could monopolize supply and reap enormous profits.

In this volume, Thomaz describes the state that was the most spectacular creation of the fifteenth-century commercial upturn. Melaka, as he says, "existed there because of trade, not trade because of the state." Pierre-Yves Manguin draws attention to the 500-ton junks that were the prime carriers of Southeast Asian trade during this period, and whose disappearance by the third decade of the seventeenth century was one of the most striking indicators of indigenous withdrawal from long-distance commerce.

New Military Techniques

Advances in technology are most quickly borrowed in the military sphere; it is a question of survival. Firearms are a case in point. Their use is documented in India and China in the fourteenth century, almost simultaneously with their first impact on European battles. Naturally, cannon and bombards also came to Southeast Asia, well ahead of Vasco da Gama. U Kala's usually reliable chronicle of Burma mentions the use of firearms by Indian soldiers in Burma from the end of the fourteenth century.[15] The presence of firearms is much better documented a century later, when the Portuguese describe, perhaps with some exaggeration, the guns they encountered in the region. They claimed to have captured 3,000 pieces of artillery in Melaka in 1511, mostly of bronze, including a huge bombard sent as a present to the sultan from the ruler of Calicut, in southern India. Many cannon were

---

[15]Victor Lieberman, "Europeans, Trade, and the Unification of Burma, c. 1540–1620," *Oriens Extremus* 27 (1980), 211.

imported by Muslim traders from India, the Middle East, and even Europe, and others of an ornate dragon type were brought in by the Chinese. Nevertheless, there were also gun founders in the city, allegedly as good as those in Germany.[16]

Although in this respect as well the beginnings of change predated 1500, the remark made by an Italian historian in the 1520s about Europe would have applied equally to Southeast Asia: "Before the year 1494, wars were protracted, battles bloodless, . . . and although artillery was already in use, it was managed with such lack of skill that it caused little hurt."[17] Hence the initial impact of the far more rapid fire the Portuguese were able to deliver in their attack on Melaka, and later Maluku, was profound.[18]

The advantage of surprise was short-lived, however. Southeast Asian states quickly devoted themselves to acquiring Portuguese-style arquebuses and cannon and the means to manufacture them. Foreign traders appeared the most adept at exploiting the new technology— notably Portuguese, Turks, Gujaratis, Japanese, and local Muslim minorities such as Chams, Malays, and "Luzons" (Muslim Tagalogs). These outsiders were bribed or forced to become artillerymen in the campaigns of the more ambitious kings of the sixteenth century, eventually forming the first professional armies of the region. Two successive Toungoo kings who unified Burma in the period 1531–81, Tabin-shwei-hti and Bayin-naung, made especially effective use of both foreign mercenaries and firearms. An Italian visitor claimed that Bayin-naung had accumulated 80,000 arquebuses and adapted them effectively for firing from elephants.[19] These military achievements undoubtedly helped create a state of unprecedented power, which at its height ruled most of present-day Burma and Thailand. To a lesser degree the same methods aided Demak in becoming dominant in Java during the reign of Sultan Trenggana (1520–51) and Aceh, Makassar, and Ayutthaya (Siam) in becoming relatively centralized powers in the early seventeenth century. Nguyen Hoang's creation of a state in central Vietnam, as ex-

[16]*The Commentaries of the Great Alfonso Dalboquerque*, trans. W. de Gray Birch, 4 vols. (London, 1875–84), 3:127–28.

[17]Francesco Guicciardini, cited in Geoffrey Parker, *The Military Revolution: Military Innovation and the Rise of the West, 1500–1800* (Cambridge, 1988), p. 10. See also Anthony Reid, *Southeast Asia in the Age of Commerce*, 2 vols. (New Haven, Conn., 1988–93), 1:121–28.

[18]"Sejarah Melayu or 'Malay Annals'," trans. C. C. Brown, *JMBRAS* 25 (1952), 167; Antonio Galvão, *A Treatise on the Moluccas (c. 1544), Probably the Preliminary Version of Antonio Galvão's Lost História das Molucas*, ed. and trans. Hubert Jacobs (Rome, 1971), p. 171; Lieberman, 1980, p. 215.

[19]"The Voyage and Travell of Master Caesar Fredericke, Marchant of Venice, into the East India," in *The Principal Navigations, Voyages, Trafiques, and Discoveries of the English Nation*, ed. Richard Hakluyt, Everyman's Library edition (London, 1907), p. 248.

plained here by Keith Taylor, also owed much to his mobilization of the new weapons.

The Archipelago states were particularly attracted to the largest possible cannon. In the late sixteenth century, Aceh gun founders, having been instructed in the 1560s by Turkish craftsmen, were manufacturing cannon bigger than European visitors had seen. Very large cannon were also being made in Manila when the Spanish took it in 1570, and Mataram and Makassar in the seventeenth century each cast a cannon more than five meters long.[20] Poorly mounted and virtually immobile, these monsters were appreciated not so much for the targets they hit as for the awe their semimagical powers inspired.

New naval technologies were also introduced in the sixteenth century. Chief among them were the fast war galleys adapted from the Mediterranean model, with both Turks and Europeans playing a role in their spread. Manguin documents in detail the scores of large galleys available to the rulers of Aceh, but this type of vessel had an even longer history in Maluku, where the *kora-kora* dominated naval warfare from the sixteenth century to the nineteenth. There appears to have been little use of firearms on shipboard prior to the European intrusion. Asian vessels adopted small cannon quickly thereafter, but naval firepower and mobility remained one area in which the Europeans retained a decisive edge.

The other such area was fortification. By introducing to Southeast Asia the new European ideas of defense behind low but thick walls surmounted by batteries of guns, with bastions projecting to provide a field of fire along the walls, the Portuguese made themselves impregnable in Melaka, Ternate, and elsewhere; the Spanish in Manila and Zamboanga; and the Dutch in Batavia, Makassar, and Maluku. During the early modern period these remained enclaves with little direct influence on their hinterlands, but they provided a permanence few indigenous dynasties could match. Local rulers responded by building forts more substantial than any traditional defense works, but these proved ultimately incapable of defending their major ports against sustained Dutch offensives.

New States

Southeast Asia was a place of "options," as Taylor argues in his essay. In such a place states rose and fell relatively frequently. The early

---

[20]Anthony Reid, *Europe and Southeast Asia: The Military Balance* (Townsville, Australia, 1982), p. 4; Denys Lombard, *Le carrefour javanais: Essai d'histoire globale*, 3 vols. (Paris, 1990), 2:179–82.

modern period witnessed the rise of many of the states that have defined Southeast Asia's modern identities, both national and ethnic. The careful studies of the rapid growth of Melaka by Thomaz, Ternate by Leonard Andaya, the Nguyen state in what is now central Vietnam by Taylor, and Jambi by Barbara Andaya enable us to see some of the especially significant factors at this time and place in history.

In all these cases the new military techniques played a part in enabling dynamic rulers to come to the top. The expansion of commerce was also a factor in every case, but in different degrees. Thomaz sees fifteenth-century Melaka as a new type of state created by commerce, its capital not on a river but directly on the sea (like contemporary Gresik in Java and, later, Ternate, Makassar, and Banten), its import tariffs low, its population inherently urban and pluralistic. The other three states discussed all arose during the most intense period of commercial competition and expansion (c. 1560–1630) and could not have done so without the cloves of Maluku, the pepper of Jambi, and the Sino-Japanese trade of Faifo in the Nguyen dominions. But all three authors are at pains to point out that the story is more complicated than that.

Other factors aided these unprecedented concentrations of power— Islamic and European models in Maluku (and implicitly Jambi) and the personal character and relationships of Nguyen Hoang in Vietnam. More important for these authors, however, is the intersection of these new factors and states with established cultural and ecological patterns. For Taylor, the critical conjunction is between the established Vietnamese Confucian tradition of the north and the multiple options presented by the south. For Leonard Andaya, Ternate rose to something akin to a modern state under Babullah, but within older and more durable cultural boundaries that had been established by the "true tales" common to much of Maluku. For Barbara Andaya, the key to understanding Jambi is the tension between the upstream and downstream foci of the state. The new factors sketched above gave downstream commerce the upper hand in the late sixteenth and early seventeenth centuries, but the Minangkabau-dominated agricultural areas upstream eventually escaped from that attempt to construct a centralized state. Moving to the older established states of the Mainland, Yoneo Ishii draws attention to the revisionist scholarship of Nidhi Aewsrivongse, which pushed the effective centralization of the Thai polity forward from the fifteenth century of conventional history to the reign of Naresuen (r. 1590–1605), when the commercial and military factors already discussed were in full play. The Burma depicted by Victor Lieberman underwent the same move toward political centralization and cultural homogenization in the sixteenth century. He makes

the case, however, for the continuation of this process with little inter-
ruption into the seventeenth and eighteenth centuries, even though
the proportion of revenue the state derived from trade declined after
1630.

Scriptural Orthodoxies

There is broad agreement that the strong kings of the early modern
period favored, as Lieberman puts it, "textually based, externally validated . . . sources of authority over local traditions". Whether they
always succeeded in moving popular belief in that direction is less
clear, however. Taylor argued in the conference paper that preceded
his essay here that in Vietnam "the Neo-Confucian ideology adopted
by fifteenth-century kings actually retreated before a resurgence of
Buddhism and animism" in the subsequent two centuries.

The best documented case of dramatic religious change is the conversion of the lowland Philippines to Catholicism in the period roughly
1580–1650, though the conversion of much of eastern Indonesia to
Islam in the same period is hardly less spectacular. I argue in my essay
that the advances of scriptural Islam and Christianity form part of a
pattern related (in very complex ways) to the peak of the commercial
upswing. How the commercial pressure affected popular values can
only be guessed at. More demonstrable factors were the new direct
contacts with the sources of the scriptural traditions, the interests of
centralizing rulers in legitimation by some external point of reference,
and a militant polarization between the two faiths which drew sharp
religiopolitical boundaries.

The tendency toward unification of the Theravada Buddhist *sangha*
(monkhood), through state patronage of reforms and reordinations on
the Sri Lanka model, has some analogies with the mass religious
change in insular Southeast Asia.[21] Clearly the process was less sudden and dramatic in most cases, however, particularly because the
confrontation between Theravada orthodoxy and animist sacrifice
lacked the urgency of that between Islam and Christianity. My argument that there was a retreat of this scriptural trend in the Archipelago
in the late seventeenth century is rejected by Lieberman, and implicitly

---

[21]In addition to the material cited by Lieberman and Ishii in this volume, see Donald K.
Swearer and Sommai Premchit, "The Relation between the Religious and Political Orders in
Northern Thailand (14th–16th Centuries)," in *Religion and Legitimation of Power in Thailand, Laos,
and Burma*, ed. Bardwell L. Smith (Chambersburg, Pa., 1978), pp. 20–33, and Than Tun, ed.,
The Royal Orders of Burma, A.D. 1593–1885, Part 2, A.D. 1649–1750 (Kyoto, 1985), pp. x–xii.

by Ishii, for the Buddhist societies. They show rather a continuing trend toward cultural uniformity and royal control into the eighteenth century and beyond. Nevertheless, the secular advances they identify in the late seventeenth and eighteenth centuries (through royal examination of monks and a tendency toward lay writing in the vernacular rather than monastic writing in Pali) may have parallels in contemporary trends in Southeast Asian Islam and Christianity.[22]

Capitalism and the End of a Period

Though we should not expect every part of a highly complex region to march in step, Southeast Asia as a whole offers a fine laboratory to look at some of the crucial global questions of the early modern period. Did the tendencies I have remarked above continue until they were overtaken by the rise of industrialization and modern imperialism (affecting Southeast Asia chiefly after 1800), or did they reach some kind of crisis or resolution that we might take as the end of the early modern period? Much of the debate in this book and the discussions preceding it are about whether the seventeenth century should be regarded as a watershed for the region. Though alternative, more fundamental, turning points are not advanced in these essays, they are implicitly the ones already identified by historians—the European intrusion around 1500 and the impact of an industrializing Europe around 1800. The candidates for major turning points are thus not different from those argued by European and comparative historians, and the choice, as Wallerstein points out, has much to do with our presuppositions about the modern world.[23]

From a Southeast Asian standpoint, the argument for a turning point around 1650 rests on the region's relations with other peoples (primarily Europeans, but also Chinese) and on the place of international commerce in the life of states. In 1600, Southeast Asians interacted as equals with Europeans; in 1700, the inequalities were already manifest. This change in the balance of power became apparent sooner "below the winds" than elsewhere in Asia because of its maritime character and its reliance on the world market for spices and aromatics, but it was essentially a change in the relations between northwestern Europe

---

[22]There is not only a shift in Islamic writing from Arabic to Malay and Javanese in the seventeenth century but a further shift from Malay into local vernaculars—notably Acehnese and Bugis—in the eighteenth.

[23]Immanuel Wallerstein, *The Modern World-System*, vol. 2: *Mercantilism and the Consolidation of the Modern World-Economy, 1600–1750* (New York, 1980), p. 7.

and the rest of the world. The debate continues as to the causes of this shift. Was it the rise of capitalism in Europe, a decline or critical failure in Asia, or some combination of the two? Were military, economic, technical, or cultural factors more central to the outcome?

Jeyamalar Kathirithamby-Wells compares Southeast Asia directly with Europe, particularly in relation to key features of merchant capitalism and the nation-state. Great wealth came into the ports and cities of the region in the sixteenth and early seventeenth centuries, she finds, but it did not produce accumulations of capital in productive crafts, mines, or transport networks as in Europe. Power remained personalized to a high degree even in the more centralized states that marked this period, and there was consequently no security of property for a merchant or manufacturing class. Manguin investigates one particular dilemma—the disappearance in the sixteenth century of the large Malay and Javanese trading junks. He concludes that the naval victories of Portuguese fleets over these junks were a relatively minor factor in their disappearance. More important was the competition of Gujarati and Chinese shipping and the increasing concentration of wealth in the royal courts, which expended much of it on massive war fleets and armaments rather than cargo vessels.

Barbara Andaya also shows the effects on one state of the decline of pepper prices in the late seventeenth century and the rise of Dutch power. The attempt of downstream (*hilir*) kings to impose their authority by use of trade wealth and imported weapons failed, largely because of their dependence on a single buyer and protector, the VOC.

Most historians would accept that the monopoly the Dutch established over supplies of nutmeg (in 1621) and clove (by the 1650s), their conquest of such key commercial centers as Makassar (1669) and Banten (1682), and their strong-armed quasi-monopoly over most of the other export centers of the Indonesian Archipelago constituted a major setback to indigenous commerce in the Islands and weakened the control of maritime states over their hinterlands. The Spanish conquest of the Philippine Archipelago was still more profound an eclipse of indigenous polities and their commercial involvement. The open question is whether these losses were part of a more general crisis for Southeast Asia (and perhaps some other parts of Asia), of which military defeat was only one aspect.[24]

Lieberman examines this possibility carefully for Burma. He concludes that there was some discontinuity in the seventeenth century,

---

[24]As I have argued in "The Seventeenth Century Crisis in Southeast Asia," *MAS* 24, no. 4 (1990), 639–59.

through the removal of the capital far inland and the reduced role seaborne commerce played thereafter in the revenues and calculations of the Burmese state. In his view the continuities were still more striking, however. The integration of Shans and Mons into a Burman-dominated polity, begun by the First Toungoo kings in the sixteenth century, was continued in the seventeenth and eighteenth, with a steadily increased degree of cultural homogeneity. Despite reduced interest in maritime trade, the monetization of the economy continued to increase throughout the eighteenth century.

Dhiravat na Pombejra's essay on Siam, like Lieberman's on Burma, is able to show that older Western strictures about a retreat into isolation and stagnation are wide of the mark. European trade with Siam certainly languished after the 1688 revolution, but Chinese and Muslim trade continued and may even have grown to fill the gap. Though there was an administrative decline after 1688 in terms of the crown's ability to control its subjects, the mid-eighteenth century was a period of great cultural flowering.

Any conclusion must reemphasize that Southeast Asia was a region united by environment, commerce, diplomacy, and war but diverse in its fragmented polities and cultures. In this it had more in common with Europe than with the great landmasses of Asia. Part of its fascination is the diversity of its reactions to the pressures of the period. Generalizations are always suspect. The balance of evidence in this book seems nevertheless to suggest that the seventeenth century, particularly its middle decades, was critical for Southeast Asia's reactions to increased military and economic pressure from the new Dutch-dominated world-system. These reactions necessarily involved some degree of retreat from what came to appear an excessive reliance on international commerce. In global terms, the share of Southeast Asians in that commerce was undoubtedly reduced. When the region is seen in its own terms, however, words such as "decline" and "stagnation" are entirely inappropriate. There was constant change and adaptation to difficult circumstances. The cultural and political achievements of the eighteenth century were at least as remarkable as those of the seventeenth or sixteenth. Many of the trends set in motion during the early modern era were developed into the foundations of modern Southeast Asia.

PART 1

Forming New States

The fifteenth and sixteenth centuries were marked in Southeast Asia by the rise of numerous new states, including Ternate and the southern Vietnamese regime known to Europeans as Cochinchina, both discussed in this section, and Melaka and Jambi, examined in the following section. The reasons advanced for this phenomenon have usually been external: the rise of international commerce, the spread of firearms, and the influence of Islamic models.

The two essays in this section demonstrate that internal factors were also critical in creating and defining these states, and that in the indigenous record they tend to predominate. The shared myths of the Maluku region defined the possibilities of Ternate, and Nguyen Hoang's personal interpretation of Vietnamese political tradition did the same for the state he founded.

1

Cultural State Formation in Eastern Indonesia

Leonard Y. Andaya

When Donald Lach in his *Asia in the Making of Europe* decided to refer to Maluku as "the Spiceries," he found a satisfactory solution to the problem of seeking some type of unified description for the "profusion of islands which lie scattered in the seas south of the Philippines, east of Borneo and Java, north of Australia, and west of New Guinea." Whereas in the past historians found "neat archipelagoes" about which one could talk intelligibly, Lach found that "the eye and the mind working in harmony have great difficulty . . . in combining these unordered spots into comprehensible and manageable patterns," and that the "task is rendered even more complex when it is necessary to group the islands into unities which pay some deference to the focal points of the region."[1] His solution, therefore, was to focus on the single item the Europeans and other foreigners in the past associated with Maluku: spices.

The problem and the solution were very much a Western academic exercise. For the people of Maluku, however, there was no doubt about what bound the many islands and ethnic groups together. Their identity was clearly and precisely presented in different types of local traditions that described their link to a specific island community and to a wider Maluku world. Though these cultural perceptions have served to legitimize later political expansion, their significance was in providing the basis for common action without political coercion in vast areas encompassing many different cultures and peoples. In this regard these cultural unities were neither political states nor "stateless" soci-

[1]Donald F. Lach, *Asia in the Making of Europe*, 5 vols. (Chicago, 1965), 1:2.592.

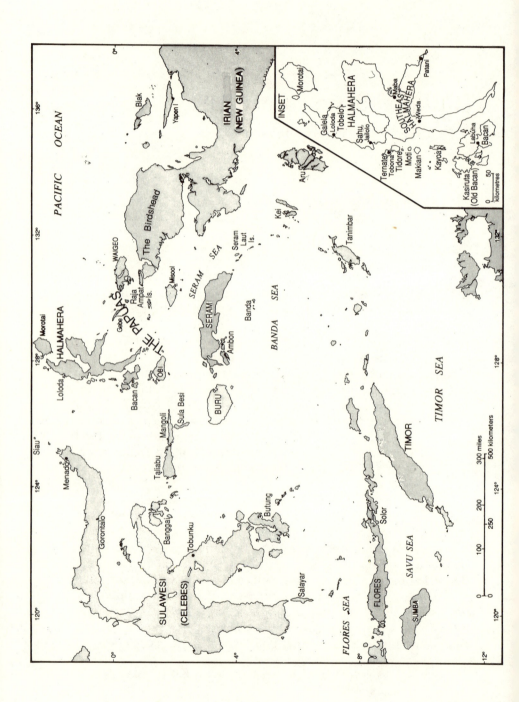

eties, the latter being a term used to refer to the ethnic solidarity of groups such as the Batak.[2] Attention to these cultural perceptions of unity, rather than to events, may be useful in helping us understand the process of later political state formation in certain parts of Southeast Asia. This is certainly the case for Maluku in eastern Indonesia, where geographic isolation and a proliferation of ethnic groups and cultures eschew any unities based on political force or a common ethnic identity. Instead, unity is forged through a common adherence by these different groups to legitimizing myths that establish the physical and spiritual parameters of their world.

The Legitimizing Traditions

Three types of traditions describe the formation of an island-wide, an area-wide, and a region-wide unity in Maluku. There are no extant indigenous sources from the sixteenth or the seventeenth centuries, and the only detailed foreign accounts are from the pens of contemporary Portuguese, Spaniards, and Dutch. The earliest account of the type of tradition describing the creation of a unified island community comes from the seventeenth-century Dutch clergyman François Valentijn, who recorded the story of Ternate. In the beginning the island was wild, without many villages, and inhabited by only a few people. The earliest settlement was Tobona, which was located on the top of the mountain and founded by a headman called Guna. One day as Guna went to the forests to tap the areng palm tree (*Arenga pinnata*) to make toddy (*tuak*), he came across a golden mortar and pestle. He brought these back to the village, and they soon became objects of great curiosity. So many people came to see them that Guna could no longer cope. He therefore decided to give them to Momole Matiti, who was head of the village of Foramadiyahi, halfway down the mountain. Once Momole Matiti accepted the unusual objects, he too was besieged with visitors, so he in turn gave them to Cico, head of the coastal village of Sampalu. Although many came to Sampalu to view the golden mortar and pestle, Cico was able to deal with them admirably and was honored by all the other heads of the island. He was therefore asked to become the principal head, with the title of *kolano*.[3]

Certain features of this tale reveal something of the way island uni-

[2]Lance Castles, "Statelessness and Stateforming Tendencies among the Batak before Colonial Rule," in *Pre-Colonial State Systems in Southeast Asia*, ed. A. Reid and L. Castles (Kuala Lumpur, 1973), pp. 67–76.

[3]François Valentijn, *Oud en Nieuw Oost-Indiën*, 3 vols. (The Hague 1856–58), 1:282–83.

ties were created in North Maluku. Earliest settlements were located on mountaintops for security; the steep mountains with barely accessible paths were formidable barriers against an invading force. The gradual move down the mountainside eventually to the coast is described in terms that would have been readily understood by the Malukans. The leader of the group is given the special name Guna, a Malay word meaning "fortune." The use of the name "fortune" would have been in keeping with his special attributes, which made possible the finding of the unusual, and therefore god-given, mortar and pestle. Throughout Southeast Asia the identification of the extraordinary individual is contained in the name, such as Hang Tuah ("The Lord Possessing Fortune"), or Bhumipon ("Person of Merit"). It is this individual who, through favor with the gods, is able to bring about significant changes to the society. Guna, then, is the Ternaten culture hero who discovers the golden mortar and pestle that transform the island.

The golden mortar and pestle is a reference to the riches that came to the island through the clove. The shape of the pestle sitting in a mortar resembles the clove, and the image would not have escaped the Ternaten listeners of the tale. The clove attracts vast numbers of people, but the location of the settlement on the mountain makes such traffic unnecessarily burdensome. Eventually, then, the principal settlement is moved to the coast, and its head becomes acknowledged as *kolano* by his peers because of his success in handling the increased activity associated with the burgeoning clove trade. It is no coincidence that the name of the headman is a Malay word, since the Malay traders in the fifteenth and early sixteenth centuries were principally responsible for the greatly increased international trade in cloves.

This seventeenth-century tale thus captures in essence the process by which the people on Ternate under their various heads (*momole*) became united under a *kolano*. A similar tradition recorded by the Portuguese in the early sixteenth century is found in the other major island in North Maluku, Tidore. In this tale from Tidore the original settlement was sited on the mountain at Mareku and then moved to the coast because of foreign traders coming in large numbers in search of the clove.[4]

The second type of tradition deals with the unity of a specific area in Maluku, that of present-day North Maluku. In 1682 the Dutch governor in Ternate, R. Padtbrugge, recorded a list of epithets of places in the area.[5] There was no story associated with the list, but its coherence and significance appeared in the epithets themselves:

[4]João de Barros, *Da Asia*, 24 vols. (1777; rpt., Lisbon, 1973), 6:322.
[5]Koloniaal Archief of the Algemene Rijksarchief, VOC 1376, R. Padtbrugge, "Memorie van Overgave," 31 Aug. 1682, fols. 262v-263r.

Loloda, *Ngara ma-beno* ("Wall of the Gate")
Jailolo, *Jiko ma-kolano* ("Ruler of the Bay")
Tidore, *Kië ma-kolano* ("Ruler of the Mountain")
Ternate, *Kolano ma-luku* ("Ruler of Maluku")
Bacan, *Kolano ma-dehe* ("Ruler of the Far End")

The antiquity of these titles was evident not only in the inability of any local informant at the time to explain their meanings adequately but also by the inclusion of Loloda. Though a Raja Loloda still existed, only a vague memory of a former kingdom remained. At first glance the meanings given for the titles appeared to be based purely on geographic considerations. Loloda's title was puzzling since "wall" and "gate" seemed to have been transposed.[6] Since the gate aspect was emphasized, the title was popularly interpreted as meaning "the Beginning," hence the beginning point of Maluku in the north in Loloda. Bacan's epithet, too, caused some debate because it meant literally the "farthest end." Informants explained that since Loloda was the "gate" and "the beginning" in the north, Bacan was logically the "exit," being in the south. Jailolo's name, "Ruler of the Bay," seemed appropriate since the town was located on the bay, and Tidore's title, "Ruler of the Mountain," also appeared purely descriptive. The largest and most prominent mountain in North Maluku is on the island of Tidore. What was easiest to explain in the seventeenth century was the identification of Ternate with the epithet "Ruler of Maluku," since Ternate was then the strongest kingdom in Maluku.

If, however, one were to examine these names more closely, one would be able to recognize in them a survival of another true tale now long forgotten. In creation myths there is often a description of a time of frequent intercourse among those inhabiting the three different spheres of life—the upperworld, the earth, and the underworld. The upperworld is depicted as being separated from the earth by a wall. It is through the gate in the wall that access is gained. Loloda's title, "Wall of the Gate," is most likely a reference to the gate dividing the upperworld and the earth within the world of Maluku. Similarly, in creation myths the gate to the underworld regions is often referred to as the "farthest end," the "exit." Bacan, then, would have been regarded as the exit, hence the gateway to the underworld.[7] In this cosmological scheme, Loloda represents the upperworld and Bacan the

---

[6]One scholar clearly unhappy about the literal meaning of the epithet suggests that perhaps what was meant was the "Gate of the Wall" (*Beno ma-ngara*); see Ch. F. van Fraassen, "Ternate, De Molukken en de Indonesische Archipel," Ph.D. diss., University of Leiden, 1987, p. 19.

[7]Mircea Eliade, *Images and Symbols: Studies in Religious Symbolism* (New York, 1969), pp. 40–41.

underworld—hence forming an upper–lower dualism. In the middle is the earth, occupied by the remaining three kingdoms, with Jailolo representing the sea and Tidore the land—hence forming a bay/sea–mountain/land dualism. Ternate occupies the center, linking both dualisms into a whole. Its epithet, "Ruler of Maluku," is unlike the other epithets in ignoring Ternaten syntax and using perhaps a popular term to refer to its assumed superiority in the area. The formation of these dualities suggests an origin extending far back in time. A linguist has demonstrated that the principal directional markers in proto-Austronesian were *laSud, "toward the sea," and *Daya, "toward the interior," a pattern that was retained in North Maluku.[8] The other duality, of upper and lower, must be of equal antiquity since it obviously refers to a creation myth of the community.

In these dualities, Bacan and Tidore would have been regarded as the superior partners because of their identification with the land. Both Bacan's underworld and Tidore's mountain had their source of power in the energies associated with the spirits of the soil. Mountains are believed to represent the earth deity impressively made manifest among the people.[9] One striking example of the prominence of mountains to Southeast Asians is the name "Funan," which the Chinese gave to a complex of early settlements in southern Cambodia. The term is believed to be derived from the old Khmer term *bnam* (mountain) and seems to have been the name with which the people of the area identified themselves.[10]

In Maluku, too, the people identify with their mountains, whose destructive force is only too apparent in these volcanic isles. Living under the constant threat of eruption, the people have come to place the well-being of their community in the hands of the mountain, which they regard with great awe and veneration. During a recent major eruption in 1980 in Ternate, the ruler led his people on a sacred circumnavigation of the mountain (*kololi kië*), in effect the entire island, to appease the mountain and preserve the community.[11] In this regard, Ternate and the North Malukan islands have much more in common with Bali, certain parts of Java, and Pacific high-island societies such as Hawaii than with many other areas of Southeast Asia. It is therefore not difficult to see how the mountain in Maluku has become syn-

[8]K. A. Adelaar, "Malagasy Culture-History: Some Linguistic Evidence," author's copy, p. 5, to appear in *The Indian Ocean in Antiquity*, ed. J. E. Reade.

[9]Paul Mus, *India Seen from the East: Indigenous Cults in Champa*, ed. I. W. Mabbett and D. P. Chandler (Monash, 1975), pp. 10–24.

[10]G. Coedès, *The Indianized State of Southeast Asia* (Honolulu, 1968), p. 36.

[11]"Gamalama 'Ditenangkan' Dulu dengan Korakora," *Kompas*, 30 September 1980.

onymous with the group. In the past, letters from rulers of the various kingdoms often referred to their kingdom and their mountain as one— hence the revealing Sahu comment that they originated from their mountain. This conception is so strong among the people of Maluku that it is possible to reason, as does an anthropologist about Sahu, that it was not people who owned land, but land people.[12]

Of the five kingdoms, Ternate's position is unique in being depicted as the linchpin of the group. Ternate's claims to supremacy did not, however, go unchallenged. In the late seventeenth century the Dutch noted that, though the ruler of Tidore was referred to as Kië ma-kolano ("Lord of the Mountain"), his more common title was Kaicili' (Lord) Maluku.[13] Tidore was now the true rival of Ternate as a result of changes that occurred in the course of the sixteenth century. When Jailolo lost its independence to Ternate in 1551, a new dualism arose between Ternate and Tidore, one that took the form of an east-west opposition. This became evident in the expansion of these kingdoms, with Ternate's fields of conquests in the west and Tidore's in the east. The unity of North Maluku was thus restructured to represent the four cardinal points: Loloda (north), Bacan (south), Ternate (west), and Tidore (east). Within this new cosmological construct Ternate came to be acknowledged as the superior partner in its identification with the west, the source of creation and life.

A third tradition concerns the unity of the entire region of Maluku. The earliest rendering of this Maluku myth was in 1537 by Antonio Galvão, captain and governor of the Portuguese community on the island of Ternate between 1536 and 1539. Galvão commented that the local inhabitants had no tradition of written chronicles or histories but preserved their past in "aphorisms, songs, and rhyming ballads, of which they are very fond." This tale, the inhabitants told Galvão, was true, as were all their "poetic fables."[14]

In this "true tale,"[15] the setting is in the southernmost clove-producing island of Bacan. It begins in a period when there are no

---

[12]Leontine E. Visser, "Mijn Tuin is Myn Kind: Een Anthropologische Studie van de Droge Rijstteelt in Sahu (Indonesië)," Ph.D. diss., University of Leiden, 1984, pp. 11–13.

[13]Valentijn, 1856–58, 1:244–45.

[14]Antonio Galvão, *A Treatise on the Moluccas (c. 1544)*, ed. and trans. Hubertus F. Jacobs (Rome, 1971), pp. 83–85.

[15]Mircea Eliade, an early scholar of myths and religion, offers a convincing explanation for "true tales" among many oral and semiliterate societies. According to Eliade, a "true tale" concerned "realities," or the fact of the existence of a certain thing or custom that in itself is a demonstration or proof of the veracity of the tale. In such a tale the sacred and supernatural elements penetrate into the present world, "creating" it and making humankind what it is. The supernatural beings and their sacred activities become the exemplary model for all meaningful action by the group. Mircea Eliade, *Myth and Reality* (London, 1964), pp. 6, 9.

kings and when the people live in kinship groups (*parentela*) governed by elders. Since "no one is better than the other," dissension and wars arise, alliances are made and broken, and people are killed or captured and ransomed. In time, some become more powerful than others, and captains and governors are created, but there are still no kings.[16] One day a prominent elder of the island, named Bikusagara, goes sailing on a local double-outrigger vessel (*kora-kora*). He spies a clump of beautiful rattan growing near a precipice by the sea and sends his men ashore to cut some stalks. But when they arrive at the spot, the rattan is nowhere to be seen, and so they return to the *kora-kora*. Exasperated, Bikusagara himself goes ashore and immediately locates the clump of rattan. He orders his men to cut down some of the stalks, but as soon as they start to hack into the rattan blood starts to gush from the cuts. Startled by this strange phenomenon, Bikusagara jumps back and notices four serpent eggs hidden among the rocks. When he approaches these eggs, a voice orders him to take them home with him because from them will emerge individuals of great distinction. Mindful of the command, Bikusagara carefully places the eggs in a rattan box called a *totombo* and brings them home, where they are guarded with great care. After some time the eggs bring forth three males and a female. When they grow up, one of the men becomes the king of Bacan, the second the king of the Papuas, the third the king of Butung and Banggai, and the woman becomes the wife of the king of Loloda. From these original four descend all the kings of these islands, "and ever since they have paid great honor to Bikusagara and to the rocky precipice, and they consider them a very holy thing, consecrated to the gods."[17]

By Galvão's time, Bacan, the Papuas, Butung-Banggai, and Loloda were politically insignificant, and yet the tale was still being recited and regarded as culturally true in Maluku. The sacred mythic quality of the tale may account for its longevity in the society. In an earlier time there were elders who governed the communities, but there was one in particular who was favored by the gods to mediate in their affairs. His special quality is evident in his revelation of the sacred rattan. The image of the rattan, or in other Indonesian tales bamboo, is usually associated with spiritual forces that provide the progenitors of a ruling dynasty.[18] The discovery of the serpent eggs in the rocky precipice by the sea combines all the elements of the underworld so prominent in this tale. The serpent, or *naga*, is an ancient mythic element found in

---

[16]Galvão, 1971, pp. 77–79; João de Barros, 1973, 5:576.

[17]Galvão, 1971, pp. 80–83.

[18]See especially the discussion of parallel stories from Kutai, Sukadana, Melaka, Kedah, and Pasai in *Hikajat Bandjar: A Study of Malay Historiography*, ed. J. J. Ras (The Hague, 1968), chap. 4.

India and Southeast Asia associated with snake spirits and sacred sites. The rocks too are a familiar feature, regarded as the "divinization of the energies of the soil" and hence a partial manifestation of the earth deity.[19] Through the recitation of these sacred elements, this tale was regarded as true and as legitimizing the boundaries of the Malukan world and the peoples who belonged to it. By the first half of the sixteenth century, new political alignments and power centers that no longer reflected the central importance of Bacan were already coming into existence. Yet the tale continued to be recounted precisely because it was a true tale and dealt with sacred activities creating exemplary models for the group within the wider Maluku world. What was essential was the preservation of the unity to assure the continuing well-being of the whole community.

All three of these traditions draw a cultural boundary defining those who belong and those who do not. In these myths the clove, the mortar and pestle, the mountain and the sea, and the snake and the eggs form a male-female sexual metaphor for the unity of the world of Maluku. The ruler, or *kolano*, is characterized by his possession of fortune, which enables him to control the golden mortar and pestle, the symbol of the clove, as well as the reproductive capacity of the community.[20] Historical sources confirm this imagery in describing the wealth that flows from the clove trade and the established pattern of the communities providing women for the ruler. In the opposite direction go prestige items in the form of imported cloth, iron, and other goods, as well as titles and institutions. The maintenance of this male-female relationship thus becomes the guarantee of the continuing prosperity of the group.

There is, however, no suggestion of a political unity. Instead, the emphasis is on the separate parts, the sacred four, with occasionally an added fifth to represent the center. The five areas mentioned in the epithets are acceptable since, in the construction of sacred space, there are four places at the cardinal points and one in the center.[21] Although by the mid-sixteenth century only three of the original kingdoms of the tradition still existed as separate political entities, the belief in the unity of the four (or five) was still maintained. Only in the late eighteenth

[19]Mus, 1975, pp. 10–15; A. L. Basham, *The Wonder That Was India* (New York, 1959), pp. 298, 317.

[20]I am grateful to Mark S. Mosko for demonstrating the common sexual symbolism all three myths share. He is a far more acute observer than I of such imagery, as is excellently demonstrated in his book *Quadripartite Structures: Categories, Relations, and Homologies in Bush Mekeo Culture* (Cambridge, 1985).

[21]William H. Alkire, "Concepts of Order in Southeast Asia and Micronesia," *Comparative Studies in Society and History* 14, no. 4 (1972), 484–93.

century, when the political and economic situation had become intolerable, was there a declaration that the sacred unity had been broken. This provoked a rebellion by Prince Nuku of Tidore which was expressed in terms of the need to restore the four kingdoms and hence the welfare of the Maluku world.

Dominance of the Center

The adherence to the various myths defining cultural unities in Maluku provided both a legitimation and a model for the growth of dominant centers and the expansion to the periphery. From the mid-sixteenth century, Ternate and Tidore had become the two most important centers in North Maluku and had begun to incorporate several neighboring areas under their control. The expansion was made possible as a result of specific external developments. The first of these was the rapid increase in the trade in cloves, the dried flower bud of a tree (*Eugenia aromatica*) said to be indigenous to the islands of North Maluku. Small quantities were reaching the outside world from an early period, as can be attested in foreign sources. In the third century B.C. a Chinese emperor of the Han dynasty ordered his courtiers to have cloves in their mouths when they addressed him.[22] K'ang Tai, one of the two envoys sent by the Wu government of southern China to Funan in the third century C.E., reported that the clove came from the islands to the east.[23] Though the clove was going in small quantities to both China and India and beyond in the early period, a major development in the spice trade seems to have begun in the late fourteenth century. It was then that the central and eastern Javanese coastal towns, with their ruling Chinese, Arab, and Javanese elite, became the major nodes of a vibrant interarchipelago trade network that linked the Spice Islands to the rest of the world. The prosperous Malay entrepôt of Melaka (c. 1400–1511) became the major collection and distribution port of the clove and other Southeast Asian spices and contributed greatly to the prosperity of Maluku.

The wealth from the clove trade, which began to flow to the royal Malukan households through customs collected and gifts from traders, provided the rulers with such highly desired items in the eastern islands as Indian cloth and iron implements. Having control over the redistribution of these goods enabled the rulers to draw many of the

[22]I. H. Burkill, *A Dictionary of the Economic Products of the Malay Peninsula*, 2 vols. (London, 1935), 1:961.

[23]O. W. Wolters, *Early Indonesian Commerce* (Ithaca, N.Y., 1967), p. 39.

outlying communities closer to the center. For many places in Maluku, barkcloth was slowly being replaced by Indian cloth and by the coarse Bima cloth being brought to Maluku by Javanese and Malay traders.[24] The roughness of the texture of the Bima cloth would have approximated the barkcloth, but it would have been far more durable. As is the case in the Pacific, where the process was more recent and therefore better documented, the substitution of imported cotton fabrics for barkcloth would have released the women from the never-ending chores of tapa making. Importation of cloth would have relieved the burden of acquiring sufficient quantities of bark, not only for clothing but also for gift exchange and burial.[25] The women in Maluku would then have been able to devote their time to the collection and preparation of cloves to pay for imported cloth and other useful foreign trade items.

Iron, the other highly valued import, became a crucial element in forging links between the center and the periphery. The association of iron with the dominant centers of Ternate and Tidore is explicit in some local Malukan traditions.[26] Effective, durable iron implements and weapons enabled the clearing of forests and the cultivation of the land. The advantages of those possessing iron were obvious, and any ruler who controlled the supply could easily entice a community to offer allegiance in return for a guaranteed delivery of that metal. Until fairly recently, the people from Tidore were well known as ironsmiths in Maluku, indicating a long history of identification of iron.[27] The ability of both Ternate and Tidore to control the redistribution of iron contributed to their increasing importance vis-à-vis the other Malukan areas in these early centuries. Iron supplies came mainly from Tobunku in southeastern Sulawesi, where the quantity and accessibility of that metal was fabled. Europeans reported that iron was so plentiful that the inhabitants simply waited for a boat to dock before digging up the iron and smelting it into the desired weapons or tools.[28]

European demands for a regular delivery of spices in large quantities and of a particular quality had significant repercussions on the center. The Portuguese, for example, were no longer satisfied to accept the

[24]Tomé Pires, *The Suma Oriental of Tomé Pires*, ed. and trans. Armando Cortesão, 2 vols. (London, 1944), 1:206–7.

[25]Simon Kooijman, *Tapa in Indonesia* (Honolulu, 1972), pp. 410–21; Douglas L. Oliver, *Ancient Tahitian Society*, vol. 1: *Ethnography* (Honolulu, 1974), p. 148.

[26]See for one example Naomichi Ishige, "Limau Village and Its Setting," in *The Galela of Halmahera: A Preliminary Survey*, ed. N. Ishige (Osaka, 1980), p. 7.

[27]F. C. Kamma and Simon Kooijman, *Romawa Forja, Child of the Fire: Iron-Working and the Role of Iron in West New Guinea (West Irian)* (Leiden, 1973).

[28]VOC 1345, "Daghregister, brieven, resolutiën, etc. . . . voorgevallen op de reyse van den Gouverneur der Moluccos met ZH Amsterdam naar Tambukko, Tidore, Mackian, enz., beginnende 1 Aug 1678 en eindigende 8 Maart 1679," fol. 286.

lower quality *cravo de bastão* (stalk of the clove) but demanded the more valuable *cravo de cabeca* (head of the clove). Finally, they succeeded in persuading local rulers to institute a new method of gathering and preparing the clove, though it incurred opposition at first because it was more time consuming than simply taking the whole stalk.[29] But the higher quality clove brought more revenue and hence greater strength to the center.

The new European requirements for the delivery of cloves brought not only economic benefits to the center but also an increasing organization and strengthening of human resources. The cloves had to be ready for loading when the ships arrived because of the latter's dependence on the monsoon winds. Officials were appointed in the center to undertake the organization of the clove trade and the supervision of the needs of the foreign traders in port. This was a much more intricate task than simply managing the royal household, which earlier had been the function of an official known as the *pinate*. Although Galvão had remarked on the importance of the *pinate*, by the mid-sixteenth century the role had clearly been eclipsed by others, reflecting changes occurring in the center. The *syahbandar* (harbormaster) in charge of foreign trade was now the crucial functionary, and the duties of *hukum* (magistrates) came to be expanded beyond the purely Islamic judicial functions to those of coordinating the activities between the center and the outside settlements. The royal port became the true hub of the kingdom and quickly outstripped the other settlements in wealth and population.

The clove trade was an important factor in strengthening the center in Maluku. Another was Islam. The ruler of Ternate was the first to embrace the new religion, sometime in the last quarter of the fifteenth century, and his fellow rulers soon followed. Islamization began in the courts and only very gradually spread to the rest of the population. According to Tomé Pires writing from Melaka between 1512 and 1515, 10 percent of the population in Ternate and Tidore was Muslim and only the ruler of Ternate used the title of *sultan*.[30] It became a practice for the sultan to appoint a brother or relative to the post of chief *casis*, the principal Islamic official of the kingdom. As Islam grew in importance, two new posts were created which bore the Islamic title *hukum*. These *hukum* served as administrators and magistrates and became increasingly vital in the maintenance of links between the periphery

---

[29]Gabriel Rebelo, *Informação sobre as Malucas*. Text 1 (1st ed., 1561), in *Documentação para a História das Missões do Padroado Português do Oriente: Insulíndia*, vol. 3, ed. Artur Basílio de Sá (Lisbon, 1955), p. 297.
[30]Pires, 1944, 1:213–21.

and the center.[31] Islam also brought major economic benefits to the sultan, thereby increasing the power of the center. Muslim traders preferred ports where they were assured a mosque for worship and the protection of a Muslim ruler. The sultan's settlement therefore became the principal gathering place of foreign Muslim traders.

A third major factor contributing to the dominance of the center was the European notion of the proper authority of monarchs. Equating Malukan rulers with those in Europe, Europeans made all economic and political arrangements with them. If duties were to be paid, they were paid to the royal treasury; if arms were to be sold, they were sold to the ruler; if any private trading arrangements were made, they involved the ruler. Letters were exchanged between the Malukan sultans and the sovereigns of Europe, placing the former, at least on paper and in the eyes of the Europeans, within the exclusive category of royal beings Europeans could understand. Any formal political arrangements, such as treaties, could therefore properly be legitimized only by these rulers. As a consequence, Malukan sultans were treated with a dignity not shared by the other local *kolano*. Treaties became a useful vehicle for clever monarchs to call legitimately on the Europeans to accomplish political goals, such as maintaining order on their borders or suppressing "rebels." The frequency of so-called rebellions in the sixteenth century was less a phenomenon of increasing dissatisfaction among local communities than one of the rulers' reliance on the treaty to consolidate their growing social dominance. In the art of diplomacy, as in the art of war, the Malukans proved to be excellent students of the Europeans. By the last quarter of the sixteenth century, the Ternate rulers were becoming much more like the image the Europeans projected of kings. Sultan Hairun (r. 1535–70) dressed like a Portuguese, spoke Portuguese fluently, and governed his kingdom with great assurance bred of long familiarity and friendship with that nation. Ternate was seen as the leader of the Malukan world, since it was by far the most impressive economically and politically of the kingdoms.

As a result of the clove trade, Islam, and European political perceptions, both Ternate and Tidore became exemplary centers in the wider Maluku world. Their greater economic strength enabled them to reinforce by material goods their position in the cosmological hierarchy of relationships created by the true tales. As they expanded into the region culturally mapped out by the traditions of unity, they recreated the center in the periphery. They brought Islam, Islamic and central (Ternate or Tidore) titulature, and Islamic (Malay and North Malukan)

[31]Galvão, 1971, pp. 87, 113.

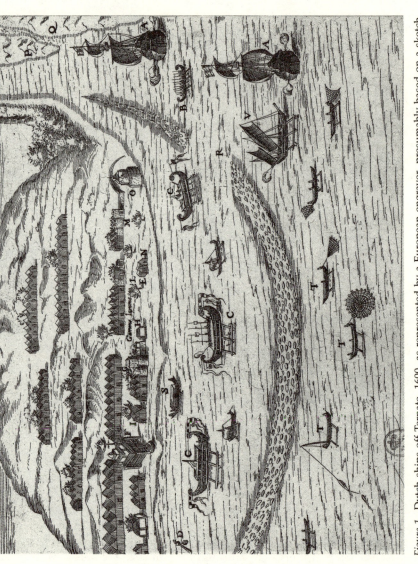

Figure 1. Dutch ships off Ternate, 1600, as represented by a European engraver, presumably based on a sketch from life that marked certain locations, including the passage through the reef (R), various local galleys (*kora-kora*, C), and a merchant ship (V); ashore, from left, the great mosque (F), the house put at the disposal of the Dutch visitors (I), the stone palace (G), the market held under the shade of a large tree (E), the house of the king's interpreter, a Chinese who spoke Portuguese (N), a monastery built by the Portuguese (L) and a tower with

dress, and they made the periphery part of the center. But this process did not occur over night; there was at first considerable resistance, expressed in the rejection of Islam, to the centralizing tendencies of Ternate and Tidore. Despite the fact that Islam was introduced some-time in the last quarter of the fifteenth century, by 1512 only the sultans and their own kin-based settlements had converted.[32]

In North Maluku in the sixteenth century there was a transitional period in the power of the sultans. The centralizing process began early in the century and reached its culmination in the rule of Sultan Babullah (r. 1570–83). Before 1570 the sultan was still very much a kin-based leader, a primus inter pares among other kolano, despite his Islamic title and pretensions. He was unable to act effectively without the consensus of the many settlements under the leadership of their elders. The sultans of Ternate and Tidore hoped to become as powerful and impressive as their western Archipelago counterparts by formally recognizing several sumptuary laws. Such laws were, however, only enforceable within the sultan's own settlement, and even here it would have been more likely that the allegiance was offered because of the sultan's position as a clan leader. His dependence on the other communities was still great, and the royal kin-based settlement was simply one among many others on the island.

For the sultan to gain consensus, he had to maintain links, preferably through marriage or blood, with the leaders of the communities. He was able to do this through the female members of his family, and it was not uncommon for a sultan to have a wife in every major settlement in the kingdom. Galvão spoke of rulers with harems filled with hundreds of royal and secondary wives.[33] On his release from the fortress, Sultan Hairun's first priority was to travel throughout his land to obtain wives. It was difficult for the Jesuits to understand why Hairun refused to give up these women, and they assumed that he was attached to "carnal vices." Hairun's contemporary, the Sultan Tidore, was also said to be married to the daughters of all the kings and nobles, while his daughters and sisters were married to all the other kings.[34] This practice was continued in the seventeenth century and was particularly noteworthy in the reign of the Ternaten ruler Sultan Amsterdam (r. 1675–90). An important means of reaffirming links after marriage was through the practice of allowing women of leading families throughout the land to suckle the sultan's baby at their breast.[35]

[32]Pires, 1944, 1:213.
[33]Galvão, 1971, pp. 87–89.
[34]de Sá, Documentação, vol. 1 (Lisbon, 1954), no. 62, "Cartas dos moradores de Ternate a El-Rei D. João 111," Ternate, 20 Feb. 1546, pp. 477–78.
[35]Galvão, 1971, pp. 120–21.

Through milk and blood the sultan was able to secure his position and assure consensus in the kingdom.

The culmination of the tendencies toward a strong sultan and the dominance of the royal settlement was reached under Sultan Babullah. When the Portuguese killed Sultan Hairun, the Ternaten court mobilized resources of which the Portuguese themselves were unaware. The Ternaten council was able to reach a decision quickly to appoint a successor acceptable to all, and the council managed to summon a force of sufficient power to besiege the Portuguese successfully. Babullah did not stop with the removal of the Portuguese from Ternate, but expanded the conflict to other kingdoms in Maluku. What had begun as an attack on the Portuguese to avenge his father's death became the vehicle for a campaign to make Ternate the single center in the Malukan world. After subduing Bacan and Tidore, Babullah sent a fleet westward and conquered Banggai, Tobunku, Butung, and Salayar. Though he threatened the Makassar kingdom of Goa, a treaty of friendship was signed between the two, ending all hostilities. The strong fleets of the Sula islands under the Cappalaya were a decisive factor in the victory of the Ternatens overseas. Through these conquests, as well as those he had accomplished under Sultan Hairun in northern Sulawesi, Babullah was dubbed by the Portuguese as the "Lord of Seventy-Two Islands."[36]

Babullah's remarkable achievement could not have been accomplished without the centralization of resources, wealth, and power made possible by the clove trade, Islam, and the Europeans. In 1579, Francis Drake was witness to the transformation of the *kolano* in his meeting with Babullah. Drake was impressed by Babullah's richness of dress, the wealth apparent in the variety of cloth in the reception hall (*baileu*), and the great esteem showed Babullah by his subjects. He was no longer simply a prominent *kolano* among his fellow chiefs but a sultan of considerable authority and prestige. The presence of resident Muslim traders in Ternate to oversee "continuall traffique" was evidence of the established place Ternate had now gained in the international trade in cloves.[37] It was from this trade that Ternate obtained the wealth to surpass the other Malukan kingdoms in strength of arms and brilliance of court. But, more important, this wealth provided the means for the Ternaten ruler to become less dependent on kin-based loyalties by creating a new basis of loyalty to the *kolano* as sultan, a privileged, god-given status that overrode all kinship considerations.

---

[36]Valentijn, 1856–58, 1:358–59.
[37]Richard Carnac Temple, *The World Encompassed and Analogous Contemporary Documents Concerning Sir Francis Drake's Circumnavigation of the World* (1628; rpt., London, 1926), pp. 66–72.

How successful Babullah was in wedding kinship loyalties to personal ones, determined principally by wealth and political prowess, was more than satisfactorily demonstrated by his expansion abroad and his proud appellation.

Accounts of Babullah's reigns have focused on his conquests and the expansion of Ternate's "empire," but what is striking is the subsequent history of this campaign. In time northern Sulawesi, Salayar, and Tobunku broke away because they regarded themselves as belonging to a different sphere. Banggai and Butung proved troublesome from time to time but always acknowledged a special relationship with Ternate because of their common adherence to the Bikusagara myth. In the late seventeenth century, a Butung sultan proudly proclaimed that he was a descendant of one of the original serpent eggs.[38] When Tidore began its expansion, it moved into the "Papuan" areas of southeastern Halmahera,[39] eastern Seram, the Seram Laut islands, the Raja Ampat islands, and the coasts of New Guinea. Though the Papuans were ethnically different from the people of Tidore, they shared a similar cultural tradition in myths of serpent eggs linking the four Papuan Raja Ampat kingdoms.[40] In their respective expansions, Ternate and Tidore encompassed the whole of the Maluku world as defined by the traditions, with Ternate expanding generally north and west while Tidore went south and east. Such an expansion was regarded as right and proper since the two islands represented the center of the world of Maluku and in their complementary dualism assured the maintenance and welfare of that world. The myth, then, served as both a cultural map of the limits of the Maluku world and a spiritual rationale for the relationships thus established.

By the beginning of the seventeenth century, the perception of a unified world of Maluku persisted, but one that was becoming increasingly dominated by Ternate and Tidore. Nevertheless, the memory of four important *kolano* centers remained, even after the conquest of Jailolo in 1551 and its incorporation into Ternate. The view that there were still four pillars—Ternate, Tidore, Jailolo, and Bacan—upholding the world of Maluku demonstrates the strength of the perception first expounded in the tale of Bikusagara from Bacan. Although the four had changed to reflect the political realities of the time, the earlier four (Bacan, Loloda, the Papuas, and Banggai-Butung) continued to sub-

[38]Valentijn, 1862, 1:223.

[39]Although southeastern Halmahera was inhabited by non-Papuan groups, it was classified by the Dutch as part of the Papuan world since it had great prestige and assumed leadership among the Papuan islanders.

[40]A. C. van der Leeden, "The Raja Ampat Islands: A Mythological Interpretation," in *Halmahera dan Raja Ampat sebagai Kesatuan Majemuk*, ed. E. K. M. Masinambow (Jakarta, 1987).

scribe to the legitimizing myth that linked them through a supernatural origin. The all-embracing cultural myth remained to define the familial relationships in an area extending from Butung-Banggai in the west to the coast of New Guinea in the east. The political aspect of this unity was clearly less important than the spiritual and cultural aspects. The belief continued to persist that, as long as there were four kingdoms in Maluku, all was well with their world.

Implications for State Formation in Eastern Indonesia

In discussing state formation in Southeast Asia, one must be careful not to focus simply on the political and economic bases of unity. The case of Maluku demonstrates the usefulness of examining cultural myths to provide an equally valid appreciation of early state formation in Southeast Asia. For Maluku, a common myth that defined a specific world and the proper place of each group within it was the vital ingredient for unity. This "cultural state" was a practical solution offering optimum economic and political arrangements within a difficult geographic region inhabited by many competing cultures and peoples. Not only were the distances great between many of the islands, but one had to contend with the treacherous winds and currents that made any contact a mammoth undertaking. In addition to the numerous small islands there were a few large ones like Halmahera, Buru, and Seram, of which the interior tribes could be contacted only when they so desired. For these communities in the wider Maluku world, a political overlord was unnecessary and meaningless since contact was so rare. What did matter to them, however, was the maintenance of the well-being of the community through the appeasement of the spiritual forces.

The belief in the spiritual efficacy of the Bikusagara tale, as well as the persistence of the memory of the epithets of the four kingdoms, suggests that the ritual creation and preservation of the Maluku world were the crucial components that held groups together. Both Ternate and Tidore relied on traditional cultural means to maintain control: they subscribed to and reinforced common myths and implemented measures to highlight the sacred nature of the links between center and periphery. No centralized political entity arose to weld the various parts together until well into the nineteenth century. Before then Maluku remained a cultural unity that was basically a loosely structured, flexible familial alliance of communities. This cultural state linked vast areas of eastern Indonesia, from Butung-Banggai and southeastern Sulawesi in the west to the northern coast of the Birdshead in New Guinea in the east, thereby making the later task of incorporating this vast and complex area into Netherlands India and the unitary state of Indonesia less daunting than it otherwise would have been.

Lach may have been unable to perceive this unity in Maluku because he was searching for some more fixed political or economic framework to define the whole. What he overlooked was the common adherence to a cultural truth that was even more widespread and durable than any political or economic entity.

2

Nguyen Hoang and the Beginning of Vietnam's Southward Expansion

Keith W. Taylor

Nguyen Hoang (1525–1613) lived during a particularly tumultuous era in the histories of the kingdoms of mainland Southeast Asia. The Toungoo empire arose among the Burmans and Mons of the Irrawaddy plain and reached out in conquest over the Tai peoples of the Chaophraya and middle Mekong plains. In response, Ayutthaya initiated an imperial momentum of its own that reduced the Khmer kings of the lower Mekong plain to vassalage. These events, however, were of peripheral interest to Nguyen Hoang, for he was himself involved in a military confrontation that, unlike the fluid movement of armies in the more sparsely populated Theravada Buddhist world, was prolonged with a tendency to settle into deadlock. Just as Bayin-naung introduced Portuguese cannon and musketry into his wars of conquest, Nguyen Hoang used Portuguese cannon to demolish the fortifications of his enemies. But victory was never as easy to define for Nguyen Hoang as it was for his contemporaries elsewhere in Southeast Asia. His was a world of constraints and minimal alternatives. His enemies were defined for him by others and they were hydra-headed; for him there was no clear-cut exhilaration of success. In the end, he made a fateful choice that in retrospect seems so natural and unavoidable that we may lose interest in why it was so difficult. In effect, he opted to turn his back on the world in which he was raised and in which he had exercised his ambitions for more than half a century. This was possible because an alternative world beckoned, a world as yet undefined but fated to be the place where Vietnamese found escape from traditional imperatives in what their historians described as a littoral paradise of peace, prosperity, and foreign merchants.

42

This is not the place for a full biography of Nguyen Hoang. I will simply focus on three "moments" in his career when he was faced with alternatives and suggest a possible reading of how he understood what he was doing. I am using two annals. The *Dai Viet su ky toan thu* was compiled in the second half of the seventeenth century from the perspective of the Le court at Hanoi and provides a critical appraisal of Nguyen Hoang; I shall call this the "northern annal." The *Dai Nam thuc luc* was compiled in the early nineteenth century from the perspective of the Nguyen court at Hue and regards Nguyen Hoang as the exemplary founder of the imperial house; I shall call this the "southern annal." Although not strictly contemporary, the two annals represent regional versions of significant episodes in national history; their accounts of Nguyen Hoang reveal diverging regional points of view.

Instead of using the terms "northern annal" and "southern annal," I could instead speak of the "seventeenth-century annal" and the "nineteenth-century annal." This would draw attention to how the boundaries of official historiography were shifted over time to accommodate new regional points of view. A third alternative would be to emphasize dynastic perspectives with the terms "Le dynasty annal" and "Nguyen dynasty annal." This would indicate how the vision of the past changed when the focus of political ascendance shifted from a "northern" to a "southern" dynasty. Recognizing that these alternative terminologies may be as fruitful as those I have chosen to employ here, I must nevertheless leave them for exploration another time.

Nguyen Hoang was the second son of Nguyen Kim, who in the 1520s began a movement to restore the Le dynasty in opposition to the Mac clan that had gained control of Hanoi and claimed imperial status. Nguyen Kim established the Le court at Tay Do, in Thanh Hoa. He was poisoned in 1545 by Mac agents and leadership of the Le restoration movement was thereupon assumed by Nguyen Hoang's brother-in-law Trinh Kiem. In his youth, Nguyen Hoang distinguished himself in the fighting between the Le and Mac forces, but then, according to southern historians, he feigned insanity to avoid the jealous attention of Trinh Kiem. The date conventionally understood as decisive in Nguyen Hoang's career is 1558, when he obtained appointment as garrison commander of Thuan Hoa, which corresponds to the modern province of Binh Tri Thien, and led his entourage south, establishing his headquarters at Ai Tu near the modern city of Quang Tri. This is the first moment I examine.

The second moment came during a critical three-year period in 1569–72 when Nguyen Hoang returned north to obtain from the dying Trinh Kiem authority over Quang Nam, which covered the Vietnamese terri-

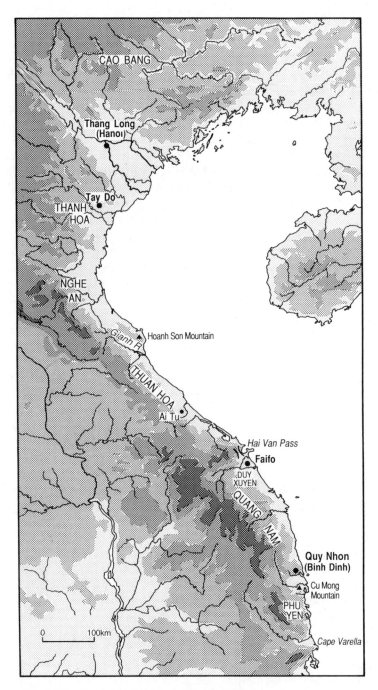

Map 4. The Nguyen and Trinh domains in Vietnam

tories south of Thuan Hoa; he also repelled an armed attack in his jurisdiction by forces pledging allegiance to the Mac and established good relations with the new Le overlord, his nephew Trinh Tung.

The third moment was Nguyen Hoang's final return to the north in 1593 after the Mac emperor had been driven from Hanoi. He stayed for seven years during which he was occupied with military operations against Mac forces. Finally, in 1600 he made his ultimate break with the north and returned south for the last time. The Mac would resist the Trinh for another seven decades from their sanctuary in Cao Bang, on the Chinese border, and Nguyen Hoang's sons and grandsons would do the same from their sanctuary in the south.

I am interested in how Nguyen Hoang and politically alert Vietnamese of his time and later understood the alternatives he faced and the decisions he made. Our northern annal shows us a man more clever than loyal, a capable man who can no longer be governed by appeals to his ancestors, a man grown arrogant by his familiarity with wealth and the power it confers. Our southern annal shows us a hero who against all odds survives the bloody affairs of a cramped, impoverished polity and leads his people into a land of peace and plenty, a man who knows how to command the loyalty of others, a man who understands foreign merchants. Nguyen Hoang has been ignored by modern Vietnamese historians because he does not exemplify the theme of national unity and resistance to foreign aggression that has been central to the modern Vietnamese experience. But in him we see the beginning of a southern version of being Vietnamese, and because Vietnamese today are no longer able to ignore the differences between north and south within their own tradition his place in history may become more significant as a key to understanding these differences. Nguyen Hoang's career may also show us how larger regional trends affected the growth of a southern variant of the national tradition.

The northern annal records that, in the tenth month of 1558, the chancellor (*thai su*) Trinh Kiem requested of the Le emperor that Nguyen Hoang, identified as the second son of Nguyen Kim and a duke (*quan cong*), be sent to lead soldiers to Thuan Hoa "to stand guard against the eastern pirates" and "give mutual aid" to the duke in charge of Quang Nam; "all local matters whether great or small and including all tax assessments, everything," were placed in Nguyen Hoang's hands and he was instructed "to receive each year the taxes that are due."[1] Here the emphasis is on the throne charging Nguyen

---

[1] *Dai Viet su ky toan thu* [hereafter *TT*], Chen Chingho edition (Tokyo, 1984–86), Ban Ky 16, p. 856.

Hoang with responsibility for a vulnerable frontier jurisdiction. The text does not explicitly identify the "eastern pirates"; perhaps they were a local manifestation of the Japanese-led operations that were at that time reaching their climax along the coasts of China, but, even if they were participants in a larger pirate culture along the coasts of the Asian mainland, the southern annal indicates that they were local groups claiming legitimacy as partisans of the Mac court. The Mac were active along the southern coasts in their efforts to distract the Le partisans during military operations in the north. The northern annal sees the appointment of Nguyen Hoang to be commander of Thuan Hoa as a straightforward administrative act, and this is the first mention of Nguyen Hoang in the annal.

In contrast, the southern annal begins with an extensive biography of Nguyen Hoang, including accounts of the careers of his father and grandfather. It explains that he was raised and educated by his maternal uncle, who became his most trusted adviser and eventually accompanied him south. He excelled in battle and is credited with killing a Mac general; he was accordingly promoted to the rank of duke. After the death of his elder brother, his uncle advised him to feign insanity to avoid the suspicion of the Trinh clan.

The annal also contains a story about Nguyen Hoang sending a messenger to Nguyen Binh Khiem to ask for advice. Nguyen Binh Khiem (1491–1585) served at the Mac court from 1535 to 1542, after which he retired to his home in a remote locality northeast of Hanoi, attracted disciples, and, standing aloof from public affairs, became known as the greatest scholar and writer of his age; his counsel was sought by all parties. In 1558, Nguyen Binh Khiem reportedly advised Nguyen Hoang that "in the region of Hoanh Son [a mountain on the traditional southern border] is room to stand for thousands of years." With a move to the south thereby legitimized by a figure whom all Vietnamese factions recognized as a spokesman for the ethos of the realm, Nguyen Hoang asked his sister to speak with her husband, Trinh Kiem, about assigning him command of Thuan Hoa. The southern annal explains that Trinh Kiem was worried about Thuan Hoa because, although the Le court had established representatives there, "the loyalties of the people were not one." The annal includes the text of what is presented as Trinh Kiem's request to the throne on Nguyen Hoang's behalf. In this request, Trinh Kiem says:

> Thuan Hoa is a strategic territory where soldiers and treasure drain from the kingdom; in the past, we have protected it in order to perfect the task of government, yet now the people still cherish rebel-

lion in their hearts and many followers of the Mac come floating across the sea, so we fear that some rebel leader will arrive and a good general will not be available to defend the area. The Duke of Doan [Nguyen Hoang] is from a family of military men; he has ability and foresight and can be sent to stand guard in this place; he and the commander of Quang Nam, the two of them providing mutual assistance to each other, will look after all our worries in the south.[2]

Whereas the appointment of Nguyen Hoang to go to Thuan Hoa is briefly recorded in the northern annal as simply one of many administrative acts at a busy royal court with priorities directed elsewhere, the southern annal features the appointment as a legitimizing inauguration for its narrative of the "great south" (Dai Nam). Southern historians preserved more of the textual record for the 1558 appointment, and their narrative includes explanatory tales that make it more than an administrative act. The southern account adds three themes that do not appear in the northern account. First, the untimely death of his elder brother makes Nguyen Hoang the leader of his clan and, with the attribution of this death to the ambition of Trinh Kiem, legitimizes enmity with the Trinh clan and provides a pretext for the decision to go south. Second, Nguyen Hoang cunningly initiates his own appointment; he feigns insanity to disarm his enemies and then enlists the assistance of his sister in obtaining the appointment from Trinh Kiem. Third, the imperial appointment is overshadowed by the counsel of Nguyen Binh Khiem, who is invoked as the highest endorsing authority for Nguyen Hoang's decision to go south. For the southern annal, the imperial appointment was simply a mechanism to implement an act already determined by Nguyen Hoang after consultation with the one man who, amid the prevailing political disorders, wielded a moral authority acknowledged by all contending parties. The southern narrative reveals Nguyen Hoang as the active agent and minimizes the significance of the imperial appointment; Nguyen Hoang's ability is the decisive factor and he is anointed by Nguyen Binh Khiem, the sage of the realm, to be the ruler of the south. In contrast, the northern annal reveals Trinh Kiem as the active agent and focuses entirely on the imperial appointment. Furthermore, and this already foreshadows the accusation of unfilial behavior that became the most damning Trinh complaint against Nguyen Hoang, the northern annal justifies the appointment not simply on Nguyen Hoang's "ability and foresight" but, more importantly, upon the fact that he is the son of Nguyen Kim;

[2]Dai Nam thuc luc, 9 vols. [hereafter TL] (Tokyo, 1961–74), 1:5–6.

Nguyen Hoang deserves the consideration of the court not because of anything he has done but rather because of the merit of his father.

In 1568, the duke in command of Quang Nam, the only Vietnamese jurisdiction south of Thuan Hoa, died, and the Le court appointed a man from the north to replace him.[3] In the following year, as Trinh Kiem drew near his own deathbed, Nguyen Hoang returned north and obtained the Quang Nam command from the Le court. The northern annal emphasizes the blood bond between Nguyen Hoang and Trinh Kiem. It notes that, as Nguyen Hoang proceeded to present himself at the Le court in Tay Do, he stopped along the way and greeted Kiem with "brotherly affection." Hoang's appointment to assume command of Quang Nam came not from the Le emperor but directly from Kiem in what was recorded as his last act, only one month before his death. The northern annal records Kiem's words on this occasion as follows: "The nation commits this great responsibility [to you]; from first to last there must be one flag. Exhaust [yourself] to the utmost in service to your earliest loyalties and assist the imperial house."[4] This statement uses terms for "nation" and "imperial house" that emphasize familial bonds; furthermore, its appeal to Hoang's "earliest loyalties," literally "first heart," invokes the family ties between the Nguyen and Trinh clans that were forged during the time of Nguyen Kim in the early years of the anti-Mac affair. But probably the most urgently telling phrase in these last words of Trinh Kiem is "from first to last there must be one flag." The image of one flag symbolizes imperial appointment at an abstract level and military command at a more prosaic level. This appeal belies a recognition and fear of the political separation of south from north that the assignment of Quang Nam to Nguyen Hoang appeared to encourage. Kiem exhorted Hoang to continue to regard himself as under obedience to the flag wielded by the Trinh.

Hoang returned south just before the death of Trinh Kiem and the outbreak of a succession dispute between two of Kiem's sons, Trinh Coi, who was eventually defeated and took refuge with the Mac, and Trinh Tung, who consolidated his control of the Trinh clan and the Le court, in the course of which the Le emperor took the field against him and was killed. During the two or three years of this disorder, Mac agents arrived on the southern coasts, recruiting and leading armies against the authority of the Trinh and Nguyen clans. The southern annal includes a story of how Nguyen Hoang achieved victory over this threat with the assistance of a female water spirit, for whom he

---

[3]This is recorded in both the northern and southern annals.
[4]*TT*, Ban Ky 16, p. 862.

thereupon built a temple and instituted a cult for formal worship.[5] This tale is significant, because it is the kind of episode that in Vietnamese annals is associated with founders of dynasties; it is evidence that Hoang had sufficient spiritual virtue to gain the attention and assistance of supernatural forces. He is depicted as cunning and alert, a man with his own karma, not dependent on royal favor or the merit of his ancestors.

Nguyen Hoang's success in defeating Mac intervention in the south during this critical time in the fortunes of the anti-Mac alliance was acknowledged in both the northern and southern annals with descriptions of Hoang's rule of the south in idealized terms. The northern annal reads as follows:

> Hoang soothed and governed for more than ten years. He ruled with geniality; seaborne merchants favored him; he applied law with impartiality, kept the local strongmen in check, and put an end to the cruel and crafty; the inhabitants of the two provinces [Thuan Hoa and Quang Nam] were influenced toward compassion and virtue and public morality was improved; people did not become bandits, doors were not locked, seaborne merchants from foreign kingdoms all came to buy and sell, a trading center was established; military discipline was strict, everyone worked hard. From that time, men of Mac did not dare come for plunder and the borderlands were at peace.[6]

This account contains many clichés of good government commonly utilized by Vietnamese historians; it also contains a perception of Hoang's jurisdiction as a place where international trade prospered. But the reason this glowing account of Nguyen Hoang is included in the northern annal is to explain how the problem of Mac intervention in the south was finally solved.

The southern version of this passage reads as follows:

> Hoang was on duty [in Thuan Hoa] more than ten years. His rule was liberal and tranquil. Military discipline was strict and dignified. The people all dwelt at peace and were content with their lot. The market did not have two prices [i.e., there was one fixed price]. People did not become bandits. The boats of merchants from all kingdoms gathered. Consequently, a large city was established.[7]

[5]TL, 1:10–12.
[6]TT, Ban Ky 16, p. 868.
[7]TL, 1:12.

This version is an abbreviation of the northern passage, and it was abbreviated because the southern historians had other interests. There is no mention of the Mac threat being solved. Rather, the point of the passage is to explain how it happened that "a large city was established."

In a separate passage, the southern annal echoes the preoccupation of the northern annal: following Hoang's defeat of a Mac intervention, Hoang "had much prestige, was cunning and seized opportunities, maintained strict discipline, and kept close guard; for these reasons, rebel soldiers did not dare to plunder the borders and the two places of Thuan Hoa and Quang Nam were at peace."[8] Here, Hoang's ability to keep peace in the south is explained not by appeal to clichéd historiographic devices or an exotic perception of foreign merchants but by an earthy evaluation of Hoang's mode of operation; he had a battlefield reputation that discouraged potential rebels.

The mention of a large city being established can refer only to the gathering place for Chinese, Japanese, Portuguese, and other merchants at the place known to Europeans as Faifo and today called Hoi An by the Vietnamese, not far south of the modern city of Da Nang. This entrepôt was conveniently located on the route between Melaka and Macao, which the Portuguese established as their primary means of access to China and Japan during the last half of the sixteenth century.[9] Yet Nguyen Hoang never resided at this place. As I have occasion to note later in this essay, he made one brief visit to the area in 1602 to establish a garrison under the command of one of his sons. His headquarters remained at Ai Tu, around 170 kilometers north of Faifo by land route. Although an entrepôt was prospering under his jurisdiction, there is no evidence that Nguyen Hoang took a personal interest in it; his priorities were directed elsewhere. In fact, although the southern annal tends to nurture an image of Nguyen Hoang after 1558 as a man whose destiny awaited him in the south, it is clear from both annals that Nguyen Hoang did not finally renounce his ambitions in the north until 1600. And even after that fateful decision was made, his descendants never chose to rule from their entrepôt but rather kept it at arm's length; it was for them a source of enrichment and nothing more.[10]

[8]*TL*, 1:8.

[9]Pierre-Yves Manguin, *Les Portugais sur les côtes du Viet Nam et du Campa* (Paris, 1972), pp. 184–87.

[10]The southern annal (*TL*, 1:13–14) records the only direct contact between Nguyen Hoang and Europeans as a military affair in 1585. A "Western Sea Kingdom [European] bandit chieftain" with the foreign title of Hien Quy (Chinese Hsien-kuei) arrived at the mouth of the Viet river in northern Thuan Hoa with five big ships. Hoang's sixth son and eventual successor

When, in 1572, Trinh Tung was occupied with tracking down the fugitive emperor and enthroning a pliant successor, he had the Le court send an official to visit Nguyen Hoang. Both annals record this as a successful encounter. Whereas the northern annal appears to treat the episode as an emblem of the continuing fraternal bond linking the Trinh and Nguyen clans, the southern annal takes the occasion to emphasize northern recognition of Hoang's accomplishments in the south. At a time when Trinh forces were closing in on the fleeing emperor not far from the Thuan Hoa border, the northern annal says that the envoy was sent to "inspect" and "speak kindly" to the southern troops; Hoang assembled his soldiers and held a feast for the envoy during which they "exhausted reminiscences and emotions from the old days and were very glad."[11] According to the southern annal, the envoy came to "congratulate" the southern soldiers for their victories over the Mac forces, and Hoang received him "with joy" and "sent him away with many gifts."[12] Here again the northern annal emphasizes the ancestral link between Trinh and Nguyen, the "old days" before Nguyen Hoang was assigned to the south; yet in using the expression "old days" it admits that things had changed. The southern annal features the many gifts Hoang bestowed on the envoy, recalling the theme of southern prosperity in contrast to northern poverty during the 1580s that appears in the southern annal.

The southern annal records the visit of a tax collector sent by the Le court in 1586; this is not recorded in the northern annal. The southern annal features the episode as an indication of Nguyen Hoang's ability to deal successfully with legal claims upon him from the north. The "inspector general" arrived "to investigate the cultivated fields and to collect the tax due"; in a note, the annal explains that at that time field taxes in Thuan Hoa and Quang Nam were not yet fixed, so every year at harvest officials were sent to inspect and collect. The annal then says that Hoang treated the tax officer "with esteem and respect"; the officer was "deeply moved, and consequently did not again calculate [the tax due] [but] allowed each district and village to prepare their own registers."[13] In this episode, the annal proposes that the southerners avoided the direct scrutiny of a northern tax collector because Nguyen

---

attacked with over ten boats and destroyed two of the alien ships, whereupon Hien Quy fled. Whether Hien Quy can be equated with some Portuguese or Spanish name or title I do not know. The annal, in a note, indicates that Hien Quy was a foreign title and not the personal name of the chieftain.

[11]*TT*, Ban Ky 16, p. 869.
[12]*TL*, 1:12.
[13]*TL*, 1:14.

Hoang's conduct caused him to be "deeply moved" and accordingly indulgent toward local autonomy. Behind this theme of relations between northern tax collectors and southern tax payers, again, was the perception of the north as an impoverished land and of the south as a land of plenty. Furthermore, the ability to neutralize the activities of northern inspectors suggests that southern cunning was superior to northern authority.

Fighting between the Mac and Le restoration forces led by Trinh Tung became increasingly intense as the 1580s wore on. In the southern annal this is characterized as a time when the Trinh became economically dependent on Nguyen Hoang. The following observation is recorded under the year 1589: "At that time, year after year there were abundant harvests; the people were satisfied and prosperous. [But] year after year, the Le emperor did not have enough men and supplies for military operations. [Hoang] ordered the collection of taxes to assist with military expenditures, yet there was no lack or deficit. [The Le court] relied on [this assistance]."[14] In 1592, after nearly seventy years of warfare, Mac forces were driven from Hanoi. This brought fighting to all parts of the Hong River plain as Trinh Tung strove to pacify areas that had been loyal to the Mac for two or three generations and to push remaining Mac forces into the mountains. At this critical moment, Nguyen Hoang went north with a well-provisioned army to add his weight to the power struggle.

Nguyen Hoang's arrival in the north is related differently in the two annals. The northern annal emphasizes the material reinforcement brought to the anti-Mac struggle: Hoang "arrived at the capital from Thuan Hoa to pay respects to his superiors, personally leading soldiers, elephants, horses, and boats; he conveyed and offered up provisions for troops, valuables and property, gold and silver, pearls and gems, and the storehouse records for the two commands of Thuan Hoa and Quang Nam."[15] This passage reads much like the stereotyped descriptions of Viet Nam in early Chinese sources that feature an exotic image of their south as a place where tropical luxury goods are available and fortunes easily gained; perhaps it partakes of the historiographic tradition of Chinese perceptions of the south. But the point of the passage is revealed in what immediately follows it: Trinh Tung requests that the court promote Hoang to the rank of grand duke (*quoc cong*) and then orders him to proceed against Mac forces entrenched in a coastal area where Trinh generals had been stymied by an enemy

[14]*TL*, 1:14.
[15]*TT*, Ban Ky 17, p. 899.

wall. Hoang uses "large cannon of all types" to destroy the wall; Mac forces are "scattered." There is an air of the exotic and the marvelous in the northern annal's perception of Nguyen Hoang's arrival. He bursts with amazing wealth and wonderful engines of war into a scene straitened by poverty and powerful enemies; he is from another world. Yet he is also under the command of Trinh Tung.

The southern annal contains nothing of this perception of Nguyen Hoang as a bearer of wealth, supplies, and weapons. Rather, Hoang "led naval forces and went to visit the Le emperor," who "praised him," saying: "You have protected two regions; the people trust you and are at peace. Your merit is great." The emperor then promoted him to grand duke.[16] Trinh Tung does not figure in this scene as he does in the northern annal. Instead, the emphasis is on the emperor praising Nguyen Hoang. Furthermore, Nguyen Hoang is portrayed in the southern annal as attacking Mac forces without reference to a command from his superiors as is emphasized in the northern annal. Instead of mentioning the use of cannon, the southern annal simply says that he defeated his foes, but adds something ignored by the northern annal—that Hoang's second son was killed in the fighting. From these observations, we can see the northern perception of Hoang as an exotic yet subservient figure who is valuable because of his wealth and military prowess, while in the southern annal he is portrayed as a recipient of royal recognition for his successful rule in the south and a loyal servant of the king at great personal sacrifice.

From 1593 until 1600, Nguyen Hoang remained in the north. Why? Both annals offer similar descriptions of his activities during this time. He was primarily occupied with military operations against the Mac; but whereas the northern annal records that each time Hoang took the field against Mac partisans he was sent by Trinh Tung, the southern annal makes no mention of him being sent by a superior authority but rather makes it appear as if he acted by his own volition. In 1596 and 1597 there were a series of intense diplomatic contacts with Ming China regarding Ming recognition of the Le court and the status of the Mac clan; Nguyen Hoang participated in these activities as a prominent member of the Le emperor's entourage during two trips to the Ming border. The two annals do not diverge significantly in their accounts of these episodes and both record that, "from that time, relations were again established between the two countries of South and North [Le Viet Nam and Ming China]."[17]

[16]TL, 1:15.
[17]TT, Ban Ky 17, p. 909; TL, 1:18.

What most significantly differentiates the two treatments of Nguyen Hoang during this time is their visions of his past and the loyalties he owed that past. The southern annal is not much interested in tying Hoang to his past, but it does briefly note that the first thing he did after greeting the emperor on his arrival in the north was to go to Thanh Hoa to visit the tombs of his ancestors and report to them.[18] The northern annal, however, includes the text of an imperial edict written for Nguyen Hoang to announce at the tomb of Trinh Kiem conferring on Kiem a posthumous promotion. The northern annal briefly adds that someone (an officer whose name does not appear elsewhere in the annal) was also sent to announce a similar promotion at the tomb of Nguyen Kim, Hoang's father, but the scene at Trinh Kiem's tomb is placed stage center in the annal.

The edict Nguyen Hoang read to his deceased brother-in-law, Trinh Kiem, begins by announcing the general principle of posthumous recognition: "Great ministers of state accumulate merit by being sincerely concerned with the aspirations of the people; the court examines what happened in the past and must record those who have earned merit and accordingly publish their deeds for all to know, and it is fitting to do this with great splendor."[19] Here is the well-established rule of just rewards for service rendered, which is prominently featured in Chinese and Vietnamese historiography; but the emphasis is not on rewards to Kiem, who in any case is already dead, but on proclaiming his merit "for all to know" and "with great splendor." The message is for the living, not for the dead. But it is a message that calls on the living to think about the past and to consider the past as containing figures worthy of emulation; the behavior of the living should follow patterns set by the dead, the dead have a claim on the living. This became the heart of the Trinh argument with Nguyen Hoang. The edict then addresses Trinh Kiem, describing him as a "proud and stately tree, from a great clan, wrapped with courtly honors." The imperial voice then proceeds: "From the beginning [you] responded to our banner, persevered in difficulty, seriously put in order the affairs of [your] time, assisted in restoration of the correct pattern, earned great merit toward the [Le dynasty]." The edict then cites two exemplary figures from T'ang history with whom Trinh Kiem can be compared: Li Sheng (727–93), who recaptured Chang-an from rebels for the T'ang emperor in 784, and Kuo Tzu-i (697–781), who was prominent in the suppression of the An Lu Shan rebellion. These citations shed light on the historical

---

[18]*TL*, 1:15.
[19]*TT*, Ban Ky 17, p. 901.

image nurtured by the Trinh: they posed as loyal servants of the Le throne, struggling with the forces of rebellion and disorder to "restore" the proper order. They looked to the mid-T'ang crisis in China as an age comparable to their own, a time when the legitimate ruler was challenged by rebels and had to rely on loyal and talented ministers to put things right again. By announcing this edict, Nguyen Hoang was publicly identifying himself with this Trinh conception of restoration. The edict then identifies Nguyen Hoang as its assigned bearer and proceeds to announce Trinh Kiem's promotion. It ends with the following comment: "Furthermore, [we] request that, in receiving and displaying [our] praise, [you] will strive to plan for and with sincerity assist the eternal prosperity of the state." Although ostensibly a prayer addressed to Trinh Kiem by the Le emperor, this could equally be an appeal addressed to Nguyen Hoang by his nephew, Trinh Tung. This edict—and the spectacle of Nguyen Hoang announcing it before the tomb of Trinh Kiem—is a token of the northern annal's view of what was lacking in Nguyen Hoang. His perceived lack of loyalty to the past and to the vision of the future embodied in that past was the northern explanation of his eventual rejection of the authority in whose name the northern annal was compiled.

From a twentieth-century vantage, it may appear odd that Nguyen Hoang stayed in the north for seven years, entering the eighth decade of his life, apparently under the command of his nephew, expending his men and treasure in a military confrontation that showed few signs of abating. What is not generally realized is that he had ambitions of supplanting the Trinh and uniting all the Vietnamese lands under his hand. When he finally released this ambition, he quickly lost interest in events in the north and hastened back to his base in the south. What led him to make this decision?

In the fourth month of 1599, Trinh Tung was promoted to the rank of king (*vuong*), a rank previously reserved for members of the imperial family. The northern annal contains the text of the edict that announced Tung's promotion and praised his merit.[20] Prior to this event, although Tung held military titles that placed him ahead of Hoang in the chain of command, both men were grand dukes. This unprecedented elevation of Tung's status is a clear indication that in the competition for position at the Le court Tung was pulling ahead of Hoang. In the eighth month of the year, the emperor died. According to the northern annal, Trinh Tung and the court decided that the crown prince was "not intelligent" and so passed over him and enthroned his

[20]*TT*, Ban Ky 17, p. 918.

younger brother instead. Just eighteen days before, the court was ordered to prepare a roster of worthy officials; such a measure implies the application of a new criterion for excellence and suggests the possibility that Trinh Tung was identifying those he could trust. The imperial succession was accompanied by a lengthy edict that contains three points of interest.[21] First, the new emperor, who was twelve years old, would be assisted by the "virtue" (*duc*) of Trinh Tung and the efforts of all the other officials; Tung was clearly designated to preside over a regency. Second, the edict shows a fresh determination to institute a larger measure of discipline over officialdom with rewards and punishments; Trinh control over the court would be translated into Trinh control of all officialdom. This theme is ostensibly related to the abated yet continuing hostilities with Mac partisans, but its most immediate effect would be on the competition with Nguyen Hoang for influence within the official class. Third, there is an acute sensitivity to the question of the unity of the realm. The edict ends on a rather surprising note of anguish and hope: "Alas! Orthodoxy began with the great unification of Spring and Autumn. Now [we] inquire about the present time, to obtain a kingdom united under the Yin Hsi calendar, thus gathering an unbroken flood of blessings. [This edict] is published far and near that all may hear and know." The "great unification of Spring and Autumn" and the "Yin Hsi calendar" are classical emblems of a united and well-regulated realm and of orthodoxy. "Alas" indicates that the present time has not yet attained this orthodoxy; one of the intents of the edict is to announce the principles by which orthodoxy is to be defined, and these principles require acceptance of Trinh Tung's authority. The edict reveals that Trinh Tung's authority was not yet accepted "far and near." But it also reveals that he had now achieved a position of supremacy at the Le court and claimed the right to define orthodoxy.

Shortly after Tung's promotion and the proclamation of his regency, Nguyen Hoang made the decision to return south. To do so, he would be forced to defy the authority of Tung; the struggle for power that had heretofore been waged in private would become a public affair. According to the northern annal, in 1600 Nguyen Hoang "secretly instigated" an uprising of Mac partisans in a coastal region south of Hanoi. It then records subsequent events as follows: "Hoang, wanting to carry out his private scheme, deviously requested authorization to pursue and attack [the rebels]. Burning his barracks, he secretly returned to Thuan Hoa. Because of this, there were disturbances in the kingdom

[21]*TT*, Ban Ky 17, pp. 919–20.

and the feelings of the people were shaken. The king [Trinh Tung] thereupon escorted the emperor to [Tay Do] and made plans for defense."[22] What is interesting about this passage is its testimony about the effect of Hoang's actions on the political situation in the north. That his sudden escape from Trinh supervision should be the cause of "disturbances" and shake the "feelings" of "the people" reveals that Hoang was indeed a figure of some political potency in the north. The northern annal attributes the uprising of Mac partisans to Nguyen Hoang's secret plotting; it was simply a screen for his departure. This account suggests that Hoang was perceived as someone with contacts and influence among those who had previously followed the Mac, which included nearly everyone in the Hong River plain. Tay Do was the fortress in Thanh Hoa near the ancestral home of Nguyen Hoang where the Le emperors had dwelled during the years Hanoi was in the hands of the Mac. Why Tung's first response to Hoang's disappearance was to hasten to Tay Do is explained in the southern annal.

The southern annal's account of these events gives no hint that Nguyen Hoang had a hand in instigating the uprising of Mac loyalists. Unlike the northern annal, which sees Hoang's treacherous hand behind all the difficulties of that time, the southern annal lays the blame elsewhere: Hoang "was at [the capital] during eight years; he attacked and subdued all four quarters. Because his merit was great, the Trinh hated and envied him."[23] According to the southern annal, Trinh jealousy rather than Nguyen treachery was behind the rupture between north and south. The southern annal then recounts the outbreak of the uprising: Hoang "took the occasion to mobilize his soldiers, advanced to attack, and then, leading all his officers and men, embarked in his boats and returned directly to Thuan Hoa by sea." The southern annal immediately adds that Hoang left behind his fifth son and a grandson as "pledge" but that the news of his departure "disturbed the people"; Trinh Tung "feared that Hoang intended to occupy Tay Do, so he took the emperor and rushed to Tay Do and secured it." Tung's initial thought was that Hoang had finally come out into the open to challenge his supremacy at the Le court, and the most logical move for Hoang in such a scenario would have been to establish control of Tay Do. Both annals reveal that the political tensions were extremely high at the time of Hoang's departure. The idea of Hoang raising his standard against the Trinh was widely understood as a likely possibility. Hoang apparently had a choice of going to war with the Trinh or

[22]*TT*, Ban Ky 18, p. 923.
[23]*TL*, 1:19.

resting content with his possession of the south. His decision to renounce further ambitions in the north came only when it was clear that, unless he did, war would inevitably ensue. That he chose to avoid open confrontation is characteristic of his preference for subtle stratagems, and it may also suggest the strength of the Trinh appeal to ancestral ties upon him.

According to the southern annal, Trinh Tung encountered Hoang's son and grandson on the road as he departed from Tay Do after realizing that Hoang had gone south. Hoang's son explained his father's actions by saying that he had "returned to Thuan Hoa only out of his concern for defense of the frontier; there was truly no disloyal scheme." The southern annal then notes that "this [explanation] was accepted and [the situation] calmed down."[24] The northern annal makes no mention of this episode or even that Hoang had left behind a son and grandson as pledge. The southern annal is careful to show that Hoang had endeavored to maintain the forms of a continuing relationship with the Le court.

The accounts in the two annals of the contacts between Tung and Hoang that followed these events were designed to establish public attitudes toward the unprecedented degree of separation that was thereafter perceived between north and south. The northern annal nurtures an image of Hoang as a treacherous, arrogant, and ambitious man who threatened the peace and order of the realm, a man who could not be moved by appeals to ancestral loyalties. The southern annal portrays him as a man who did as he wished and who was feared by the Trinh; this much is not contradicted by the northern view. But it also shows Hoang as a man with a destiny beyond the horizon of his ancestors, a man who resonated with the landscape of a new land, the supernatural powers that dwelled in it, and the opportunities available there.

According to the northern annal, within a month of Hoang's return to the south Tung sent him a letter. The text of this letter is included in the annal and constitutes an official statement of the Trinh complaint against Hoang.[25] It is a long document and deserves careful study, but here I can only summarize the main points that serve to draw our discussion toward a close. In this letter, Tung addresses Hoang as "uncle," or more precisely "my mother's brother," and refers to himself as "nephew," or "your sister's son." He begins by appealing to the "obligations of close family relations" and the importance of such

[24]*TL*, 1:19.
[25]*TT*, Ban Ky 18, p. 923–24.

obligations among high ministers of state for the welfare of the realm. This opening is followed by a historical narrative beginning with the merit of Nguyen Kim, Hoang's father, in serving the Le dynasty and recounting that after the death of Kim, Trinh Kiem, Tung's father, carried on the task begun by Kim while Hoang was assigned to protect Thuan Hoa and Quang Nam. Tung notes that Hoang ruled the south well, kept his jurisdiction in peace, and was unstinting in sending taxes and eventually in personally assisting the Le cause against the Mac. This affirmation of Hoang's past merit is an important part of the Trinh argument with Hoang; his later deeds were a betrayal of an established pattern of loyalty. Tung affirms that, in recompense for his good service, Hoang had been assigned a fief not far from the capital; Tung claims that it had been his intention that Hoang, along with another prominent general, serve as his right and left hands in governing the realm. Tung then notes the uprising that precipitated Hoang's departure and informs Hoang that it was quickly suppressed, but he refrains from attributing it to Hoang's instigation. Here is his version of what happened and his judgment of Hoang:

> We [your sister's son and my mother's brother] were occupied in arranging military affairs to attack and destroy the rebels. Unexpectedly, [you] no longer responded to commands but, acting privately and without authority, returned [to Thuan Hoa], stirring up and exciting the local people. I do not know if this was your own intention or the result of the scheming of others, in which case I have misunderstood; which is it? [You] are surely able to fully recognize your fault and to repent of your error. Consider the merit of your ancestors. [I] am sending a messenger to present this letter [to you] and to superintend the gathering of wealth and taxes [from you] as a contribution to the nation, whereby [you] may gain merit to cancel your transgression. The court has laws and regulations [about transgressions like yours], but in consideration of [your] former loyal service, it is possible [for you] to be completely restored [to favor] and the fame of [your] merit will endure for generations and never be forgotten. If this way is not taken, then, following the usual procedure for attacking rebels, the court will use its best soldiers! In that case, how will it go for [your] name and reputation? You are familiar with military affairs and you also pay attention to the classics and histories; look into and consider all these things and do not hand down remorse to your posterity.

In this letter, all Tung's resentment and anger surface. He interprets Hoang's escape from his supervision as an act of rebellion. He is willing to entertain the face-saving formula of Hoang not being personally responsible for what had happened, but he insists that payment be made before the affair can be forgiven, and he ends with threats of military operations if Hoang fails to repent. This letter is strikingly similar to letters sent by Chinese rulers to Vietnamese rulers, beginning in the tenth century, to explain why Chinese armies were being mobilized to attack them. The sense of betrayal, the appeal to ancestral loyalties, the enumeration of transgressions, the exhortation to repent, and the threat of dire consequences are all familiar in Vietnamese historiography; now, for the first time, they are being used not by a Chinese ruler to intimidate a Vietnamese ruler but by one Vietnamese ruler against another. This suggests the significance of what was happening in Viet Nam at this time. A new version of being Vietnamese was in the process of formation; it was identified by the traditional center of Vietnamese culture and polity, at Hanoi, as something that had slipped out of its control, a contradiction of, and a threat to, its claim to define what Vietnamese could and could not do on the stage of political action.

Unlike the occasions of such letters from Chinese rulers, war did not immediately break out. Fighting between the Trinh and Nguyen would not begin for more than twenty years, and then under the leadership of Tung's and Hoang's sons. But a letter such as this was a declaration of war, and northern historians had to explain why there was no war. Their explanation turns on an anecdote, about Hoang's reception of the envoy bearing the letter, which embodies the defeat of Hoang in a battle of wits with the envoy; for northern historians, one of Hoang's prime attributes was his cunning, and the ability of the northern envoy to overcome Hoang's cunning with his own was for them a metaphor of what they chose to interpret as Hoang's subordination to northern authority. According to the anecdote, Hoang had foreknowledge of the letter and wished to avoid receiving it, in which case he would be forced to publicly acknowledge the Trinh complaint against him and respond to it.[26] The envoy "knew that Hoang invariably employed many schemes" and so, when he arrived in the south, he hid the letter in a bamboo tube secreted in a thick clump of trees in the open country. Hoang "schemed to snatch the letter and thereby disgrace the envoy"; he sent a thief at night to seize all the envoy's baggage. When the letter was not found in the baggage, Hoang sent the thief back to burn down the place where the envoy was sleeping, believing that the letter would be lost in the flames. But the envoy's precautions enabled him to present the letter to an astonished Hoang the next morning. Hoang ac-

[26]*TT*, Ban Ky 18, p. 924.

knowledged the envoy's success by saying, "Heaven gives birth to men with military talent, but the court has real men." These words, attributed to Hoang by northern historians, constituted an admission by Hoang of his own inferiority as a man with merely "military talent," unable to match wits with the kind of loyal man found at the Le court. The northern annal ends this account with the following observation: "From that time, [Hoang] never again looked down [on the Trinh] with ambitious disdain." This comment suggests a defensive, vulnerable perception of Hoang as a clever, unpredictable adversary; the "never again" contains a sigh of relief that Hoang had now confined his ambitions to the south.

The southern annal does not record the text of Tung's letter, nor does it record the anecdote about its delivery. Rather, it records simply that the Le emperor sent an envoy with an edict directing Hoang to "stand guard" in the south "as usual" and to collect taxes for the court; a letter from Tung was also received "advising" Hoang to pay taxes. This emphasis on the northern request for taxes became a large part of the explanation of southern historians for the eventual outbreak of hostilities; the southern annal perceives the north as the source of constant demands on their wealth, and resistance to northern demands was eventually justified on the basis of the immoderation of these demands. But in Hoang's lifetime there was no open resistance. He had spent his life in loyal service to the Le court, and in the south there were more interesting things to do than nurture confrontation with the north. The southern annal records that Hoang "generously entertained the envoy and sent a messenger to thank the emperor; he also sent a letter to Trinh Tung proposing a covenant treaty and promising to give bond for it by a marriage alliance." Within half a year, Hoang sent one of his daughters to wed Trinh Trang, Tung's son and eventual successor. The southern annal sums up the situation after this marriage as follows: "From that time [Hoang] did not go to [the capital] again. Members of the Le court repeatedly talked about settling the affair, but Trinh Tung shrank from using soldiers and dared not take action."[27] Southern historians explained why war did not break out by describing Hoang's successful negotiating strategy and noting Tung's fear of Hoang's military prowess. For them, Hoang continued to be the active agent in the situation.

Hoang lived thirteen more years after his final departure from the north. He disappeared from the northern annal. The southern annal records many details of his activities during these years, which can be

[27]TL, 1:19–20.

summarized under three headings. First, he built five temples in various parts of his domain; there is reference to his "enjoyment of the scenery" in areas where temples were built and to his visiting temples for "fasting and penance" and to "give alms." These were ostensibly Buddhist temples, but not exclusively. One was built at the dwelling place of a female spirit with great supernatural power; this spirit had previously made known by oracle that "a great ruler will come and build a temple here," and Hoang accordingly built a temple for the worship of the spirit and the Buddha.[28] This linking of the ruler with local animist cults and Buddhism is nothing new in Vietnamese history; the same kind of thing occurred in the eleventh century when the early Ly rulers were building their dynastic authority. Hoang is portrayed by southern historians as being in the same mold as earlier dynastic founders in Vietnamese history. The idea of founding a new dynasty had been defeated in the north by the Le restoration; in the south, there was yet room for this change-affirming strand of Vietnamese historiography. The anecdotes recorded about Nguyen Hoang encountering local spirits and establishing places of worship for them suggest the application of a particular Vietnamese way of establishing a new locus of authority and legitimacy, now for the first time in the former Cham territories of the Vietnamese south.

A second kind of information in the southern annal from Hoang's final years concerns the continued expansion of Vietnamese control farther south. In 1611, hostilities with the Chams resulted in the formation of Phu Yen, a new jurisdiction in the region of modern Tuy Hoa.[29] Before this time, Binh Dinh had been the southernmost command of Hoang's domain with the border at Cu Mong. With the acquisition of Phu Yen, the border was shifted to the cape called Varella. The southern border was easily expanded, in contrast to the fixed line that marked the northern border both of the Le realm with China and of the Nguyen lands with the Trinh domain. The experience of an expanding frontier is reminiscent of the broadening horizons experienced by the early Ly kings during the eleventh century, before the Sino-Vietnamese border was clearly defined.[30] But it also drew the Vietnamese away from the source of their own traditions and exposed them to a non-Vietnamese world with possibilities of being Vietnamese in nontraditional ways.

A final episode worthy of comment from Hoang's later years is his

[28]*TL*, 1:20–21.
[29]*TL*, 1:22–23.
[30]K. W. Taylor, "Authority and Legitimacy in 11th-Century Vietnam," in *Southeast Asia in the 9th to 14th Centuries*, ed. D. Marr and A. C. Milner (Singapore, 1986), pp. 149–50.

only recorded visit south of Hai Van Pass, to Quang Nam in 1602.[31] The southern annal begins by observing that in Quang Nam "the land was fertile and well populated, material goods were abundant, tax revenue greatly exceeded what could be collected in Thuan Hoa, and soldiers there were more than half the number of soldiers in Thuan Hoa." This image of prosperity, which we have encountered several times already, appears as a metaphor for opportunity. According to the annal, "Hoang often thought about how to govern this land," and eventually he traveled south to see it for himself. After examining the situation, he selected a site between 15 and 20 kilometers upriver from the entrepôt at Faifo, in the district of Duy Xuyen. There he built a garrison and a storehouse, erected a temple, and assigned his sixth son, and eventual successor, to take command. After interviewing the man in command of the southernmost garrison at Binh Dinh, he returned to Thuan Hoa. Although we know from non-Vietnamese sources that the port of Faifo was a thriving center of international commerce, and although Vietnamese sources repeatedly refer vaguely to foreign merchants gathering at some unidentified place under Nguyen Hoang's jurisdiction, and one even mentions a "large city," nowhere in Vietnamese sources is this city identified by name or location.

Nguyen Hoang finally established the direct presence of his family in Quang Nam only in 1602, shortly after his final fateful departure from the north. But the fact that he placed his most competent son in command of the garrison there reveals the importance he attached to the place. We have already noted that the southern annal describes Quang Nam as more prosperous and productive than Thuan Hoa; surely the presence of foreign merchants was not unconnected with this perception. Hoang selected a site for his son's headquarters that was admirably located to supervise the port—without being dominated by it.

The evidence forces us to draw a curious conclusion: the port of Faifo was a prosperous international entrepôt for half a century before Nguyen Hoang established a direct administrative presence in its vicinity. Before he did this, Hoang surely took an interest in the place and sent officers to supervise it to some extent; at least we can assume as much from the comments in the annals about Hoang maintaining order and discipline in the south, the reference to fixed prices being enforced in the market, and repeated mention of foreign merchants. Yet Hoang's interest did not go beyond order, security, and profit. He did not perceive Faifo as a proper place for either himself or his son to reside. Nothing attracted his attention sufficiently for him to believe that there

[31]*TL*, 1:21.

his authority could be measurably enhanced by a more direct and active exploitation of opportunities for enrichment. And the same can be said for his descendants. We may feel compelled to try to explain this disinterest by citing a presumed bias in Vietnamese culture for agriculture and control of land rather than commercially generated wealth. But this compulsion surely rests on cultural assumptions of our own. Is it necessary to explain why someone might not be eager to exploit the marketplace? Must we regard other priorities as anomalous and in need of rationalization? These questions bring me to my final two points.

First, Nguyen Hoang's exposure, along the coasts of what is now central Viet Nam, to the larger world of Southeast Asia enabled him to establish a new version of being Vietnamese distinguished by relative freedom from the Vietnamese past and the authority justified by appeals to that past. In the context of values announced from the traditional seat of Vietnamese authority, he was a rebel because he did not honor his obligations to the dead; he broke free from the bond of merit that linked him with his ancestors. He turned his back on efforts to draw him into the constraints of a restoration mentality that nurtured an idealized vision of the past. Instead of depending on ancestral merit, he lived by his wits. In this way, he participated more fully than his Trinh kinsmen in a world of options and choices. His decision to go south in 1600 is a metaphor for all the decisions that going south would make possible, simply because, in rejecting the traditional definition of a "good Vietnamese," options for being another kind of "good Vietnamese" could be explored. The social discipline required for survival in close proximity to the Chinese border began to relax. Talent and ability began to count for more than birth and position. This was, in effect, an escape from ancestors, an escape from the past. For Nguyen Hoang, the result was a greater reliance on his own abilities, a shifting of the burden of moral choice from the past to the present.

Nguyen Hoang was confronted with options not sanctioned in what had become the Vietnamese political tradition, and he was in a position to exercise his own discernment in measuring these options. In a word, his encounter with the larger world of Southeast Asia bestowed a new experience of freedom. He dared to risk being pronounced a rebel, because he had found a place where such pronouncements no longer mattered. At the intersection of Southeast Asia and Viet Nam was room to explore options without a coercive model of how things ought to be. In the south, Hoang was free to be the center of a new Vietnamese realm. He was free to travel about, to be inspired by new scenery, to dream visitations of new spirits and establish personal relationships with them, to build new temples, to taste the sensory and imaginative powers of unexplored terrain—all reminiscent of activities ascribed to the early Ly kings in the eleventh century.

A good example of this freedom is the 1572 episode recorded in the southern annal, mentioned above, of Hoang defeating a Mac partisan with the assistance of a local female spirit. In this story, Hoang noticed a spot near his encampment where the river made a crying sound like "trao trao." He regarded this as "strange" and possibly evidence that a spirit dwelled there. Accordingly, he uttered a prayer that, if a river spirit be there, it help him destroy his enemy. That night he dreamed of a "woman dressed in green holding a white silk fan in her hand," who promised assistance with supernatural powers if he would employ a beautiful woman to entice his enemy into an ambush. When Hoang awoke, he related his dream to his entourage, and subsequently a palace woman famed for both beauty and cleverness was sent to entice Hoang's enemy to the place where the river made the "trao trao" sound. Hoang's enemy, ignoring the warnings of his followers, fell into the trap and was killed. Hoang thereupon rewarded the woman, conferred a title on the water spirit, and built a shrine for it. This story follows a pattern found in many tales from the Ly dynasty:[32] the ruler takes interest in some scenic or unusual feature of the landscape and calls on any spirits that may be residing there; the spirit appears to the ruler and offers assistance; and the ruler responds by establishing a place of worship for the spirit. This relationship between supernatural and temporal powers reveals a religious or cultural basis for initiating authority of long standing in the Vietnamese tradition.

My second and final point, in conclusion, is to suggest that Nguyen Hoang's career offers a clue to what may be a significant feature of Southeast Asia at that time, namely, the diversity of options open to ruling-class people and the diversity of choices exercised on those options.

[32]*TL*, 1:10–11; Taylor, 1986, pp. 156–69.

PART 2

Commerce and the Southeast Asian State

Chinese and European demand for Southeast Asian products rose markedly in the fifteenth century and peaked in the global trade boom of 1570–1630. The states around the busy Straits of Malacca, through which most trade between eastern Asia and the rest of Eurasia had to pass, were particularly affected by these currents.

In the fifteenth century the Sultanate of Melaka became the archetype of a Southeast Asian port-state benefiting from the trade upturn. Luis Filipe Thomaz describes the commercial communities and methods concentrated there in the remarkable moment of its flowering on the eve of the Portuguese advent.

In the later boom period, several "pepper states" arose to meet the great expansion in demand for pepper, especially from Europe. Barbara Andaya shows how the downstream river capital of Jambi flourished as a result of its pepper exports, which in turn transformed its delicate relationship with the ethnically complex upstream areas where pepper was grown. The power of the capital over this hinterland grew as a result of the pepper trade, but by the late seventeenth century European monopoly pressures for lower prices strained the relationship to breaking point.

Jeyamalar Kathirithamby-Wells directly addresses an issue our other contributors explore obliquely: how far Southeast Asia developed, or might have developed, in a capitalist direction. She shows that rulers were as concerned with trade there as in any part of the early modern world, but she also delineates several institutional preconditions for movement toward merchant capitalism which were present in Europe and Japan but absent in Southeast Asia.

3

The Malay Sultanate of Melaka

Luis Filipe Ferreira Reis Thomaz

The history of the Sultanate of Melaka, although not always clear in its details, is at least better known than that of other sultanates of the Malay world in the fifteenth to seventeenth centuries. In fact, we have not only a quite detailed local chronicle, the *Sejarah Melayu*[1] but also a valuable body of data collected by early Portuguese geographers and chroniclers, of whom the most valuable is Tomé Pires.[2] Besides such narrative sources, there are also extensive Portuguese archival records (letters, orders, receipts, account books), most dating from the first quarter of the sixteenth century, which contain many interesting elements for the study of daily life in the town during the first two decades of Portuguese rule. Provided that we use them carefully and critically, it is often possible to extend the conclusions that can be drawn from them to the period preceding the downfall of the sultanate, especially when they reveal customs, habits, and institutions alien to Portuguese practice. These records often stress that things were done in a certain way "since such is the custom in this town." In fact, the Portuguese crown was by then more interested in setting up a maritime trade network than in creating a true land-bound empire, and

---

[1]"*Sejarah Melayu* or 'Malay Annals'," trans. C. C. Brown, *JMBRAS* 25, nos. 2–3 (1952). The text in Malay has been edited by Sir R. Winstedt, *JMBRAS* 16, no. 3 (1938), and also by A. Samad Ahmad, *Sulatus Salatin (Sejarah Melayu)* (Kuala Lumpur, 1979).

[2]Tomé Pires, *The Suma Oriental of Tomé Pires*, ed. and trans. Armando Cortesão, 2 vols. (London, 1944); new edition (in Portuguese): *A Suma Oriental de Tomé Pires e o Livro de Francisco Rodrigues* (Coimbra, 1978). Book 6 of the *Suma* is devoted to Melaka and is one of our main sources of information. Another important work on Melaka at the beginning of the sixteenth century is the text by Manuel Godinho de Eredia, *Malaca, l'Inde méridionale et le Cathay: Facsimilé du manuscrit autographe de la Bibliothèque Royale de Belgique*, ed. L. Jansen, 2 vols. (Brussels, 1881–82).

it therefore avoided any significant change in the status of its new subjects; it preferred, in general, to maintain local customs, considering itself the heir of the powers it had replaced, as regards their duties as well as their rights. Accordingly, at least during the first century of Portuguese dominance, Melaka was to some extent still ruled by Malay law. The Portuguese records of the sixteenth century are therefore interesting despite the scarcity in them of direct references to the preceding period.

We must nevertheless emphasize that the importance of Melaka's history does not lie merely in our comparatively better knowledge of its internal conditions; it also lies in the originality of its characteristics and in the influence it exerted on contemporary political formations in the Malay world, which viewed Melaka as a model. This is true not only for the heyday of its hegemony over the seas of the Archipelago but even after the fall of its capital to the Portuguese. The role of Melaka as a model becomes evident, for instance, when we compare its law code[3] with those of other Malay sultanates.

This does not mean that Melaka was unusually culturally creative in Asian history. On the contrary, it seems a typical example of that "soft underbelly of Asia" on which the great civilizations of India, China, and the Muslim world imprinted many traces of their influence. Perhaps this readiness to embrace exogenous patterns and to adopt solutions already tested elsewhere enabled the sultanate to adapt to new conditions and needs more quickly than did older civilizations like China, where the weight of a rich cultural heritage seems to have frequently hindered institutions from keeping pace with economic and social evolution.

Even in the context of Southeast Asia, the most noteworthy features of the Sultanate of Melaka were not original. A similar type of economic structure based on trade rather than agriculture seems to have prevailed some centuries before in Funan, Champa, and Srivijaya. Nor was Melaka the first Muslim state in the Malay world: the conversion of the rulers of Pasai had taken place more than a century earlier. The cosmopolitan character of Melaka's society already appears, to some extent, in the entrepôts that existed at the fringes of many ancient empires.

Nevertheless, nowhere can we find such features so consistently combined into a large institutional system as in fifteenth-century Melaka. Here, I believe, lies the foremost historical originality of the Malay sultanate of Melaka.   •

---

[3]*Undang-undang Melaka: The Laws of Malacca*, ed. Liaw Yock Fang (The Hague, 1976).

A Mercantilist Kingdom

The image of the sultanate given by our sources is that of a mercantile state in which the whole ruling class as well as the sultan himself was engaged in trade.

On the eve of the Portuguese conquest, Melaka had become a very large city, with a population estimated at 100,000 to 200,000 souls.[4] This concentration, which grew up in the short space of a century, is not explained by any economic development of the surrounding region, most of it still covered by jungle, but essentially by long-distance trade. In fact, the maritime networks that intersected at Melaka embraced the whole Indian Ocean, from the Red Sea and the Persian Gulf to the Pacific archipelagos of Ryukyu, the Philippines, and Maluku. The city profited not only from its situation in the zone of equatorial calms, where it provided a comfortable port of call for vessels awaiting the favorable monsoon, but also from its strategic position on the main maritime passage between two merchant realms—those of the Indian Ocean and the South China Sea. This favorable conjuncture, put to good use by a judicious regime, enabled the hamlet of fishermen and corsairs that was Melaka at the beginning of the fifteenth century to become in the space of a few decades the largest urban center in Southeast Asia. Such remarkable growth would not have been possible without the accumulation of movable wealth.

It is also noteworthy that the town depended almost entirely for its subsistence on its long-distance maritime network, since even a staple as vital as rice was imported—mainly from Java, Siam, and Pegu. To encourage the importing of foodstuffs, ships conveying provisions were granted exemption from duties, and the exemption was perhaps sometimes extended to the rest of their cargo. Nevertheless, Por-

---

[4]Fernão Lopes de Castanheda, in *História do descobrimento e conquista da India pelos Portugueses* (Coimbra, 1551–61; rpt., Coimbra, 1924–33, 4 vols.), 2:112, puts the number of households in Melaka at 30,000, that is, a total population of at least 120,000 inhabitants. Gaspar Correia reckons it at more than 200,000 people during the monsoon season, when the city was bustling with ships and merchants; see *Lendas da India* (Coimbra, 1923), chap. 29, p. 253. Pires (1944, 1:143–44) reckons the population of Pasai at 20,000 souls and specifies that Melaka is ten times as populous, which confirms Correia's estimate; elsewhere (p. 260) he considers that 100,000 men-at-arms can be called up in the district of Melaka, which would indicate a population of about 400,000 souls, over half of whom probably lived in town. Only one estimate differs markedly from the preceding: Rui de Araújo, imprisoned in Melaka in 1510, in his letter to Afonso de Albuquerque dated 6 February 1510, puts the number of households in Melaka at 10,000, which would correspond to only 40,000 or 50,000 inhabitants; see ANTT, *Gaveta* 14–8–21; published in *Documentação para a História das Missões do Padroado Português do Oriente—Insulíndia*, ed. Artur Basílio de Sá, 5 vols. (Lisbon, 1955–58), 1:21; *Cartas de Afonso de Albuquerque seguidas de documentos que as elucidam* ed. Raymundo António de Bulhão Pato, 6 vols. (Lisbon, 1884–1915), 3:5–12. Malayan sources tend to agree with Correia: the"Sejarah Melayu" (1952), p. 157, puts the Melaka population at 190,000 souls.

tuguese writers stressed that the Melaka region, being flat and wet, was appropriate for rice cultivation provided that clearing and drainage works were carried out, but the inhabitants never bothered to do this. This means that no such enterprise merited the interest of either the state or the propertied classes, who were oriented, rather, toward the sea.

Melaka shared some features with the ancient entrepôts of southern Asia. Like them it was a pivot between ecologically complementary regions: the tropical and equatorial islands of Indonesia, which abounded in spices and precious woods, and the subtropical old worlds of China and India, which although not so well endowed by nature were more developed in manufactures such as porcelain and textiles. Melaka was also, like the ancient entrepôts, a kind of neutral territory for foreign powers, where merchants from abroad were welcomed and protected by the state. This neutral character did not hinder Melaka from building up its own empire, but it certainly contributed to the particular mood assumed there by Islam, at least during the brightest days of the sultanate. There was in Melaka an official procedure for the reception of foreign ships and traders, and special magistrates, the *syahbandar,* entrusted with that task; but nothing suggests that the control of foreigners involved the inquisitorial aspects often observed in ancient empires, where suspicion toward foreigners and dread of polluting contacts were the rule.

At the same time, everything in Melaka points to a market economy rather than an administered trade as in ancient empires. The merchants conducted their business on their own account, not on behalf of their sovereigns. One could become a merchant by free choice, not by royal appointment. For the most part prices were fixed by the laws of supply and demand rather than by the convention among rulers. In brief, the sultanate was a vigorous, expanding nucleus of monetary economy, not an archaic survival of the ancient entrepôt that operated as a privileged place of exchanges between states (as some have argued for Calicut in southern India). The state existed there because of trade, not trade because of the state.

Some Melaka practices were the direct opposite of "administered trade." For instance, whenever a ship called at Melaka in a hurry, afraid of missing the monsoon, it was possible with royal permission to evaluate the cargo in bulk and pay the customs accordingly. For this purpose an ad hoc committee of ten merchants, five Muslim and five Hindu, was appointed and made its evaluation before the *temenggong* (senior judge). Often, too, the cargo of such a ship was sold wholesale, by a kind of auction among ten or twenty commissioned merchants, who afterward shared the cargo pro rata and retailed it to other merchants.[5]

The Melaka sultanate could be described as a mercantilist state. This does not necessarily mean that its structures were in any manner inspired by mercantilist doctrines. As far as we know, no economic theory had developed in Melaka in this period; but in Western Europe too the theory was preceded by the practice, and states that may be described as mercantilist appeared in the late Middle Ages, one or two centuries before the embodiment of the doctrine. In this regard the sultanate was quite similar to Portugal in the same period—a feature that helps to explain the fairly easy incorporation of many Malay institutions and customs into the Portuguese regime. In both cases the state—that is, the sovereign—played an active role in commerce alongside private merchants.

The boundary between the private and public sectors was set by the ruler somewhat autocratically, and therefore free competition between the two was problematic. Nonetheless, both coexisted within an essentially market economy. In short, mercantilist states dealt with commerce and movable wealth more or less in the way traditional agrarian states did with real estate. They kept a kind of reserve, as a basis for the livelihood of the sovereign, the court, and dignitaries, and left the rest to private holders. It is not impossible that certain royal monopolies represented a survival of "administered trade," the system of exchanges among chiefs that prevailed in societies organized into chiefdoms and even in some centralized ancient empires. A noteworthy survival of this type of trade, the tribute paid to Chinese emperors by several Southeast Asian states, lasted as long as the empire itself.

In less traditional states such as Portugal and Melaka in the fifteenth and sixteenth centuries, the involvement of the state in trade probably arose chiefly from the wish to possess liquidity—to pay for everything from retainers to weapons and from troops to luxury articles. We know, for instance, that the sultanate used Javanese mercenaries to defend its capital against the Portuguese in 1511. The natural tendency of rulers was to increase their cash expenditure, but in economies not entirely monetary the possibilities of acquiring liquidity through taxation were limited, since overtaxation of monetary sectors such as overseas trade would asphyxiate commerce and thus all economic activity. Hence the tendency of sovereigns to imitate the merchants by going to the very sources of the nation's prosperity.

The state of Melaka shared the benefits of commerce in several ways.

---

[5]Pires, 1944, 2:273–74.

First, indirectly, as a sovereign power, through its customhouses: every ship coming from the countries "above the winds," from India and the Middle East, paid a 6 percent import duty. An additional tax of 2 percent, referred to as *peso* (weight) in Portuguese texts, was levied on certain merchandise, both incoming and outgoing.

Ships coming from the countries "below the winds" (Indonesia, peninsular Southeast Asia, and the Far East) paid no duty but were subject to the *beli-belian* system (which was maintained by the Portuguese until 1542). They had to sell 25 percent of their cargo to the state, at the market price reduced by 20 percent. Payment was made in merchandise destined for export, evaluated at the market price plus 20 percent. This was equivalent to a 5 percent tax, levied on both imports and exports, unlike customs duties paid by ships from the countries "above the winds." A typical mercantilist feature, it is at the same time an imposition owed to the state as a sovereign entity and a means of providing merchandise for the trade carried out by the sultan, who was "the first merchant of his state."

Existing documents do not allow an exact evaluation of the revenues of the sultanate on the eve of the Portuguese conquest, but it is clear enough that levies on commerce represented the lion's share of the state's income. If the list of tributes paid to the sultan by provincial governors (*mendelika*) and vassal kings is given accurately by Tomé Pires, the total income of more or less land-based origin was equivalent to 3,820 Portuguese cruzados. But we know from a text of 1515 that the supplementary 2 percent tax represented by the *peso* (which by then had reincorporated the brokerage fees suppressed by the sultan) yielded 10,000 to 12,000 cruzados a year.[6] We have no figures for customs duties and *beli-belian*; after 1540, however, when the Portuguese administration combined the two, they yielded an average 40,000–50,000 cruzados a year. Yet we know from Pires that on the eve of the conquest the commodities imported from Gujarat, southern India, and Bengal added up to about half a million cruzados a year; they would therefore have yielded some 30,000 cruzados in import duties. We can thus reasonably estimate the annual movement of merchandise through the port of Melaka at one to two million cruzados and the total income of the customhouse and the *beli-belian* at 40,000–50,000 cruzados a year. If these estimates are correct, the levies on commerce represented 90–95 percent of state revenues in Melaka.

These figures do not include the profits derived by the sultan from

[6]A letter from Governor Lopo Soares de Albergaria to the captain of Melaka, Jorge de Brito, in December 1515. ANTT, Cartas dos Vice Reis, no. 132.

his own trading activity. He owned a fleet of merchant ships, regularly dispatched to different quarters. At the ports of destination they conducted their business in free competition with private traders; at Melaka, however, they enjoyed exemption from duties, as did the sultan's commercial partners and even his sailors. Nevertheless, we find virtually no trace of real royal monopoly, a form of state intervention in trade that would later become important in other sultanates such as Aceh.

The Sultanate of Melaka was thus in a sense a large mercantile enterprise with many staff, mainly slaves. They numbered 1,600, or even 3,000 according to another source; the latter figure would almost equal the total of 3,500 private slaves owned by merchants.[7] Moreover, as the number of royal slaves was apparently insufficient, private slaves were often requisitioned by the state for tasks in the public interest, such as manning galleys for the defense of the Straits. According to several Portuguese accounts, the main employment of public slaves was in seafaring and trade: the *hamba raja* (honorary slaves) were entrusted with the management of merchandise; the *belati* (cash-bought slaves) served as sailors in the ruler's junks, as oarsmen, dockers, and so forth.

The Layout of the Realm

Among the Malay traditions concerning the nebulous beginnings of the sultanate, recorded in both Malay and Portuguese sources, one is particularly important for an understanding of its evolution. It is reported that its center was formerly at Bertam, on the banks of the Melaka River, roughly one league upstream from the present-day town.[8] The original shape of the realm was thus that of a traditional Malay state: it coincided with the hydrographic basin of a river system, the area ruled from the lower course of the river. Near the sole outlet to the sea of this basin dwelt the ruling classes and the power center.

Later, the capital shifted onto the very shore of the Straits. This was, as far as we know, an innovation, since even such important thalassocracies as Srivijaya were based on rivers, at some distance from the mouth. The shift of Melaka to the coast suggests a stronger mastery of the sea and greater confidence regarding piracy or other dangers coming from the sea.

[7]de Bulhã Pato, 1884–1915, 3:357–76; also Pierre-Yves Manguin, "Manpower and Labour Categories in Early Sixteenth Century Malacca," in *Slavery, Bondage, and Dependency in Southeast Asia,* ed. Anthony Reid (St. Lucia, Qld., 1983), p. 210.
[8]For example, Pires, 1944, 2:233–37.

Thenceforth Melaka used the Straits, instead of a river, as the axis of its realm; but we can, perhaps, discern a trace of the traditional Malay conception of space in the fact that one of the suburbs of the town, which stretches along the seaside southeast of the center, has been called *hilir* (downstream) right up to the present. In any case, it was from its new position on the coast that Melaka built up her empire on both sides of the Straits.

Since land revenue formed but a small percentage of the sultanate's income, it seems that the main aim of its conquests on both sides of the Straits was not so much the acquisition of territory as the occupation of strategic positions. By doing this Melaka prevented the growth of rival trading centers or marauding economies living as parasites on its main trade artery. This is clearly shown by the location of its territories along the Straits.

The realm of the sultanate was broadly made up of three concentric circles. The inner one, around Melaka, was formed by territories directly ruled by the sultan; the middle one was formed by territories administered by mandarins and *mendelika* appointed by the ruler; and the outer one was formed by tributary, vassal, and allied kingdoms, some of which were ruled by kinsmen of the sultan.

The contribution of each unit to the whole political system was determined by its staple product; the system was thus based on the complementarity of specialized regions. The west coast of the peninsula, northwest of Melaka, was already in this period the main zone of tin mining. Its *mendelika* paid their tribute to the sultan in tin, which was minted in Melaka, being thus one of the pillars of Melaka's monetary system and economy. Apart from tin, the economy of this region was based on subsistence agriculture, so its inhabitants sent to Melaka's market only small amounts of rice, sugar, sugarcane, bananas, *arak* (distilled rice wine), chickens, and goats.

A group of vassal states paid tribute in gold: on the east coast, Pahang produced its own; Sumatra, Kampar, and Inderagiri were the eastern outlets for the mining zone of Minangkabau. Gold, although not coined, had currency as money and was therefore even more crucial than tin in the economy of the sultanate. The trade from these tributaries consisted in commodities useful for Melaka's shipbuilding and long-distance commerce—sulphur and alum from Pahang; eaglewood, pitch, honey, wax, and some rice from the Sumatran dependencies.

The rest of the realm was largely maritime, formed by river basins on both sides of the Straits and a handful of islands between them. Instead of tribute it provided the sovereign with soldiers and especially rowers for his fleet of *lancharas* (galleys). These men, like the slaves of merchants requisitioned by the state, earned no wages but only their daily food. This part of the realm was mostly made up of territories ruled on the sultan's behalf by mandarins appointed by him. Nevertheless the control of Melaka over the *orang laut* (called in Portuguese *celates*, from Malay *selat*, "straits") who peopled the coast of Sumatra and the islands seems to have been incomplete. There is evidence that piracy was one of the mainstays of their livelihood—undoubtedly harmful for the security of Melaka-based trade. But they also used the city as a market for their surplus foodstuffs—fish (especially shad), fruit, meat, and some rice—and supplied some honey and wax, rattan, eaglewood, and gold.

In short, Melaka's dominions ensured safety for travel through its Straits, currency for its transactions, seamen for its fleet, soldiers for its army, and provisions for its inhabitants. In return Melaka provided its dominions with protection, a market for their surplus crops, and a share in its prosperity. These relations, founded on the basis of a certain reciprocity, seemingly acted as centripetal forces. They were to some extent offset by centrifugal forces, such as the aspiration of vassals for independence, the propensity of coastal populations to piracy, and the jealousy of lesser trading centers. Some of the latter, such as Siak, Kampar, and Pahang, harbored their own colonies of foreign merchants and apparently competed with the metropolis. This muted rivalry subsisted under Portuguese rule.

The sultans often organized punitive expeditions against recalcitrant vassals. They also tried to secure the latters' allegiance by offering them a share in their commercial profits through the system of sleeping partnerships. These were used by the kings of Kampar and Pahang to share in their overlord's commercial ventures. This system, which provided the sultan with up to a third of the capital he needed for his trading expeditions, thus seems to have been a factor promoting economic solidarity not only among different social classes but also between the kingdom and its dependencies.

A Pluralistic Society

The cosmopolitanism of Melaka was a byword in Asia. Pires reports that in a single day people there were heard speaking eighty-four different tongues.[9]

[9]Pires, 1944, 2:269.

The official policy of the sultanate was to promote the settlement of foreign traders in the city. The resident merchants and those who had their families in Melaka enjoyed a reduction of import duties; they paid only 3 percent ad valorem instead of 6 percent. That this policy was continued by the Portuguese after their conquest indicates that it was driven by deep structural reasons as opposed to conjunctural motivations. We know, for instance, that in 1521 Captain Garcia de Sà sent a messenger to persuade secretly the merchants living in Pahang to settle in Melaka. The following year his successor, Jorge de Albuquerque, proclaimed in the ports of the Coromandel coast that "great liberties" would be granted to every merchant who decided to settle in Melaka. To attract more merchants to the town, Pero de Faria announced in 1537 that they would be allowed to participate in the fleet that was being prepared to sail to China. Curiously, Hindu and Muslim merchants paid just 6 percent in customs duties to the Melaka customhouse, whereas Christians paid 10 percent. The crown probably wished by this measure to prevent the Portuguese from becoming merchants, thinking that one more merchant meant one less soldier. During the first half of the sixteenth century at least, Portuguese policy, like that of the sultanate, wagered on the development of foreign merchant communities.

It is possible to discern several reasons for this policy. More merchants meant a greater volume of trade and thus more state revenue through the customhouse. There was also the matter of economies of scale: the investment capacity of the local population being meager, new settlers and new capital would be to the general advantage. But the main reason appears to have been sociocultural: the know-how of resident foreigners, their knowledge of the markets and political conditions of their own countries, the trust they enjoyed among their compatriots. This latter aspect must have been essential, since operations such as long-distance orders, deferred payments, and *commenda* (entrusting capital) could not be carried out without a basis of mutual confidence and a common code of moral values, if not a common system of law. Hence the importance of religious solidarities among merchants, which explains in part how by the fifteenth century the Indian Ocean had become a sort of Muslim lake. This also helps explain the bad reception of the first Portuguese to reach the Indian Ocean, in 1498, once they were identified as Christians at their first Muslim port of call, Mozambique. Worse than ancestral foes and potential competitors for the established trading networks, they disturbed the common ethic that prevailed in that ocean, where from Sofala to Java all swore on the same Koran.

Melaka had become the pivot of the whole Asian trade "for a thousand leagues on every hand," as Pires says hyperbolically,[10] because it acted as the hinge linking two solidarities: on one side, the ethnic and religious solidarity that connected each foreign colony of the town to its mother country; on the other, the solidarity of neighborhood that bound them together under the local ruler and local law.

Such a structure led naturally to a policy of wide religious tolerance. Islam had been the official religion of Melaka since its beginnings as a maritime power; but the prevailing Islam was open and permissive in character. It could appear impure in the eyes of stricter Muslims from the Middle East, such as Ibn Majid: "They have no culture at all. The infidel marries Muslim women while the Muslim takes pagans to wife. You do not know whether they are Muslims or not. They are thieves for theft is rife among them and they do not mind. The Muslim eats dogs for meat for there are no food laws. They drink wine in the markets and do not treat divorce as a religious act."[11] Some of these charges, such as the marriages between infidels and Muslim women, are confirmed by Portuguese authors.[12]

Koranic *fiqh*, being in general stricter than Malay *adat*, or customary law, was apparently regarded in Melaka as a subsidiary law, to which it was possible to resort when a need of further severity was felt. The expression "this is the custom of the country; but according to God's law" (*itulah adatnya negeri; tetapi pada hukum Allah*) occurs more than a dozen times in the *Undang-undang Melaka*, always to introduce a harsher penalty as an alternative.[13] Even apostasy, regarded by the *fiqh* as a major crime punished by death, is viewed with some tolerance, and the transgressor given three occasions for repentance. We find in Melaka no traces of discriminative taxation against infidels, such as the *kharâj* and *jizya* of orthodox *fiqh*, or of exemption from customs duties granted to vessels coming from Muslim countries, as was the practice in some Indian ports. In later Malay law codes, albeit based on that of Melaka, such alternatives disappear and the option between *fiqh* and *adat* is enacted in the very clauses of the code. This change apparently means that in later Malay sultanates, less cosmopolitan than the Melaka sultanate, the problem of managing foreign communities was less urgent.

[10]Pires, 1944, 2:286.

[11]Shihab al-Din Ahmad Ibn Majid, "al-Mal'aqiya" (1462), translated in *A Study of the Arabic Texts Containing Material of South-East Asia*, ed. G. R. Tibbetts (Leiden, 1979), p. 206.

[12]For example, Pires, 1944, 2:268.

[13]See *Undang-undang Melaka*, for example, sects. 5, 3; 7, 2; 8, 2–4; 10; 11, 3; 12, 2–3; 14, 1–2; 15, 7; 16, 1; 18, 4; 36, 1; 44, 6. Sometimes *hukum kanun* is encountered instead of *adat negeri*.

Searching for a historical or mythic pedigree, the young sultanate tried to insert itself into the Islamic tradition through the legend of Iskandar Zulkarnain, whom the *Sejarah Melayu* points to as an ancestor of the royal lineage of Melaka.[14] It is, however, noteworthy that other traditions with a Hindu flavor could coexist with this one, including the story told in the *Hikayat Hang Tuah* which ascribes the origin of the dynasty to Sang Perta Dewa, a semidivine king who came down from the Paradise of Indra.[15] Even if this syncretism was not consciously designed, it fit well with the pluralistic character of Melaka society.

Nevertheless, the authorities were Muslim, and the positions of the different religious communities were not the same in their sight. We know from Portuguese records the names of a dozen Muslim merchants of Melaka, most of them of Javanese or Luzon origin, and some twenty-five Hindu traders from southern India. The former often bear Malay titles of nobility, mainly that of *adiraja*, which shows a certain osmosis between the trading class and the aristocracy, also shown by the involvement of the sultan and the mandarins in trade. On the contrary, Hindu merchants always bear the title *nina* or *naina*. The origin of this term seems to be the Sanskrit *nayana* (leader, guide), but the word had lost its military or feudal connotation and become a bourgeois title (corresponding to Persian *khawja* or *khoja*, which was sometimes used in Melaka for Jewish, Armenian, and Middle Eastern merchants). We can infer from this difference of titles that non-Muslim merchants were farther removed from power.

Pires counted several thousand foreign traders settled in Melaka: 1,000 Gujaratis; a total of 4,000 Bengalis, Persians, and Arabs; perhaps 1,000 Keling or Tamils; certainly several thousand Javanese; as well as many lesser communities.[16] The foreign colonies were assembled into four groups around the most influential communities, the Gujaratis, Tamils, Javanese, and Chinese. Each of the four had a *syahbandar* who was entrusted with the reception of merchants coming from his own country of origin and its neighbors. He presented them to the prominent officials (*bendahara*), provided them with godowns and in certain cases elephants, and helped them dispatch their commodities. The official brokers who formerly acted as middlemen in transactions, having been convicted of corruption, were suppressed by Sultan Mahmud Syah shortly before the Portuguese conquest.

In Portuguese Melaka the *syahbandar* also had a military function. In wartime they gathered, armed, and commanded their communities,

---

[14]"Sejarah Melayu," pp. 13–17.
[15]*Hikayat Hang Tuah*, ed. Kassim Ahmad (Kuala Lumpur, 1966), pp. 1–6.
[16]Pires, 1944, 2:254–55.

who served in war with their own slaves and dependents. Probably it was already so in the days of the sultanate, since there was no permanent army. In this as in other matters the Portuguese, whose budget allowed for only five hundred men as a permanent garrison of Melaka, maintained the traditional organization of Southeast Asian armies, formed by the armed dependents of mandarins and notables.

The largest merchant colonies in Melaka under the sultans were Muslim Gujaratis, Hindu Tamils (Kelings), recently Islamized Javanese, and Chinese, about whom much has been written.[17] Less known are the smaller communities, some of which continued to live in Melaka after the Portuguese conquest. The small Luzon colony was relatively prosperous. A community of some 500 souls lived at Minjam, a small port situated somewhere between Bruas and Klang, northwest of Melaka; they were involved in trade and perhaps tin mining. In Melaka the community had just assembled around a wealthy merchant, Aregimuti Raja, on the eve of the Portuguese arrival. In 1513 he dispatched junks to Siam, Brunei, Sunda, and China and a smaller vessel (*penjajap*) to Pasai; after his death in the same year, his widow sent a junk to Sunda and his father-in-law dispatched others to China. Another Luzon merchant, Kurya Diraja, annually sent to China a junk with 1,000 *bahar* (nearly 200 metric tons) of pepper, probably imported from Sunda. Luzon merchants seemed especially involved in commerce in the South China Sea, although not especially with Luzon.

More surprising is the fact that all the Luzon inhabitants of Melaka were Muslim—since, as far as we know, Islam had not yet penetrated into Luzon and the Sultanate of Manila did not yet exist. Islam is believed to have been introduced there via Brunei, whose inhabitants, at least since their conversion at the beginning of the sixteenth century, acted as middlemen in the intercourse between Melaka and the islands now called the Philippines. Nevertheless, it is not impossible that Islam was introduced from Melaka by the endeavors of these Muslim merchants, who were certainly already converted when they arrived in Melaka. Noteworthy, at any rate, is the connection between the expansion of the mercantile network of Melaka and the spread of Islamic nuclei throughout the Archipelago.

There are also fleeting references to Armenians—such as the merchant Khoja Iskandar, who in 1517 led two Portuguese from Melaka to Saint Thomas the Apostle's grave in Mylapur, Coromandel. It is difficult to discern whether they were true Armenians or Nestorian Chris-

---

[17]Most recently in Luis Filipe Thomaz, "Malaka et ses communautés marchandes au tournant du 16ᵉ siècle," in *Marchands et hommes d'affaires asiatiques dans l'Océan Indien et la Mer de Chine 13ᵉ–20ᵉ siècles*, ed. Denys Lombard and Jean Aubin (Paris, 1988), pp. 36–39.

tians from Mesopotamia, since the Portuguese normally used the name "Armenian" to refer to both. According to Pires they already frequented Melaka in the days of the sultanate. Perhaps some of them settled there; in 1610 the Portuguese found the remains of an old Nestorian or, less likely, Armenian church.

There were also a few Jews. Some of them were "white" and came from the Middle East by the Red Sea route; others were "black" and came from Malabar, where the presence of Jewish communities is documented since the first century of the Christian era. A Jew known as Khoja Azedim worked in Melaka as a moneylender in 1514 and had probably done so since the days of the sultanate.

Trade, Slavery and Land

We know little about merchants who were not shipowners; they could participate in overseas trade by hiring *pétak* (compartments) in junks belonging to other merchants. All the members of the crew of a junk, both slaves and freemen, enjoyed by custom the right to use certain *pétak* freely or at a reduced rate, according to their rank. These customs remained under Portuguese rule; two account books of junks that voyaged between Melaka and Pegu in 1512–13 and 1514–15 provide us with many interesting details on this practice.[18]

Another procedure, apparently the most widespread, was to entrust funds to shipowners sending their junks to a foreign port. The investor was a sleeping partner who did not interfere in their administration but bore the loss in the case of shipwreck; in a successful voyage he received the invested sum plus a percentage, previously contracted, which depended on the port of destination. The commission was from 35 to 50 percent for voyages within the Archipelago, 80 or 90 percent for India, and up to 200 percent for China. This system presented both financial and social advantages. It provided for the pooling of small savings and their investment in trade, and it enabled even poor people to share in the benefits of commerce. It remained in force under the Portuguese regime, and many Portuguese sailors and soldiers, often illiterate, made use of it, investing sometimes considerable sums with Hindu or Luzon merchants. In the days of the sultanate, according to Pires, the ruler himself used this procedure to finance up to a third of

[18]Luis Filipe Thomaz, *De Malaca a Pegu: Viagens de um feitor português (1512–1514)* (Lisbon, 1966).

his trading ventures, exempting his sleeping partners from custom duties.

The sultan employed his bondsmen as dockers, workmen in his shipyards, and sailors in his vessels; undoubtedly he also used them in his court as waiters, singers, pages, and retainers. The merchants used their slaves as seamen, dockers, domestic servants, agricultural workers in their orchards (*dusun*), and concubines. The total number of public and private slaves was about 6,500, representing less than 7 percent of the city population. Slavery was thus not the basis of the whole economic system, but rather a kind of supplementary labor, valued chiefly for heavy labor and menial tasks. Often slaves were purchased to display power, wealth, and prestige. Slaves usually earned wages, often equal to those of free workmen of the same craft but sometimes slightly lower. If there was a difference—in wages paid in cash as well as in rice rations—it was between masters (*tukang*) and common workers.

State-owned slaves were quite often entrusted with tasks of public utility, such as rowing in the *champanas* and *calaluzes* that patrolled the Straits, clearing the river and removing trees that had fallen down from its banks, or twisting ropes in the royal ropeyard. Whenever they were not sufficient for those tasks, private slaves belonging to the merchants were requisitioned according to local custom. In 1511–12 the Portuguese fortress was built in this manner, the merchants supplying one-tenth of their slaves every day. A few years later the same system was used to obtain oarsmen for patrol boats and workmen for the ropeyard. Unlike the royal slave sailors on the king's junks and other vessels, who earned wages, these requisitioned slaves received only rice.

Although competing with merchants, often unevenly as all the mercantilist states did, the sultanate offered them in return the protection of its fleet, at least along the Straits. In this particular it went further than most of the Indian trading states of the same period, where, according to ancient Hindu tradition, the realms of the ruler and merchants were clearly separated: "land for kings, sea for traders." The latter had thus to organize their own defense overseas. In Hindu ports such as Cananor and Calicut, war fleets were owned and commanded not by the sovereigns but by Muslim merchants appointed as admirals, the *aliraja* in Cananor and the *kujali* in Calicut. The former finally succeeded in overthrowing the king and seizing the throne; the latter was surrendered to the Portuguese by his sovereign, frightened by the example of Cananor. In Melaka the links between economics and policy were thus closer, and a practice such as the requisitioning of private slaves to man the sultan's vessels was probably regarded as a contribution to tasks of common interest rather than as an arbitrary imposition.

The debt bondsmen must be considered apart. We know of a single document referring to this institution, which was recognized by Hindu law as well as by Malay *adat*, though it was unknown in Koranic and Portuguese law. This document, written in Italian and conserved in Venice, is a sort of travelogue dictated in 1518 by "Francesco del Bocchier," who is probably the same Francisco de Albuquerque we encountered in 1511 organizing the requisitioning of slave labor for the construction of the Portuguese stronghold "A Famosa."[19] Here is my translation of his text:

> The wealth of the merchants in this country is their slaves; and he who has the greatest number is considered the richest; to obtain the aforesaid slaves they proceed thus: if a poor man has need of a certain sum of money, he goes to a merchant and asks him for 10 ducats or more or less according to his need; and binds himself as a slave to give him every month one ducat per ten ducats. And he is bound to every task of his master, either ashore or overseas, giving him nevertheless the 10 percent a month which the aforesaid slaves are obliged to. . . . If he wishes to be redeemed, he must make restitution of all the money that has been lent; and this is done because many poor men are found here.

This system demonstrates a widespread monetary economy. It also confirms what we already know from other sources, that slaves earned wages and were legally able to own goods. Moreover, it proves that the amount of labor slaves were bound to provide was far from the physical maximum—since they were expected to secure their own livelihood and to pay the interest of the loan and also the capital if they wished to redeem themselves. For the merchants this system presented three advantages: it allowed investments at a high rate of interest, perhaps more profitable and safer than trading ventures; it provided stable labor for both inland and seafaring tasks; and it enabled them to display power and wealth, and therefore to vie with mandarins and Malay patricians.

As to landed property, there are only a few records concerning estates on the outskirts of the city, within the territory occupied by the

---

[19]"Referir de Francesco del Bocchier, quando ando in India," reproduced in Jean Aubin, "Franciso de Albuquerque, un juif castillan au service de l'Inde portugaise (1510–1515)," *Arquivos do Centro Cultural Português* (Paris) 7 (1974), p. 197.

Portuguese. These estates, numbering 1,150, are regularly called *duções* (i.e., *dusun*) in our records and are famous in Portuguese literature for their fertility and refreshing air. Most of them were along the rivers or in glades amid the jungle and were accessible only by narrow paths. They are often described as places of pleasure, where mandarins and rich merchants dwelt most of the time far from the bustle of the town, and where they had their offices and their godowns.

Some *dusun* were of great value indeed. In 1515, Captain Jorge de Brito attempted to confiscate the estates supposed to have been illegally occupied in 1511, when many Malay patricians withdrew following their sovereign into exile. The Luzon merchant Kurya Diraja offered half a *bahar* (90 kilograms) of gold, worth about 9,000 Portuguese cruzados, to keep the *dusun* he held. Such a great sum suggests that many of these estates were not merely pleasure grounds but also agricultural enterprises employing slave labor, although their role in Melaka's economy was minor compared to commerce. Perhaps merchants owned them not only to emulate traditional land-bound aristocrats but also to gain a supplementary source of income, more secure than trading ventures although less lucrative. In addition, real estate could be used as a pledge or insurance against commercial failure.

The hoarding of large treasures of precious metals, often referred to in our records, seemingly had the same functions. At the end of the sixteenth century, for example, Diogo do Couto noted that in Melaka local merchants, especially Indians from Benua Keling, formerly amassed quite impressive amounts of gold, some of them possessing as much as twelve or fifteen *bahar* (two and a half to three metric tons).

Besides the large estates owned by rich merchants or granted to local notables by the sultan, smaller properties also existed on the outskirts of Melaka. Apparently at least some of their holders were not outright owners but rather tenants; it seems that land had been granted them by the ruler freely, without any known quid pro quo such as payment of rent or rendering of services. It also seems that these tenancies were de facto hereditary. In 1527, in fact, Captain Jorge Cabral, while preparing a complete *tombo* (cadastral survey) of the territory, begged the Portuguese king to give poor Malays full ownership without payment of groundrent of the land they had inherited from their parents, based on original grants from the sultan. Unfortunately, as far as we know, the *tombo* is lost; we can, however, infer that Jorge Cabral's request was granted from the fact that sixteenth-century Portuguese budgets for Melaka do not include any land taxes.

As to the crops grown on these properties, Portuguese documents specifically refer to tropical fruits, emphasizing the goodness of durians and mangosteens, which are described as the best fruits in the world. This probably means that agriculture around Melaka was of a market garden type, specializing in vegetables, fruits, and other perishable foodstuffs that could not be transported long distances. Yet the region was not self-sufficient in produce, which was, as we have seen, partly imported from the neighboring coast of Sumatra by Javanese food dealers.

References to the hinterland are rare in sixteenth-century texts. At the beginning of the next century it was virtually uninhabited, with the exception of a few glades and the corridors formed by river banks. Even in these nooks, uninhabited by human beings, forestry, sporadically carried on, provided some useful commodities such as camphor, benzoin, agalloch and calambac, dragons blood, some oleaginous trees, and several kinds of palms such as coconuts and nipa. Most of these products seem to have been important for local crafts, especially for shipbuilding, rather than for export. In any case, the economic role of Melaka's hinterland seems minor compared to that of the port, and to some extent subsidiary to the latter.

It is also noteworthy that the purpose of the cadastral survey, which had been ordered in 1515 by the Portuguese governor of India, Lopo Soares de Albergaria, was not to assess land for taxation but to avoid irregular occupation of plots abandoned following the upheavals of 1511, so that Portuguese settlers might be installed there. This indifference on the part of both the sultanate and the Portuguese administration toward land assessment wholly confirms the impression given by other sources, that the essence of the Malay economy did not lie in land but on the sea. Many texts stress this feature, which in the sixteenth century must have seemed quite uncommon, even in the eyes of a seafaring people: written in Venice, the "Referir de Francesco del Bocchier" nevertheless found it remarkable that nothing grew in Melaka, which lived by its harbor. But the most apt expression of the astonishment of the Portuguese toward a society that lived wholly on seafaring and trade is undoubtedly that of Jorge de Albuquerque, the second captain of Melaka: "Malacca has nothing of its own, and has everything of the world."[20]

Fiscal Policy

One of the most noteworthy features of the sultanate was undoubtedly its policy of low custom duties, practiced from the reign of Mansur

[20]Letter from Melaka to the king, 8 Jan. 1515, in de Sá, 1955–58, 1:76.

Syah (r. 1458–77). According to Pires, this policy brought great prosperity to Melaka. Since the realm was not self-sufficient in food supplies, these were not subject to duty. This policy was continued by the
Portuguese, who quite often extended this exemption to the full cargo
of junks conveying victuals in order to stimulate commercial relations
with countries supplying foodstuffs. Other commodities paid, as we
have seen, 6 percent ad valorem if conveyed by foreign vessels, 3
percent if conveyed by ships equipped in Melaka.

The contrast between these rates and those practiced in more traditional agricultural kingdoms is striking. According to Pires, in Bengal
customs duties reached 37.5 percent ad valorem and in Siam 22.2 percent; even in Pegu, to some extent a seafaring state, they attained 12
percent.[21] In such countries external commerce was seemingly viewed
rather as a means to obtain luxury items for the consumption of the
ruling class and liquid resources for the royal treasure. Demand for
luxury items is normally quite inelastic, since their purchasers are rich
people who tolerate the increase in price due to high taxation.

By contrast, the low tax policy of Melaka was based on mass trade. It
consciously sacrificed the ruler's income per unit, expecting that the
low price thus retained by the merchandise would increase demand
and therefore the aggregate volume of trade and the total income of the
customhouses. Such reliance on mass trade seems quite modern when
compared with the traditional fiscal policy of Asian states.

Crisis and Downfall of the Empire

The troubles that arose in Melaka on the eve of the Portuguese
conquest—rumors of bribes, plots, and conspiracies, schemes between
merchants and mandarins, execution of the bendahara and then of the
Tamil syahbandar—were but symptoms of a deeper social and political
malaise, probably starting a few years before, roughly from the beginning of Sultan Mahmud's reign. Pires, who certainly reflects the public
opinion in Melaka of his time, makes Mahmud out to be the black
sheep of an otherwise bright lineage of wise and righteous rulers. It is
likely that his evil deeds were, at least in part, the result of the difficult
conditions he had to face rather than of his bad character.

Pires reports that Melaka's sultans generally abdicated as soon as the
heir to the throne came of age and married. Sultan Mahmud did this in
about 1510, as is proved by coins minted with the name of his successor, Sultan Ahmed. But he soon resumed power, an irregular proce-

---

[21]Pires, 1944, 1:93, 99, 104.

dure disclosing a deep-seated political crisis. That the *Sejarah Melayu*, contrary to all the Portuguese sources, places the resumption of power by Sultan Mahmud after the Portuguese conquest probably means only that official historiography wished to remove from him the responsibility for defeat. It was quite easy to do so, since Sultan Ahmed, who in fact led the resistance against the Portuguese, was subsequently murdered by order of his father. In any case, this harsh struggle for power reveals deep cleavages in Melaka society. It may be that Melaka was suffering from having reached the limits of its own type of commercial growth.

Perhaps Sultan Mahmud's imperialist views around 1510 can be understood as a search for a solution. Seemingly his plan was to overwhelm Haru, on the northern border of his Sumatran domains, and perhaps also to intervene in Pasai, where civil war seemed imminent. Pasai, though somewhat fallen from its former greatness, was still an important trading center. It competed with Melaka, which explains the warm welcome it bestowed on the Portuguese in 1509. By contrast, Haru could not compete with Pasai and Melaka and resigned itself to the role of parasite, basing its economy on piracy. Sultan Mahmud's designs appear to have aimed at full control over the seafaring networks that passed through the Straits. Rather than a shift toward territorial imperialism, these plans may represent an endeavor to maximize commercial profits. We can infer from the high profits yielded to investors in silent partnerships that investments in overseas trade still involved considerable risk. An increase in security would have reduced costs and improved profits.

If such was its aim, this policy had no opportunity to bear fruit. The requisitioning of Chinese vessels for the campaign against Haru annoyed the Chinese community, which had less interest in that passage toward the west, and led it to welcome the Portuguese as partners in 1509 and to support them as liberators in 1511.

During Mahmud's reign there also appears to have been a tendency to stress the Islamic component of Melaka's policy. We know from the *Sejarah Malayu* that shortly before the Portuguese attack an embassy had been sent to Pasai—which still enjoyed the prestige of being the Muslim pioneer in the Malay world—asking for clarification on certain obscure points of Islamic theology. Nevertheless, Melaka longed to replace Pasai as the Muslim center of the region. Even the place of Mecca was to some extent challenged. Unlike his predecessors, who often nourished plans of pilgrimages to Mecca, Mahmud conceived the idea of making Melaka a place of pilgrimage. This idea gained some acceptance overseas, as the Javanese legend of the nine *wali* (saints) who introduced Islam into Java testifies. The young Sunan Bonang and Sunan Giri had decided to pay a visit to Mecca. But first they stayed for some time in Melaka with Wali Lanang, who instructed them in the faith. This holy man dissuaded them from fulfilling their vows of pilgrimage and sent them back to Java.[22]

In the sultanate's policy, the expansion of Islam and that of Melaka-based trade were closely linked. Even if internal religious toleration remained, a foreign policy of this nature could be enough to exasperate the non-Islamic communities of Melaka. In fact, insofar as religious solidarity formed the basis of commercial trustworthiness, Muslims from the city tended to have privileged relations with the new Muslim ports around Melaka; other communities could therefore feel marginalized by this policy.

When in 1509 the Portuguese appeared on the political scene, the reactions were opposite. Diego Lopes de Sequeira's expedition had diplomatic and commercial purposes. Because the viceroy, Dom Francisco de Almeida (1505–9), was interested in trade rather than warfare and inclined to negotiation rather than to conquest, Portuguese policy had not yet taken up the imperialistic trend it assumed during the governorship (1509–15) of Afonso de Albuquerque. In Melaka, all they requested was a treaty of commerce, probably as most favored nation. For the merchant communities of Melaka the question was, therefore, to admit or not to admit one more partner. Some merchants—the Chinese, some Tamils, and a few Javanese, supported by the *laksmana* (admiral)—were inclined to accept the newcomers. They foresaw the opening of new markets and an increase in demand for the commodities they conveyed from eastern Asia and the Indonesian archipelago, and perhaps also a counterweight against the mounting influence of the party sponsored by the *bendahara*. Briefly, this faction saw the Portuguese entry into the commercial system of Melaka as an alternative to the Islamic expansionism of Sultan Mahmud, which seemed harmful to their interests.

The other party, led by the Gujaratis and supported by the powerful *bendahara* and the *temenggong*, his brother, foresaw increasing competition on the western trade routes, a threat to the moral solidarity between the sultanate and its satellite seaports, and the installation of the ancestral foe of the Muslim people in the very heart of the city that was endeavoring to make itself a sacred capital. The arrival of the Portuguese only sharpened the tensions already existing among commu-

[22]*Babad Tanah Djawi. Javaans Rijkskroniek*, trans. W. L. Olthof, ed. J. J. Ras (Dordrecht, 1987), p. 22.

nities and factions, probably stimulating the upheavals of 1510–11. By seizing all the Portuguese they could in 1509, with the eventual approval of the sultan, the party led by the *bendahara* and the Gujarati community won only a provisional victory that kept the Portuguese away for two years. When they reappeared in 1511, Sultan Mahmud had not yet been able either to carry out his projects of expansion or to appease the quarrels and redress the balance. Furthermore, the Portuguese now came with stronger forces and more ambitious views. In that crucial moment the Malay dependencies of the sultanate did not disavow their allegiance to their suzerain, but part of the urban core of the realm continued to gamble on overturning the status quo—exactly as the nineteen Portuguese kept as hostages since 1509 had foreseen six months before.

The arrival of the Portuguese on the historical stage at this very moment may have been the catalyst that sharpened the tensions already prevailing inside the sultanate and hindered its reorganization on a new basis. In a sense, the conquest was an anticlimax.

4

Cash Cropping and Upstream-Downstream Tensions: The Case of Jambi in the Seventeenth and Eighteenth Centuries

Barbara Watson Andaya

Historians have long recognized the importance of river systems in linking the coast and interior of many Southeast Asian states, especially in the larger islands of the Malay Archipelago, where mountainous terrain and dense jungle made overland access to the hinterland difficult. In what we have come to see as the typical maritime state, the rivers provided a route by which products could be transported from the interior to the downstream port and there exchanged for goods brought by incoming traders. Societies that inhabited the upstream (*hulu*) and downstream (*hilir*) ends of the river retained their own cultural characteristics, often heightened by adaptation to contrasting ecological environments and by the greater exposure to outside influences among coastal settlements. Nonetheless, because of his strategic position near the mouth of the river, the downstream chief, or

The present essay could not have been written without the unfailing assistance of the staff of the State Archives in The Hague and the Koninklijk Instituut in Leiden. My understanding of the Jambi situation was greatly aided by my visit there in 1986–87, during which time I received valuable support from the personnel of the Indonesian Institute of Sciences as well as local authorities. I received financial support for research from Auckland University, the Japan Society for the Promotion of Science, and the Joint Committee of Southeast Asia of the Social Science Research Council and the American Council of Learned Societies with funds provided by the Ford Foundation and the National Endowment for the Humanities. To all these bodies I wish to express my deep gratitude.

raja, was normally able to exercise a degree of economic and political control over the people living along the length of the major waterway. The perception of the river as the fulcrum of authority is well depicted in a Malay map of 1876 showing the Perak River as a broad straight road around which the principal officeholders of the state are grouped.[1]

In general terms this picture can be applied to many of the small states that sprang up along the trading routes of island Southeast Asia and has often been invoked to help explain the nature of political development on the Malay Peninsula[2] and to a lesser extent in Sumatra, Borneo, and some of the Philippine Islands. At the same time, students of individual "upstream-downstream" societies have pointed to the numerous variations of what can sometimes be presented in a rather simplified form. For instance, despite the *hilir's* access to the sea, political authority in some states was exercised from the *hulu,* which was removed from the often fever-ridden swamplands of the coasts and less subject to the threat of enemy attack. Royal capitals in the state of Perak did not begin to move downstream until the mid-eighteenth century.[3] In other areas the role of the river itself as a link between coast and interior may be much less important than sometimes thought. Along the west coast of Sumatra, for example, the *hulu-hilir* distinction is better rendered as "upland-lowland," for here the shallow and fast-flowing rivers that tumbled down from the highlands were unsuitable for transport, and the principal means of communication were jungle tracks rather than waterways.[4] Again, in several cases the dominance of the main river could be countered by the complexity of its tributaries, each with its own upstream localities connected to the headwaters of neighboring river systems. In the hinterland of every coastal *hilir* could therefore lie a number of different *hulu.* The inter-

[1]Barbara Watson Andaya, *Perak, the Abode of Grace: A Study of an Eighteenth Century Malay State* (Kuala Lumpur, 1979), Map 3.

[2]See J. M. Gullick's classic, *Indigenous Political Systems of Western Malaya* (London, 1958), p. 21.

[3]Andaya, 1979, pp. 24–25. Perak was by no means unique: centers of political control elsewhere were frequently some distance from the coast. For a discussion on the interior as the source of political legitimacy, see Kenneth R. Hall, "The Coming of Islam to the Archipelago: A Reassessment," in *Economic Exchange and Social Interaction in Southeast Asia: Perspectives from Prehistory, History, and Ethnography,* ed. Karl L. Hutterer (Ann Arbor, Mich., 1977), pp. 223–25.

[4]See further Jane Drakard, *A Malay Frontier: Unity and Duality in a Sumatran Kingdom* (Ithaca, N.Y., 1990), pp. 2, 16; M. A. Jaspan, "From Patriliny to Matriliny: Structural Change among the Rejang of Southeast Sumatra," Ph.D. diss., Australian National University, 1964, p. 13. The importance of mapping jungle paths is often overlooked in studies of riverine states, but they frequently provided easier and faster routes than rivers for transport between exchange centers.

weaving of such river networks and the extent of internal communication encouraged the growth of thriving secondary and tertiary exchange centers that could give the people of the interior considerable economic power.[5]

The east coast of Sumatra provides the best examples of this multi-*hulu* environment. All the main rivers flowing into the Straits of Malacca—the Rokan, Siak, Inderagiri, Kampar, Batang Hari, and Musi—represented the confluence of several distinct interior riverine systems that were in turn linked by jungle pathways. The people who lived in the *hulu* were thus not tied to one *hilir* area, since they had access to several different ports on the east coast and could also make their way down to other exchange centers on the west coast. This multiplicity of choice significantly affected relations between the *hulu* inhabitants and the principal downstream settlements, for the latter always depended on interior collectors to supply the exotic jungle products so desired by foreign traders. Successive generations of *hilir* kings had found that the most effective way of promoting political and economic ties with the hinterland was the provision of an attractive trading environment where people came by preference, not by force. From the sixteenth century, however, the expansion in the *hulu* of pepper as a cash crop increased the incentives of coastal rulers to attract upland growers to their ports. Vying with their neighbors to profit from the increased international demand, downstream kings now sought to tighten their hold over the interior. Some, encouraged by the growing numbers of Europeans who began to frequent the region, believed that it was indeed possible to tip the balance in favor of the *hilir*, to enforce its dominance of the *hulu* and thus ensure command of the valuable pepper trade. In the most favorable commercial circumstances this would have been extremely difficult, for geography militated against the *hilir*'s physical control of the *hulu* districts. But the attempts to extend downstream authority were impeded further because the very economic changes that encouraged *hilir* extension into the *hulu* injected new tensions into their relationship. It is the nature of these changes and the way they affected the interaction between upstream and downstream that is my concern in this study of the Sumatran state of Jambi during the seventeenth and eighteenth centuries.

[5]A possible model has been proposed by Bennet Bronson, "Exchange at the Upstream and Downstream Ends: Notes towards a Functional Model of the Coastal State in Southeast Asia," in Hutterer, 1977, pp. 39–54. Such economic centers may well have also acted as foci for religious ceremonials that helped regulate commerce between potentially hostile people. John Miksic, "Classical Archaeology in Sumatra," *Indonesia* 30 (Oct. 1980), 43–66.

Jambi as an Upstream-Downstream State

The dominance of the upstream-downstream apposition in local thinking was one feature of Jambi that struck Western observers in the nineteenth century. "People will say they are going downstream even when there is no water to be seen" and "[indicate] the situation of places by a simple reference to the ascent and descent of the river."[6] In terms of this essay, Jambi also provides an object example of the multi-*hulu* state. The Batang Hari, the longest river in Sumatra, meanders down from the Minangkabau highlands, linking the interior uplands, the descending coastal plain, and the swamp forests that in premodern times formed a wide band along the coast, in places well over a hundred kilometers wide. The Batang Hari is the only major waterway in the *hilir*, and its junction (or *muara*, "mouth") with the Tembesi was commonly regarded as the dividing point between *hulu* and *hilir*. Its very name (literally, "the main stream of the river") points to the existence of secondary branches, for beyond Muara Tembesi the Batang Hari divides into a web of tributaries. Many of these are important rivers in their own right, as indicated by the fact that they too are termed *batang* to distinguish them from *air* and *sungai*, both used to refer to the numerous lesser rivers making up their tributaries. The most extensive of Jambi's river systems is that emanating from the Batang Tembesi, which rises in the hills to the southeast along the border with Palembang and is fed by several other rivers, notably the Batang Merangin flowing down from the Kerinci highlands.

In the seventeenth century the phrase "Jambi with its nine rivers"[7] was a common way of referring to the territory over which Jambi kings claimed jurisdiction, but early European descriptions make it apparent that the hinterland was divided into a number of virtually autonomous districts under local heads whose ties with the center were often tenuous. Indeed, the archaeological record suggests that many areas in the *hulu* had long provided a local economic and cultural focus. The well-known Karang Berahi stone, for example, is strategically cited on the Merangin, indicating that this now little-frequented river once pro-

---

[6]H. T. Damsté, "Het landschap Loeboe Oelang Aling aan de Batang Harie in 1897," *Tijdschrift voor het Binnenlandsch Bestuur* 31 (1906), 327; John Anderson, *Mission to the East Coast of Sumatra* (Kuala Lumpur, 1971), p. 390.

[7]Traditionally said to be the Batang Tembesi, Merangin, Asai, Tabir, Tebo, Bungo, Uleh, Jujuhan, and Siau. "Silah-Silah Keturunan Radja-Radja Djambi jang Keradjaannja Bernama Keradjaan Melayu Djambi," from a typescript dated 1954, kindly lent by Tsuyoshi Kato, which had been copied from another dated March 1900. The original manuscript was obtained from the wife of Sultan Taha, the last ruler of Jambi.

vided important trading connections. The thirteenth-century *Nagarakrtagama* lists Tebo, at the junction of the Tebo River and the Batang Hari, as a vassal of consequence, and people in this area still point to remains of old *candi* (shrines) and statuary that recall legendary settlements of the past. Jambi folklore reinforces the impression of considerable independent political and economic development in the interior. As elsewhere in Sumatra, a common theme in such stories is the wandering hero who finds burned twigs floating down the river, only to discover that they come from a thriving settlement upstream. Legends also speak of independent confederations of *hulu* societies, like the Pemuncak Tiga Kaum at the foothills of the Kerinci plateau which drew together several communities that had only intermittent links with the downstream port.

In Jambi the enforcement of control over the *hulu* by downstream kings could never have been a real possibility. Despite all the advantages of modern transport, much of the province remains difficult of access, and it is no coincidence that the Bangsa Duabelas, the "Twelve Groups" traditionally said to be the direct subjects of the *hilir* king, were originally drawn only from places along the Batang Hari. The independence of *hulu* areas from the coast was accentuated during the dry season when the water level in the upland river systems fell drastically. Until the rains came it was almost impossible for larger boats or rafts to navigate the shallow waters of several Batang Hari tributaries and occasionally of the main river itself. For several months in the year, contact between the downstream and the *hulu* could thus be severely limited.

The continuing maintenance of trading links with the interior was nonetheless essential for the survival of the downstream port, for the *hulu* supplied the gold and jungle products that helped make Jambi into a port well known to Indian and Chinese traders. The interior was also the primary source of manpower. As elsewhere in east coast Sumatra, the downstream region was very lightly populated because acid peat soils and tidal flooding made agriculture impossible except in thin bands along the river banks and levees. For any task involving labor, whether building a palace or raising an army, *hilir* kings had to look upstream. As long as the demands of coastal rulers were acceptable, and as long as there were identifiable advantages in accepting Jambi's nominal overlordship, the interior peoples willingly participated in the upstream-downstream association. The delicate nature of this relationship, however, was to become openly exposed with the development of pepper as a cash crop.

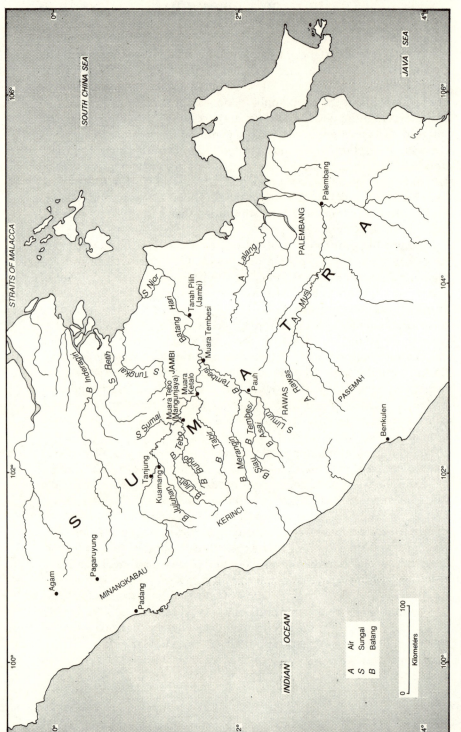

Map 5. Jambi and Palembang

The Advent of Pepper Cultivation in Jambi

By the turn of the seventeenth century, the *hulu* had assumed greater economic importance than ever before, because it was in the upstream districts that the cultivation of *Piper nigrum* (black pepper) began, probably in the first half of the sixteenth century. Tomé Pires, describing Jambi in 1512, noted that it was a source of aloe wood and gold, but he made no mention of pepper.[8] At least by 1545, however, Jambi was known to the Portuguese as a pepper producer, and twenty years later pepper growing had become sufficiently established for orders to be issued to the Melaka captain to buy supplies from Jambi. Nonetheless, the Portuguese may not have begun to frequent Jambi in any numbers until the 1580s, when the port of Sunda (a prime pepper-producing region) was closed for a time to Christian trade.[9] For a generation after this the Portuguese conspired to keep any knowledge of access to Jambi secret from their European rivals, but in 1615 the English and Dutch discovered the elusive entrance to the Nior River which wound through dense swamp forest to the main settlement of Jambi, Tanah Pilih, about a hundred kilometers from the sea. Now the English East India Company and the Dutch VOC entered the lists as eager purchasers of Jambi pepper, along with Chinese, Portuguese, Malays, Makassarese, and Javanese. Meanwhile, world consumption continued to rise. In 1611 it was said that the European market could absorb around 1.5 million kilograms of pepper, a figure that more than doubled in ten years. The market in China had also expanded rapidly and annual imports were estimated at between 10,000 and 12,000 *pikul*, which suggests a widespread mass market for this spice.[10]

The competition fostered by the increased number of purchasers and rising profits encouraged the spread of pepper growing along the upstream rivers. By the 1630s it was being cultivated down the Batang Hari as far as Muara Ketalo, and around the same period cultivation also began along the Tembesi.[11] But it was in the court of the ruler

---

[8]Tomé Pires, *The Suma Oriental of Tomé Pires*, ed. and trans. Armando Cortesão, 2 vols. (London, 1944), 2:154.

[9]I am indebted to Jorge Manuel das Santos Alves of the Instituto de História de Além Mar, New University of Lisbon, for informing me of the 1545 date; José Wicki, "Duas relações sobre a situação da Índia Portuguesa nos anos 1568 e 1569," *Studia* 8 (July 1961), 148; B. N. Teensma, "An Unknown Portuguese Text on Sumatra from 1582," *BKI* 45, nos. 2 and 3 (1989), 317; *Livro das Cidades e Fortalezas que a coroa de Portugal tem nas partes da India*, ed. Francisco Paul Mendes da Luz (Lisbon, 1960), fols. 96r-v, 105.

[10]John E. Willis, *Pepper, Guns, and Parleys: The Dutch East India Company and China, 1662–1681* (Cambridge, Mass., 1974), p. 10; Kristof Glamann, *Dutch Asiatic Trade, 1620–1740* (The Hague, 1958), p. 74. A *pikul* measures about 62.5 kilograms.

[11]VOC 1115 Jambi to Batavia, 4 Sept. 1634, fol. 773.

Figure 2. An *orang kaya* (aristocrat) of the pepper-growing areas of Sumatra, as perceived by a seventeenth-century European engraver. Note at left a pepper vine using the support of planted bamboo. From *Begin ende Voortgangh van de Vereenighde Neerlandtsche Geoctroveerde Oost-Indische Compagnie,* ed. I. Commelin (Amsterdam, 1646).

downstream, rather than in the pepper-growing districts, that the benefits of this increased trade were most obvious. Much of the new wealth came from customs duties, gifts, and port dues from traders who now came directly to Jambi so that there was no longer any need to ship local pepper to Banten or Patani.[12] It took some time, but the Jambi ruler eventually realized the advantages he could draw from the increased volume of trade. In 1616, 10 percent was paid on all exports with no charge on any incoming goods. By 1628 this export toll had been raised to 12.5 percent, plus a levy of 10 percent payable by those delivering pepper from the interior.[13] A second reason for the increase in the prosperity of the court was the entry of the royal family and nobles into the pepper market. With advances of cloth and money from both the Dutch and English, they and their agents could go into the countryside or collect incoming pepper from tollhouses set up along the rivers, usually for prices well below those being paid in Jambi

---

[12]In Patani the lack of pepper became so marked that in 1622 the VOC closed its post there.
[13]H. T. Colenbrander and W. Ph. Coolhaas, *Jan Pietersz. Coen. Bescheiden omtrent zijn Bedrijf in Indië,* 7 vols. in 8 parts; vols 1–6 by Colenbrander (The Hague, 1919–34); vol. 7 by Coolhaas (The Hague, 1952–53).

itself. The VOC estimated that through imposts of various kinds the king made a profit of 30 to 35 percent on the pepper he sold them.[14]

Even at the time, the growing wealth of the Jambi court aroused comment. In 1616 local people could still remember a time when the king had been poor, but a description of Jambi that same year describes it as the second port in Sumatra, after Aceh.[15] The prosperity of Jambi's ruler had become a byword and a Dutch captain complained about the unbridled luxury of Jambi court ladies, especially the royal wives, widows, and concubines.[16] Their demands for novel items, like European-style jewellery and rare and expensive cloth, reflected a lifestyle in growing contrast to that of the interior peoples.

The headiness engendered by the expanding market for pepper tended to cloud the dangers inherent in economic reliance on one crop, particularly one in many respects unsuited to the kind of society that typified the Jambi interior. Despite its demographic superiority to the coast, the *hulu* was still an area of low population, where families were small and the most common form of cultivation was a modification of the slash-and-burn type. But pepper growing demanded a high labor input and a degree of supervision at the early stages of planting which must have placed considerable strain on small kinship units. In addition, pepper proved vulnerable to variation in weather patterns. Young plants could well die if deprived of water for long periods, but should they be sited too close to a river they could be subject to flooding during the wet season. The failure of a pepper crop represented the loss of a considerable investment, because pepper plants did not mature for four to seven years. Since they ceased to bear after thirty years, the preparation of new gardens had to be carefully planned in advance. The adjustments needed to cultivate this slow-growing crop rather than the annually harvested rice and cotton were considerable.

Further difficulties were introduced into *hulu-hilir* relations because pepper cultivation along the upper Batang Hari was largely in the hands of Minangkabau migrants. The border between Minangkabau territory and Jambi was fixed at the settlement of Tanjung, but by the mid-sixteenth century at least the area below Tanjung had become a Minangkabau *rantau*[17] occupied by two federations, the so-called Fed-

[14]Ibid., 5:392.

[15]VOC 1061 Jambi to Batavia, 17 July 1616, fol. 271v; J. H. Glazemaker, trans., *De Rampspoedige Scheepvaart der Franschen naar Oost-Indiën* (Amsterdam, 1669), p. 131.

[16]VOC 1099 Jambi to Batavia, 1 Jan. 1630, fol. 117v; *Dagh-Register Gehouden int Casteel Batavia vant passerende daer ter plaetse als over geheel Nederlandts-Indië, 1624–1682*, ed. J. A. van der Chijs et al., 31 vols. (The Hague, 1887–1931), 1636, p. 44.

[17]*Rantau* in this context refers to frontier areas containing Minangkabau settlements regarded as lying on the fringes of the Minangkabau heartland.

eration of Nine Towns (Kota Sembilan) and the Federation of Seven Towns (Kota Tujuh). According to traditions collected earlier this century, Kota Sembilan and Kota Tujuh were descended from nine daughters and seven sons of a Pagaruyung king, "siblings from one womb," which had once formed a single kingdom under a king who reigned at Kuamang, downstream from Tanjung. In turn, Kota Sembilan and Kota Tujuh had become the "mother" and "father" of several nearby settlements, including those along the Sumai River. These two groups claimed that they had never been included among the Bangsa Duabelas, the *orang berajo*, or king's people.[18] In the seventeenth century, the only service they agreed to provide to downstream rulers was assistance in defending the capital from enemy attack.

The independence of this region also reflects the fact that economically it could easily stand apart from *hilir* Jambi. Although Tanjung and Kuamang were twenty-five days from the downstream capital of Tanah Pilih, they were only fifteen from Agam, a major Minangkabau market. In addition, this area lay just upstream from Muara Tebo, which marked the confluence of the Batang Hari and the Tebo rivers. Muara Tebo was the most important trading center in the *hulu* and was in turn linked to Inderagiri and Tungkal by the Sumai River and by jungle paths. During the dry season, when trade with Jambi was cut off by the low river levels, Muara Tebo acted as an exchange point for gold coming down from Minangkabau; pepper from Tanjung, Kuamang, and Sumai; and textiles and salt supplied by Indian traders in Johor, which Malays brought overland from Tungkal. The Tebo area, in fact, was so closely locked into the Malay trading network that it was sometimes called "little Melaka." For the pepper growers on the upper Batang Hari, therefore, Jambi was simply one of several possible trade outlets, and they were quite willing to stay away if they felt the commercial environment was unsatisfactory. In 1625 the Minangkabau claimed their "king" had forbidden them to come down to Jambi because two or three of their number had been attacked and robbed there, and they similarly boycotted Inderagiri where they had been "badly treated."[19]

The fragility of the linkages between the upper Batang Hari and the *hilir* was not simply economic in nature. In most other highland-lowland relationships in Southeast Asia, the lowland center came to be regarded as culturally superior to the uplands. This was not the case in Jambi or in any of the coastal states adjoining the fertile volcanic highlands of central Sumatra inhabited by the demographically dominant

---

[18]B. J. Haga, "Eenige opmerkingen over het adatstaatrecht van Djambi," in *Feestbundel uitgegeven door het Koninklijk Bataviaasch Genootschap*, 2 vols. (Batavia, 1929), 1:238. Other scholars have disputed this; see J. Tideman, *Djambi* (Amsterdam, 1938), p. 66.

[19]VOC 1087 Jambi to Batavia, 3 Dec. 1625, fols. 154v, 156v.

Minangkabau. Early statues of Minangkabau kings suggest their claims to demonic powers, and still in the eighteenth century Minangkabau in general were commonly believed to possess the secret arts of sorcery, invulnerability, and second sight.[20] Their rulers, "the kings over the green mountains," traced their descent directly from Alexander the Great (Iskandar Zulkarnain) and were traditionally attributed with spiritual authority equal to the kings of Turkey and China. Furthermore, Minangkabau living in *rantau* areas like the Sumatran coasts or the Malay Peninsula continued to regard the Yang Dipertuan Sakti, the "Emperor of the Minangkabau," or the even more revered queen mother, Puteri Jamilan, as their rightful lords. Any individual who presented himself as their envoy could rely on Minangkabau support, regardless of where they had settled. It was thus extremely difficult for Jambi rulers to command the loyalty of Minangkabau communities in the area over which the downstream laid claim. On several occasions the boundary between Jambi and Minangkabau at Tanjung was affirmed but all the upper Batang Hari remained in the awesome shadow of Minangkabau prestige. Just beyond Tanjung, for instance, three regents, with such titles as Baginda Ratu and Yang Muhammad Kecil, governed as representatives of Pagaruyung, and in 1642 the "Raja Pagaruyung, the greatest King of Minangkabau," was even reported to have appeared personally at Tanjung to collect tribute.[21]

The cultural and economic independence of the upper Batang Hari was not easily laid aside. Differences between *hulu* and *hilir* would have been further accentuated by the pronounced Javanese influence in the Jambi court, made evident when the Jambi ruler insisted that "the people of Kuamang, Tujuh Kota, and elsewhere," who had previously been permitted to appear at court in Malay clothes, should now dress in the Javanese style. Twenty years later, the Minangkabau inhabitants of upstream Jambi were still saying that they preferred to trade with the "Malay" king in Inderagiri. When the ruler of Jambi attempted to appoint his own representatives in the Kota Tujuh districts, a rebellion broke out and a thousand people reportedly fled back to Minangkabau.[22]

There were limited ways by which Jambi kings could strengthen

[20]A Minangkabau leader in Rembau on the Malay Peninsula in 1677, for example, claimed to be able to "poison the wind and make it blow wherever he willed in order to do men to death, bewitch cannon and firearms so that they could not be fired, harden his warriors to such a degree that they could not be wounded . . . that he himself could change his shape three times a day and even make himself invisible." "Report of Governor Balthasar Bort on Malacca 1678," trans. M. J. Bremner, ed. C. O. Blagden, *JMBRAS* 5, no. 1 (1927), 69.

[21]VOC 1138 Jambi to Batavia, 8 April 1642, fol. 602.

[22]P. A. Tiele, *Bouwstoffen voor de Geschiedenis der Nederlanders in den Maleischen Archipel*, 3 vols. (The Hague, 1886–95), 11:114; VOC 1244 Jambi to Batavia, 31 Dec. 1663, fol. 2629; 1246 Jambi to Batavia, 22 Feb., fol. 169.

their hold over a territory where the inhabitants had only loose ties with the downstream court. A royal envoy, or even the ruler himself, might go up personally to encourage people to come downstream to trade, but if persuasion failed, force was rarely effective. A few villages might be burned and local leaders punished, but basically the pepper growers held the trump card. If they refused to bring their harvest down, the effects on the port economy were immediate and far reaching. In 1615, for example, it was said that it was forty years since there had been so little pepper because the Minangkabau had not appeared, and the situation only began to improve when they arrived once more in 1619.[23]

Hilir Jambi could lay claim to other upstream districts which in the early seventeenth century were less subject to direct Minangkabau influence, but relations with them were equally sensitive. Much of the upper Tembesi had previously been under Palembang, but several villages had been transferred to Jambi with the dowry of a Palembang princess. The cultivation of pepper, however, had transformed this area into one of prime economic importance, and subsequent Palembang kings were naturally anxious to reassert their previous authority here. They were assisted by the fact that *hulu* Tembesi was only about eight days' travel from Palembang, whereas it was twelve from Jambi. Furthermore, local inhabitants were fully prepared to shift allegiances according to the overlord who offered the most advantages. In fact, the people along the Tembesi moved back and forth between Jambi and Palembang so frequently that they were called the Suku Pindah, the "moving tribes."

Another important pepper district was located along the Merangin, the Tembesi's major tributary. In the first half of the seventeenth century this area was the appanage of a branch of the royal family whom many *hulu* people regarded as having greater claims to the throne than the ruler himself. The head of this family was sometimes termed "the pepper king" because he alone had exclusive trading rights in Merangin, where pepper harvests allegedly yielded around 1,500 *pikul* of pepper per annum. The rulers of Merangin came to independent arrangements with the Dutch, employed their own agents to buy up pepper, and maintained a lifestyle similar to that of the court. Possessing "almost the same power as the king," they were naturally unwilling to accept a position of subservience to the downstream ruler.[24]

[23]J. W. J. Wellan, "Onze eerste vestiging in Djambi," *BKI* 82 (1926), 359; Colenbrander and Coolhaas, 1919–34 and 1952–53, 1:178, 7:113.

[24]VOC 1131 Jambi to Batavia, 29 Oct. 1639, fol. 1382; 1386 Jambi to Batavia, 10 July 1683, fol. 987v.

The geography of Jambi thus encouraged the development of local centers of authority in the interior which had long traditions of near-independent government. The extent of riverine and overland communications across southern and central Sumatra also meant that the great new crop of the sixteenth and seventeenth centuries, pepper, was easily carried to ports on both the east and west coasts. Because *hulu* Jambi could essentially operate independently of the *hilir*, and because important economic areas had become the preserve of migrant groups, *hilir* claims to overlordship in the upstream districts could never be too strident. The strains that could result if acceptable demands were exceeded became increasingly obvious after the establishment of Dutch and English trading posts in Jambi in 1615.

The Effects of the Dutch and English Presence

From the time of their arrival in Jambi, the English and Dutch demonstrated their determination to dominate the pepper market. Their first aim was to limit Chinese competition. At the same time, the northern Europeans were also attempting to force a lower price for pepper (around 6.5 reals per *pikul*), whereas the Chinese who came to buy pepper in Jambi were willing to pay up to 9.5 reals. From 1620, following the establishment of Batavia, Chinese junks were actively driven away, despite the objections of the Jambi ruler. Freedom from direct Chinese competition enabled the northern Europeans to exert a progressively tighter hold on the market. In 1626 the English and Dutch reached an agreement by which they would pay only 6.5 reals per *pikul*, and in 1629 VOC ships forced a besieging Portuguese fleet to retreat, thus confirming the Dutch and English as the dominant European traders.

The commanding presence of the northern Europeans in Jambi was to have a fundamental effect on the economic relations between interior and downstream. In Banten, Chinese had already begun traveling inland to the pepper districts before the European arrival, but this was not the case in Jambi, where growers themselves brought their products downstream. But the Dutch and English, both anxious to gain first access to the pepper harvests, were not content to wait for the interior people to appear at Tanah Pilih. Increasingly they began to send agents to the *hulu* to buy up pepper from growers themselves or to gain promises of the forthcoming crop. Occasionally these agents were Europeans, but it was more common to employ local Chinese to whom cloth was "trusted out." Laden with piece goods, they went upstream to buy up pepper on behalf of Europeans, sometimes carrying debts themselves for several years. The ruler and his nobles rapidly followed suit, employing agents of their own. By the mid-1630s the Minangkabau had become so accustomed to having Chinese come upriver with goods to advance for pepper that "it was unlikely they will come downstream again as they used to do in the past."[25]

The expanding use of middlemen meant that the growers themselves received much less for their product than the official prices for pepper suggest. This was not so apparent in the first decades of the century, when pepper prices were high, but that situation soon began to change. The expanding market of the early seventeenth century resulted in increased pepper production in much of the western Archipelago, and with larger amounts for sale in Europe prices inevitably dropped. In 1636 the price per *pikul* in Jambi had fallen to four reals, and by the 1640s there was an overall trend downward. Despite occasional recoveries, the heady days associated with the early seventeenth century never returned. In 1652, Europe was said to be glutted with pepper, with a surplus sufficient to last for at least three years.[26] As the century progressed, overproduction ensured that the market remained depressed. In the 1680s an English surgeon commented that in India pepper was as plentiful "as stones in the street, and only serves for the ballast very often and to pack up the other goods tight. . . . sometimes several whole shiploads of it are thrown into the sea, and many hundred thousand poundweight of it is burnt."[27] Unpredictable falls and occasional rallies in the price of this slow-maturing crop increased the risks involved in its cultivation because growers could not respond quickly to fluctuations in the market as they could with an annual like cotton. They not unreasonably resented orders from downstream that they must plant pepper despite the adverse economic climate.

The strains in the *hulu-hilir* relationship resulting from falling pepper prices were exacerbated by other developments that were indirect outcomes of the changing economic environment. Probably the change that most affected growers was an increasing use of coinage in commercial transactions. When the Dutch and English first reached Jambi, they found that the most common unit of currency was the lead *pici*, which had apparently been introduced to Java by Chinese traders

[25]*Generale Missiven van Gouverneurs-Generaal en raden aan Heren XVII der Verenigde Oostindische Compagnie*, 9 vols; vols 1–8 ed. W. Ph. Coolhaas; vol. 9 ed. J. van Goor (The Hague, 1960–88), 1:541; see also D. K. Bassett, "The Factory of the English East India Company at Bantam, 1602–1682," Ph.D. diss., University of London, 1955, p. 103.

[26]Glamann, 1958, pp. 63, 74, 81.

[27]Cited in D. W. Davies, *A Primer of Dutch Seventeenth Century Overseas Trade* (The Hague, 1961), p. 55.

around 1590. *Picis* were bundled together in packets of a thousand, known as a *paku*; the *paku* was then given an exchange value in relation to silver Spanish reals. Initially *picis* were brought in by the Chinese, but soon they were being manufactured in Jambi itself, and in 1640 the ruler even sent up 100,000 *picis* to the interior in a deliberate attempt to encourage their usage. Difficulties occurred in Jambi as elsewhere, however, because of fluctuations in the exchange rate between reals and *picis*. In Jambi in 1619, 8,500 *picis* were equivalent to one real; by 1636 the rate had dropped to about 6,900 to each real. Since pepper was priced in reals but purchased with *picis*, this degree of movement obviously disadvantaged growers. A person who had stored *picis* (despite their limited life) might even find that they were worthless; in 1642, for instance, the Jambi ruler decided to make *picis* heavier and to abolish the smaller ones then in use.[28] Perhaps predictably, the coinage used by the Europeans, which bore a value related to its metal content, became preferred to *picis* not simply in commercial exchanges but be-cause it could be used as jewellery or melted down for prestige items such as kris heads. Even so, it was found that the highly prized reals could prove counterfeit. In 1655, for instance, a batch of "silver" reals arrived in Jambi from Batavia but included several that were all copper and others that weighed light.[29] The bewildering array of different forms of coinage introduced to Jambi during the seventeenth century and the uncertainty as to their value only served to foster a view among many *hulu* people that traders from downstream could not be trusted.

Another area of suspicion concerned weights, for the lack of standardization in the seventeenth century made this a sensitive area. In the VOC books, for instance, a Jambi *bahara* weighed 122 Dutch *pond*, while a Melaka *bahara* weighed 125. In times of shortages the Jambi ruler might permit weights to be changed, so that a *last* of unhusked rice normally reckoned at 3,000 *pond* could be rendered at 8,050 *pond*.[30] In the view of many *hulu* people, the arbitrariness of weights worked to their disadvantage when it came to selling their pepper harvest. By 1632 the people of the upper Batang Hari were so convinced that the scales used in Jambi were false that they gave this as another reason for

[28]*Dagh-Register*, 1640, p. 63; VOC 1141 Jambi to Batavia, 13 Aug. 1642, fol. 333v.

[29]VOC 1209 Jambi to Batavia, 13 March 1655, fol. 293. A detailed study of how the introduction of *picis* affected the circulation of coinage in Banten is found in Leonard Blussé, *Strange Company: Chinese Settlers, Mestizo Women, and the Dutch in VOC Batavia* (Dordrecht, 1986), pp. 35–48.

[30]VOC 1099 Jambi to Batavia, 10 Jan. 1631, fol. 151v. One Dutch *pond* here is equal to 0.494 kilograms, so Jambi *bahara* would weigh about 60.2 kilograms and the Melaka *bahara*, 61.75 kilograms.

refusing to come down.[31] Their suspicions were not without basis. In 1643 a VOC official going upstream to buy pepper was ordered to weigh with a different scale, five *kati* heavier than that used in Jambi, in order to compensate the Company for the heavy costs involved in the trip to the interior.[32]

The major cause of *hulu* hostility, however, concerned the repayment of debts and the manner of debt collection. The practice of extending credit for the next season's crop encouraged upstream growers to purchase large amounts of goods or cloth. A bad season, sickness, or simply misplaced optimism often meant that these debts could not be repaid. Sometimes several seasons could pass before pepper was finally delivered, and even then it could well be under duress. Europeans considered local attitudes to indebtedness (for the Protestant English and Dutch a sign of imprudency and even dishonesty) to be casual in the extreme. They felt quite justified in forcibly seizing cargoes of pepper from suspected debtors, and even in pursuing those who owed them money or pepper into the interior.

The Europeans were, however, quite wrong in their view that in Jambi society debts were readily forgotten. The critical difference was in the perception of how debts should be repaid. From the indigenous standpoint, the balance between debtor and creditor could be rectified not only by recompense of pepper or money but (for instance) by loyal service and the presentation of gifts. Furthermore, such repayment need not be made by the debtor himself but could be rendered by anyone who was in turn beholden to him.[33] It was also felt that rich creditors like the Europeans should always be ready to forget the debts of someone in obvious need; by the same token, to refuse credit (as the Europeans did when the debts of any individual reached unacceptable levels) was regarded as a deliberate attempt to humiliate.

The readiness of the Europeans to supply credit was a principal factor in what might be termed Jambi's growing "trade imbalance." Less than a decade after their arrival, the Dutch and English were already concerned about the indebtedness of the Jambi ruler and his nobles, and by 1632 the combined court owed the VOC 5,603 reals.[34] Under continued pressure to make good the amounts owed, Jambi kings found that the Europeans were not satisfied by many traditional

---

[31]*Dagh-Register*, 1631–34, pp. 68–69.

[32]VOC 1151 Orders for J. J. Pars, 6 Nov. 1643, fol. 468. A *kati* is about 0.617 kilograms.

[33]To cite Raymond Firth's classic example, in the long term, the payment owed by B to A may be paid back by C to D. "Here B may be the father-in-law of A, D the son of A and C the brother of B." *Elements of Social Organization* (London, 1951), p. 143.

[34]VOC 1195 Jambi to Batavia, 11 Feb. 1632, fol. 114.

means of repaying debts, such as the bestowal of courtly titles, adoption as a royal son, or gifts of women. On one occasion the Dutch Resident even publicly read out a letter from Batavia in which it was proclaimed that Jambi would never be restored to VOC favor until its debts were repaid. The debts of the ruler produced a chain reaction. Having distributed goods to his nobles and agents, the king was now compelled to insist on immediate payment in a tangible form so that he could reimburse his European creditors. Increasingly he came to relate to his people as a debt collector, not only for amounts owed to him but to the Europeans as well.[35] A treaty signed between the VOC and Jambi in 1644, for example, established that anyone owing money to the Company should be compelled in the king's name to pay back what they owed. By the 1650s a special court official was appointed to collect all debts according to a list the Dutch Resident drew up. The ruler demanded that his debtors (including his own family) should pay him on pain of losing all their slaves and goods. Court nobles and even his mother were told that they should sell their necklaces, earrings, and bracelets to make good the amount owed.[36]

The growing dependence of the Jambi ruler on income derived from pepper cultivation brought far-reaching changes to his relationship with the interior peoples. Previously he had been a distant figure, collecting tolls and customs and mediating in disputes but rarely impinging directly on the lives of ordinary villagers. Now, however, they were compelled to assume part of the burden of the royal liabilities, for in 1662 the Jambi king ordered that each household contribute five-eighths of a real to defray his debts.[37] Court hunting or fishing expeditions to the *hulu* grew in frequency and became a pretext for the forcible collection of debts. If these could not be paid, then the debtor or his family became the ruler's bondsmen. As elsewhere in Southeast Asia, such status was usually assumed unwillingly, for the duties and obligations of "king's men" could transform an individual into little more than a royal asset. Furthermore, determined to ensure the eventual repayment of money, goods, or pepper owed him, the ruler was far less willing to tolerate the seminomadic lifestyle of groups such as

[35]The pressure for payment within a specified time may also be a feature of a growing monetized economy. The *Tuhfat al-Nafis*, for instance, describes the conflicts in eighteenth-century Mempawah when a Bugis trader attempted to regain debts owed him by upstream Dayaks. The reason he required immediate payment, he said, was because of pressure placed on him by merchants in Batavia. Raja Ali Haji, *Tuhfat al-Nafis (The Precious Gift)*, annot. trans. Virginia Matheson and Barbara Watson Andaya (Kuala Lumpur, 1982), pp. 72–80.

[36]VOC 1195 Jambi to Batavia, 1 Feb. 1652, fol. 389v; 1202 Jambi to Batavia, 24 Jan. 1654, fol. 362v.

[37]VOC 1246 Jambi to Batavia, 22 Feb. 1664, fol. 169.

the Suku Pindah. In 1655, for instance, on hearing that the inhabitants of seven pepper-growing villages in *hulu* Tembesi were fleeing to Palembang, the Jambi ruler, the Pangeran, went upstream with an armed expedition and succeeded in capturing two hundred people.[38] A Minangkabau pepper trader in an eighteenth-century story from the Lampung region of southern Sumatra probably expressed the feelings of many of his contemporaries when he advised his son to cut wood or catch fish to sell in order to raise capital, but never to become "indebted to the Raja or the Company."[39] Even at the time, a Jambi prince recognized the growing indebtedness of the interior pepper growers, but he blamed the Chinese who, he said, sold cloth too cheaply in their capacity as agents, giving little attention to how ultimate repayment would be made.[40] Indeed, it was the Chinese who often felt the brunt of popular anger. In 1639, for example, two *hulu* men had planned an attack on the Chinese community living in Kuamang.[41]

The response of the pepper cultivators to perceived impositions from downstream was continuing low-level but insidious resistance. As early as 1629 the Minangkabau of Tanjung and Kuamang told the Jambi ruler that they would destroy their pepper gardens and plant rice if they did not receive higher prices. In 1654, when growers were offered only 3 reals per *pikul*, they said that if the situation did not improve they would shift to cotton.[42] Low returns and "unfair" scales encouraged the use of another weapon, the adulteration of pepper. When the Dutch had first arrived in Jambi, its pepper had been considered remarkably clean, but a generation later there were continual complaints about the admixture of dirt, stones, and rubble, which could make up to 6 percent difference in weight. Often, too, the pepper was picked too early or poorly dried so that it simply molded in the sacks. Enterprising locals even responded to the recurring shortages of Spanish reals by minting their own quite passable copies. The ruler's efforts to strengthen his hold over the pepper trade by persuading the Minangkabau of Tanjung and Kuamang to sell their harvest in Jambi "as of old" were fruitless. Not only did they remain obdurate in their refusal to carry their pepper downstream, they also set up their own toll system, placing rotans across access paths so that downstream traders

[38]VOC 1209 Jambi to Batavia, 1 Feb. 1655, fol. 289.

[39]G. W. J. Drewes, *De Biografie van een Minangkabausen Peperhandelaar in de Lampongs* (The Hague, 1961), p. 105.

[40]VOC 1257 Jambi to Batavia, 20 Oct. 1666, fol. 708.

[41]VOC 1131 Jambi to Batavia, 16 Sept. 1639, fols. 53–54, 55–56, 84.

[42]VOC 1098 Jambi to Batavia, n.d. Dec. 1629, fol. 14v; 1202 Jambi to Batavia, 31 Oct. 1654, fol. 383.

could not pass without paying 10 percent tolls.[43] But probably the most telling reply to the deteriorating pepper market in Jambi was the rise in "smuggling" to alternative ports on both east and west coasts where Malays, Javanese, and Chinese were prepared to offer higher prices than those offered in *hilir* Jambi. An indication that the glut in Europe was not worldwide is suggested by the fact that, when a Chinese junk managed to slip past Dutch patrols and reach Tanah Pilih, its crew was reportedly buying up pepper for around 9 reals per *pikul*.[44]

Rupture Between *Hulu* and *Hilir*

Until the 1670s a total breakdown in *hulu-hilir* relations was prevented by the prestige of Jambi's ruler, the Pangeran or prince who succeeded as a young man in 1630 and reigned until 1679. Despite the many unpopular measures he adopted in regard to the pepper trade, *hulu* communities were apparently willing to forgive him much because he was an important mediator in local disputes and because the economic environment still provided opportunities for trading profits. His principal wife apparently had connections with Muara Tebo, and this may have been another factor in his ability to maintain a loose overlordship over most *hulu* areas.[45] Certainly Dutch records make it clear that upstream leaders did feel free to come down to Tanah Pilih, where many of their grievances were openly debated at court. This ruler was also greatly respected outside Jambi. Because of his wealth and longevity he came to be regarded as one of the senior princes in the region, his standing so high that the kings of Makassar and Banten requested Jambi princesses in marriage and the VOC recruited his services as mediator in their quarrels with Banten. In 1677 he publicly registered his high status by adopting the title of Sultan Agung, the "great sultan."

Sultan Agung's lifestyle, however, bequeathed to his successor debts amounting to several thousand reals. His death in early September 1679 laid bare deep-seated economic and diplomatic difficulties that had been kept at bay only by his personal influence. Shortly before he died, simmering enmities with Johor had already come to a boil. Johorese fleets had sailed up the Batang Hari, razed the capital, and even

[43]VOC 1142 Jambi to Batavia, 12 Nov. 1643, fol. 465; 1118 Jambi to Batavia, 6 Sept. 1635, fol. 486.

[44]*Dagh-Register*, 1636, p. 168; VOC 1138 Jambi to Batavia, 17 Jan. 1642, fol. 587v.

[45]She seems to have retired to Muara Tebo after his death.

set fire to the English lodge. The latter was never to be reopened, and
the new ruler, Sultan Ingalaga, could therefore no longer play one
European power against another as his father had often done. Two
years later, pressured by the Dutch, he agreed to a contract that gave
the VOC a monopoly of Indian cloth and fixed the price of pepper at
the unprecedented low figure of 3 rijksdaalders per *pikul* in cash, and
3.5 if paid in cloth. Continuous raids mounted by Palembang in an
effort to regain control of the rich Tembesi pepper districts merely
served to worsen the situation. In 1683 the VOC intervened to bring
about a partial reconciliation, using their financial hold over Sultan
Ingalaga to force the transfer of several rich pepper-growing districts to
Palembang, with whom the VOC also had a monopoly contract.

These years of conflict with both Johor and Palembang took their toll
on *hulu-hilir* relations, for in defense of his interests Sultan Ingalaga
became ever more dependent on the manpower represented by his
interior subjects. In 1680, fearing an attack by Palembang forces, he
was said to have ordered "all the bovenlanders in Jambi" downstream.
No sooner had they returned than another summons came for them to
again come down to build stockades. The Dutch Resident himself noted
the apprehension of upstream villagers as they fled to escape the king's
"pressers," parties of men sent up to make forcible recruitments.[46]

A more serious aspect of the continuing wars was the concerted
effort by both Johor and Palembang to drive traders away from the port
of Jambi by lying in wait for seagoing vessels. As trade declined and
the costs of food rose, the Chinese who had acted as a mainstay of the
pepper trade began to leave. The VOC account books provide telling
evidence of the extent to which Jambi's economy was affected. Between August 1683 and 31 July 1684, the Dutch lodge in neighboring
Palembang made a profit of 37,570 guilders from pepper purchases and
cloth sales, while from 1 August 1684 to 31 July 1685 Jambi made only
2,868 guilders.[47] The piles of textiles that lay unsold and rotting in the
Dutch warehouse told their own story, and native traders fared little
better than the VOC. In 1680, five ships arrived from Johor with 5,000
reals' worth of Indian cloth but found few buyers; on another occasion
an Indian brought in 4,000 *pikul* of cloth that had to be put into storage
for lack of customers.

The marked drop in royal income resulting from the decline in trade
served to increase the demands on the *hulu*. Sultan Ingalaga attempted
to control what pepper he could by forbidding merchants to go into the

---

[46]VOC 1361 Palembang to Batavia, 2 Jan. 1681, fol. 4v; 1403 Jambi to Batavia, 17 Feb. 1684,
fol. 303v.
[47]*Generale Missiven*, 5:19.

interior, but his expeditions upstream merely served to heighten resentment as he and his three unpopular wives forcibly bought up supplies far below the current price. The VOC hierarchy in Batavia saw the remedy for Jambi's problems in a change of ruler, and this decision was confirmed when Sultan Ingalaga became involved with a Minangkabau prince who had fled from Pagaruyung after a succession dispute. Sultan Ingalaga's association with this Yang Dipertuan Sakti, known to be talking of holy war against the VOC, was Batavia's signal for action. Following the king's refusal in May 1687 to surrender his Minangkabau ally, a VOC blockading force was sent to Jambi, and Tanah Pilih was eventually overcome in September 1687. While Sultan Ingalaga fled to Muara Tebo, the VOC installed his eldest son as Sultan Kiai Gede. In March 1688, however, Sultan Ingalaga was persuaded to come to the Dutch lodge, where he was arrested by the Resident. Shortly afterward he and his family were exiled to Batavia, where they remained until his death in 1699.

In a generation, the relationship between *hulu* and *hilir* in Jambi had been radically altered. The downstream capital had now been claimed by the VOC as their preserve, and the king who ruled there was a Dutch nominee. The VOC had hoped by this means to confirm their pepper monopoly in the *hulu*, but two factors brought about a complete rupture between upstream and downstream. The first was the continuing rule of the unpopular Kiai Gede downstream at Tanah Pilih, reliant on his position as a VOC protégé. Among the interior peoples in particular there was a widespread feeling that Kiai Gede's *derhaka* (disloyalty to the king, his father) was responsible for Jambi's decline. Court circles too were less than enthusiastic in their support for Kiai Gede, especially since he did not possess the sacred Jambi regalia, which had been taken by Sultan Ingalaga to Batavia. In 1687 some nobles had said they would rather see the kingdom go to Palembang or Johor, and in 1692 they even asked the VOC to supply them with another king. Their opposition was also due to the steady deterioration of the downstream economy. By 1695 there had been no trade between Jambi and Melaka, Johor, or elsewhere for a year. Without the incoming ships that provided such goods as cloth, porcelain, ironware, and salt, it was impossible for Tanah Pilih to attract upstream pepper growers. In seven months of 1705, only 96 *pikul* found their way down to the VOC post, compared with hundreds a century earlier.[48] The measure of popular protest could be seen in the flight of manpower and debt bondsmen from the center. In 1695 it was said that there were 600 men in Tanah

---

[48]VOC 1711 Palembang to Batavia, 3 April 1705, fol. 9.

Pilih who could carry arms, but a year later this had fallen to 400. A few years afterward when the Dutch asked for 58 soldiers, Kiai Gede said this was impossible. If he lent these to the Dutch he would have no people left.[49] Even the *orang laut* who normally patrolled the mouth of the river melted away. Nowhere, however, was the rejection of the downstream center greater than among the jungle people, the *orang kubu*, whom the Dutch called the "wilde menschen." Angry because Kiai Gede had sold some of their children as slaves, they mounted raids on the capital which became so severe that the inhabitants were afraid to go out and work in their rice fields. The normally lucrative trade in jungle products such as rotans, which the *orang kubu* collected, simply came to a halt. It must have seemed like an omen in 1693 when there was a widespread epidemic and Kiai Gede's wife died in childbirth, together with her newborn son and several other court ladies. As a measure of the nadir to which Jambi had fallen, the VOC decided in 1697 to close the Jambi lodge and to place the supervision of Dutch affairs there under the Resident of Palembang.

A second factor contributing to the upstream-downstream division was the opposition to Kiai Gede from his brother, Pangeran Pringgabaya. The latter had retreated to Muara Tebo, where he set up a new capital named Mangunjaya and was installed by the Minangkabau ruler as "king of Jambi from the sea to Minangkabau."[50] Equipped with its own ruler, Mangunjaya became the focus of *hulu* loyalties and mounted a direct challenge to Tanah Pilih. Already advantaged by established trading links with both the east and west coasts, Mangunjaya now developed into an exchange point for Bugis traders arriving with supplies of opium from Benkulen, where the English had recently opened a post. A new administration was established, a feature of which was the Raja Sembilan Belas (the Nineteen Kings), who were given control over the upland rivers.[51] In all, Pringgabaya was said to rule in the interior "with more glory and might" than did his brother downstream. *Hulu* leaders were quick to attach themselves to this prosperous settlement, and even the people of Tungkal, an area over which Jambi's hold had never been strong, now claimed connections with Mangunjaya and said they wished to be under the son of their former lord.[52] A united attempt by Kiai Gede and Dutch forces to take Mangunjaya was a complete failure.

[49]VOC 1569 Jambi to Palembang, 31 Jan. 1695, fol. 38; 1808 King of Jambi to Jambi Resident, received 12 June 1711, fol. 96.

[50]*Generale Missiven*, 6:63.

[51]VOC 1759 Abraham Patras to Batavia, 5 March 1708, fol. 15.

[52]VOC 1728 Pangeran Suta to Kiai Gede, received 5 Dec. 1706, fol. 73.

For the next thirty years Jambi was divided into two kingdoms, despite Minangkabau-sponsored efforts to restore the country "as it was in the time of Sultan Agung." It was not long, however, before many *hulu* people, notably those with ready access to the Batang Hari, began to press for a revival of previous trading links because Tanah Pilih remained for them a conveniently located port. For their part, the Dutch were also anxious to see a reunion of upstream and downstream. Memories of earlier profits provided compelling arguments for a VOC return to Jambi, and in 1706 the lodge was reopened. Through Dutch intervention a reconciliation of sorts took place between Sultan Kiai Gede and his brother, Pringgabaya, but the VOC hierarchy now felt that in order to gain the cooperation of the interior an *hulu* prince should be installed as ruler. Accordingly, in 1708 it was decided that Sultan Kiai Gede should relinquish any real authority and act simply as "older ruler," while his brother, Pringgabaya, was to be the true king of Jambi.

From 1708, at least in theory, there was only one ruler in Jambi. But the potentiality for *hulu-hilir* conflicts remained. The crux of the problem was the inability of the downstream kings to maintain sustained links with core economic areas like the upper Batang Hari, Tebo, Merangin, and Tembesi. The Dutch return did nothing to resolve the worsening *hulu-hilir* relationship; if anything, it exacerbated the inherent tensions. Pringgabaya and successive *hilir* kings were placed on the Jambi throne by the Company, which in return hoped to use them as agents who would help enforce the VOC's trading monopolies. Rulers were pressured to lend their weight to support Dutch projects such as the "extirpatie" of cotton bushes in favor of pepper, and royal orders regarding the pepper trade usually originated from Company officials, bearing the VOC seal as well as that of the king. In pursuit of *hilir-hulu* cooperation, the VOC was quite prepared to use force, and in 1712 a Dutch-led expedition destroyed Mangunjaya and transported 2,500 people from the surrounding "new villages" to Tanah Pilih. When such measures failed to bring the upstream under *hilir* control, the VOC saw their only recourse as a change of ruler. In the following decades kings were imprisoned, deposed, exiled, reinstated, and reexiled as the Dutch attempted to find an individual who would be acceptable both to them and to the people of Jambi.[53]

But the closer the cooperation between a ruler and the Dutch, the greater was the likelihood of his alienation from his subjects. The VOC vision of a kingdom controlled by a downstream port that was in fact

---

[53]See the appendix to this chapter.

economically moribund was simply unacceptable to the *orang hulu*. What makes the Jambi case of particular interest is the vehemence with which this hostility was expressed. Refusal to cultivate pepper, for example, reached open defiance. In 1720 a local head in Jambi complained that despite the king's orders his fellow villagers would not let him clear the jungle to make pepper gardens. The eighteenth century saw a continuing preference for the growing of cotton and rice as well as other fast-maturing crops like tobacco and gambier which enabled the cultivator to respond more quickly to changing market prices.

The Minangkabau Movement into Jambi

As I suggested earlier, the *hulu* opposition to the center in Jambi cannot be attributed to economic factors alone. A glance at Jambi's neighbor, Palembang, helps make the point more clearly. In Palembang downstream rulers were manifestly more successful in obtaining recognition of their overlordship in the interior districts. It must be remembered, however, that the Musi is the only river in southeast Sumatra which does not lead up into the Minangkabau heartlands. From the early eighteenth century Jambi rulers, unlike those in Palembang, were faced with the formidable task of establishing their authority over a population that was rapidly becoming more Minangkabau in character and thus more closely linked with "the kings behind the green mountains."

The Minangkabau movement down into Jambi gained momentum from the 1660s, when the Dutch removed Acehnese control on both sides of Sumatra. Migration was further encouraged by disputes within the Minangkabau ruling elite and the flight of several Minangkabau princes with their often considerable following into the *rantau* areas. These bands of wandering Minangkabau were drawn to Jambi because it was known that gold could be found not only in the older *rantau* areas of Tabir, Tebo, and Bungo but in previously unworked districts such as Limun and Pauh in the upper Tembesi. One story from the upper Merangin, for instance, describes how a Minangkabau man came to Jambi via Kerinci because he had "heard from friends who had made the *merantau* of a place where there was much gold and where it could be collected by digging or by panning."[54] By the early eighteenth century their migration into Jambi had become a flood, and in 1728 the

[54]"Himbauan untuk pergi merantau," a typescript kindly lent by Ibu Nuraini, formerly Penilik Kebudayaan, Sungai Manau, Jambi.

ruler claimed gold diggers could be reckoned in the thousands. Already many of these people had settled in the *hulu*, "up to fifteen or twenty people in one village," and by 1761 the Minangkabau movement into the Jambi interior was so extensive that it was even claimed that "all bovenlanders" were Minangkabau.[55] The appearance of Minangkabau adventurers, claiming grandiose titles and purporting to be delegated envoys of Pagaruyung, became commonplace, and on several occasions Minangkabau rulers themselves made apparent their deep interest in Jambi politics.

It is clear that the influx of Minangkabau into Jambi served to feed the undercurrent of unrest, contributing to *hulu* resentment of *hilir* overlordship. A basic reason for this was the favoritism rulers showed to newly arrived Minangkabau even in cases of conflict with existing communities. Since the death of Sultan Agung, there had been a growing tendency by downstream kings to grant interior appanages to their clients, thus displacing traditional hereditary heads who came from local families. This much-resented practice was now extended in an effort to win the support of Minangkabau leaders and the bands of young unmarried males, sometimes numbering a hundred or more, who appeared seasonally to pan for gold. The privileges such newcomers received naturally aroused the hostility of long-time residents (including those in older established Minangkabau villages). In 1722, for example, Sultan Astra Ingalaga gave a Minangkabau regent who lived outside Jambi rights over important gold mines around Tebo, despite the objections of local inhabitants who said these mines had provided them with an income "from olden times."[56] It was later said that this decision played a major role in opening the way to increased Minangkabau migration into Jambi, but it is not difficult to understand why downstream rulers were anxious to gain Minangkabau cooperation. Dominating all aspects of the gold trade, which was rapidly replacing pepper as Jambi's most valued export, Minangkabau controlled a good proportion of commercial dealings between coast and interior. In the absence of large numbers of Chinese in Jambi, the Minangkabau in addition became the principal traders in the addictive drug opium, for which they exchanged their gold. In this situation, however, disputes regarding debt collection commonly involved Minangkabau traders on one side and local residents on the other.

The social and economic independence of Minangkabau communities in Jambi was underscored because their leaders sought legit-

[55]VOC 3059 Jambi to Batavia, 8 Dec. 1761, fol. 19.
[56]VOC 1961 Jambi to Batavia, 4 Nov. 1721, fols. 19–20; 1996 Jambi to Batavia, 28 April 1722, fol. 34.

imacy not from downstream Jambi but from some Minangkabau regent, and occasionally from Pagaruyung itself. This practice created several new centers of allegiance in the *hulu* which often refused to give even token recognition of Tanah Pilih's authority. For example, it was only with the intervention of the Minangkabau ruler in 1729 that the four heads of Limun's gold districts agreed to recognize Sultan Astra Ingalga as their overlord, although they continued to request that their leaders be installed by the Minangkabau regents beyond Tanjung. The king of Jambi thus still complained that he could not persuade the *hulu* people to bring their gold downstream "because they come from other districts and are under different kings, since my country is only from Tanjung downward."[57] *Hilir* efforts to attract gold miners downstream were further impeded as new paths were cut through the jungle to link Limun with Palembang and the west coast, increasing the opportunities of *hulu* people to trade elsewhere. Now Minangkabau gold miners found that they could effectively blackmail the Jambi ruler by promising to bring gold down to the capital if certain demands were met, or by refusing to trade if they were not. Using this weapon, representatives from Limun successfully obtained the release from prison of one of their leaders and forced the dismissal of an unpopular royal representative.[58]

The defiance of the interior toward the *hilir* capital became more noticeable after 1708 as the VOC and the kings it supported attempted to exert greater control upstream. In 1709, 1,500 uplanders were reported to be organizing a rebellion in the Tanjung region, not to establish their independence from Tanah Pilih but to express their desire for a king who would reign in accordance with the "old ways," as they had existed "in the time of Sultan Agung." To some extent this was a vague reference to a kind of golden age believed to have existed in the past, but it conjured up memories of a period when pepper prices were high and the involvement of the *hilir* in *hulu* life comparatively limited. Now there had been nearly forty years of economic decline and increased downstream demands. Like the Dutch, the interior people believed that the fault lay with the *hilir* king. The VOC itself had demonstrated that an unacceptable ruler could be deposed or exiled, and it may have been from Dutch actions that the *orang hulu* took their cue. In 1716 the people of Tujuh Kota told the Dutch Resident that they would no longer acknowledge the king because he was not governing them by their

---

[57]VOC 2193 King of Jambi to Dutch Resident, received 6 March 1731, fol. 39; 3059 Jambi to Batavia, 8 Dec. 1761, fol. 19.

[58]VOC 2239 Jambi day register, 20 Dec. 1733, fol. 163; 2100 King of Jambi to heads of Limun, 19 Aug. 1728, fol. 72; 2133 Jambi to Batavia, 18 Oct. 1729, fol. 133.

old laws and customs. Furthermore, they were now prepared to use force to put in place the kind of government that would restore the upstream-downstream relationship they believed had existed in former times. In 1719 the VOC bowed to the wishes of an *hulu*-led resistance movement that involved around 8,000 people and installed Raden Astrawijaya, Pringgabaya's son, as ruler with the title Sultan Astra Ingalaga. When the latter was imprisoned by court nobles in 1725, an upland "army" again appeared downstream to come to his support. The Dutch stood helplessly by while *hulu* headmen forced the *hilir* leaders to swear never again to take up arms against the interior. In March 1727, a Minangkabau "king," widely believed to come from Pagaruyung, arrived in state at Tanah Pilih to ensure that Sultan Astra Ingalaga was released from confinement and to oversee his reinstallation as ruler of Jambi.

From 1729 there was a general peace in Jambi, but the *hulu-hilir* relationship was clearly weighted in favor of the upstream. In a situation where the *hilir* was so obviously dependent on continuing economic links with the interior, real economic power was with the *hulu*. Efforts to force traders to come to Tanah Pilih by forbidding salt to be carried upriver proved futile, for upstream people retaliated in kind. Dutch records show that they not only failed to bring down supplies of gold and pepper but also withheld tribute and refused to carry out corvée duties. Increasingly, too, they would not accept goods from the ruler on credit against future deliveries. As one VOC official observed, they knew that to do so would effectively render them the king's slaves.[59] *Hulu* leaders coming downstream had even given their written authority (*piagem*, "verband briefjes") to the Dutch Resident to ensure that nothing in them would be changed.[60] It was the boldness of the interior groups that struck the author of the *Hikayat Bandjar*, a text written from the point of view of another upstream-downstream state. He had no doubt that the disrespect of Jambi's rural people for the "city folk" (*orang kota*) and the king's officials was due to the fact that they grew pepper.[61]

Lacking the ability to compel obedience, Jambi rulers were forced to use other means to win the favor of the interior. Gifts from the center had always been an important way of confirming *hulu-hilir* ties, but

[59]VOC 1776 Patras to Batavia, 28 Feb. 1709, fol. 63.

[60]VOC 1945 Jambi to Batavia, 3 Sept. 1720, fol. 4. These *piagem* are a heritage from the period of Javanese influence in Jambi. They were usually inscribed on copper or silver and confirmed the holder's office or privileges.

[61]*Hikayat Bandjar: A Study in Malay Historiography*, ed. J. J. Ras (The Hague, 1968), pp. 331, 375. This text also sees a similar situation in Palembang, although this is not supported by VOC records of the period.

now honors bestowed by the king became so common that by the 1730s local heads in Tembesi and Rawas regions commonly had the court-bestowed title of Dato. Other important concessions were also made. In 1728, Sultan Astra Ingalaga had promised to consult with the Minangkabau of Limun "concerning their customs" in order that trade in gold, pepper, and rice could proceed smoothly, and in 1741 old promises that Minangkabau would receive special privileges were confirmed.[62] Any talk of "extirpatie" of cotton was abandoned and orders were given that cotton could be grown freely if pepper was also cultivated. The inhabitants of Merangin were told that tribute, previously submitted annually, need now be brought to court only every three years as long as pepper was grown. In 1740 a general order that uplanders need not come down for corvée except for defense was extended so that people in the *hulu* were released from all court service when they agreed to plant pepper.[63]

Granted largely because of pressure from the Dutch, these concessions made marked inroads on established royal privileges, especially regarding access to manpower. *Hilir* kings, themselves receiving scant respect in the interior, became increasingly resentful of VOC demands. By the mid-eighteenth century, Sultan Anum, who had succeeded in 1742, could see little advantage in the continuing association with the VOC. In 1758 he said categorically that "Jambi is my land and no one has anything to say about it except me." When the Dutch threatened reprisals for his lack of cooperation, he reminded them of the protection the environment afforded him. The Dutch, he said, need not imagine that Jambi would be like Java, where people could be more easily subdued. In Jambi "the river flows high up, and it will be difficult to follow me without harm to the Company. During past expeditions the company has already experienced how many people can die, not through the might of my subjects but through the power of the spirits [*duyvels*]."[64] A stalemate had been reached. After a decade of gradually worsening relations, the Dutch lodge was attacked in March 1768 by about a hundred men acting under Sultan Anum's orders.

The subsequent VOC decision to close the lodge in Jambi deprives the historian of vital material which would make possible a more detailed reconstruction of the *hulu-hilir* relationship in the late eighteenth

[62]These privileges included promises by the ruler that he would not confiscate the goods of Minangkabau who died, that they would be permitted to return home at any time, that slaves and female servants could not be taken by the court, and that Minangkabau traders would be under the jurisdiction of their own leaders.

[63]VOC 1911 Jambi to Batavia, 19 Jan. 1718, fol. 28; 2502 Jambi day register, 27 Sept. and 30 Oct. 1740, fol. 43.

[64]VOC 2965 Jambi to Batavia, 29 Nov. 1658, fol. 6; 22 Feb. 1659, fols. 1–2.

century. Scattered sources suggest that, although the upstream districts nominally recognized a king in Tanah Pilih, in the aftermath of the Dutch departure Jambi as a whole was regarded as a Minangkabau vassal. It is apparent, however, that no developments occurred during this period to restore the long-lost prosperity of the downstream center. By contrast, the *hulu* continued to thrive, and in 1833 when the Dutch signed a treaty with the Jambi ruler it was in the hope of gaining access to the rich interior trade. The ability of the upstream to stand apart thus remained, so that a return to a division like that of the late seventeenth century was always possible. In 1858 this became a reality when Sultan Taha set up his capital at Muara Tebo in resistance to the downstream king, who was again shored up by Dutch strength.

In this essay I set out to examine the nature of the *hulu-hilir* relationship in one Indonesian state in the seventeenth and eighteenth centuries and to assess the degree to which this relationship was affected by changing economic circumstances. Although the Jambi case has unique features, a comparison with other upstream-downstream states, including those on the mainland, would no doubt reveal many points of similarity as well as contrast.[65] One feature probably typical of all such areas in early times was the economic partnership between upstream and downstream in which the stress was on cooperation rather than the dominance of the coastal market over the producers.[66] The only way *hilir* kings could maintain the loyalty of interior people was to provide an attractive trading environment that would be patronized by choice and that was more appealing than alternative centers nearby. It was on this basis that the pepper trade in Jambi initially developed, with the upstream growers bringing their products down because the relatively convenient market at Tanah Pilih offered good prices and customers who could provide a range of desired products. During the seventeenth century, however, the increasing dominance of Europeans, and especially the VOC, combined with other factors to bring about the fall of pepper prices and the collapse of local trade. As *hilir* kings became more closely associated with the Dutch, they also began to adopt many European trading practices and to commit themselves to supporting unpopular economic policies in order to ensure themselves of VOC backing. The inevitable result was the rejection by *hulu*

---

[65]See, for instance, Susan D. Russell ed., *Ritual, Power, and Economy: Upland-Lowland Contrasts in Mainland Southeast Asia* (DeKalb, Ill., 1989).

[66]Consider, for instance, the peace pacts between lowland Ilocano and upland Igorot traders discussed in William Scott, *Cracks in the Parchment Curtain* (Quezon City, Philippines, 1982), pp. 148–58.

dwellers of *hilir* claims to authority over them. The Jambi experience encapsulates a basic problem of many coastal rulers who found themselves caught up with a European power. Any alliance between them was bound to increase tensions as the Europeans attempted to manipulate or recast traditional upstream-downstream relations to attain specific commercial goals.

But it was not only the European association that contributed to interior resistance to kings in upstream-downstream states, for frequently opposition to perceived imposition was fostered by cultural differences. In the Malay-Indonesian Archipelago, downstream communities were commonly Muslim but dependent on non-Muslim groups for supplies of local jungle products. Conflicts could well arise because of differing trading practices that were in turn shaped by contrasting cultural backgrounds. The disputes between Malay-Bugis traders and upstream Dayaks described in sources from southwestern Borneo could thus be seen as evidence of the kinds of problems that could arise in interaction between a relatively isolated *hulu* society and inhabitants of the more commercialized and monetized coastal ports.[67] In other areas where the headwaters of main river systems interlocked, economic and demographic shifts could mean that *hulu* regions long linked to one *hilir* ruler could be incorporated into the economy of a neighboring coastal state. In eighteenth-century Perak, for instance, the rich tin mines of the *hulu* were taken over by enterprising workers from Kedah who refused to acknowledge the authority of the Perak king.[68]

What makes the Sumatran case of special interest is the cultural and economic dominance of the interior highlands, a situation more akin to New Guinea than to the Malay Peninsula or Borneo. For those Sumatran states adjoining the Minangkabau heartlands, upstream-downstream differences were rendered particularly acute because the *hulu* frequently developed into a Minangkabau *rantau*. The Minangkabau migration into Jambi is certainly not unique. For example, one Malay text describes attempts by Minangkabau in upstream Inderagiri to oust the coastal ruler and take control of the entire state.[69] The ability of these migrant groups to stage such opposition, however, was to a considerable degree dependent on their ability to call on support from their homeland. Minangkabau pepper growers also settled in the interior of Terengganu, but when disputes occurred with the downstream authorities they simply left. In Jambi, however, as in much of

[67]Raja Ali Haji, 1982, pp. 72–80.
[68]Andaya, 1979, pp. 280–85.
[69]Raja Ali Haji, 1982, pp. 118–19.

Sumatra, Minangkabau migrants settled down to assume a dominant economic position. They were not easily persuaded to become subjects of a downstream king whom they saw as inferior to the spiritually powerful Minangkabau rulers at Pagaruyung.

In seventeenth- and eighteenth-century Jambi, a combination of geographic realities, economic pressures, historical circumstances, and cultural loyalties combined to infuse tensions into the *hulu-hilir* relationship which were not easily resolved. Though the state was finally and incontrovertibly brought under the control of the downstream center in the early twentieth century, it took nearly four decades of conflict and the prolonged efforts of a colonial army. It is perhaps symbolic that today, although the provincial administration is located downstream, the burial ground of the *hilir* kings lies overgrown and forgotten; by contrast, the grave of Sultan Taha, the *pahlawan nasional* (national hero) who led nineteenth-century resistance against the Dutch, remains an honored memorial in the center of the upstream town of Muara Tebo.

Appendix: The VOC and the Royal House of Jambi, 1679–1770

1679	Sultan Agung dies, succeeded by son, Sultan Ingalaga.
1687	Conflicts between the Dutch and Sultan Ingalaga reach a head. A Dutch expedition is sent to Jambi and Tanah Pilih is taken on September 5. Sultan Ingalaga flees to Muara Tebo. His eldest son is installed by the Dutch as Sultan Kiai Gede.
1688	Sultan Ingalaga arrested and sent to Batavia.
1690	Sultan Ingalaga's second son, Pangeran Pringgabaya, establishes his capital at Muara Tebo with Minangkabau support.
1697	VOC lodge closed, with a small complement of men left behind.
1698	Attempt to reconcile the two brothers organized by the Minangkabau ruler.
1699	Sultan Ingalaga dies in Batavia.
1706	Dutch post reopened.
1708	Reconciliation between Kiai Gede and Pringgabaya under Dutch sponsorship. Kiai Gede to be senior ruler and Pringgabaya junior, but actual, ruler.

1710	Dutch exile Pringgabaya to Batavia because of alleged contacts with English and conflict with his brother.
1711	Pringgabaya exiled to Banda, where he dies in 1715. Rebellions break out in interior.
1717	Eight thousand uplanders reported to be rallying upstream, calling for return of Pringgabaya's son, Raden Astrawijaya, from Batavia. Other rebel groups threaten the capital.
1719	Raden Astrawijaya brought back. Kiai Gede dies. Raden Astrawijaya installed as ruler at insistence of uplanders with the title Sultan Astra Ingalaga. He is opposed by Kiai Gede's son, Suriadinata.
1723	Reconciliation between Suriadinata (now called Sultan Muhammad) and Sultan Astra Ingalaga.
1725	Sultan Astra Ingalaga imprisoned by nobles. Rebellion by interior people (led by Kota Tujuh) who come down and reinstall him in May. Two weeks later he is deposed by the VOC, which places Sultan Muhammad on the throne.
1726	Sultan Muhammad dies of smallpox. For some months there is no king in Jambi.
1727	Sultan Astra Ingalaga again made king with the intervention of the Minangkabau ruler.
1742	Sultan Astra Ingalaga steps aside in favor of his brother, Sultan Anum.
1768	VOC personnel leave after attack on lodge.
1770	Dutch lodge closed down.

5

Restraints on the Development of Merchant Capitalism in Southeast Asia before c. 1800

Jeyamalar Kathirithamby-Wells

There is perhaps no socioeconomic phenomenon of the modern era that links the present with the past more intimately than the growth of capitalism. The nature of this development is inherently global in its dimensions. The forces that set it on its path had their origins in European commercial and political expansion. The harnessing of resources for the same end could, to some degree, have suppressed latent forms of merchant capitalism in the third world. There were, however, internal forces that determined local responses to the growth of international trade. The vigor of early merchant enterprise which laid the foundations for the success of modern capitalism in Japan, for example, contrasts with the negative response of the equally independent regimes of Thailand and China and the anticapitalist trends that surfaced in Russia and Eastern Europe. In the case of Southeast Asia, the passive indigenous response to merchant capitalism, even preceding the era of European imperialism, was at least partly a feature of its political economy.

The World-System and Southeast Asian Response

Throughout the course of its cultural evolution, Southeast Asia's circle of trade progressively expanded, stimulated by contacts with India, China, and West Asia. By the time of the Melaka sultanate, the region was linked by maritime routes with the outer limits of long-distance trade, stretching from Venice in the west to Canton in the east. Association with Europe did indeed reach further back into antiquity, as attested in the generic name *Cinnamomum* for the exotic bark that derives its name from the Greek *kinnamomom*. Southeast Asia's new encounter with the West, beginning with the Portuguese conquest of Melaka in 1511, marked, however, a significant departure from the earlier phase of international contacts. Unlike the waves of Hindu-Buddhist and Islamic influences preceding it, European penetration was characteristically aggressive in its bid to break the conventional boundaries of segmented commercial exchange in order to gain mastery over the main girdle of exchange.

Commercial expansion generated by the Renaissance ethos ultimately linked the silver and gold mines of Mexico and Peru with the distant spice gardens and aromatic forests of Southeast Asia, via the markets of the Mediterranean and Atlantic seaboard. Notwithstanding the rivalry between Catholic and Protestant, Christian and Muslim at various points of commercial exchange and at various times, the circle of trade was successfully closed for the ramifications of a "world-system", encompassing an *economie monde*, hitherto unknown. The metropolitan base for this new and formidable structure of commercial exchange was in the capitals of Europe; but it was in Southeast Asia that the complex lines of regional, interregional, and long-distance trade converged. It was here that the crucial drama of international exchange involving the importation of bullion and valuable cloth for the high-profit investment in pepper and spices was enacted. For Tomé Pires in 1512, and his Persian counterpart Rabi ibn Muhamed Ibrahim some two hundred years later, the commercial power of Melaka and the natural wealth of Aceh, respectively, were unsurpassed.[1]

In contrast to Mexico and Peru, whose wealth was rapidly plundered and whose culture was brought to ruin, Southeast Asia's social and economic evolution took spectacular strides during the early period of European commercial expansion. Unlike South American bullion, Southeast Asian spices were widespread, with the exception of nutmeg, and could not be guarded effectively as a monopoly. Despite their initially aggressive stance, the Portuguese soon learned the importance of treaty negotiations and, failing that, entered profitable joint ventures and investments on a footing of equality with Asian merchants. The seeds of capitalist growth in Europe took root in long-term invest-

---

[1]Tomé Pires, *The Suma Oriental of Tomé Pires*, ed. and trans. Armando Cortesão, 2 vols. (London, 1944), 2:237; *The Ship of Sulaiman*, trans. John O'Kane (London, 1972), p. 174.

ment in luxury goods, which generated the necessary market and monetary facilities. Nonetheless, the reduction of risk through the provision of military protection for trading vessels was a basic feature of European commercial expansion. Such protection was interpreted broadly when other methods failed to secure implementation of preferential treaties and monopolies coerced from local powers. European methods of associating arms with trade were matched by Southeast Asia's resistance. The purchase and manufacture of arms for defense against external threats became a major concern of the rulers of Patani, Aceh, Banten, Makassar, and Ayutthaya, though their use for internal political ascendancy, such as by the First Toungoo empire at Pegu (1535–99), was not unknown.[2]

In the commercially oriented states of Southeast Asia, territorial expansion, greater administrative centralization, increased manpower and arms, royal monopoly of produce—in short, royal absolutism— were direct reactions to the Western commercial challenge. Nowhere else in Asia did absolutism function so widely and effectively on the basis of commerce. Sultan Iskandar Muda's (r. 1607–36) contempt for and suspicion of European traders in reaction to their methods of engrossing the market were shared by other rulers, namely, Pangeran Ranamanggala of Banten (r. 1608–24), Sultan Hasanuddin of Makassar (r. 1653–69), and King Narai of Siam (r. 1656–88), all of whom turned the situation to advantage by playing off one commercial group against another.

Commercial growth led to unprecedented expansion of cash crop cultivation along the coast and in the hinterland, particularly pepper in western Java, Sumatra, and Borneo, as well as increased extraction of tin in the Malay Peninsula and sappanwood and deerskin in Siam. Urban growth was the logical consequence,[3] along with expansion of regal wealth, evinced by the spectacle and splendor of the contemporary courts of Ayutthaya and Aceh.[4] In Europe, as in Southeast Asia, commerce expanded under the patronage of rulers. The ruler's interest in the affairs of commerce proved, in fact, an important basis for nascent capitalism in Europe. What then went wrong with the impeccable models of regal participation in Southeast Asian commerce?

Despite the vigorous and expanded system of market exchange at

[2] V. B. Lieberman, *Burmese Administrative Cycles: Anarchy and Conquest, c. 1650–1760* (Princeton, N.J., 1984), pp. 26–29.

[3] Anthony Reid, "The Structure of Cities in Southeast Asia," *JSEAS* 2, no. 2 (1980), 238.

[4] J. Kathirithamby-Wells, "The Courtly Wealth of Seventeenth Century Southeast Asia, with Special Reference to Aceh, Ayutthaya and Banten," *Sarjana*, University of Malaya, 1992 (in press).

the height of Southeast Asian commerce, it lacked the more important ingredient—a certain kind of society, as Fernand Braudel defines it, to foster the growth of merchant capitalism.[5] In Japan, social and economic forces in the Ashikaga period (1368–1573) established roots for the later growth of merchant capitalism.[6] In contrast, a substantial indigenous class of merchants to match the wealth and influence of resident foreign entrepreneurs was lacking not only in the Melaka sultanate[7] but throughout Southeast Asia. The indivisible nature of trade and politics, peculiar to the environment and the times, dictated the domination of ruler and state in the administration of commerce, restraining the growth of indigenous merchant enterprise. Trade was critical to the Southeast Asian economy, including that of the agrarian states with interior capitals. Pagan ran a vital line of commerce with Yunnan through the Shan states, exchanging cotton for silks. Sukhothai laid claim to the southern Menam Chaophraya leading to the seacoast; and the power of Mataram was sustained only as long as it controlled the north Javanese *pasisir* (coast).

It was different with the agrarian-based economies of China and Mughal India. There commercial revenue and tributary goods were a boon that enhanced the splendor and prestige of the respective courts, but they were not central to their political economies. The large export industries—south Chinese ceramics and cloth production in the Coromandel—were both at coastal locations, away from the respective royal capitals. Intermittent suspension of trade did not seriously damage the Chinese economy. In India, the Mughal rulers and officials were casual traders who formed private partnerships with indigenous merchants.[8]

The very different pattern in the Southeast Asian capitals controlling upstream-downstream movements stemmed from economic and environmental factors. The location of Mataram, Pagaruyung, Pagan, and Ava in the heart of the interior ricelands ensured control over communication along valley orientations and over the resources generated by large population concentrations. Generally, the prevalence of wet rice (*sawah*) cultivation in lower riverine locations, providing food and manpower resources, favored the strategic location of capitals at river

[5]Fernand Braudel, *Civilization and Capitalism, 15th-18th Century: The Wheels of Commerce*, trans. Sian Reynolds, 2 vols. (London, 1979–84), 2:600.

[6]Mikiso Hane, *Japan: A Historical Survey* (New York, 1972), pp. 115–20; Norman Jacobs, *The Origins of Modern Capitalism in East Asia* (Hong Kong, 1958), pp. 60–61, 70; Braudel, 1979–84, p. 589.

[7]M. A. P. Meilink-Roelofsz, *Asian Trade and European Influence in the Indonesian Archipelago between 1500 and about 1630* (The Hague, 1962), p. 58.

[8]Ashin Das Gupta, "Indian Merchants and the Trade in the Indian Ocean, c. 1500–1750," in *Cambridge Economic History of India*, ed. Tapan Raychaudhuri and Irfan Habib, 2 vols. (Cambridge, 1982), 1:422.

Figure 3. Dutch impression of Asian merchants in Banten, 1596: Malay merchant (D), southern Indian or Keling merchant (E), and Javanese woman (F). From *De eerste schipvaart der Nederlanders naar Oost-Indië onder Cornelis de Houtman,* vol. 1, ed. G. P. Rouffaer and J. W. Ijzerman (The Hague, Linschoten-Vereniging, 1915).

mouths or a few miles inland, away from coastal swamps and controlling movement of goods up and down river.

Rulers earned some revenue from rice, paid as tax and tribute, and from trade in surplus exported to regional markets, as by Mataram to the Spice Islands. These revenues, in turn, financed the purchase of cloth and other luxury goods, predominantly silk and porcelain, from outside the region. Lucrative currency earnings more commonly came from the export of pepper, spices, and a variety of natural resources. By the beginning of the fifteenth century, Phnom Penh was fast developing as a trading center with a substantial population of Chinese, and probably Malay-speaking Chams, engaged in the exportation of jungle produce, mainly ivory and aromatics from the upper Mekong.[9] External trade in Cambodia, though not crucial to the peasant economy, brought revenues and luxuries for the ruler and elite.[10] Ayutthaya supplemented revenues from rice through a spectacular expansion of trade in sappanwood and deerskin during the seventeenth century.

In most areas where the interior population relied on external

[9]Ibid.; David Chandler, "Cambodia before the French: Politics in a Tributary Kingdom, 1794–1848," Ph.D. diss., University of Michigan, 1973, p. 33.
[10]David Chandler, *A History of Cambodia* (Boulder, Colo., 1983), pp. 78–80.

sources of salt, cloth, and other necessities, the riverine capitals that serviced them became politically influential. Palembang functioned in this way with reference to Pasemah, and Jambi serviced Kerinci and the primitive forest-produce gatherers, the Kubu. The traditional symbiosis between coast and interior was greatly enhanced with the wider culti-vation of pepper as a cash crop in Sumatra. Reduced subsistence culti-vation and heavier reliance on external supplies of food and luxuries brought increased dependence on coastal centers by hinterland and surrounding populations.

Commerce and Political Power

Economic growth generated by the expansion of Muslim trade, as from the fourteenth century, laid the foundations for a new cycle of state formation in maritime Southeast Asia which extended into the eighteenth century. The variety of polities arising from riverine chief-doms ranged from the principalities of Pedir, Pasai, Inderapura, the Javanese *pasisir*, the Malay Peninsula, Banjarmasin, and Magindanao to the more extensive maritime kingdoms of Brunei, Johor, Aceh, Banten, Ternate, Makassar, and Sulu. There were also the older polities of Palembang and Jambi, which drew a new lease on life from the cash crop economy. In all instances, commercial growth was directly super-vised by the riverine or coastal chief or ruler, whose political influence increased in direct proportion to revenues from trade.[11] For adminis-tration, the commercial hierarchy was extended through the develop-ment of subsidiary centers of trade in adjoining river basins and at interior river junctions. The incorporation into the administration of local chiefs for the supervision, collection, and movement of produce was the logical consequence.

The fluvial orientation of settlement, administration, and general activity in Southeast Asia did not necessarily imply facility of communi-cation even in areas where rivers were abundant. Fluctuations between the seasonal drying up and flooding often rendered river communica-tion difficult. In contrast to the earlier specialization in high-value gold, camphor, wax, and aromatics traded for small luxuries, the bulk trade in pepper, tin, hardwoods, and deerskin in exchange for equally cum-

[11]J. Kathirithamby-Wells, "Royal Authority and the 'Orang Kaya' in the Western Archi-pelago," *JSEAS* 27, no. 2 (1986), 265–67; John Villiers, "The Cash-Crop Economy and State Formation in the Spice Islands in the Fifteenth and Sixteenth Centuries," in *The Southeast Asian Port and Polity: Rise and Demise*, ed. J. Kathirithamby-Wells and John Villiers (Singapore, 1990), p. 91.

bersome loads of rice and other necessities made transportation a serious problem. A natural emphasis became the organization of manpower, from corvée and slave labor, for the complex movement of goods by river boats and rafts and by portage along footpaths over the watersheds. The same infrastructural organization was involved in the collection of marine produce at Brunei, Johor, and Sulu. Trade was inherently a political affair in Southeast Asia. Latent in the system was the potential for political tension and conflict. The mere stimulation of the market economy was sufficient to upset the balance between reciprocity and redistribution. Development of commerce and the concomitant rise of subsidiary power centers at strategically located river junctions (Malay, *pangkalan*), for example, on the long reaches of the east Sumatran rivers created conditions for political tension. Around 1700 a power struggle within the royal house of Jambi led Pringgabaya to install himself as Sri Maharaja Batu at Muara Tebo, on the upper reaches of the Batang Hari, in opposition to his elder brother, Sultan Kiai Gede, at the capital of Tanah Pilih.[12]

The importance of appropriating a commercial resource base for establishing political power cannot be overestimated in the Southeast Asian context. In Sumatra this was evident as early as the mid-fourteenth century when Adityawarman from Java moved up the Inderagiri to control Pagaruyung, the important resource base in Tanah Datar, for the export of gold to the Straits of Malacca.[13] By the turn of the seventeenth century, with the decline of the gold trade in Pagaruyung, both Raja Kecil and Ahmad Syah ibn Iskandar, who claimed connections with the Minangkabau royal family in the highlands, attempted to establish their power base at the lower end of the commercial network. In doing so their aim was to galvanize the natural and manpower resources of the Jambi and Siak river valleys.[14]

The impact of European commercial expansion on producer states was inevitable. The search by European companies for bigger supplies on the monopoly principle was aimed at higher profit margins, involving large capital outlays, complex financial partnerships, and substantial borrowing. It reciprocated readjustment within the indigenous

[12]Stamford Raffles, *The Memoirs of Sir Stamford Raffles* (London, 1935), p. 333; J. Tideman, *Djambi*, VKI 42, (Amsterdam, 1938), pp. 29–30; J. Kathirithamby-Wells, *Thomas Barnes' Expedition to Kerinci in 1818*, Centre for Southeast Asian Studies, University of Kent at Canterbury, Occasional Paper no. 7 (1986), pp. 21–22. See also Barbara Andaya, Chapter 4 in this volume.

[13]Christine Dobbin, "Economic Change in Minangkabau as a Factor in the Rise of the Padri Movement," *Indonesia* 23 (1977), 10.

[14]J. Kathirithamby-Wells, "Ahmad Shah ibn Iskandar and the late 17th Century 'Holy War' in Indonesia," *JMBRAS* 53, no. 1 (1970), 51, 54, 61–62; Leonard Andaya, *The Kingdom of Johor, 1641–1723* (Kuala Lumpur, 1975), pp. 262–63, 279, 281–82, 288.

structure for greater resource mobilization through territorial expansion, increased cultivation, and efficient control over movement and sale of produce. Through shrewd leadership and organization a ruler could engross the principal imports and exports as royal monopolies, determining their prices and holding sole authority for the issue of licenses and commercial concessions. As well as enacting his traditional role through offering commercial facilities he had occasionally exploited for personal investment, he was now the chief trader.

Given the irrevocable link between commerce and wealth in maritime Southeast Asia, the interest of the nobility and officials in gaining a share of the increased profits from trade was a natural outcome. Even in the days preceding the age of monopoly, the Tamil harbor master or *syahbandar*, Raja Mendaliar, was "easily the richest" in the Sultanate of Melaka. The wealth Bendahara Mutahir acquired from commercial investment was rated second only to that of the *syahbandar*: "Bendahara Sri Maharaja was in fact always engaging in business and never once did he come to grief in any of his enterprises."[15] The new age of commerce opened an even wider range of opportunities for enrichment. In the absence of a salaried bureaucracy, the nobility and officials earned commercial privileges and a share in the increased revenues. There evolved through this process an identifiable group of men of influence, *orang kaya*, in the Banda Islands, Ternate, Aceh, and Johor.[16] The law codes of Melaka and Aceh provide an interesting insight into the changing perception of the participation of an administrative elite in commerce.

The *Undang-undang Melaka*, first compiled in the reigns of Sultan Muhammed Syah (r. 1424–44) and Sultan Muzaffar Syah (r. 1445–58) and used widely in the Malay world, was evidently designed with a view to ordering a society with just and equitable laws congenial to free trade. The way Sultan Mahmud Syah (r. 1511–29) invested in the purchase of cloth in the Coromandel appeared to be through fitting out an occasional ship, much in the way Emperor Aurangzeb and the Mughal Prince Khuram did to Aceh and the Nawab Comeetchan of Bengal did to the Malay Peninsula a century later.[17] Participation by the official elite was casual and provision was made to prevent the engrossment of trade by any single party. Prospective buyers of a particular commodity

---

[15]*Sejarah Melayu: "Malay Annals,"* trans. C. C. Brown (Kuala Lumpur, 1970), p. 154.

[16]Villiers, 1990, p. 91; Kathirithamby-Wells, 1986 ("Royal Authority"), pp. 256–67.

[17]*Sejaruh Melayu*, 1970, p. 134; B. Schrieke, *Indonesian Sociological Studies*, 2 vols. (The Hague, 1957), 1:390, n. 112.; *Generale Missiven van Gouverneurs-Generaal en raden aan Heren XVII der Verenigde Oostindische Compagnie*, ed. W. Ph. Coolhaas, 9 vols. (The Hague, 1960–88), 3:551, 19 March 1683; Om Prakash, *The Dutch Factories in India, 1617–23: A Collection of Dutch East India Company Documents Pertaining to India* (New Delhi, 1984), p. 155.

were obliged to make a combined purchase of the whole cargo at an agreed price.[18] To prevent the *syahbandar*, in particular, from misusing his position, a clause in the *Undang-undang Melaka* limited his investment in tin, presumably one of the most valuable exports, to a total value of 112.5 reals.[19]

When the Melaka Digest was compiled in 1595 for the Sultan of Pahang, 'Abd al-Ghafur Muhaiyu'd-din Syah, the ruling elite had begun to take a more aggressive and direct role in trade. The preamble to this document stated categorically the obligation of port officers to protect foreigners "who bring trade to the ruler and chiefs" against ill treatment.[20] By the reign of Sultan Iskandar Muda (r. 1607–36) the *syahbandar*—the "father and mother" of foreign merchants—and the *laksamana* (naval commander) were taking bribes from foreign traders for using their influence with the ruler to secure licenses.[21] The privileged position of the ruler and port officials at Banda Aceh had become by now a legal right. The *Adat Aceh,* which declared the closing of all ports except Banda Aceh to foreign traders, also obliged the latter to make presents to the sultan in stipulated items, such as cloth and gun powder.[22] By the reign of Safiyyat ad-Din Taj ul-Alam Syah (r. 1641–75), when the ruler's powers were greatly reduced by the influence of the *orang kaya* at court, the latter gained a significantly larger share of perquisites from trade. Senior administrators, including the *panglima bandar* (chief civil officer) and the *penghulu kawal* (head of garrison), claimed a share of the taxes levied on foreign imports of cloth in addition to receiving presents in common with junior port officials such as the *penghulu kunci* (keeper of the keys).[23]

Increased trade, which brought the introduction of monopolies and greater efficiency in the collection of taxes and tribute, meant the extension of central administrative control beyond the capital. Sultan Iskandar Muda of Aceh stationed *panglima* (provincial heads) and *uleëbalang* (military and territorial chiefs) in the provinces and Sultan Abdulfath Abdul Fattah Ageng of Banten (r. 1651–82) commissioned representatives (*jenang*) to southern Sumatra. In Jambi, the extension of the rul-

---

[18]Pires, 1944, 2:273–74.

[19]*Undang-undang Melaka*, ed. Liaw Yock Fang (The Hague, 1976), p. 171.

[20]J. E. Kempe and R. O. Winstedt, eds., "A Malay Legal Digest, Compiled for 'Abd al-Ghafur Muhaiyu'd-din Shah, Sultan of Pahang, 1526–1614 A.D. with Undated Additions," *JMBRAS* 21, no. 1 (1948), 4.

[21]John Harris, *A Complete Collection of Voyages and Travels, Containing the Memoirs of Admiral Beaulieu's Voyage to the East Indies,* 2 vols. (London, 1748), 1:731–74; F. C. Danvers and W. Foster, eds., *Letters Received by the East India Company from the Servants of the East,* 6 vols. (London, 1896–1902), 3:195–217.

[22]G. W. J. Drewes, ed., *Adat Atjeh, VKI* 24 (The Hague, 1959), p. 23.

[23]*Adat Atjeh,* 1959, pp. 24, 26.

er's commercial influence inland into Kerinci resulted in the appointment of *'depati* or *adipati* (village heads) to the *mendapo* (geneologically derived village federations).[24] Similarly, the expansion of maritime trade in Syriam under King Tha-Lun (r. 1629–48) of Burma saw the appointment of provincial officers in the form of *akauk-wun* to administer toll and harbor duties.[25] In Siam during the reign of King Narai (r. 1656–88), the *okya phrakhlang*, or minister in charge of the foreign department, including trade, was the most powerful official. It was he who put the royal seal of approval on licenses and commercial concessions.[26]

In the absence of a salaried bureaucracy with recruitment based on training and merit on the mandarin model, administrative extension reinforced the traditional patron-client network involving the nobility, officials, and other men of influence. Their services were rewarded by commercial privileges and commissions, which they frequently abused to the disadvantage of competing merchant enterprise. Entitlements to commissions collected in kind, such as cloth and foodstuffs from Indian traders visiting Aceh, were lucrative items for reinvestment in the local market. The additional revenue required to support this growing bureaucracy raised tax burdens at all levels of commercial transaction, entailing reduced profit margins for ordinary traders unable to earn exemptions outside the circle of patronage. The Orang Kaya Seri Maharaja Mangkubumi and the *panglima bandar* shared the hefty monthly tax of one *mas* imposed on market stalls in Banda Aceh. Even the *kadi*, Malikul Adil, was entitled to part of the weighing charges.[27]

Titles and positions were, strictly speaking, not hereditary, so that winning the personal favor of the ruler was the only guarantee of security of status and office. At the same time, in the absence of firm rules for royal succession, access of the elite to social advancement through acquisition of wealth and manpower could jeopardize the ruler's position. Men of wealth and commanding influence were often the initiators of court intrigues in support of a parvenu. In Aceh, following the death of Sultan Ala'ad-din Ri'ayat Syah al-Kahar (r. 1539–71), the *orang kaya*, who had amassed a rich inheritance in lands and houses as well as cannon, arms, gold, and silver, dethroned five rulers in the space of ten years. The trend was arrested by the repressive measures of Sultan Ala'ad-din Ri'ayat Syah Sayyid al-Mukammil (r. 1589–1604),

---

[24]Kathirithamby-Wells, 1986 (*Thomas Barnes*), p. 21.

[25]Lieberman, 1984, pp. 60, 118, 124.

[26]Jurrien van Goor, *Koopleiden, Predikanten & Bestuurders Overzee* (Utrecht, 1982), pp. 31–34; Dhiravat na Pombejra, "A Political History of Siam under the Prasatthong Dynasty, 1629–88," Ph.D. diss., University of London, 1984, p. 60.

[27]*Adat Atjeh*, 1959, p. 29.

which involved the massacre of *orang kaya* and confiscation of their possessions. While, therefore, obliged to buy the services of the elite by allowing them a share of the trade, rulers were quick to restrict their accumulation of wealth.[28]

The custom of appointing foreigners to the post of *syahbandar*, as in the Melaka sultanate, had the obvious advantage of facilitating trade for visiting merchants. Appointment of foreigners to these and other commercial positions soon became commonplace, offering rulers a means of preventing the indigenous elite from exploiting these positions to gain power. In Banten, the *syahbandar* and *laksamana* during the rule of the protector, Pangeran Ranamanggala (1608–24), were both Kelings. By mid-century, the *kapitan cina*, "Caitson," who adopted the Muslim name Abdul Gafur, was *syahbandar*.[29] In Siam a Turk was governor of Bangkok during the 1670s and 1680s. At Phuket and neighboring Bangkhli, important sources of tin, two Indian Muslims, Muhammed Beg and Islam Beg, were appointed regents. The influence gained in the court of King Narai by the Persian merchant Aqa Muhammad was considerable. The man who succeeded him after his death in 1679 as the king's favorite was a Greek, Constantine Phaulkon, who held the coveted position of *okya phrakhlang*.[30]

The substantial role Chinese and Indian traders played in the Southeast Asian commercial scene was under the strong patronage of local rulers. The Chinese often traded in partnership with, or acted as agents for, indigenous rulers. In addition to long-distance trade with Canton, they were also active in intraregional and interior trade. They gained a clear advantage, particularly in the internal sector of trade, by introducing around 1590 a small cheap currency in the form of the lead *picis* to replace the declining circulation of the Chinese copper *cash*, in the absence of a comparable medium of local exchange. Due to the high value of silver currency used mainly in wholesale transactions, internal trade was largely on a barter system until the appearance of the *picis*. The new currency rapidly monetized the subsistence and cash crop economy in areas outside direct royal monopoly.[31] With the high value placed on *picis* as a circulating medium of trade, the Chinese soon

[28]Anthony Reid, "Trade and Problems of Royal Power in Aceh, c. 1550–1700," in *Pre-Colonial State Systems in Southeast Asia*, ed. A. Reid and L. Castles, Monograph of the Malayan Branch of the Royal Asiatic Society, no. 6 (1975), pp. 47–49.

[29]J. Kathirithamby-Wells, "Banten: A West Indonesian Port and Polity during the Sixteenth and Seventeenth Centuries," in Kathirithamby-Wells and Villiers, 1990, pp. 113–14.

[30]Dhiravat na Pombejra, "Crown Trade and Court Politics in Ayutthaya during the Reign of King Narai, 1656–88," in ibid., p. 78.

[31]Leonard Blussé, *Strange Company: Chinese Settlers, Mestizo Women, and the Dutch in VOC Batavia*, VKI 120 (Dordrecht, 1986), pp. 36–41.

cornered the market for both the purchase of cash crops and the sale of essential provisions in Sunda and the southern and eastern Sumatran interior. Because of their business skills and success in penetrating the regional markets, often in the interior, enduring physical hardships, they emerged as indispensable commercial brokers for the rulers of Banten and Jambi.

To the more commercially successful and influential Chinese, popu-larly known as *kapitan cina*, licenses were farmed for tax collection, gambling, and opium smoking. These licenses were effectively out of the reach of indigenous entrepreneurs.[32] The gambling monopoly held by the Teochiu merchant Cheng Yung in Ayutthaya enabled his family to gain wealth and political influence. His son, Taksin, whose mother was Siamese, was appointed provincial governor before he rose to be ruler at the new capital of Thonburi (opposite modern Bangkok) after Ayutthaya's fall in 1767.[33]

In Siam, with a substantial agrarian economy, the nobility (*khun-nang*), who derived a secure income from the cultivation of land, gener-ally considered it beneath their dignity to participate in trade. Trade was left largely to foreigners in the absence of local navigational exper-tise or any official-cum-merchant class comparable to the *orang kaya* of the Malay world. The crown trade in which the queen also participated was conducted almost exclusively by Muslims and Chinese, with Eu-ropeans employed on occasion as factors and sea captains. These for-eigners also enjoyed monopoly privileges like that for the trade in eaglewood.[34] The importance of Chinese trade in Ayutthaya is attested in a report of the last quarter of the seventeenth century: out of some twenty vessels in the harbor, half were crown-owned, but nearly all the rest belonged to Chinese.[35]

The Indian merchant community, whose activity was confined large-ly to urban centers and interregional trade, was less numerous than the ubiquitous Chinese. Faced with the increased rigor of the Dutch pass system during the second half of the seventeenth century, these South Asian traders, including Hindus, Chulia Muslims, and Armenians like Albertus, known as Koja De La Croux (Croix), sailed to Banten,

---

[32]By contrast, in the Coromandel such licenses constituted an important source of capital among the merchant community; Sinnappah Arasaratnam, *Merchants, Companies, and Com-merce on the Coromandel Coast, 1655–1740* (Delhi, 1986), pp. 216, 222–26.

[33]Chingho A. Chen, "Mac Thien Tu and Phraya Taksin: A Survey on Their Political Stand, Conflicts, and Background," in *Proceedings of the 7th International Association of Historians of Asia* (Bangkok, 1977), p. 1539.

[34]Pombejra, 1984, pp. 40–42.

[35]*Java Factory Records*, India Office Records (IOR), Foreign and Commonwealth Office, Lon-don, G/21/7A fol. 28.

Makassar, Manila, and Ayutthaya carrying cloth under cover of English and Danish passes.[36] Similarly, their collusion with indigenous chiefs frustrated Dutch efforts to collect gold and pepper from Inderagiri through their agent, "Chietu," at Banten.[37] By the last quarter of the century, following the loss of Makassar (1667) and Banten (1682) to the Dutch, Madras traders, often in partnership with English East India Company officials, strengthened links with the ports of Burma and the Malay Peninsula, mainly Pegu, Mergui, Phuket, and Kedah.[38] Besides their carrying trade and commercial investment, the Hindus in particular complemented the services of the Chinese at brokerage, accounting, and moneylending at the main commercial centers.

As long as they retained their separate identity, foreign merchants posed less of a threat to the ruler than their influential counterparts from among the indigenous elite, who had manpower and factional loyalties at their command. Should the loyalty of a foreigner be in doubt at any time, he could be cast aside with impunity. The Persian merchant Abdu'r-Razzaq, who commanded a high position at court during the reign of King Narai, was later imprisoned when he discredited himself.[39] For his part, Constantine Phaulkon, despite his earlier prominence in Siamese affairs, was summarily executed in 1689 when his political machinations and commercial intrigues affected royal interests.[40] The ambiguous position of the foreign trader in Southeast Asia is explicit in the Malay term *orang dagang*, which conveys the dual meaning of "foreigner" and "trader."

Insecurity of Wealth and Property

Despite the significant contribution of foreign Asians to commercial growth, transmission of large profits to their countries of origin constituted a serious drain of cash and capital from Southeast Asia. Astrappa Chetty, one of the foremost merchants of the Coromandel, died in 1634, leaving his brother a considerable legacy that originated from trade with the Malay Peninsula and other regions across the Bay of Bengal, which had earned him the appellation "Malay Chetty."[41] Coro-

[36]Arasaratnam, 1986, pp. 127–29; *Generale Missiven*, 24 Nov. 1678, 4:233.

[37]*Generale Missiven*, 24 Nov. 1677, 4:195; 15 Feb. 1679, 4:232; Andaya, 1975, pp. 108, 147–48.

[38]D. K. Bassett, "The British 'Country' Trade and Local Trade Networks in the Thai and Malay States, c. 1680–1770, *MAS* 23, no. 4 (1989), 632, 635–37.

[39]*The Ship of Sulaiman*, 1972, p. 97.

[40]van Goor, 1982, pp. 44–47; Holden Furber, *Royal Empires of Trade in the Orient, 1600–1800* (Minneapolis, 1976), pp. 117–18; Pombejra, 1990, pp. 138–39.

[41]*Generale Missiven*, 3 March 1631, 1:298, n.2; Arasaratnam, 1986, pp. 222–23.

mandel traders in particular took advantage of their proximity to Southeast Asia to retain their capital base in the Indian subcontinent. The lack of security for property inheritance and the harsh laws of escheat affecting all, foreigners and indigenes alike, would have discouraged permanent settlement. In Siam, a law of 1635 allowed the king to appropriate all property belonging to officials ascribed with four hundred or more *sakdina*, or "dignity marks." Generally, *khunnang* lost, on their death, more than a third of their property.[42] The *Undang-undang Melaka*, though providing for the settlement of claims between individuals and the protection of royal rights and property such as slaves, did not provide any security of individual property against arbitrary claims of the king.[43] Wealth could not be inherited intact. A family could lose all or, at best, acquire a part inheritance.

Foreigners with wealth and property were at even greater risk. In Aceh, when a foreign merchant or ship captain died, his house and property were sealed by the harbor master until such time as an inventory was prepared and the death duty imposed. During the reign of Sultan Jamalul Alam (r. 1704–26) the rate was fixed at 83 *tahil* 12 *mas*, to be shared by various officials.[44] On the Peninsula, Saudagar Priya reported in 1792 the unfortunate case of a deceased relative, Nasaruddin, who had been commercial agent to Sultan Mansur Syah (r. 1741–93) of Terengganu. According to him, the death had brought the wholesale appropriation by the ruler of Nasaruddin's house and property, leaving his family destitute. Saudagar Priya, though the legal representative of the deceased, failed to gain any part of the property for the family.[45] Although the foreign merchants who actively traded in Southeast Asia were numerous, few established local merchant dynasties. The wealth and influence of the Bunnag family in Ayutthaya, which originated with the Persian merchant and court favorite Aqa Muhammad and continued into the Chakri period, was more the exception than the rule.[46]

State and Monarchical Restraints

Ironically, the organization of commerce in Southeast Asia that stimulated several independent port polities also restrained development of indigenous merchant enterprise. Free market forces and security for

[42]Pombejra, 1984, pp. 35, 53.
[43]See *Undang-undang Melaka*, 1976, p. 169.
[44]Drewes, 1959, p. 31.
[45]William Marsden, *A Grammar of the Malayan Language* (London, 1812), pp. 145–46.
[46]David Wyatt, *Thailand: A Short History* (New Haven, Conn., 1984), pp. 108–9, 142–43.

property and wealth, vital ingredients for commercial initiative and profit accumulation, were not to be found within the framework of royal absolutism and monopoly. Even at the primary level of produce collection, state agents intervened to organize the purchase, preventing the development of an independent agency or brokerage system comparable to that flourishing on the cloth-producing Coromandel coast. On the Minangkabau coast of western Sumatra, some *penghulu* (headmen), who traditionally were members of the *penghulu's* council, had indeed, in the absence of royal interference, emerged as brokers for visiting Gujarati traders. From the wealth accrued many became *orang kaya*. But with the extension of Acehnese and later Dutch control, they were appointed official agents, which curtailed their initiative and independence.[47]

The system of monopoly that subsequently prevailed on the Minangkabau coast arrested the development of a robust chain of commercial activity linking the producer with the local trader, the broker, and ultimately the merchant within a competitive system. West Sumatran *penghulu* maintained their position as the chief indigenous traders but only by virtue of their role as the VOC's commercial agents for the distribution of cloth and salt.[48] They had much less economic opportunity than the independent Minangkabau traders of the highlands who traded to the east coast. There was, in fact, no indigenous merchant class on the Minangkabau coast comparable in prosperity to the Chinese at Padang. Unlike the many Minangkabau traders who sought their fortunes abroad, often through migration, the *penghulu* and itinerant traders who linked the coastal trade with the highlands were reconciled to "circulatory migration."[49] Their habitations of bamboo and thatch, in contrast to the wooden and brick residences of the European and Chinese merchants, suggest both their impermanence and economic limitation.[50] Modest fortunes earned on the coast would have been set aside to enable them to return to their home villages with investment in clothes, jewellery, and perhaps sufficient means to secure an extended residence and slaves to work additional *sawah*, purchased as *harta pencarian* (acquired wealth). These resources provided the hospitality and entertainment necessary for acquiring and bolstering status, leaving insufficient surplus for large investment.

[47]Christine Dobbin, *Islamic Revivalism in a Changing Peasant Economy: Central Sumatra, 1784–1847* (London, 1983), pp. 71–75.

[48]Ibid., pp. 85–103.

[49]Tsuyoshi Kato, *Matriliny and Migration: Evolving Minangkabau Traditions in Indonesia* (Ithaca, N.Y., 1982), pp. 29–30.

[50]H. G. Nahuijs, *Brieven over Bencoolen, Padang het Rijk van Minangkabau, Rhiouw, Sincapoera, en Poelo-Pinang* (Breda, 1826), pp. 37–38, 41; Dobbin, 1983, pp. 97–98.

The free trade policy adopted in Johor and Riau as a foil to the Dutch monopoly system provided greater potential for development of the mercantile activities of *orang kaya*. But here again the influence of powerful cliques under the patronage, in turn, of Sultan Abdul Jalil Ri'ayat Syah (r. 1623–77), the *laksamana* Tun Abdul Jamil, and his rival, *bendahara* Tun Habib Abdul Jalil, emphasized the inherent links between trade and politics.[51] Restriction of indigenous capital investment to rulers and a select group of *orang kaya*, trading by commenda, was the norm. In Ayutthaya the ships sent by King Prasatthong (r. 1629–56) as far as China and the Coromandel were in partnership with his brother.[52] In Johor, the Raja Muda, Raja Indra Bongsu, was, during the reign of Sultan Abdul Jalil Ri'ayat Syah (r. 1699–1719), the spearhead of commercial resistance against the Dutch, trading actively as far as India. He is estimated to have invested as much as 8,000 guilders in a commercial venture to Negapatnam which he lost through shipwreck.[53] In Banten, the strained relations between Sultan Abdul Fattah and his son, Prince Haji, were exacerbated by business rivalry.[54] In Jambi, the *ratu mas*, mother of the ruler, the *pangeran ratu*, Pringgabaya, was for a good part of the second half of the seventeenth century the chief trader in pepper. While Jambi's rulers were preoccupied, first with the Johor war and later with upriver rivalries over pepper supplies, it was the *ratu mas* who exercised a firm control over exports and prices at the capital. She cleverly played off one party of foreign traders against another, leading the English to complain that they were obliged to advance credit for pepper supplies to compete successfully with Indian Muslims.[55]

Servicing the trade of the Jambi royalty were a network of *orang kaya* and Chinese merchants, licensed to collect produce in the interior.[56] English attempts to buy the services and loyalty of individual traders like Nakhoda Tangoo (Tengku?) were unsuccessful because the traders could not break with powerful patrons such as Pangeran Mangku Negara.[57] Sanctions and permits for trade could be obtained only through

---

[51]J. Kathirithamby-Wells, "The Johor-Malay World, 1511–1784: Changes in Political Ideology," *Sejarah* (Kuala Lumpur) 1 (1988), 45–49.

[52]Pombejra, 1984, p. 40.

[53]Diane Lewis, "The Dutch East India Company and the Straits of Malacca, 1700–1784: Trade and Politics in the Eighteenth Century," Ph.D. diss., Australian National University, 1970, pp. 112–13; Andaya, 1975, p. 220.

[54]D. K. J. de Jonge, *De Opkomst van het Nederlandsch gezag in Oost Indië*, 13 vols. (The Hague, 1870), 7:civ.

[55]*Generale Missiven*, 20 Jan. 1645, 2:257; 25 Jan. 1655, 2:775; 11 Dec. 1679, 2:366; 31 May 1684, 2:685; 28 Feb. 1687, 2:80; *Java Factory Records* (IOR), G/21/5 fol. 42.

[56]*Java Factory Records* (IOR), G/21/5 fol. 27.

[57]*Java Factory Records* (IOR), G/21/5 fol. 11.

the influence of such patrons. The extension and enforcement of political patronage formed part of the resistance of ruling authorities to European monopoly restrictions. A significant feature of the times was the strengthening of traditional links between royal princes and the *orang laut* (sea nomads) for the protection of native trade. But the individual trader remained vulnerable to internal political rivalry. In 1675 the Johor *laksamana*'s son assembled fifty vessels at the mouth of the Batang Hari to intercept and rob vessels in a bid to punish those operating outside the Johor commercial network.[58]

The Southeast Asian economic structure was based on patronage and manpower, foundations different from those that fostered the growth of early capitalism in Europe. There was no evolution toward parliamentary institutions, constitutional regulations, and the security of law to guard the interests of individual liberties[59] in the Southeast Asian state system. In the spirit of the *dewaraja* cult of an earlier era, Southeast Asian states were centered in the ruler rather than in the Thammasat (Buddhist law) or Shari'a (Islamic law). Initiative for the protection and implementation of the respective religious laws rested entirely with rulers.[60] Nevertheless, in maritime-oriented Muslim states aspects of the Shari'a pertaining to commerce and investment which were of direct interest to the ruler appear to have been implemented, perhaps because of increased competition in trade after the coming of the Portuguese. Evidence of this is found in the Pahang Malay Legal Digest of 1595, which is more Shari'a-inclined than earlier editions of the *Undang-undang Melaka*. The nature of these laws, though not explicitly favoring monarchical capitalism, served to encourage it.

The basic Islamic commercial law adopted in the Malay Legal Digest of Pahang was the prohibition of usury (*riba*): "Trade is lawful, but the taking of interest unlawful."[61] Trade was the obvious avenue to invest capital without engaging in usury. Large commenda investment (entrusting capital to a partner) originating from Islamic times, the *al-mudārabah* or *al-muqāradah*, involving the services of an agent-manager, gained popularity in the Muslim world. According to this contract, the investor (*rabb al-māl* or *commendator*) or group of investors (*arbāb-al-māl*) entrusted capital or merchandise to an agent-manager

[58]*Generale Missiven*, 31 Jan. 1675, 4:3.

[59]For a recent discussion of this with reference to Britain, see Alan Macfarlane, "The Cradle of Capitalism: The Case of England," in *Europe and the Rise of Capitalism*, ed. J. Baechler, J. A. Hall, and M. Mann (Oxford, 1988), pp. 197–98.

[60]Stanley Tambiah, *World Conqueror and World Renouncer* (Cambridge, 1976); A. C. Milner, "Islam and the Muslim State," in *Islam in Southeast Asia*, ed. M. B. Hooker (Leiden, 1983), pp. 33–42.

[61]Kempe and Winstedt, 1948, p. 10.

(*'āmil, muḍārib*). In the wider understanding of commenda trade, as also in pre-Islamic times, the *commendator* and agent-manager could share the capital involved in the *al-muqāradah* contract. Islam prohibited this practice because it allowed for illegal personal enrichment by the agent. At the same time, to guard against the arbitrary demands of a *commendator*, Islamic law required that the investor's share of the profits, in addition to the principal sum, be agreed on at the time of the contract, leaving any profits in excess to the agent.[62] The adoption of the institution of *al-muqāradah* thus provided for merchantile activities within the framework of Islamic jurisprudence and gave commercial contracts the weight of legal sanction. In Banten during the mid-seventeenth century, contracts were reported to have been engraved with a needle on tree bark and stored either rolled up or folded four-square between two boards, secured very neatly with "pack thread."[63]

One can surmise that the restriction placed by Shari'a law on bilateral investment would have restricted opportunities for indigenous royal agents, working solely on commissions, to accumulate sufficient profit to emerge as independent merchant entrepreneurs. At the same time, the absence of dynamic indigenous entrepreneurship enhanced opportunities for Chinese and Indian merchants to control the long-distance trade. They took advantage of the lack of prohibition against agents chartering vessels in partnership with investors to forge alliances with local rulers. By jointly chartering or owning vessels, the contracting parties mutually reduced risks; the foreign merchants maximized gains by combining agency services with investment in a private cargo. Proposing such a partnership to Francis Light in Penang at the end of the eighteenth century, Saudagar Nasaruddin suggested chartering a vessel in partnership with the ruler of Terengganu, with each party taking a third share.[64] Islamic law, which did not hold an agent responsible for the loss of a cargo in circumstances beyond his control, favored such joint ventures: "If the capital is lost or if there were losses, he [the agent], need not compensate for (the loss of) the business or the loss of property, (provided that) it was not due to any negligence on his part."[65]

The absence of an indigenous class of merchants and long-distance shippers comparable to that which developed, for example, in Surat,

[62]Abdullah Alwi bin Haji Hasan, "*Al-Muḍārabah* (Dormant Partnership) and its Identical Islamic Partnerships in Early Islam," *Hamdard Islamicus* 12, no. 2 (1989), 13–14; *Undang-undang Melaka*, 1976, p. 146.

[63]Glanius, *A New Voyage to the East Indies: Containing an Account of Several of Those Rich Countries, and More Particularly the Kingdom of Bantam* (London, 1682), pp. 69–70.

[64]Marsden, 1812, p. 142.

[65]*Undang-undang Melaka*, 1976, p. 147.

Bengal, and the Coromandel,[66] gave the foreign entrepreneur a distinct advantage. When Sultan Mahmud Syah of Melaka (r. 1488–1511) commissioned Hang Nadim to buy cloth for him in India, the latter sailed in a vessel belonging to a native, Hang Isak.[67] But shipping passed into foreign hands by the seventeenth century. The Sultan of Banten, Abdulfath Abdul Fattah Ageng (r. 1651–82), besides purchasing freight on English vessels sailing to China[68] entered business partnerships for long-distance trade with Coromandel merchants and resident Chinese, like the merchant-cum-shipowner Sim Suan.[69] In Siam, the king and queen owned about ten vessels between them, but their maritime and mercantile ventures were handled almost exclusively by Chinese.[70] In Perak during the same period, the Chulia merchant Siddie Lebbie used his position as *saudagar raja* to gain virtual monopoly of the trade in tin that found its way to Porto Novo and Cuddalore in Chulia vessels.[71] In Johor alone did the *orang kaya* play a significant role in maritime activity, though the political problems that beset the kingdom undermined their vigor and durability. Johor's trade continued to prosper at the free port of Pancor in Riau; but any boost to indigenous enterprise through the influx of Bugis commercial activity was in the sector of small-scale peddling trade. Once again, the benefits were more apparent from foreign participation. By the turn of the seventeenth century the influence of the Indian merchant had spread farther in the Peninsula into Kedah, Perak, and Terengganu, where they frequently organized the commercial ventures of local rulers.[72] In Riau in 1713 the *saudagar raja* was an Armenian.[73]

Apart from commercial laws that were of particular relevance to the vested interests of the ruler, the punishments prescribed in the Shari'a for theft were also rigorously implemented where this helped enforce royal authority. *Panglima* guilty of corruption or lax in enforcing the monopoly during the reign of Sultan Iskandar Muda suffered the same fate as fourth-time offenders for theft, the loss of all four limbs.[74] These and other brutal punishments were notorious for crimes committed

[66]A. Das Gupta, "India and the Indian Ocean in the Eighteenth Century," in *India and the Indian Ocean, 1500–1800*, ed. A. Das Gupta and M. N. Pearson (Calcutta, 1987), pp. 135–37, 143, 147.

[67]*Sejarah Melayu*, 1970, p. 134.

[68]*Java Factory Records* (IOR), G/21/7A fol. 17.

[69]Kathirithamby-Wells and Villiers, 1990, pp. 111–13.

[70]*Java Factory Records* (IOR), G/21/7A fol. 27.

[71]Arasaratnam, 1986, p. 147.

[72]Ibid., pp. 118–120.

[73]Barbara Andaya, "The Indian *Saudagar Raja* in Traditional Malay Courts," *JMBRAS* 51, no. 1 (1978), 20.

[74]*Letters Received*, 1896–1902, 3:210–26, 5:170, 6:68.

against the royal person.[75] Yet there was no legal provision for the safety of property and person from the arbitrary will of the ruler.

The dependence on political patronage for nearly everything that mattered—land, commercial privileges, security, and inheritance of title and property—ruled out opportunities for the development of a separate bourgeois merchant class like that evolving in Europe. Braudel has drawn attention to the use of royal patronage by the bourgeoisie and French *noblesse de robe*, the forerunners of capitalism in Europe, through the purchase of favors, estates, property, and offices from kings.[76] It was different in Southeast Asia, where any entitlement to a privilege or right was a personal favor, or *anugerah*, which could be forfeited at any time. Being, strictly speaking, neither salable nor transferable, property and title could not form the basis for cumulative inheritance and capital accumulation as in Europe.[77]

Not only did institutional factors work against accummation of wealth; property in the maritime capitals was also at risk from theft and fire. Both could be attributed to the ubiquity of wooden structures, since stone was scarce and reserved largely for use by the ruler for fortifications as well as religious and prestigous edifices.[78] Because stone buildings were valuable and afforded superior protection of person and property, their ownership was a royal favor. In Aceh, a prohibition was imposed by the ruler against the ownership of stone buildings by *orang kaya* in reaction to their construction of private fortifications. In Banten the few stone dwellings available were owned largely by foreigners. The two-story house rented by the English East India Company in 1626, which served both as a dwelling and a place for storing goods, belonged to a foreign merchant, Koja Ali Hassan.[79] The enormous losses the Dutch and English East India companies suffered from theft and fire during the period preceding their acquisition of stone factories are fair indication of the hazards of property ownership among ordinary citizens to whom the privilege of owning stone

[75]William Dampier, *Voyages and Discoveries*, ed. and introd. C. Wilkinson (London, 1931), 1:97; and see Anthony Reid, Chapter 6 in this volume.

[76]Braudel, 1979–84, 2:594.

[77]Perry Anderson, *Lineages of the Absolutist State* (London, 1974), pp. 33–34. The appropriation of hereditary rights by the *ulëëbalang* of Aceh after the mid-eighteenth century was a symptom of their challenge to central authority and the rise of diffuse centers. It was not, therefore, a feature of the unified state. See Takeshi Ito and Anthony Reid, "From Harbour Aristocracies to 'Feudal' Diffusion in Seventeenth Century Indonesia: The Case of Aceh," in *Feudalism: Comparative Studies*, ed. E. Leach, S. N. Mukherjee, and J. Ward (Sydney, 1985), pp. 203–5.

[78]J. Kathirithamby-Wells, "The Islamic City: Melaka to Jogjakarta c. 1500–1800," *MAS* 20, no. 2 (1986), 335–36.

[79]W. N. Sainsbury, ed., *Calendar of State Papers, Colonial Series, East Indies and Persia, 1625–29* (London, 1884), p. 1.

buildings was denied. Given this material insecurity, there was greater wisdom in investing surplus assets in service and manpower to win the ruler's favor for the acquisition and guarantee of titles, offices, and appanages, or *jajahan* as they were known in the Malay world. The alternative course of aggressive merchant enterprise, in competition with the ruler, would have courted his jealousy and disfavor.

Within the structure of trade in sixteenth-century Southeast Asia, indigenous traders—with the exception of some nobility, chiefs, and officials—were by and large limited to peddlers, brokers, and *nakhoda* (supercargos) of small coastal vessels. After the Portuguese capture of Melaka, many such traders settled at Makassar under the patronage of the ruler, Tumapa'risi Kallonna of Goa (r. 1512–48), and their numbers swelled in the next century with the imposition of stringent Dutch commercial restrictions in the Spice Islands and Straits of Malacca.[80] Following the treaty of Bongaya in 1667, however, they lost the commercial supremacy they had shared with the Javanese in eastern Indonesia. Apart from those indigenous peddlers confined to specific sectors of trade involving investments of local patrons, there were a multitude who led a free-wheeling existence, moving within the Malay-Minangkabau and Bugis commercial diaspora. Trading on their own account and working on very small capital, they lived as adventurers, taking high risks and earning meager profits. In Patani during the early sixteenth century, the Minangkabau trader Syeikh Gombak was put to death for flouting the royal decree against the exportation of copper, which was reserved for casting cannon.[81] A graphic portrayal of the fluctuations in the fortunes of the typical Minangkabau adventurer is found in the memoir of Nakhoda Muda.[82] Originating in Bayang to the southeast of Padang, his family moved abroad during the mid-eighteenth century to ply trade in various parts of Borneo. Eventually unstable conditions there forced them to migrate to Lampung. The important commercial position Nakhoda Muda established for himself at Semangka, through exporting pepper to Banten, soon drew him into local politics and culminated in his appointment as the sultan's official agent, with the title of Kiai Demang Perwasidana. On later losing favor with the sultan's Dutch protectors, he moved to British Benkulen in 1765.[83]

---

[80]John Villiers, "Makassar: The Rise and Fall of an East Indonesian Maritime Trading State," in Kathirithamby-Wells and Villiers, 1990, pp. 152–56.

[81]"Hikayat Patani: The Story of Patani," trans. and ed. A. Teeuw and D. Wyatt, *Bibliotheca Indonesica*, no. 5 (1970), 2:153–55.

[82]William Marsden, *Memoirs of a Malay Family Written by Themselves* (London, 1830; rpt., London, 1968).

[83]Ibid., pp. 72–82.

Monetary and Currency Restraints

One of the most serious problems for the development of indigenous trade related to money and currency. Despite the indispensability of commerce to Southeast Asian rulers, the monopoly system they subscribed to did not encourage full commercialization and free monetization of the internal economy. This partly accounts for the absence of rational monetary policies, with adverse effects on the indigenous economy, particularly in the face of the bullionist policies pursued by Southeast Asia's trading partners. Sumatra was proverbially a source of gold, as attested by the large amounts brought to the markets of Aceh and the Straits of Malacca. Gold had traditionally financed cloth imports from India. During the seventeenth-century era of absolutism, when gold was declared a royal monopoly, it was put to several uses. Some gold was fashioned into jewellery that only royalty had the privilege to don; some, in the form of gold bars, was hoarded as treasure.[84] A small amount went into coinage, but a greater part seems to have left the region as commodity rather than currency. Throughout the eighteenth century the Dutch, for example, relied on Minangkabau gold, which they paid for in cloth, to produce the Coromandel gold *pagoda* (coin worth 4–4.5 rupees).[85] Though a variety of small currencies were coined locally, gold currency was the only form of international monetary exchange issued under regal tender at Aceh, Ayutthaya, Banten, Makassar, Patani, and Terengganu; it enjoyed prestige more than practical value. In the Southeast Asian commercial scene—dominated, on the one hand, by foreign investors using silver as the international medium of exchange and, on the other, by the multitude of peddlers dealing in small currency units—the gold *dinar* or *mas* had restricted circulation. As one visitor to Aceh during the mid-eighteenth century observed, "they make their payments oftener in pieces of Gold at Aceh than in coin, and therefore, the rate You intend to receive and pay Gold at, and the Kati you buy and sell by must be expressed in the contract. It would be very tedious receiving one thousand pound in gold mas."[86]

The outflow of gold as a commodity, the poor circulation and scarcity of gold currency, and the hoarding of gold as noncirculating treasure gave imported silver dollars superiority as the chief medium for large commercial transactions. In India during the same period, the Mughal coinage of silver, to support the collection of land rents, stimulated

[84]Kathirithamby-Wells, 1992, in press.
[85]Dobbin, 1977, pp. 2–4.
[86]Captain Cope, *A New History of the East Indies with Brief Observations on Religion, Customs, Manners, and Trade of the Inhabitants* (London, 1754), p. 106.

monetization of the economy.[87] Under the Southeast Asian system of surplus extraction in the form of services and produce, paid as tax and tribute rather than as rents in money, there was little advantage to the rulers in putting a high-value currency into circulation. It was more profitable to settle payments for monopoly produce in the form of salt and cloth, the import monopolies for which rulers also engrossed. Even with increased monetization of taxation in Burma and Thailand after the mid-eighteenth century,[88] no currency of high value was brought into circulation to stimulate free enterprise or the integration of the internal economy with external commerce. The *ganza*, a copper-lead alloy, and the "lump silver" of Burma, though popular, were confined to local market exchange. So was the cheap *picis* the Chinese imported into the Archipelago and the range of other small coinage with restricted circulation, namely, the *kupang* and *picis* minted by various rulers. Spanish dollar earnings from international exchange and taxes from the coastal ports were reserved largely for financing cloth imports and purchasing arms and ammunition by rulers. This meant that, effectively, a dual economy functioned with the ruler, official agents, and licensed foreign merchants mediating as chief brokers between the domestic and external sectors of trade. Apart from expenditure on the purchase of imports, large amounts of silver went out of circulation, as in Burma, when they entered the royal treasure house.[89] Substantial sums in silver earnings from local markets were also exported via Batavia to China, where they serviced land tax.[90] In 1604 the English factors at Banten reported that *picis* were cheap but silver reals were dear because the Chinese had "sent all the reals they could for China."[91] The policy of the Dutch to limit the importation of specie in favor of financing purchases of pepper with Indian cloth put a further strain on silver needed for outlays on arms, ammunition, and ceremonial expenses to bolster monarchical power.[92]

Factionalism, succession disputes, and civil wars, brought to a head by European interference in internal politics, effected an additional drain on monarchical resources, resulting in widespread indebtedness.

[87]Irfan Habib, "The Monetary System and Prices," in Raychaudhuri and Habib, 1982, 1:363.

[88]*Burmese Sit-Tans, 1764–1824: Records of Rural Life and Administration*, ed. and trans. F. N. Trager and W. J. Koenig, Association for Asian Studies, Monograph no. 36 (Tucson, Ariz., 1979), pp. 134–39; see also Victor Lieberman, Chapter 9 in this volume.

[89]Michael Symes, *An Account of the Embassy to the Kingdom of Ava Sent by the Governor-General of India in the Year 1795* (London, 1800; rpt., Farnborough, Hants., 1969), p. 316.

[90]Blussé, 1986, p. 116.

[91]Samuel Purchas, *Hakluytus Posthumus or Purchas, His Pilgrimes*, 20 vols. (Glasgow, 1905), 2:459.

[92]Kathirithamby-Wells, 1992, in press.

The Islamic law of *salam* sales involving "a contract sale, causing an immediate payment of the price and admitting a delay in the delivery of the wares,"[93] found liberal interpretation for noncompliance or tardiness in the fulfillment of contractual agreements in the Malay world. In the production sector, delays in payment at the secondary and tertiary market levels aggravated problems of inadequate returns from cash cropping among cultivators. Reliance on imports of rice and other necessities at high prices and the inability to cover living costs encouraged evasion of monopoly. The periodic suspension of cultivation during periods of flight and migration and the search for new patrons or markets were some of the main reasons for produce shortage and sharp price fluctuations characteristic of the anti–free-market forces the monopoly system had unleashed.

In a region irretrievably committed to trade, the lack of a sophisticated monetary and financial tradition would seem a paradox, but it was consistent perhaps with the involvement of the indigenous populace predominantly in the subsidiary levels of small market exchange. The money changers in Aceh, like the merchandise brokers in the commercial ports of Southeast Asia such as Saigon, were frequently local women, who sat in the marketplace, with a shrewd eye to profit.[94] The more complicated business of accounting, money changing, and shroffing at the capital cities was left largely to the Indian *banya* (commercial agent) of Gujarat, Sind, and the Coromandel.[95] In Ayutthaya the king's chief accountant in 1679 was a Persian, and those who transacted his other commercial affairs, including the warehouse keepers, were nearly all Chinese.[96] The more successful participation of foreigners in commerce and financial management can best be explained by institutional features of Southeast Asian society which emphasized values other than money among indigenes. Where power was based on manpower control and the purchase of favor, wealth functioned as a means rather than an end. The importance of gift giving, conspicuous consumption, and fulfillment of the material needs of clients underplayed the virtues of parsimony—a necessary foundation for the growth of merchant capitalism.

[93]K. N. Chaudhuri, *The Trading World of Asia and the English East India Company, 1660–1760* (Cambridge, 1978), p. 256.

[94]Dampier, 1931, p. 92; John White, *A Voyage to Cochin China* (London, 1824; rpt., Kuala Lumpur, 1972), p. 245.

[95]Cope, 1754, p. 104; Purchas, 1905, 4:171; Anthony Reid, "Economic and Social Change, 1500–1750," in *Cambridge History of Southeast Asia*, ed. N. Tarling, vol. 1 (Cambridge University Press, 1992), p. 479.

[96]*Java Factory Records* (IOL), G/21/7A fol. 27.

Immutability of Southeast Asian Commercial Politics

If monarchical capitalism, the outgrowth of the peculiar institutional features of Southeast Asia, put the strongest curbs on merchant capitalism, did the decline of royal absolutism by the end of the seventeenth century release more positive mercantile forces? Aceh and Minangkabau, which continued to flourish commercially after the decline of monarchical power, offer interesting case studies. In Aceh, the greater sharing of wealth from trade by the *orang kaya* under four successive queens (r. 1641–99) did not assist the evolution of a non-bureaucratic independent merchant elite. On the contrary, the political link between commercial wealth and administrative power was reinforced. This was demonstrated in the rise to power during the eighteenth century, as agriculture and commerce expanded through the country, of the three *panglima sagòë*. These were chiefs of the XXII, XXV, and XXVI *mukim* (*ulèëbalang* federations) in Aceh Besar. The decline of trade and royal power in the capital provided the opportunity for the devolution of economic initiative to local power centers. Their chiefs were crucial in manipulating the nominal power of the sultan at Banda Aceh over his vastly shrunken territories. In 1771, the Indian trader Po Rahman of Meulaboh was vested by a royal warrant (*sarakata*) with the rank of *keudjruen tjhi'*.[97] The same period saw the rise of an independent port chief, Leubé Dapa, who by the turn of the century gained virtual control over the whole coast from Susoh to Singkil by conducting a properous trade in pepper, benzoin, and camphor. The commercial power wielded by the various coastal chiefs and the *panglima sagi*, headed by the powerful Panglima Polim of the XXII *mukim*, extended the arena of dynastic conflict well beyond the confines of the capital.[98] The lack of a clear delineation, as in this case, between mercantile and administrative-cum-political functions bred internal conflicts and instability which, in the long run, proved detrimental to the consolidated growth of an indigenous merchant elite. In contrast to the inherent conflict of interests within the indigenous power sphere, Western commercial agencies in the region, be they chartered companies or licensed "country traders," operated under crown or official patronage. In

---

[97]G. W. J. Drewes, *Two Achehnese Poems* (The Hague, 1980), p. 53.
[98]Lee Kam Hing, "Acheh's Relations with the British, 1760–1819," M.A. thesis, University of Malaya, 1969, pp. 41–42, 80–81; John Anderson, *Acheen and the Ports on the North and North East Coasts of Sumatra* (London, 1841; rpt., Kuala Lumpur, 1971), pp. 50–53, 63.

Southeast Asia there was no semblance of the protectionism known to early capitalist enterprise in Europe under mercantilism.

It seems that the almost unique example found in the Minangkabau political system, which provided monarchical patronage and protection for indigenous merchants, would have encouraged the growth of nascent capitalism.[99] Any such potential was effectively brought to naught with the loss of influence, by the end of the eighteenth century, of the Pagaruyung court. By the early nineteenth century it became, in fact, a prime concern of the *padri*, the leaders of the Minangkabau Islamic revival, to bolster threatened social stability and commercial security. The prosperity and order introduced in Agam by the merchant regime of the *padri* was impressive even in the eyes of Dutch officials.[100] Nonetheless, *padri* political control and socioreligious influence, through commerce, brought them into a tense relationship with the *penghulu* as traditional authorities. This situation of conflicting roles and interests, not uncommon in Southeast Asia, ruled out conditions for a mutually supportive separation between public and private agencies and their respective spheres of influence which had, to a large extent, fostered early merchant capitalism in Japan and the West.[101]

Southeast Asian states from roughly the mid-fifteenth century to the end of the eighteenth appear to have been characterized by a prosperity based on commerce, but without the development of indigenous merchant capitalism. The sociopolitical characteristics, shaped by environmental, economic, and cultural factors, remained preeminent and were even strengthened by the stimulus of European commercial expansion. The Southeast Asian case demonstrates that spectacular commercial and economic expansion was not sufficient in itself for the germination of merchant capitalism.

[99]For a discussion of the role of Pagaruyung rulers in maintaining the coherence and stability of the Minangkabau world (*alam*) through protection of *adat* institutional traditions, see J. Kathirithamby-Wells, "Myth and Reality: Minangkabau Institutional Traditions in the *Rantau*," in *Change and Continuity in Minangkabau*, ed. L. L. Thomas and F. von Benda-Beckmann, Monographs in International Studies, Southeast Asia Series 71 (Athens, Ohio, 1985), pp. 121–30.

[100]Dobbin, 1983, pp. 126, 135–36.

[101]Jean Baechler, "The Origins of Modernity: Caste and Feudality (Europe, India, and Japan)," in Baechler, Hall, and Mann, 1988, pp. 57–58.

PART 3

Religious Change

The most dramatic permanent change to Southeast Asia in the early modern period was the establishment or strengthening of the scriptural religions that still dominate: Islam, Christianity, and Theravada Buddhism. How this religious change was linked to economic changes is one of the major issues in the field.

Anthony Reid argues that the period 1550–1650 was critical in the establishment of Christianity in the Philippines and some of Maluku and Vietnam and of Islam in most of present-day Indonesia and Malaysia. The chief reasons, in his view, were the increase in commerce and the polarization between Iberian Catholicism and Islam.

The Theravada world changed more gradually, but Yoneo Ishii argues that Siam underwent a major transformation during the seventeenth century, culminating in the reign of Narai. Centralized control was for the first time established over the whole country. In this process, the king's use of Buddhist symbols and his subordination of the monkhood to royal authority were crucial weapons.

6

Islamization and Christianization in Southeast Asia: The Critical Phase, 1550–1650

Anthony Reid

The extensive debate about the Islamization of Southeast Asia has focused principally on the presumed earliest manifestation of Islam in various places and how and from where it became established. European scholarship accepted until recently that Islam came to Southeast Asia through the filter of India, beginning with the small port-states of thirteenth-century Sumatra. Southeast Asian Muslim scholars have generally preferred to see Arabs as the mediators and have attempted to push the dates for Islamization back as far as the evidence could bear—and sometimes farther.

This excessive emphasis on the "first steps" has given rise to a healthy reaction stressing the extreme gradualness of the process of conversion. Merle Ricklefs's "Six Centuries of Islamization in Java" makes the forceful point that the process that began in the fourteenth century is still continuing,[1] and A. C. Milner argues that the Malay state absorbed and used Islam on its own terms rather than being transformed by it.[2] No one with Southeast Asian experience can doubt

Much of this essay was prepared when I was a Rockefeller Fellow at the Center for the Comparative Study of Islamic Societies and Cultures at Washington University in St. Louis. I thank John Bowen, Cornell Fleischer, and other colleagues there for their stimulus and assistance. Bruce Cruikshank and Jennifer Brewster helped with the material on Christianity, and Humphrey Fisher and Anthony Johns made valuable comments on the draft.

[1]Merle C. Ricklefs, "Six Centuries of Islamization in Java," in *Conversion to Islam*, ed. Nehemia Levtzion (New York, 1979), pp. 100–128.

[2]A. C. Milner, "Islam and the Muslim State," in *Islam in South-East Asia*, ed. M. B. Hooker (Leiden, 1983), pp. 23–49.

the continuing importance of compromises with pre-Islamic beliefs, which literal Muslims still regard as in need of conversion.

Similarly in the Philippines the coexistence of Catholic and animistic practices and rituals in what is often called folk Catholicism is frequently remarked.[3] The prayers of both the scriptural religions have been widely incorporated into rituals of propitiation of spirits; Islamic and Catholic leaders tactfully leave important ceremonies after having said their prayers, so as not to witness rituals they could not approve.

From these phenomena the inference should not be drawn that conversion to scriptural religion never really occurred, or that the process of religious change has been a slow, almost imperceptible, progression whereby ever greater numbers grafted ever more elements of the new religions onto their existing belief system. On the contrary, religious change is by its nature discontinuous. In certain periods dramatic conversions occur on a large scale, whereas others witness an everyday process of disillusion, backsliding, skepticism, or apathy. There is no doubt that many individual Southeast Asians entered Islam and Christianity passively through marriage, conquest, or the cultural example of their leaders. The crucial turning points for whole societies, however, were of relatively short duration and should be described not simply as adhesion but conversion—which I define as a conscious repudiation of a past identified as evil in favor of an externally defined new ideal. Such conversion is typically associated with profound disruption of the social order. Clifford Geertz summarized Max Weber's arguments about the advances of the world's major religions: "This sense . . . that the traditional conglomerate of rituals and beliefs was no longer adequate, and the rise to consciousness of the problems of meaning in an explicit form, seems to have been part, in each case, of a much wider dislocation in the pattern of traditional life. . . . The process of religious rationalization seems everywhere to have been accompanied by a thorough shaking of the foundations of social order."[4]

I argue that the period 1550–1650 was such a period of dislocation in Southeast Asia as a whole (though shorter periods were critical in specific areas), one that stimulated a remarkable period of conversion toward both Sunni Islam and Catholic Christianity. It is helpful to look at both religions in this context, to separate more clearly the underlying processes from the cultural specifics. Despite the lead in this respect

---

[3]Among others in Landa F. Jocano, "Conversion and the Patterning of Christian Experience in Malitbog, Central Panay, Philippines," in *Acculturation in the Philippines*, ed. Peter Gowing and W. H. Scott (Manila, 1971), pp. 43–72; Alfred McCoy, "Baylan: Animist Religion and Philippine Peasant Ideology," *PQCS* 10 (1982), 141–94; Fe Susan Go, "Mothers, Maids, and the Creatures of the Night: The Persistence of Philippine Folk Religion," *PQCS* 7 (1979), 186–203.

[4]Clifford Geertz, *The Interpretation of Cultures* (New York, 1973), p. 173.

Figure 4. Modes of dress in the Christianized Philippines. From left, a Spaniard with his retainer, a prominent Filipino or mestizo, and a pair of Christian Filipinos engaged in the favored sport of cock-fighting. To the rear are animist hill people. From the 1734 map of Murillo Velarde, Bibliothèque Nationale, Paris, Cartes et Plans.

given by historians of Africa, it is surprising that Southeast Asianists have not attempted to analyze Islamization and Christianization as part of a similar process.[5] In addition to these advantages of perspective, the relative richness of the sources for Christian conversion helps greatly to shed light on the poorly documented passage into Islam.

The importance of this period is not difficult to demonstrate for Christianity. Virtually nothing was achieved among the indigenous population until the 1540s, when Antonio Galvão impressed many eastern Indonesians during his period as captain of Ternate (1537–40), Antonio de Paiva converted several Bugis-Makassar rulers, and Saint Francis Xavier preached effectively in Ternate and Amboina.[6] The Je-

[5]Robin Horton, "African Conversion," *Africa* 41, no. 2 (1971), 85–108, and "On the Rationality of Conversion," *Africa* 45 (1975), 219–35, 373–99; Humphrey J. Fisher, "Conversion Reconsidered: Some Historical Aspects of Religious Conversion in Black Africa," *Africa* 43, no. 1 (1973), 27–40.

[6]Antonio Galvão, *A Treatise on the Moluccas (c. 1544). Probably the Preliminary Version of Antonio Galvão's Lost História das Molucas,* trans. H. Jacobs (Rome, 1971); Antonio de Paiva, Letter to the Bishop of Goa, in Hubert Jacobs, "The First Locally Demonstrable Christianity in Celebes, 1544," *Studia* 17 (1966), 282–302; Francis Xavier, Letter from Ambon 10 May 1546, in *Epistolae S. Francisi Xaverii Aliaque eius Scripta,* ed. G. Schurhammer and J. Wicki, 2 vols. (Rome, 1944–45), 1:318–35.

suits claimed up to 70,000 converts in the Ambon region in the period 1540–65;[7] the Dominicans about 50,000 in the Solor-Flores region from 1559 to 1605;[8] Spanish Franciscans and Jesuits about 10,000 in Siau and Sangihe Besar (northeast of Sulawesi) from 1613 to 1665. In the half-century after the Spanish capture of Muslim Manila (1571), virtually the whole of the lowland population of Luzon accepted Christianity, with the process complete in the Visayas by 1650. The rapidity of this Christianization has been hailed as unparalleled before the late nineteenth century.[9] In Vietnam in the period 1625–40, Alexandre de Rhodes and his (mainly Jesuit) colleagues claimed 39,000 converts in the southern (Nguyen) state and 82,000 in Tonkin.[10]

The gains of Islam in this period are generally thought of in terms of eastern Indonesia only. Islam was adopted by the rulers of southwest Sulawesi (1603–12), Kaili, Gorontalo, and other coastal states of central and northern Sulawesi, Butung, Lombok, Sumbawa, Magindanao, and eastern Borneo. Less frequently considered is the high tide of political Islam on the Mainland, with the Cham king (already tributary to Vietnam) becoming Muslim sometime between 1607 and 1676,[11] Cambodia having a Muslim king in the years 1643–58, and Muslims enjoying a peak of influence in the Thai capital at the same period. Unlike many of the shadowy earlier acceptances of Islam, those of this period tended to be self-conscious conversions involving a decisive abandonment of one kind of lifestyle and value system for another. The sources are explicit about the exact moment in 1605 when the rulers of Tallo and Goa (the two royal lineages of Makassar) pronounced the *shahada* (confession of faith) and became Muslims, and about the seriousness with which they took up the new faith. The unusually matter-of-fact Makassar chronicle recorded this of "the first Muslim" (Sultan Awwal-al-Islam), Karaeng Matoaya:

> He was adept at reading and writing Arabic [script] and well-read in Islamic literature; from the time he embraced Islam until his death he never once missed the ritual prayer; only at the time he had a swollen foot and an Englishman treated him by giving him liquor did he omit to pray. . . . [one of his widows] said he performed at least two and at most ten *raka'* each night. He performed the supererogatory *tasbih* on the eve of each Friday and in the month of Ramadan each night.[12]

[7]Cornelius Wessels, *Histoire de la mission d'Amboine* (Louvain, 1934), p. 70.

[8]*Sejarah Gereja Katolik Indonesia,* 4 vols. (Jakarta, 1974), 1:300–307.

[9]John Schumacher, *Readings in Philippine Church History* (Manila, 1979), p. 193, and "Syncretism in Philippine Catholicism: Its Historical Causes," *Philippine Studies* 32, no. 3 (1984), 252.

[10]Georges Taboulet, *La geste française en Indochine,* 2 vols. (Paris, 1955–56), 1:15.

[11]Pierre-Yves Manguin, "L'introduction de l'Islam au Campa," in *Bulletin de l'Ecole Française d'Extrême Orient* 66 (1979), 255–69.

[12]J. Noorduyn, "Makassar and the Islamization of Bima," *BKI* 142 (1987), 315.

Within a generation of this solemn initial entry into Islam, the old (transvestite) ritual specialists were driven out of the Makassarese realm and habits of dress, devotion, literature, and sexual behavior had completely changed.[13] The new faith provided the ideological basis for an unprecedented intervention by Makassar in the Bugis states of Wajo, Soppeng, and Bone, all of whose ruling elites, at the minimum, were obliged to pronounce the *shahada* and renounce pork. Though force was clearly necessary to push them over the brink, the ruler of commercially inclined Wajo had already moved intellectually toward monotheism,[14] and the new ruler of Bone embraced Islam so enthusiastically (if perhaps selectively) that he insisted that all Muslim slaves be freed immediately.[15] Another indication of the effectiveness of Islam in abruptly changing lifestyles in southwest Sulawesi is the absence of buried ceramics from grave sites after about 1620, contrasting sharply with burial practice in the two previous centuries.

How deeply Islam penetrated society before what I call the critical period is difficult to establish. The evidence of Islamic tombstones, coins, chronicles of later date, and the reports of external visitors demonstrates that there was a substantial group of Muslims speaking Malay or Javanese in the port cities on the major trade routes; among their number were the most important port rulers of Sumatra, the Malay Peninsula, northern Java, and Maluku. In Java around 1500 there was constant warfare between these Muslim beachheads and the remaining Hindu states of the interior. As late as 1596 the first Dutch visitors to Java were told that the Muslims were only on the north coast, while the interior was "heathen."[16] Elsewhere there appears to have been a complex interplay between Muslim ports and animist hinterlands. Rulers often played a mediating role, patronizing the mosque of the city traders, abandoning pork, adopting a Muslim name and dress, but not renouncing the supernatural attributes that gave them power with their interior peoples.

Christian sources frequently point out that Islam was a minority affair in Maluku and the eastern Archipelago in general, and that even that minority had little but the name of Muslims. Tomé Pires reckoned

[13]*The Travels and Controversies of Friar Domingo Navarrete, 1618–1686* [1676], trans. J. S. Cummins, 2 vols. (Cambridge, 1962), 1:110n; Anthony Reid, "A Great Seventeenth Century Indonesian Family: Matoaya and Pattingalloang of Makassar," *Masyarakat Indonesia* 8, no. 1 (1981), 13–19.

[14]Jacobus Noorduyn, *Een Achttiende-eeuwse Kroniek van Wadjo': Buginese Historiografie* (The Hague, 1955), p. 263.

[15]Ibid., pp. 116–17; Anthony Reid, ed., *Slavery, Bondage, and Dependency in Southeast Asia* (St. Lucia, Queensland, 1983), p. 169.

[16]Willem Lodewycksz, 1598, in *De eerste schipvaart der Nederlanders naar Oost-Indië onder Cornelis de Houtman, 1595–1597*, ed. G. P. Rouffaer and J. W. Ijzerman, 3 vols. (The Hague, 1915–29), 1:114.

only one in ten Malukans was a Muslim,[17] and Xavier added that "the Moros of these regions do not practice the doctrines of the sect of Mahomed; they have no *alfaquis*, and those they have know very little and are all foreigners."[18] Early Spanish observers of Muslims in the Manila area, Mindanao, and Ternate pointed out that beyond circumcision and avoidance of pork they knew virtually nothing of Islam.[19]

Arab visitors of this period were in a better position to make such judgments, but some of them did not differ greatly in their assessments. The famous Arab pilot Ahmad ibn Majid was not flattering about the people of Melaka in the late fifteenth century: "You do not know whether they are Muslims or not."[20] Although this may be less than fair, Pires confirmed the frequent intermarriage of Muslims with non-Muslims in Melaka.[21] The Melaka chronicle itself gives the impression that Melaka Malays were more relaxed than Arabs about such matters as alcohol; it makes fun of a judgmental Arab scholar, Maulana Sadar Johan, who lost a verbal duel with a drunken Malay nobleman.[22]

The Patani chronicle is one of the few Malay sources to describe Islamization in terms of a progression. It relates that the first Muslim ruler gave up eating pork and worshiping idols, "but apart from that he did not alter a single one of his kafir habits." It was only in the reign of Sultan Muzaffar (d. 1564) that the first mosque was built ("because without a mosque there is no [visible] sign of Islam") and "the Islamic religion was more widespread in all the rural areas [*dusun*] and reached as far as Kota Maligai"—still only 14 kilometers from the coast. Even then the people only gave up eating pork and worshiping idols; "heathen practices such as making offerings to trees, stones and spirits were not abandoned by them."[23]

Finally it must be noted that no Islamic texts in Southeast Asian languages which date from before 1590 have come to light. At about that time, Hamzah Fansuri began writing about the mystical path in Malay, explaining that he did so "in order that all servants of God who do not understand the Arabic and Persian languages may reflect upon

[17]Tomé Pires, *The Suma Oriental of Tomé Pires*, 2 vols. [1515], ed. and trans. Armando Cortesão (London, 1944), 1:213.

[18]Francis Xavier, Letter from Cochin, 20 Jan. 1548, in Schurhammer and Wicki, 1944–45, p. 386.

[19]Miguel Lopez de Legazpi, "Relations of the Filipinas Islands, and of the Character and Conditions of Their Inhabitants, July 1569," in *The Philippine Islands, 1493–1898*, ed. E. H. Blair and J. A. Robertson, 55 vols. (Cleveland, 1903–9), 3:60–61.

[20]G. R. Tibbetts, *A Study of the Arabic Texts Containing Material of Southeast Asia* (Leiden, 1979), p. 206; for fuller quotation, see L. F. Thomaz, Chapter 3 in this volume.

[21]Pires, 1944, 2:249.

[22]"Sejarah Melayu or 'Malay Annals'," ed. C. C. Brown, *JMBRAS* 25, nos. 2–3 (1952), 153.

[23]*Hikayat Patani: The Story of Patani*, ed. A. Teeuw and D. K. Wyatt, 2 vols. (The Hague, 1970), 1:75, 78–79.

it."[24] He may not have been the first to do so; what is clear is that there is a sudden abundance of Islamic writing in both Malay and Javanese at about the turn of the century, some sublime, some prosaic, and much explicitly propagandistic. Only at this point can we say with confidence that there was a community of Muslim scholars consciously translating Islamic concepts into vernacular texts. If earlier missionaries wrote only in Arabic and Persian, this would be the strongest evidence that their interaction with the bulk of the local population was extremely limited. Within only a half-century, however, Islamic writing in Malay reached its greatest heights in the work of Hamzah Fansuri, Syamsu'd-din as-Samatrani, Nuru'd-din ar-Raniri, and Abdur-rauf as-Singkili. Javanese Islamic texts go back to the same period. This development was strikingly contemporary with the appearance of Christian devotional literature in Malay (beginning with Xavier in the 1540s), Tagalog (from the 1580s), and Vietnamese (from the 1620s).

In the second half of the sixteenth century the boundaries of the "House of Islam" (*Dar al-Islam*) began to be much more sharply drawn. The established Islamic states, notably Aceh, Johor, Patani, Banten, Demak-Pajang-Mataram, and Ternate, extended their authority to their rural hinterlands, together with their demands for minimal Islamic conformity. In their conflicts with neighboring kingdoms the concept of *jihad* (holy war) became prominent as Islam began to assume a major role in their self-perception.

Can we identify some of the conditions that made the period 1550–1650 unique in the religious history of the region? One factor on the Christian side would certainly be the Counter-Reformation mentality, carried to Asia preeminently by the Jesuits immediately after their foundation in 1540. This influence made the character of the Spanish operation in the Philippines after 1565 utterly different from the bloody conquest of Central and South America, or from early Portuguese activity in Asia. Conversion of the inhabitants was from the beginning the most prominent item on the agenda of Miguel Lopez de Legazpi and Fr. Urdaneta. The number of missionary priests in the Philippines grew spectacularly, from 13 in 1576 to 94 in 1586 and 267 in 1594—a striking contrast to the handful the Portuguese sent to Southeast Asia even in the wake of Francis Xavier.[25] Beginning with Xavier, the Jesuits set a high standard of learning the languages of Asia; Christianity was translated into Malay, Tagalog, Visayan, and Vietnamese in the period 1550–1650.

---

[24]*Sharabu'l-Ashiqin*, cited in S. M. Naguib Al-Attas, *The Mysticism of Hamzah Fansuri* (Kuala Lumpur, 1970), p. 297.
[25]J. L. Phelan, *The Hispanization of the Philippines* (Madison, Wis., 1959), p. 56.

Nevertheless, the more important factors had to do with developments in Asia itself, which profoundly transformed the lives of Southeast Asians as well as the way the scriptural religions affected them. Of these, I focus on three.

Rapid Commercialization

What European historians call the "long sixteenth century," beginning sometime in the fifteenth and ending about 1630, was a period of expansion and rising prices in the whole global trade system. Both Europe and China certainly grew rapidly in population in this period, and their demand for imported luxuries grew even more strongly. Since Southeast Asian cloves, nutmeg, mace, pepper, sandalwood, sappanwood, and camphor were among the most valued articles in the long-distance trade in this period, the region was necessarily drawn into a rapid expansion of cash cropping for export. Southeast Asian pepper exports, in particular, grew from almost nothing around 1400 to about 8,000 tons in the middle of the seventeenth century. The production of this crop alone must have required the labor of about 200,000 people, and the trade in this and other export items supported far more.

The peak of the commercial boom for Southeast Asia occurred at the climax of this global period of trade expansion, about 1570–1630. The most clear-cut indicator was the flow of silver into the region. New methods of mercury extraction greatly increased the output of silver mines in both the New World and Japan around 1570. Some of this greatly increased production was carried by Europeans to buy Southeast Asian spices and to boost the prices for them. Most of the Japanese silver, and a substantial proportion of the American, ended up in China (where it helped fuel the "late Ming boom"), but it had to pass through Southeast Asia. The Ming court forbade direct trade with Japan, so Chinese traded their goods for Japanese silver at such Southeast Asian ports as Hoi An (Faifo), Ayutthaya, Cambodia, Patani, Manila, and Banten. American silver was carried on the annual galleon from Acapulco to Manila, where it was sold for Chinese and Southeast Asian wares. The flow of silver to and through Southeast Asia reached a peak in the 1620s. Thereafter, the output of the mines slowed, the Japanese ceased coming to Southeast Asia, the Chinese were ruinously impoverished by the mid-century crisis that brought down the Ming dynasty (1644), and the Dutch progressively established a monopoly over the key Southeast Asian exports.[26]

During the period of rapid commercialization, large trading cities developed and in turn became the centers of states of unprecedented wealth and power. From the most remote parts of the region forest products, deer hides, and cash crops flowed onto the world market, while in return Indian cottons and Chinese manufactures reached the remotest Southeast Asian markets. All of this must have done much to shake the foundations of social order in a general sense. Intense commercial interaction presented particular problems, however, for traditional Southeast Asian spirit worship.

As Robin Horton points out for Africa, Richard O'Connor for northern Tai-speakers, and Janet Hoskins for modern Sumba, animism was not readily portable.[27] Once away from his own familiar landscape, the traveler was at the mercy of unknown spirits manipulated by his enemies. He had to return frequently to his own village to attend to his ancestors. Those who left the village world for trade, warfare, cash cropping, or service to a new lord were in need of universally valid values and identity. In a pattern similar to that sketched by Horton for Africa,[28] there was a tendency for the earliest and most thorough converts to Islam to be found in the merchant communities of every port in the region. One of the earliest Javanese Muslim texts even gives support to an Islamic "Protestant ethic," with its emphasis on asceticism, hard work and little sleep, almsgiving, and not minding being considered stingier after conversion.[29] Since the port cities were also the dominant political and cultural centers of the period, their Islamic character eventually influenced all who lived within their economic orbit.

Because the first Muslims and Christians encountered by Southeast Asians were traders and warriors, they appeared both wealthy and powerful. In terms of traditional Southeast Asian religion, this could only mean that they had some advantages in invoking the help of the spirit world. As has been remarked about contemporary Ngadju Dayak religion, "if one man is richer than another they say it is because he must have sponsored the correct rituals at the right time and was

[26]Anthony Reid, "An 'Age of Commerce' in Southeast Asian History," *MAS* 24, no. 1 (1990), 1–30.

[27]Horton, 1971; Richard O'Connor, "Sukhothai: Rule, Religion, and Elite Rivalry," paper presented to 41st Annual Conference of the Association for Asian Studies, Washington DC, 1989; Janet Hoskins, "Spirit Worship and Conversion in West Sumba," in *Indonesian Religions in Transition*, ed. Rita Kipp and Susan Rodgers (Tucson, Ariz., 1987), p. 146.

[28]Horton, 1975.

[29]G. W. J. Drewes, *An Early Javanese Code of Muslim Ethics* (The Hague, 1978), pp. 28–37.

careful in his selection of spirits. . . . The more a man knows about ritual, the more he can do for his own and his family's welfare."[30] Missionaries in the seventeenth century sometimes complained that in their approach to religion Southeast Asians (in this case Filipinos) "seemed to have no heart or understanding for anything except the gaining of money."[31]

The process of religious change, therefore, was in part the natural attraction of the ritual practices of those who seemed most successful in the new world of commerce. Observing Islamization at an early stage in the Manila area, a Spaniard wrote: "some are Moros [Muslims], and they obtain much gold, which they worship as a God. . . . They believe that paradise and successful enterprises are reserved for those who submit to the religion of the Moros of Brunei, of which they make much account. . . . These are a richer people, because they are merchants, and with their slaves, cultivate the land."[32] Apparently even without any Islamic proselytism some Filipinos who had dealings with Muslim traders imitated their tabu on pork, presumably believing it to be the ritual key to their success.[33]

Direct Contact with the Heartland

In the case of Christianity, the importance of direct contact is so apparent as to need no emphasis. The Catholic Christianity of the Counter-Reformation depended on a disciplined priesthood for its expansion. The religious orders made priests available in Europe, and much of the success of Christianization depended on how many of these could be put to work in Southeast Asia. The number of indigenous priests was insignificant until the last quarter of the seventeenth century, when the French Society of Foreign Missions succeeded in ordaining Vietnamese, in small numbers and under great difficulties. With this limited exception, conversion to a wholly different lifestyle and value system was the work of foreign priests trained in Europe. Without them, Catholic communities tended to be reabsorbed into the dominant value system of their surroundings.

[30]Douglas Miles, "Shamanism and the Conversion of Ngadju Dayaks," *Oceania* 37, no. 1 (1966), 5.

[31]Diego Duarte, "Historia de la Provincia del Sancto Rosario . . . en Philipinas" [1640], in Blair and Robertson, 1903–9, 30:238.

[32]Francisco de Sande, "Relation of the Filipinas Islands" [1576], in ibid., 4:67–68; see also Guido de Lavezaris, "Reply to Rada's Opinion" [1574], in ibid., 3:267.

[33]"Relation of the Conquest of the Island of Luzon" [1572], in ibid., 3:165; Legazpi, ibid., 3:60–61.

Partly because of the booming economic conditions of the period 1550–1630, the Portuguese and Spanish crowns were able to send relatively large numbers of priests to the East. Political factors soon intervened. When the Dutch captured Portuguese Melaka in 1641, and the remaining Spanish strongholds in Maluku and Sangihe-Talaud were withdrawn in 1666, Catholic priests were excluded from the Indonesian Archipelago except on the most clandestine and occasional basis. The Dutch were not interested in missionary work themselves, and they arrested any Catholic priest they encountered. From 1645 onward, each of the Vietnamese states periodically banished foreign priests and attempted to suppress Christianity, notably during the purges of 1664–65. Thereafter it was only in the Philippines that Catholic priests were present in any large number. Even there, in the view of the Jesuit historian John Schumacher, there was a relapse toward folk Catholicism:

> Rather than an intensification of what was accomplished in the Christianization of the 16th and early 17th centuries . . . there was . . . growing stagnation from the end of the 17th century. Far from the number of priests increasing so as to make possible a fuller penetration of Catholicism, the number remained stable, for there was a failure to develop a native clergy. Even worse, the proportion of priests to people probably decreased in the face of a growing population on the one hand, and increasing difficulty in getting missionaries to come from Spain on the other.[34]

Islam has no such priesthood, and one of its great strengths has been the capacity of individual travelers—traders, soldiers, mystics, and teachers—to begin viable Islamic communities. Nevertheless, the redirection of trading routes in the period 1550–1620 and the intensity of commercial activity during this period brought the "lands below the winds" into more intense contact with the Middle East than at any time before the nineteenth century.

Before about 1490 most Moluccan spices and almost all Indonesian pepper had been exported to China. The pull of the European market changed both the quantity and direction of Indonesian exports during the sixteenth century. By 1620 more than 60 percent of the much increased Indonesian pepper crop was being taken to Europe. Some of this increase was taken by the Portuguese. From the 1530s, however,

---

[34]John Schumacher, "Some Historical Considerations on the Evangelization of the Philippines," *Contemporary Studies* 2, no. 4 (1965), 226–27.

Muslim traders based in Aceh began sending their own ships to the Red Sea, probably by way of India. By the 1550s they were sailing directly across the Indian Ocean to Arabia, avoiding the dangerous centers of Portuguese power on the west coast of India as well as the Straits of Malacca. This put Aceh in direct contact with the Hejaz, Yemen, and Egypt, as well as with its older trading partners in Gujarat and Malabar.[35]

This direct contact was short-lived but important. In the second half of the sixteenth century about a thousand metric tons of pepper were being carried from Sumatra to the Red Sea each year, with four or five ships making the annual voyages. As much pepper was flowing along this route toward Alexandria as the Portuguese were taking to Lisbon.[36] When the first Dutch, English, and French ships arrived in the Archipelago around 1600, they found traders whom they called Turks or "Rumes" (people from the Malay *Rum*, an amalgam of Rome, Byzantium, and Istanbul) established in Aceh, Banten, Banda, and Ternate. When Frederick de Houtman wanted an example for his wonderful dictionary of the way foreign traders were received in Aceh, he used the reception at court of a *nakhoda* from Mecca who, as part of the preliminaries for trade, offered the sultan of Aceh military assistance from his country.[37]

Whereas earlier Muslim apostles and scholars had come "below the winds" primarily from India, this shift in the trade routes made the Malay world directly accessible from Arabia. Hence in the 1570s and 1580s Arab scholars such as Muhammad Azhari and Syeikh Abu'l-kheir ibn Syeikh ibn Hajar of Mecca and Syeich Muhammad of Yemen journeyed to Aceh and made it their temporary home, preaching, teaching, and disputing with one another there.[38] Portuguese and Spanish sources also refer to the large numbers of "Arabian and Persian false prophets" helping to strengthen Islam in the Archipelago in the second half of the sixteenth century.[39] Similarly, Southeast Asian Muslims were able to board the pepper ships if they wished to travel to

[35]Charles Boxer, "A Note on Portuguese Reactions to the Revival of the Red Sea Spice Trade and the Rise of Acheh, 1540–1600," *JSEAH* 10, no. 3 (1969), 416–19.

[36]Ibid., p. 419; Frederick Lane, "The Mediterranean Spice Trade: Its Revival in the Sixteenth Century" [1940], in *Venice and History: The Collected Papers of Frederick C. Lane* (Baltimore, 1966), pp. 25–34.

[37]Frederick de Houtman in *Le "Spraeck ende woord-boeck" de Frederick de Houtman*, ed. Denys Lombard (Paris, 1970), pp. 27–28.

[38]Nuru'd-din ar-Raniri, [1644] in *Nuru'd-din ar-Raniri: Bustanu's-Salatin, Bab II, Fasal 13*, ed. T. Iskandar (Kuala Lumpur, 1966), pp. 33–34.

[39]Baltazar Dias [1556] in *European Sources for the History of the Sultanate of Brunei in the Sixteenth Century*, ed. Robert Nicholl (Bandar Seri Begawan, 1975), p. 32; Leonardo Argensola, *The Discovery and Conquest of the Molucco and Philippine Islands* (London, 1708), p. 103.

Mecca and Madina for pilgrimage or study. Hamzah Fansuri seems to have done this around the 1580s, and Jamalud-din of Pasai, Syech Yusuf of Makassar, and Abdur-rauf of Singkel certainly did so in the first half of the seventeenth century.[40] Each of the latter two spent about twenty years in the Hejaz, Abdur-rauf having recorded a list of the fifteen teachers he studied with during his time in Arabia, and Yusuf having left his name as the copyist in Mecca of several important Arabic manuscripts.[41]

The Dutch and English after 1600, with far more resources of ships and money, completed what the Portuguese had only half achieved. By the 1620s there were no further shipments of Southeast Asian pepper and spice along the old Muslim route to the Red Sea, and Turkey itself had to import its needs from the western Europeans.[42] Moreover, the Gujarati ships that had traded as far as Banten now went no farther than Aceh, and in decreasing numbers. A Dutch blockade excluded Gujarati ships from Aceh for several years in the 1650s and removed the supplies of tin and pepper that had made Aceh's port attractive. In the overall pattern of world trade, pepper and other Southeast Asian products were in any case less important after 1650, and long-distance shipping was shifting to other directions.

The last Gujarati ships seem to have visited Aceh in the 1690s. After the collapse of direct Acehnese shipping, these had still enabled Southeast Asians to travel in Muslim ships as far as Gujarat, where they could join the large pilgrim ships for Jidda organized by the Mughal emperors. In the eighteenth century Muslim shipping was predominantly local, and Aceh, Surat, and Jidda all became less important as commercial centers. Hence the aspiring pilgrim would have had to transship several times, and put up with considerable discomfort, to reach his goal.

Political Crusades

The arrival of the Portuguese in 1509 via India, and of the Spanish via the Americas twelve years later, gave a new political character to reli-

[40]Ph. S. van Ronkel, "Een Maleische Getuigenis over den Weg des Islams in Sumatra," *BKI* 75 (1919), 363; A. H. Johns, "Islam in the Malay World," in *Islam in Asia*, ed. R. Israeli and A. H. Johns (Jerusalem, 1984), pp. 122–26.

[41]Peter Riddell, "Abd al-Ra'uf al-Singkili's *Tarjuman al-Mustafid*: A Critical Study of His Treatment of *Juz'* 16," Ph.D. diss. Australian National University, 1984, pp. 20–22; Nicholas Heer, *The Precious Pearl: Al-Jami's Al-Durrah Al-Fahirah* (Albany, N.Y., 1979), pp. 13–15.

[42]Niels Steensgaard, *The Asian Trade Revolution of the Seventeenth Century* (Chicago, 1973), pp. 171–72.

gious identity. The Iberians had warred for several centuries against the Muslims in their homeland, so that the crusade against the "Moros" (Moors) had become part of their national mythology and culture. In addition, the Portuguese were out to take over the spice trade from the Muslims who had shipped pepper and spices to the Red Sea and thence to Alexandria for sale to Venice. Ideology and self-interest converged to make the Portuguese (and to a lesser extent the Spanish) identify the wealthy Muslim traders and the rulers who supported them as the enemy to be attacked and plundered at every opportunity.

In return, the Muslims of Southeast Asia, particularly those involved in the spice trade, tended to regroup around explicitly Islamic centers prepared to counterattack the Portuguese. The rise of Aceh is the clearest example. Portuguese high-handed intervention in Pasai and Pidië, not to mention the taking of Melaka across the Straits, drove all the more Islamic, commercial, or simply patriotic elements to support Sultan Ali Mughayat Syah in his drive to unite the north Sumatran coast during the 1520s into a new and explicitly anti-Portuguese kingdom. For more than a century Aceh remained the most consistent enemy of Portuguese Melaka, mirroring its coincidence of ideological and economic interests as the new center of the Islamic spice route. Banten in western Java was established as an Islamic kingdom at the same time and for somewhat similar reasons, after the Portuguese had sought to ally with the Hindu port of Sunda Kelapa there.

The Ottoman expansion to Egypt, Syria, and the Hejaz in 1516–17 and to Iraq in 1534–38 provided for the first time a first-class military power with an interest in defending the Muslim spice-trading route in the Indian Ocean. The attacks of sultans Sulaiman and Selim II on the Christian powers led by Spain seem to have had a galvanizing effect even as far away as Southeast Asia. The first Turkish fleet to combat the Portuguese in the Indian Ocean was launched by the governor of Egypt in 1537–38. Though it failed dismally, some of its members must have found their way to Aceh. Sultan Ala'ad-din Ri'ayat Syah al-Kahar was assisted in his wars against the Bataks in 1538 by "the hundred and threescore Turks, that a little before were come to him from the Strait of Mecca, with two hundred Sarasins, Malabars, and some Abassins, which were the best men he had."[43] The establishment of direct commercial and diplomatic relations between Turkey and Aceh in the 1560s gave a much clearer impetus to the concept of a pan-Islamic countercrusade against the Portuguese in Southeast Asia. A 1566 petition from

---

[43]Fernand Mendez Pinto, *The Voyages and Adventures of Fernand Mendez Pinto*, trans. H. Cogan (London, 1653), p. 19.

Sultan Ala'ad-din Ri'ayat Syah al-Kahar of Aceh to the Ottoman sultan pleaded with him as khalifa of universal Islam to aid the oppressed Muslims of the Indian Ocean: "The sultan [of Aceh] says that he is left alone to face the unbelievers. They have seized some islands and have taken Muslims captive. Merchant and pilgrim ships going from these islands toward Mecca were captured one night [by the Portuguese] and the ships that were not captured were fired on and sunk, causing many Muslims to drown."[44] Turkey responded to repeated Acehnese requests by sending gunsmiths and artillerymen on at least two occasions, in 1564 and 1568.[45] This short-lived Turkish intervention further stimulated the spirit of pan-Islamic solidarity in the Indian Ocean. The Muslim states of the Deccan, led by Bijapur, for the first time were able to cooperate in a 1564–65 *jihad* that overthrew the Hindu kingdom of Vijayanagar. Aceh, Japara, and (less enthusiastically) Johor in Southeast Asia concerted action with Bijapur and the Muslim community of Calicut in India to launch a series of *jihad* against the Portuguese in Melaka (1568 and 1570) and Goa (1570). Even in the neutral entrepôt of Ayutthaya, two Dominican missionaries who arrived in the 1560s were set upon by a mob of rioting Muslims, with the result that one Dominican was killed and the other badly injured, and several Muslims were sentenced to be trampled to death by elephants for their unruliness.[46] As a result of this new-found Islamic cooperation along the spice trading route, the period 1560–80 was a high point not only for the Islamic military success in Southeast Asia,[47] but also for Muslim-Christian polarization.

In eastern Indonesia by the middle of the sixteenth century the Portuguese had established an unstable modus vivendi with the Sultanate of Ternate in the clove trade which allowed Christian as well as Muslim missionaries to make some headway among the still largely animist Malukans. In the 1560s, Sultan Hairun of Ternate proved extremely irritating to the Portuguese by his ability to manipulate them to advance his own authority and that of Islam, and in 1570 they treacherously murdered him. Hairun's son, Babullah, used the outrage against this act to drive the Portuguese out of Ternate and to compel most of their Christian supporters throughout Maluku to adopt Islam

---

[44]Letter of Sultan Selim II [1568], in Saffet Bey, "Bir Osmanli Filosunun Sumatra Seferi," *Tarihi Osmani Ecumenli Mecmuasi* 10 (1912), 606–8.

[45]Anthony Reid, "Sixteenth Century Turkish Influence in Western Indonesia," *JSEAH* 10, no. 3 (1969), 395–414; Naimur Rahman Farooqi, "Mughal-Ottoman Relations . . . 1556–1748," Ph.D. diss. University of Wisconsin, 1986.

[46]Fernandus de Sancta Maria, Letter from Goa, 26 Dec. 1569, in *Exemplar Literarum ex Indiis* (Rome, 1571).

[47]Reid, 1969, p. 408.

as a sign of loyalty. Babullah had already been an effective propagandist for Islam during his father's day, but now he was able to spread it through much of the Ambon area, to Butung, Salayar, and some of the coastal kingdoms of eastern and northern Sulawesi, and southern Mindanao. According to Argensola he sent envoys to Aceh and Brunei to try to form an Islamic coalition against the Portuguese.[48] During Babullah's reign, and up to the time the Dutch arrival complicated religious loyalties considerably, there was a stronger sense than before or since that acceptance of Islam was an essential part of loyalty to the ruler of Ternate.

Portuguese and Spanish sources in the second half of the sixteenth century are redolent with hostility to Islam, but they also suggest strongly that the feeling was reciprocated. Fernand Mendez Pinto, for example, puts anti-Christian speeches into the mouths of the kings of Aceh and Demak and claims that Pahang would not allow Portuguese to be buried ashore because otherwise "their country should remain accursed, and incapable of nourishing anything, because the deceased were not purged from the hog's flesh they had eaten."[49] Spanish envoys reported that the sultan of Brunei had responded in 1578 to an arrogant letter from Manila by saying, "so this is the way that your people write to me, who am king; while the Castilians are kafir . . . who have no souls, who are consumed by fire when they die, and that, too, because they eat pork."[50] What little is written in Muslim sources about the Christian infidels in this period tends to confirm that a holy war mentality was prominent on both sides.[51]

Southeast Asians, undergoing a profound social transformation themselves, were thus confronted with two scriptural religions both at a high point of aggressive expansion, each competing consciously with the other to convince them that they had to choose one side rather than the other, right rather than wrong. The intense competition between the two sides certainly sharpened the boundary, not only between themselves, but between each of them and the surrounding environment of traditional beliefs. Several features of the period show how much more seriously the religious character of the society within that boundary was emphasized than before or for some time thereafter; to these I now turn.

[48]Argensola, 1708, p. 94.
[49]Pinto, 1653, p. 40.
[50]Blair and Robertson, 1903–9, 4:160–61.
[51]Raniri, 1966, pp. 31–32; Entji Amin, *Sja'ir Perang Mengkasar (The Rhymed Chronicle of the Macassar War)* [1670], trans. C. Skinner (The Hague, 1963), pp. 94–99.

The Use of Writing

The scriptural religions introduced writing for the first time to relatively few areas—at most Maluku, the southern Philippines, northern Sulawesi, some islands east of Lombok, and parts of Borneo. For the rest, Indic-derived scripts were already widespread. Where the new Arabic and Latin alphabets came to replace or coexist with the older alphabet, as in Luzon and the Visayas, coastal Sumatra and southwest Sulawesi, there seems little doubt that literacy was higher in the old alphabet than the new, and much higher for women.[52]

What carried weight was the sacred authority of a book. Except in Java, where sacred writings were numerous, and southwest Sulawesi, where writing was probably used primarily for preserving genealogies, the purposes of writing had been for the most part ephemeral—love poems and messages written on bamboo or palm leaf. Islam and Christianity each claimed that their authority rested on a book, and moreover a book written in an alien language that carried the extra sacral weight of impenetrability. William Marsden tells of a Sumatran spirit worshiper who challenged a Muslim fellow countryman to show how his God was any more demonstrably real than the spirits. The apparently persuasive answer was that the truths of Islam were written in a book.[53] Some ethnographers note a similar persuasiveness in modern times.[54]

Both Muslim and Christian proselytists based their own authority on their ability to read and explicate sacred texts. At the point of most rapid religious change, moreover, they generated new texts, designed to convey the essential truths of the new religion in forms that could be memorized and understood by their proselytes, in Southeast Asian languages. But these texts were for the specialists. The new religious ideas were invariably conveyed orally to new converts, with writing serving only to assist the teacher. Prayers and articles of faith were learned by group recitation, usually in a poetic or melodic form.

Saint Francis Xavier was the first of the Christian evangelists to compose in Malay a version of Christianity that could be memorized:

---

[52]Anthony Reid, *Southeast Asia in the Age of Commerce*, vol. 1: *The Lands below the Winds* (New Haven, Conn., 1988), pp. 215–25; H. H. Bartlett, "A Batak and Malay Chant on Rice Cultivation," *Proceedings of the American Philosophical Society* 96, no. 6 (1952), 630–31 (reprinted in H. H. Bartlett, *The Labors of the Datoe* [Ann Arbor, Mich., 1973]).

[53]William Marsden, *The History of Sumatra* [1783], 3d. ed. (London, 1811; rpt., Kuala Lumpur, 1966), p. 289.

[54]Hoskins, 1987, p. 146.

I taught the children and native people a "declaration" I had written on each article of the faith, in a language that all could understand, adapting myself . . . to what the people of the country newly converted could understand. This declaration I taught instead of prayers, in Melaka as I had in Maluku, to establish in them a basis to believe well and truly in Jesus Christ, ceasing to believe in vain idols. This declaration could be learned in one year, if one taught each day a little, that is, about twenty words that they could easily learn by heart.[55]

The Spanish had a similar compendium of the essentials of the faith, the *Doctrina Christiana* originally compiled in Mexico but translated into Tagalog and printed in Manila in 1593. Later versions adapted into Tagalog the popular *Dottrina Cristiana* of the Jesuit cardinal Bellarmine (1597). So that this whole document could be memorized by new Christians, question-and-answer sessions were held after masses, with the correct responses preferably being chanted by the whole congregation.[56]

Muslims also used the method of oral recitation to commit to memory the essential prayers (*salat*) as well as the Arabic Koran. Syamsu'd-din as-Samatrani (1601) wrote an Islamic creed in Malay, the *Mir'at al-Mu'minin* (1601), which used a question-and-answer form no doubt intended to be recited between a teacher and pupils and thus committed to memory. One of the most popular Persian works rendered into Malay was the "Thousand Questions" (*Kitab Seribu Masalah*), which provided crucial items of religious dogma and Islamic cosmology in the form of the questions a learned Jew put to the Prophet. Questions and answers were presented in a form that could be readily memorized.[57]

Emphasis on a Predictable Moral Universe

Just as has been argued for the Christianization of the Roman empire, the religious change in Southeast Asia helped people cope with

[55]Francis Xavier, Letter from Cochin 1548, in Schurhammer and Wicki, 1944–45, 1:389. None of Xavier's Malay writings appears to have survived; see ibid., 2:590–94; *Documenta Malucensia (1542–1577)*, ed. Hubert Jacobs (Rome, 1974), 1:14, 35. A Portuguese text of the rhyming catechism referred to here, composed in Ternate, is reproduced in Schurhammer and Wicki, 1:355–67. It probably had both Portuguese and Malay versions.

[56]Vicente Rafael, *Contracting Colonialism: Translation and Christian Conversion in Tagalog Society under Early Spanish Rule* (Ithaca, N.Y., 1988), pp. 39–54; Phelan, 1959, pp. 57–58; Schumacher, 1984, p. 253.

[57]G. F. Pijper, *Het Boek der Duizend Vragen* (Leiden, 1924), pp. 72–81; Sir Richard Winstedt, *A History of Classical Malay Literature* (Kuala Lumpur, 1977), pp. 148–52.

the constant and unpredictable assaults of demons.[58] The power of shamanistic possession presented the early missionaries with a considerable challenge. The Jesuit Pedro Chirino chronicled many contests with traditional healers and conceded that, though some were fakes, "there are also those who actually have a special pact with the devil, who aids and supports them with very special assistance, which Almighty God in his inscrutable judgement permits."[59] For Iberian priests, these unfamiliar supernatural forces could only be categorized as in league with the devil. Alarming as the phenomena often were to them, the friars believed they had to do battle with these powers of darkness, armed with the cross and the sacraments. Presumably they sometimes failed, but in their pious narratives there are numerous stories of spectacular victories over demons:

> Having planted this royal standard of our redemption [the cross] in an island greatly infested by demons, who were continually frightening the islanders with howls and cries, it imposed upon them perpetual silence, and freed all the other [neighboring] islands from an extraordinary tyranny. For the demons were crossing from island to island, in the sea, in the shape of serpents of enormous size . . . but this ceased, the demon taking flight at the sight of the cross.[60]

The assimilation of Southeast Asian spirits to Islamic ones (*jinn*), both good and bad, presented fewer problems. Even learned *ulama* did not deny the existence of spirits, but the higher path of union with God offered protection against them. Like Christianity, Islam offered a refuge from the domination of these demanding spirits in a different vision of the cosmos. This was a predictable, moral world in which the devout would be protected by God from all that the spirits could do and would eventually be rewarded by an afterlife in paradise. The powerless too would be rewarded if they lived lives of personal virtue. "The high and the low; the rich and the poor; they will all appear the same," as a Tagalog devotional poem put it.[61]

It is difficult to exaggerate the importance of this new vision in providing a "tremendous increase in distance . . . between man and the sacred,"[62] a major step toward what Weber characterized as rationaliza-

---

[58]J. N. Hillgarth, *Christianity and Paganism, 350–750: The Conversion of Western Europe* (Philadelphia, 1986), p. 12.

[59]Pedro Chirino, *Relacion de las Islas Filipinas: The Philippines in 1600* [1604], trans. Ramon Echevarria (Manila, 1969), p. 300.

[60]Pedro Murillo Velarde, "Jesuit Missions in the Seventeenth Century" [1749], in Blair and Robertson, 1903–9, 44:71.

[61]Pedro de Herrera [1645], quoted in Rafael, 1988, p. 176.

[62]Geertz, 1973, p. 174.

tion of religion.[63] For those who were making their way in a wider world of international trade, of large-scale state operations, of the exchange of ideas through literature and debate, this new worldview provided the necessary foundation.

This moral universe depended on a simple but consistent concept of eternal reward and punishment. The older view of the afterlife had been full of dangerous possibilities, against which there were no sure guarantees. By contrast, Islam and Christianity introduced the promise of a heaven that was forever safe and comfortable, "without death, only joy and happiness and life. . . . There is nothing lacking there, every wish will be fulfilled . . . without sorrow and lament, no sadness, no tribulation, nothing that is not glorious," as a seventeenth-century Augustinian wrote in one of the first catechetical poems in Tagalog.[64]

On the Muslim side, the Koran itself was the primary source of vivid imagery about heaven and hell, but these were also among the earliest concepts to be translated. The most effective work may have been the "Book of the Thousand Questions," probably reworked into Malay in Sumatra in the sixteenth or early seventeenth century but found as far away as Ambon by Valentijn. As Richard Winstedt put it, in this widely read work "the tortures of the damned are portrayed with the imagination and vivacity of Hieronymous Bosch."[65] Raniri also composed in Aceh in 1636 a popular Malay tract of over two hundred pages, the *Akhbaru'l-akhirat*, on death, judgment, heaven, hell, and the last days.[66]

There were, of course, problems. At an early stage of Filipino grappling with the new concept of paradise, a local notable who had died soon after baptism reappeared to fellow villagers—whether in a shamanistic possession or a Christian vision is not clear. His account of the paradise to which baptism gave access persuaded many to seek baptism immediately, though others rejected it because they did not want to share eternity with Spanish soldiers.[67]

Hell was even more persuasive. Chirino notes that Filipino fear of what evil spirits could do to man was such that "a well-painted picture of hell has converted a very great number of them".[68] Writers and preachers of both faiths dwelt on the torments in hell awaiting those

[63]Max Weber, *The Religion of China*, trans. H. Gerth (Glencoe, Ill., 1951), p. 226.

[64]Cited in Rafael, 1988, pp. 172–73.

[65]Winstedt, 1977, p. 151.

[66]H. H. Juynboll, *Catalogus van de Maleische en Sundaneesche Handschriften der Leidsche Universiteits-Bibliotheek* (Leiden, 1899), pp. 274–76.

[67]Juan Gonzalez de Mendoza, "History of the Great Kingdom of China," in Blair and Robertson, 1903–9, 6:148–49.

[68]Chirino, 1969, p. 297.

Figure 5. The funeral of Sultan Iskandar Thani of Aceh, 1641, as fancifully depicted by a Dutch artist. From *Reisen van Nicholaas de Graaff,* ed. J. C. M. Warnsinck (The Hague, Linschoten-Vereniging, 1930).

foolish enough to prefer earthly pleasures to their eternal welfare and those who rejected the true faith (Islam or Christianity) for its rivals.[69] Domesticating the Muslim hell in the Sumatran jungle, Raniri likened it to "a tiger with thirty thousand heads."[70]

Although the prominence of heaven and hell was new, the concepts may not have been. In their desire to find evocative terms to translate the Muslim and Christian heaven, proselytists made use of already localized words. Throughout Indonesia use was made of the Sanskrit *swarga* (the abode of Siva) and *naraka* for heaven and hell, respectively (Malay *syorga* and *neraka*). The Spanish used Tagalog *langit* (sky) or other terms implying profound peace and contentment when discussing the joys of heaven. When it came to hell, however, the shock of the unfamiliar *infierno* was evidently more effective.[71]

Execution of Unbelievers

The establishment of the Inquisition on Asian soil, at Goa in 1561, was an indication on the Christian side of the desire to keep the boundary between belief and unbelief firm. Only eight Southeast Asian cases were in fact referred to it in the period 1561–80, and only two of these suffered "severe penalties."[72] The number of non-Christians spared death because they embraced Catholicism must have been far greater.

In Manila the first bishop, Domingo de Salazar, assumed the role of inquisitor in 1580. Among the cases he investigated was that of a Spanish soldier accused of going native with Muslims of Manila, wearing a sarung and eating, drinking, and dancing with Muslims.[73] The Mexican tribunal of the Inquisition extended its functions to Manila in 1585 and endeavored to keep the boundaries of orthodoxy well defined by controlling the importation of books and the behavior and speech of Christians. The only executions of heretics, however, were of Dutch Protestants captured in Maluku in 1601, and these were technically condemned for rebellion against Spain rather than for heresy.[74]

The Islamic counterpart of this rigor is less known. The execution of

[69]See examples in Schurhammer and Wicki, 1944–45, 365; Rafael, 1988, pp. 179–84; Hamzah Fansuri, "Poems," in *The Poems of Hamzah Fansuri*, ed. G. W. J. Drewes and L. F. Brakel (Dordrecht, 1986), pp. 76, 92, 132.

[70]Cited in R. J. Wilkinson, *A Malay-English Dictionary (Romanised)*, 2 vols. (Mytilene, 1903; rpt., London, 1959), 2:799.

[71]Rafael, 1988, pp. 170–81.

[72]Luiz Filipe Thomaz, "Malaka et ses communautés marchandes au tournant du 16e siècle," in *Marchands et hommes d'affaires asiatiques dans l'Océan Indien et la Mer de Chine, 13e - 20e siècles*, ed. Denys Lombard and Jean Aubin (Paris, 1988), p. 43.

[73]F. Delor Angeles, "The Philippine Inquisition: A Survey," *Philippine Studies* 28 (1980), 258.

[74]Ibid., p. 280.

those held to be enemies of the state is a political act. But when such people are offered the choice of religious conversion or death, religion becomes defined as the essential test of political loyalty. The two issues are as difficult to disentangle in Muslim Aceh as in Protestant England in the same period. There are numerous cases throughout the period 1550–1650 of non-Muslims given the choice of accepting Islam or being executed after having been defined as enemies or criminals; it happened frequently in Aceh, and also in Banten, Mataram, Makassar, and Babullah's Ternate. This is of some importance in showing that these states did, to a greater extent than before or after, define themselves as necessarily Islamic, despite the presence of non-Muslim minorities in all of them. I believe there is also a tendency to accentuate the religious as against the political character of such executions as we move toward the middle of the seventeenth century.

One indication of this short-lived trend is Makassar, an exceptionally tolerant haven for all religions, especially Portuguese Catholicism. Yet here too, in 1658, two Portuguese were condemned to execution for murder but were offered a pardon if they became Muslim. One refused and was executed with a kris; the other was "so daunted at the sight" that he accepted Islam and was spared.[75]

Three cases where religious motives appeared to play a larger part, and about which we know more than usual, all occurred in seventeenth-century Aceh. Frederick de Houtman, leader of the first Dutch expedition to Aceh, was held captive on shore after a fight broke out between his men and the Acehnese in 1600. After some months of captivity he was told that Sultan Ala'ad-din had decided he would be killed unless he agreed to become a Muslim. When he refused, saying that one could not be forced to believe what one did not believe, the judicial officials of Aceh set about trying to convince him. They explained that Muhammad was the last of the prophets in the line of Moses, David, and Jesus and that it was as illogical not to acknowledge him as it would be to say that only the earlier kings of a dynasty were ordained by God and not the later. They asked him how Christians could worship stone idols as in Catholic Melaka, how they could believe that God had a son, and why they did not accept circumcision since Jesus himself was circumcised. All he need do was repeat the *shahada*—a greater understanding would come later. De Houtman's report declared that if he narrated the whole of the debate it would fill half a book.[76] When he remained obdurate, they took him to the river for execution, waved a sword over his head shouting "mau Islam?" and

[75]Navarrete, 1962, 2:121–22.
[76]Frederick de Houtman, "Cort Verhael" [1601], in *De Oudste Reizen van de Zeeuwen naar Oost-Indie, 1598–1604*, ed. W. S. Unger (The Hague, 1948), pp. 96–100.

threatened to trample him with elephants. Nevertheless, the sultan clearly wanted him alive rather than dead, and eventually his release was negotiated.

Portuguese usually kept clear of Aceh because of the intense mutual hostility that had built up between themselves and the sultanate. In fact, one of the first references to non-Muslims being given the Islam-or-death alternative was to a group of Portuguese traders who visited Aceh during what they thought an interval of peace, in 1565, only to find an ambassador from Turkey there who successfully urged the sultan to have them all killed if they did not embrace Islam.[77] After the death of Sultan Iskandar Muda and the accession of his son-in-law, Iskandar Thani, in 1637, however, the Portuguese viceroy sent a mission to Aceh from Goa in the hope of establishing peace, since Iskandar Thani was known to come from Pahang, a state often friendly to the Portuguese. The Portuguese were encouraged to come ashore and then were immediately imprisoned. All the sixty Europeans in the party were executed except the few who agreed to convert; the Indian Christians were evidently treated more leniently and returned to tell the story in Goa. The most detailed surviving accounts are in the pious literature about one of the two priests in the party, Denis of the Nativity (born a Frenchman, Pierre Berthelot), who was beatified by the church on account of his martyrdom. The Acehnese seem to have given particular attention to trying to convert the priest, who spoke Malay fluently. He was kept as a slave in a prominent household for a month and regularly punished and humiliated while being promised a good life and a wealthy wife if he converted. "By order of the king, one, two or several *casis*, who are their priests, were continually around him and his companions," preaching and arguing with him about the merits of Islam. According to the hagiographic literature, the Acehnese were so impressed with his sanctity that none wished to be the one to kill him, so he was eventually krissed by a Portuguese who had already converted to Islam.[78]

It is arguable that such events have nothing to do with Islamic norms, since there is nothing in the Shari'a that encourages such acts against Christian "people of the book" (*ahl al-Kitab*). Nevertheless, the theological effort put into trying to convert these unbelievers says something about the strength of Islamic ideas in the trading cities of Southeast Asia. It also contrasts markedly with the more relaxed mood

[77]*Documenta Indica*, ed. J. Wicki, 13 vols. (Rome, 1948–75), 7:33–34, 89.

[78]Philippe de la tres-saincte Trinité, *Voyage d'Orient* (Lyon, 1652), pp. 496–515; Ch. Bréard, *Histoire de Pierre Berthelot* (Paris, 1889); Denys Lombard, "Voyageurs français dans l'Archipel Indien," *Archipel* 1 (1971), 146–47.

only two decades later when Christian missionaries were allowed to operate in Aceh (though not among Muslims).

Much more unusual was the execution of a learned Muslim for heresy, presumably as an unrepentant apostate (*murtad*), for whom the obligatory death penalty had been copied into at least one Malay law code—that of Pahang in 1595.[79] I am aware of only one such clearly documented case in Southeast Asia before the nineteenth century, if we set aside the semilegendary stories of the execution of Syeh Siti Jenar and other Javanese mystics for having revealed truths that ought to be hidden—rather a different thing. This case occurred in the reign of Iskandar Thani of Aceh (r. 1637–41), which should be regarded as the extreme point of the application of Islamic norms in Southeast Asia before the nineteenth century. The incident lends greater significance to the case of the executed Portuguese that occurred in the same short reign.

It is well known that with the death of the influential *syeich* Syamsu'd-din in 1630, and still more of his patron, Sultan Iskandar Muda, in 1636, the adherents of the monistic *wujuddiya* school in Aceh lost their dominance in the city. The Gujarati champion of orthodoxy, Nuru'd-din ar-Raniri, rushed back to Aceh as soon as Iskandar Thani was enthroned. He began attacking the pupils of Syamsu'd-din and Hamzah Fansuri and had the works of these popular figures burned in front of the great mosque in Aceh. Raniri himself explained in his *Tabyan* how he debated with these mystics in front of the sultan and showed that they equated themselves with God: "All the Muslims gave a *fatwa* that they were *kafir* and would be killed. And some of them accepted the *fatwa* that they were *kafir*, and some repented and some did not want to repent. And some of those who repented had also been apostates (*murtad*), they returned to their former faith. So all the principal legions of the unbelievers were killed."[80] From Dutch sources we know that the most prominent victim of this inquisition was one "Shaikh Maldin" (Jamalud-din?). After the death of Raniri's protector, Iskandar Thani, one of this shaikh's pupils, a popular Minangkabau sufi named Saifurrijal, returned to Aceh from Surat and recommenced a bitter debate with Raniri. Popular feeling in Aceh was evidently on the side of the *wujuddiya*, and Raniri was lucky to be able to escape Aceh with his life at the end of 1643.[81]

[79]J. E. Kempe and R. Winstedt, "A Malay Legal Digest Compiled for 'Abd al-Ghafur Muhaiyu'd-din Shah, Sultan of Pahang, 1592–1614 A.D.," *JMBRAS* 21, no. 1 (1948), 53.

[80]Quoted in C. A. O. van Nieuwenhuijze, *Samsu'l-Din van Pasai* (Leiden, published dissertation, 1945), p. 200; also Iskandar, 1966, p. 8.

[81]Takeshi Ito, "Why Did Nurud-din ar-Raniri Leave Aceh in 1054 A.H.?" *BKI* 134 (1978), 489–91.

This stern imposition of a particular view of orthodoxy was thus short-lived and certainly uncharacteristic of Southeast Asia. Nevertheless, its timing is significant in marking a turning point for Aceh and perhaps the whole region. What followed was in part a reaction against the excesses of Raniri, in part a reassertion of a more moderate but still popular mysticism under the Shattariya *syeich*, Abdur-rauf of Singkel and Yusuf of Makassar, in part a long-term decline in the influence of international, commercial, and urban elements in Southeast Asian Islam.

The Application of Shari'a Law

To test the application of Islamic law three types of source exist: law codes, Southeast Asian chronicles, and the observation of outsiders. All are problematic, but all tend to support the impression of a movement toward greater implementation of Islamic laws in the late sixteenth and early seventeenth centuries and a movement in the opposite direction thereafter.

The chronicles, of which Raniri's *Bustan as-Salatin* is the most informative, record that some pious rulers imposed certain requirements of the Shari'a, though this may have meant no more than a token gesture if not backed up by legal institutions and codes. The law codes suggest that Islamic law was known by the compilers of the fifteenth and sixteenth centuries, though the Shari'a provisions are sometimes tacked on in what appears to be a learned footnote rather than a law expected to be followed. The *Undang-undang Melaka*, for example, sets out the rather lenient penalties for rape (marry the woman or pay a fine) and then adds, "But according to the law of God, if he is *muhsan* [married], he shall be stoned."[82] As cosmopolitan communities identifying strongly with Islam grew in the commercial cities (of Arab, Indian, and Chinese as well as Southeast Asian origins), they must frequently have been given the option of using Islamic law among themselves (as was still the case in the *kauman* (Muslim quarter) of Javanese towns at much later dates). A Muslim writer in one of the coastal cities of sixteenth-century Java confirmed this kind of pluralism, in a nominally Muslim polity, by insisting, "It is unbelief when people involved in a lawsuit and invited to settle the dispute according to the law of Islam, refuse to do so and insist on taking it to an infidel judge."[83] To judge from the *Undang-undang Melaka*, the *Luwaran* of Magindanao, and other codes

---

[82] *Undang-undang Melaka: The Laws of Malacca*, ed. Liaw Yock Fang (The Hague, 1976), pp. 84–85.
[83] Drewes, 1978, p. 37.

that apparently originated in this period, Islamic law was borrowed most fully in matters of commercial law, where there were presumably few local alternatives of any relevance to the cosmopolitan traders of the town. Muslim marriage, divorce, and inheritance law, laws of evidence, and laws relating to slaveholding were also widely incorporated into law codes of the period, though less widely applied in practice. Laws relating to royal prerogatives were entirely a Southeast Asian matter little affected by Islam.

The handling of what we call criminal offenses, especially theft, was perhaps the best index of change over time in the commitment of states to the Shari'a. Because Shafi'i law imposed the penalty of amputation of the right hand, left leg, left hand, and right leg for first, second, third, and fourth offenses, respectively, of theft of an item worth at least a quarter-dinar (about a gram of gold), it tended to be noticed by foreigners wherever it was applied. Hence we know from visitors to Aceh throughout the seventeenth century—François Martin and Wybrandt van Warwijck under Ala'ad-din Ri'ayat Syah al-Mukammil (r. 1588–1603),[84] Augustin de Beaulieu under Iskandar Muda (r. 1607–36),[85] Thomas Bowrey under Iskandar Thani (r. 1636–41),[86] and Peter Mundy and William Dampier under the queens[87]—that there was a system of chopping off alternate limbs which could only have been based on the Shari'a. They also note various other, crueller amputations, of noses, ears, lips, and vital organs, but these in most cases were for crimes held to touch the royal person, for which no punishment seemed too severe.[88]

Aceh was not alone in applying these Shari'a punishments. Brunei in the 1580s punished theft by cutting off the right hand, though in other respects its procedures were more traditional.[89] Banten under Sultan Ageng (r. 1651–82) applied the same penalties, and Magindanao at least included them in its law code.[90]

[84]François Martin, *Description du Premier Voyage Faict aux Indes Orientales par les francois en l'an 1603* (Paris, 1604), p. 46; Wybrandt van Warwijck, "Historische Verhaal vande Reyse gedaen inde Oost-Indien," in *Begin ende Voortgangh van de Vereenighde Neederlandtsche Geoctroyeerde Oost-Indische Compagnie*, ed. I. Commelin (Amsterdam, 1604), p. 14.

[85]A. de Beaulieu, "Mémoires du voyage aux Indes Orientales," in *Relations de divers voyages curieux*, ed. M. Thevenot, 4 vols. (Paris, 1663–72), 2:102.

[86]Thomas Bowrey, *A Geographical Account of Countries round the Bay of Bengal*, ed. R. C. Temple (Cambridge, 1905), p. 314.

[87]Peter Mundy, *The Travels of Peter Mundy in Europe and Asia, 1608–1667* [1667], ed. R. C. Temple, 5 vols. in 6 parts (London, 1907–36), 3:135, 331; William Dampier, *A New Voyage round the World*, 1697, ed. Sir Albert Gray (London, 1927), p. 96.

[88]Takeshi Ito, "The World of the Adat Aceh: A Historical Study of the Sultanate of Aceh," Ph.D. diss., Australian National University, 1984, pp. 171–83.

[89]John Carroll, "Berunai in the Boxer Codex," *JMBRAS* 55, no. 2 (1982), 7.

[90]William Dampier, *Voyages and Discoveries* [1699], ed. C. Wilkinson (London, 1931), p. 97; Najeeb M. Saleeby, *Studies in Moro History, Law, and Religion* (Manila, 1905), p. 68.

Sexual offenses were treated very differently in the Shari'a than in Malay tradition, but there are some cases among the urban elite, at least, where tough Islamic judgments were imposed. In Aceh three cases of *zina* (fornication) offenses for which the death penalty was imposed were witnessed by foreigners: in 1613 and twice in 1642. The men were painfully killed by flogging, and the women in some cases were strangled, as prescribed by Shafi'i law.[91] In Patani two young aristocrats were killed for a *zina* offense around 1601, by Malay methods of krissing for him and strangling for her.[92] In Banten and Brunei the death penalty was also imposed in this period.[93]

More important than these external signs that the Shari'a was being applied is evidence that properly constituted Islamic courts were set up and used. Here again we know most about Aceh, where there was at least one Shari'a court throughout the first half of the seventeenth century. Beaulieu in fact tells us there were two, one for offenses against the requirements of prayer, fasting, and religious orthodoxy and the other for matters of debt, marriage, divorce, and inheritance.[94] In 1636 a Dutch observer noted specifically that "the great bishop" (Syamsu'd-din's successor as judge, or *kadi*) presided over a weekly court in Aceh to judge theft, drunkenness, and offenses against royal etiquette.[95] Other sources also note the importance of the *kadi* in Acehnese affairs as early as the 1580s. Takeshi Ito shows that, although Sultan Iskandar Muda may have set up some of these institutions, it was his two successors who for the first time allowed these courts to work without the constant interference of arbitrary royal decrees. Perhaps the clearest indication of the attempt to give real force to the spirit of the Shari'a was Iskandar Thani's decree that the age-old Southeast Asian system of judging cases by ordeal (immersion in boiling oil or water was most common) be abolished in favor of the Islamic requirements for witnesses.[96]

Elsewhere there are also frequent indications that a *kadi* played a role in state affairs. The only definite evidence I have for a functioning Shari'a court outside Aceh, however, is in Banten under Sultan Ageng. There a resident French missionary reported: "They have two principal

[91]Ito, 1984, pp. 168–70.

[92]Jacob van Neck, "Journal van Jacob van Neck" [1604], in *De vierde schipvaart der Nederlanders naar Oost-Indie onder Jacob Wilkens en Jacob van Neck (1599–1604)*, ed. H. A. Forest and A. de Booy (The Hague, 1980), 1:224.

[93]*Relation des missions et des voyages des evesques vicaires apostoliques . . . és années 1676 & 1677* (Paris, 1680), p. 93; Carroll, 1982, p. 9.

[94]Beaulieu, 1666, pp. 100–102.

[95]Ito, 1984, pp. 155–60.

[96]Reid, 1988, pp. 139–44.

judges, of whom one is called the grand Chabandar [Syahbandar], who knows all commercial affairs; and the other carries the name of Thiaria [Shari'a], who extends his jurisdiction over all civil and criminal cases, and who among other crimes punishes theft and adultery rigorously."[97]

When colonial officials and the earliest ethnographers began to provide detailed information about the Muslims of Southeast Asia toward the end of the nineteenth century, they saw little evidence of Islamic law, of Shari'a courts, or of rulers publicly celebrating Islamic rituals. John Gullick's reading of the British colonial evidence on late nineteenth-century Malaya, for example, was that there were "no kathis," no evidence that the Shari'a was "effective law," and "no public rituals of Islamic content."[98] Similarly, Snouck Hurgronje emphasized that Islamic law was very seldom applied in Aceh, that justice was effectively in the hands of secular authorities (*ulèëbalang*), and that penalties for theft and *zina* such as those above were almost unheard of.[99] We should not conclude, as they tended to, that it was ever so.

[97]*Relation*, 1680, p. 83.
[98]Quoted in Milner, 1983, p. 23.
[99]Snouck Hurgronje, *The Acehnese*, trans. A. W. S. O'Sullivan, 2 vols. (Leiden, 1906), 1:93–114, 2:277–314.

7

Religious Patterns and Economic Change in Siam in the Sixteenth and Seventeenth Centuries

Yoneo Ishii

Existing recensions of the Ayutthayan chronicles all agree in enumerating as "vassals" major port-cities along both sides of the Malay Peninsula, key principalities on the northern tributaries of the Chaophraya River, and an important port town in the southeast, thereby giving the impression of Ayutthaya as a well-organized kingdom capable of extending political control over a wide area of mainland Southeast Asia even at the time of its foundation in the mid-fourteenth century.[1] Modern research proposes a more diffuse picture of the Siamese kingdom, in which political power was shared by different royal families, each controlling crucial strategic centers of the region independently, and with the stronger trying to bring the weaker under at least nominal control through rituals, marriage, and other personal linkages. The integrity of the early Ayutthayan kingdom was achieved by the appointment of blood relatives of the kings to superintend the government of the most important provinces.[2] Such a decentralized state of

---

[1] The following sixteen *müangs* are enumerated as vassals (*phraya prathetsarat*): Melaka, Java, Tenasserim, Ligor, Tavoy, Martaban, Moulmein, Songkhla, Chantabun, Phitsanulok, Sukhothai, Phichai, Sawankhalok, Phichit, Kamphaengphet, and Nakhonsawan. (*Phraratcha Phongsawadan Krung Sayam chabap Phancanthanumat (Choem) kap Phracakphatiphong (Chad)*, ed. Nai Tri Amatayakun (in Thai) (Bangkok, 1964), pp. 2, 502).

[2] Nidhi Aeusrivongse, *Kanmuang Thai samai Phra Narai* [Politics in the Reign of Phra Narai] (in Thai) (Bangkok, 1980), p. 6. See also David K. Wyatt, *Thailand: A Short History* (New Haven, Conn., 1982), p. 72.

affairs may be reflected in the diversity of recorded designations in a Chinese chronicle of those who sent emissaries to China from Siam between 1371 and 1398.[3]

The administrative centralization of Siam has long been attributed to the effort of King Trailokanat (r. 1448–88), who issued laws on the civil, military, and provincial hierarchy in 1466, now retained in the Law of the Three Seals.[4] Today scholars tend to believe that the more institutionalized system of government described in these laws was little more than theoretical and only partially implemented. It was not until the next century during the reign of King Naresuen the Great (r. 1590–1605), who successfully regained the kingdom's independence from Burma, that Siam really emerged as one of the most powerful kingdoms in mainland Southeast Asia with a more or less institutionalized polity sustained by economic strength and military power.[5] What follows is a modest attempt to relate such a political consolidation of Siam in the sixteenth and seventeenth centuries to certain religious developments that seem to have taken place concomitantly.

Development of Ayutthayan Overseas Trade

Soon after his ascension to the throne in 1368, Emperor Hung Wu dispatched envoys to transmit the Imperial Proclamation of Enthronement to Southeast Asian kingdoms including Annam (1368), Champa, Java, Hsi-yang, (1369), and Siam (1370). The Siamese responded to this call from the new Chinese dynasty quickly and appreciatively. In fifty-two years between 1371 and 1423, Siam sent as many as sixty-two envoys, most with tributes of sappanwood and pepper, to the imperial court, far more than any other Southeast Asian kingdom. After 1428, however, the recorded dispatches of the Siamese tributary missions began to slacken; from 1447 onward Siamese visits to China became sporadic. *Tai Ming Shih-lu* records fewer than fifty tributary envoys from Siam in the period of almost two centuries between 1425 and

---

[3]Between 1371 and 1398 the senders of tributes from Siam are diversely recorded as Hsien Lo Kuo, Hsien Lo Hu Kuo, king of Hien Lo Kuo or king of Hien Lo Hu Kuo with or without regnal titles, king of Suphanburi, who is the heir of the king of Hsien Lo Hu Kuo, king of Suphanburi of Hsien Lo Hu Kuo, and so forth. Riichiro Fujiwara, using *Tai Ming Shih-lu*, has prepared a detailed list of tributary missions to China in the reigns of emperors Hung Wu and Yung Lo; *Tonan Ajia-shi no Kenkyu* [Studies on the History of South-East Asia] (in Japanese) (Kyoto, 1986), pp. 27–30, 57–59.

[4]D. G. E. Hall, *A History of South-East Asia*, 4th ed. (London, 1981), pp. 195–96.

[5]Nidhi, 1980, pp. 8–9.

1619.[6] The decrease in the number of recorded dispatches of embassies does not necessarily reflect a general decline in Siamese trade with China, however, since an increasing number of private traders must have entered into these lucrative transactions as the suppressive measures formerly imposed by the imperial authorities gradually slackened under ever-growing pressure from the maritime-oriented southeastern provinces of China, where 90 percent of the population lived off the sea. The *hai-chin* official interdict on private trade was finally lifted in 1567.

In contrast to the Siamese enthusiasm, the early Ming emperor paid little attention to this Buddhist kingdom.[7] In fact, after the first visit in 1371, no official mission was sent to Siam from the Ming court until the reign of Emperor Yung Lo (r. 1403–24), who ordered the dispatch of Cheng Ho's expedition to Hsi-yang, which included Siam in its list of destinations. Between 1403 and 1421, Siam received thirteen missions from China, including two visits by Cheng Ho's fleets, in 1408 and 1421.[8] It is interesting to note in this connection that in 1497, when a Siamese tribute mission reached China, "the Foreign Languages Department had no interpreter for Thai, so Grand Secretary Hsü P'u asked for a dispatch to be sent to Kwangtung [the provincial government] to investigate whether someone there could speak and write in that language."[9] Later, in 1579, the Siamese Language Department was created at the Official Translation Office (Ssŭ-i-kuan), a measure perhaps indicative of a growing recognition by the imperial government of the importance of Siam as a trade partner within the existing tributary system.

A study of trade in fifteenth- and sixteenth-century Siam cannot be complete without proper consideration of the activities of the Ryukyuan traders, who played a significant role in linking Siam with eastern Asia commercially. Between 1425 and 1564, sixty-one Ryukyuan fleets called at the port of Siam. Dispatches were particularly frequent between 1425 and 1442, during which time twenty-nine Ryukyuan ships visited Siam. A second wave followed between 1444 and 1480, during which time eleven ships were sent. After an apparent lacuna of nearly

[6]Calculated by the present writer based on extracts from *Tai Ming Shih-lu*, ed. Zhao Ling Yang et al., *Ming-Shih-lu chung zhi Tung-nan-a Shi-liao*, 2 vols. (in Chinese) (Hong Kong, 1968, 1976).

[7]*Huang-ming tsu-hsün* (Imperial Admonition to Posterity) counts Siam as one of the *pu-chan chu-i*, "a barbarian country [so remote and unimportant as to be] unworthy of conquering." See *Huang-ming tsu-hsün* in *Huang-ming chih-shu, hsia chüan* (Tokyo: Koten Kenkyu-kai, 1967), p. 3.

[8]Fujiwara, 1986, p. 61.

[9]*Ming-shih*, bk. 324, see also T. Grimm, "Thailand in the Light of Official Chinese Historiography: A Chapter in the 'History of the Ming Dynasty'," *JSS* 49, no. 1 (1961), 9.

thirty years, which is probably due to the loss of relevant records, the dispatch of "tributary" ships to Siam was resumed, and between 1526 and 1564 thirteen visits are recorded.[10] The Ryukyuans brought Chinese porcelain to Siam in exchange for sappanwood and pepper, which they purchased in Ayutthaya for reexport to eastern Asia. The widely known low price and abundance of sappanwood in Siam seem to have been a great attraction to the Ryukyuan traders, who profited enormously from this trade.

It must be emphasized in this connection that the Siamese government, with its strict control of trade, extracted no less benefit from this lucrative business than the incoming foreign merchants. This practice was known to the fifteenth-century Ryukyuan traders as *kuan-mâi* and *kuan-mái*, "official sale" and "official purchase." The rapacity of the Siamese functionaries may be guessed from a complaint made in one of the Ryukyuan dispatches dated 1424 addressed to "the Country of Siam." The writer of this petition appeals to the Siamese authorities over the unfair treatment received by his colleagues in an earlier visit to Ayutthaya, when their entire cargo of porcelain was "traded only under government supervision, and no private purchase of sappanwood was permitted." "We hope," he continues, "that . . . you will offer sympathy to the men from afar [this time] who have to undergo the hardships of the voyage, and that you will exempt them from government control in their sale of porcelains, allow them to purchase sappanwood, pepper, and other goods, and let them come home to our country."[11] In the following century, Tomé Pires implied that these extortions still prevailed: "Through the cunning [of the Siamese] the foreign merchants who go to their land and kingdom leave their merchandise in the land and are ill paid; and this happens to them all. . . . However, as the land is rich in good merchandise, they bear some things on account of the profit, as often happens to merchants, because otherwise there would be no trading."[12]

An early seventeenth-century Chinese description of Siam suggests that royal intervention in foreign trade continued in 1617: "When a ship has arrived, a watch [stationed at the third post] sends an urgent messenger to make a report of the arrival [of the ship] to their king. . . . At the [last] post, [the visitors] are always questioned about

[10]Yoneo Ishii, "The Ryukyu in Southeast Asian Trade in the 15th and 16th Centuries," in *Asian Panorama: Essays in Asian History, Past and Present*, ed. K. M. de Silva, Sirima Kiribamune, and C. R. de Silva (New Delhi, 1990), pp. 356–57.

[11]Atsushi Kobata and Mitsugu Matsuda, *Ryukyuan Relations with Korea and South Sea Countries* (Kyoto, 1969), pp. 55–56.

[12]Tomé Pires, *The Suma Oriental of Tomé Pires*, ed. and trans. Armando Cortesão, 2 vols. (London, 1944), 1:104.

their trade with countries nearby before they pay homage to the king. At the capital, they make a symbolic tribute to the king, who is invisible, staying in the inner sanctum."[13] In 1693, Simon de la Loubère referred directly to the king's intervention in foreign trade in Ayutthaya:

> Commerce requires a certain liberty: no person can resolve to go to Siam, necessarily to sell unto the King what is carry'd thither, and to buy of him alone what one would carry thence, when this was not the product of the Kingdom. For though there were several foreign Ships together at Siam, the Trade was not permitted from one Ship to the other, nor with the Inhabitants of the Country, Natives or Foreigners, till that the King, under the pretence of a preference due to his Royal dignity, had purchased what was best in the Ships, and at his own rate, to sell it afterwards as he pleased: because that when the season for the departure of the Ships presses on, the Merchants choose rather to sell to great loss, and dearly to buy a new Cargo, than to wait at Siam a new season to depart, without hopes of making a better Trade.[14]

Technological Innovation and Political Consolidation

Technological innovations in firearms from the sixteenth century had an unprecedented impact on political consolidation in various parts of the world.[15] In Asia the successful unification of Japan by Oda Nobunaga in the latter half of the sixteenth century is generally attributed to his prescient mastery of musketry. What enabled Nobunaga to procure the several thousand muskets he used most effectively in his unifying wars was the wealth resulting from his trade promotion policy. Almost contemporaneously, the same military revolution was in progress in Southeast Asia, including Siam and Burma, where modern firearms had been introduced by Portuguese merchants. There, unlike Japan, the Portuguese not only sold firearms to the Asian kings but also hired themselves out as mercenaries. In 1538, one hundred and twenty Portuguese were employed by King Phrachai (r. 1534–46) to instruct the Siamese soldiers in musketry. The Portuguese gunners and musketeers were incorporated into the existing military hierarchy as "experts on gunnery" with relevant official titles. In readiness for a possi-

[13]Chang Hsie, *Tung-hsi yang-k'ao*, bk. 2 (Peking, 1981), p. 40.
[14]Simon de la Loubère, *The Kingdom of Siam* (Singapore, 1986), p. 112.
[15]Geoffrey Parker, *The Military Revolution, Military Innovation, and the Rise of the West, 1500–1800* (Cambridge, 1988).

ble Burmese artillery attack, the old mud wall of the Siamese capital was replaced by brick walls in 1550. King Maha Thammaracha (r. 1569–90) was also an ardent buyer of cannon from foreign merchants.[16] Thus, by the time Naresuen the Great launched his campaign for the political consolidation of his father's realm after successfully regaining independence from Burma, the Siamese royal army was well versed in the use of firearms.

It is worth noting in this connection two important types of Siamese functionaries which Nidhi Aeusrivongse mentions in his analysis of the Ayutthayan bureaucracy, namely, "administrators" and "specialists," the latter being mostly foreigners placed under the direct and exclusive control of the king. The distinction between the two was so strict that no foreign "experts" or their descendants were permitted to become administrators.[17] The experts included "Brahmans" who conducted rituals, jurists, the Chinese in charge of foreign trade (commercial commissioners and navigators), and various craftsmen. The Ayutthayan king's monopoly of these resources of expertise in the fields of state ritual, military technology, and overseas trade, at least at one stage, contributed to the strengthening of his political power and the successful consolidation of his realm.

The Strengthening of Political Integration

As noted earlier, before the first fall in 1569 of Ayutthaya to the invading Burmese army, the Siamese king had hardly exercised his direct control beyond the capital and its adjacent area (known as *wong ratchathani*), the radius of which seldom exceeded one hundred kilometers. For the rest of his realm (the *phrayamahanakhon*), provinces governed by his princes or high officials and the semiindependent tributary states, he had to be satisfied with various token gestures of their political allegiance. King Naresuen the Great, whose dynamic leadership combined with his ability to maximize available political, economic, and military resources, not only regained independence from Burma in 1590 but also undertook the herculean task of transforming the hitherto fragmented kingdom into a more or less centralized state. To forestall local rebellion led by resident princes of high rank, the king abolished the *phrayamahanakhon* and reorganized the provinces outside

[16]W. A. R. Wood, *A History of Siam* (Bangkok, 1933), pp. 102–28; "Tamnaeng Na Thahan Hua Muang 14," in Thailand Fine Arts Department, *Rüang Kotmai Tra Sam Duang* [The Law of the Three Seals] (Bangkok, 1978), p. 163.

[17]Nidhi, 1980, p. 8. The distinction between these two categories may have become blurred, however, when some descendants of the "expert" group began to covet a higher status in the bureaucracy by moving into the administrative group.

the *wong ratchathani* into three classes known as first, second, and third provinces, to which royally appointed high officials were dispatched as governors. As Nicolas Gervaise observed, the king "always reserves to himself freedom to dismiss them at his pleasure, without their ever daring to protest against their dismissal."[18] The loyalty of the new provincial administrators was assured by obliging them to come, like any other official, to drink the water of allegiance in the capital, where they were questioned by the Minister of the Palace on the administration of their respective provinces.[19] The water of allegiance bound those who drank it with fear of ominous penalties threatened not only in this life but also in the life to come. In addition, the performance of provincial governors was monitored by the king, who "often nominates commissioners to go to the province to find out how they have performed their duties and to receive statements from people who may have some cause for complaint. If they are found guilty of misappropriation or any other criminal offence, these commissioners have authority to try them and condemn them to death."[20] Gervaise reported in 1688 a case involving the governor of Phitsanulok, who was convicted of malpractice on a large scale by two royally commissioned mandarins and executed in their presence.[21] According to Jeremias van Vliet, a servant of the VOC who stayed in Ayutthaya in the 1630s, King Prasatthong (r. 1629–56) did not allow the governors of the remote provinces to reside in one place for long for fear that their authority over the local populace might grow to a point beyond his control. The same Dutch observer continues, "the great mandarins (except Oubrat who is incapable by old age) were all transferred after 4 to 8 months from one office to the other, so that they could not have an opportunity to have a stronghold in one position."[22]

Hinduism and the Enhancement of Royal Power

Hinduism, which the Siamese had adopted along with Theravada Buddhism, continued to function, with its concept of divine kingship

---

[18]Nicolas Gervaise, *The Natural and Political History of the Kingdom of Siam*, trans. John Villiers (Bangkok, 1989), p. 72.

[19]H. G. Quaritch Wales, *Ancient Siamese Government and Administration* (New York, 1965), p. 108.

[20]Gervaise, 1989, p. 72.

[21]Ibid., p. 73.

[22]L. F. van Ravenswaay, "Translation of Jeremias van Vliet's Description of the Kingdom of Siam," *JSS* 7, no. 1 (1910), 61.

accompanied by grandiose rituals, to enhance the political prestige of the Ayutthayan king. In Siam, however, the divinity of Hindu kingship was inherited without the concomitant societal checks that had been developed by the Hindus: there was no spiritual authority to act as a countercheck on the secular power of the king. Unlike their colleagues in India, the Siamese *phram*, or Brahmans, far from being superior to the king were in fact the most subservient members of the court. The absence of any counterbalancing institution may have helped produce a degree of absolutism in Siam which had no parallel in India.[23]

One way the absolute power of the Ayutthayan king was manifested was in the performance of the *indrabhiṣeka*, the consecration ceremony of the emperor. This important Hindu ceremony was practiced in ancient Cambodia, brought to Siam probably in the mid-fifteenth century after the fall of Angkor, and revived to symbolize the omnipotent power of the Ayutthayan monarch. H. G. Quaritch Wales believes that the only recorded instance of this ceremony was performed in the reign of King Ramathibodi II (r. 1491–1529).[24] From a description of this ceremony in the Kot Monthienban, or Palatine Law, we know that it was a theatrical representation of the myth of the "Churning of the Ocean" in the Ramayana, where the king sits on top of an artificial Mount Meru, the abode of Indra, and is thereby identified with that powerful Hindu deity.[25] King Ramathibodi II would have earned the performance of this imperial ritual by successfully subduing Chiengmai and laying a foundation for the greater kingdom of Ayutthaya.

Buddhism and the Enhancement of Royal Power

However effective the flamboyant paraphernalia of Hinduism in enhancing royal dignity, the Hindu guise of Siamese kingship as expressed in the *indrabhiṣeka* should not blind us to the supremacy of Buddhism in legitimating the Ayutthayan monarchy. The Siamese king was, first and foremost, a Buddhist. Buddhism has never surrendered

[23]Santosh N. Desai, *Hinduism in Thai life* (Bombay, 1980), p. 61; H. G. Quaritch Wales, *Siamese State Ceremonies* (London, 1931), pp. 54–63.

[24]Quaritch Wales, 1931, pp. 122–23. But in the Luang Prasoet version of the Ayutthayan chronicle we read, under C.S. 919 (A.D. 1557), "Indra Bhisek (inauguration) took place for the new palace." See O. Frankfurter, "Events in Ayuddhya," quoted from the reproduction of the article in *The Siam Society 50th Anniversary Vol.1 1904–1929* (Bangkok, 1954), pp. 38–64. The event falls in the reign of King Maha Chakkraphat (r. 1548–69). His regnal title is a Thai form of *cakravartin* ("universal monarch").

[25]"Kot Monthienban 171," *Rüang Kotmai Tra Sam Duang*, p. 71.

its central position in the spiritual hierarchy to any other religion adopted by the Thai. The Brahmans who officiated at court rituals were treated in Ayutthayan bureaucracy as merely one category of experts, along with a Chinese captain of the royal junk or a Portuguese gunner. Later, the court Brahmans in Siam were made Buddhist and even required to pass through the novitiate as Buddhist monks before they could officiate at court rituals.[26]

As long as the king ruled his realm in conformity with the ten kingly virtues prescribed in the Buddhist Thammasat (*dhammasattham* in Pali), he could justify himself as *dhammaraja*, the king of righteousness, and thus be entitled to the obedience of his subjects. Enhancement of Buddhist values continues to be a prerequisite for any Thai ruler. One of the most significant occasions in which the Siamese king could openly exhibit to the public his royal bounty for the benefit of Buddhism was the *thot kathin* ceremony, the annual presentation of yellow robes to the monks held in October after the Buddhist Lent. Joost Schouten has left us a detailed description of the impressive royal procession in the seventeenth century in which "the King of Siam shews himself by water and land in state to his people, going to the principal Temple of the Gods, to offer there for the welfare of his Person and Kingdom."[27] Another public event of a religious nature involving the Thai king was the annual excursion to the Phraphutthabat ("Buddha's Footprint"), an event instituted by King Songtham (r. 1610–28) following its discovery in 1623 by a hunter at the foot of a hill northwest of Saraburi. This custom was made an official event by King Prasatthong (r. 1629–56) and continued by subsequent kings. Various festivities stretched over seven days, attracting a horde of pilgrims from different parts of the kingdom. The grandiose royal procession, lasting a few days either on land or on water, must have impressed the peasants living along the route between the capital and the site of the relic. The accompanying feasts in and around the site would have renewed the Buddhist identity of the participants and strengthened social ties.

The construction of royal temples was another exemplary act of the Ayutthayan king's religious piety. Chroniclers not infrequently honor royal enthusiasm in the construction and restoration of Buddhist monasteries. Ordinary Buddhists would have been encouraged to emulate

---

[26]Quaritch Wales, 1931, p. 57.

[27]François Caron and Joost Schouten, *A True Description of the Mighty Kingdoms of Japan and Siam* (Bangkok, 1986), p. 128. It is interesting to note that, in the procession reported by Schouten consisting of "fifteen or sixteen thousand persons," there were "two hundred *Japan* soldiers," obviously recruits from the Japanese trading community established outside the island of Ayutthaya since the end of the sixteenth century.

the meritorious precedent of their ruler according to their means. A rich high-ranking official might go so far as building a large temple at his own expense. Gervaise refers to "the pagoda which the *barcalon* [finance and foreign minister] had built for the king eight or nine years ago" as "a work of extraordinary beauty."[28] In and near the city of Ayutthaya there existed, according to one contemporary document, four hundred "beautiful temples, which are adorned with many gilded towers and pyramids. . . . Some temples are covered with gold, silver, and copper, so that they look elegant and ingenious and costly." There were "four principal temples of the whole country," that is, royal temples, whose names were recorded as wat Sy-serpudt (Wat Sri Sanphet), the Nappetat (Na Phra That), wat Deun (Wat Duan), and Thimphiathey (Thung Phaya Thai). In the pointed tower of the last-mentioned monastery, people believed there was "a costly ruby, the value of which can hardly be estimated and in order that nobody may take away the buried riches from the gods there are many dead guards placed there." It was also said that the value of the treasure lying under the Buddha images of Wat Sri Sanphet and Wat Na Phra That was so great that with it even "a ruined kingdom could be restored."[29]

Royal Control of the Buddhist Fraternity

One of the institutional features of Siamese Buddhism is its monasticism, the architectural representation of which is the temple and its accessories, pagodas, and Buddha images. The members of the Buddhist fraternity (*sangha*) who reside in these buildings are dependent on the voluntary support of the lay followers who hope to better their life here and hereafter by acts of *thambun* (merit making). The pure *sangha* with its precept-abiding monks is deservedly called "the field of merit," since it promises lay Buddhists who support them an increase in their merit, too. Although in Theravada countries the distinction is respected between the *sangha* (*phutthachak*) and the secular world (*anachak*), monks have often yielded to the secular power. The same process occurred in Siam in the sixteenth and seventeenth centuries.

Royal concern about the affairs of the *sangha* was clearly expressed in the institution, probably in the fifteenth century, of the *samanasak* (ecclesiastical rank) and *ratchathinnanam* (ecclesiastical title), both given by

[28]Gervaise, 1989, p. 167.
[29]van Ravenswaay, 1910, pp. 73–74.

the king to monks of a certain rank, together with a *sakdina* grade indicating their social status in the traditional Siamese bureaucratic hierarchy. Thus in the Law of the Military and Provincial Hierarchy, the Buddhist clergy were classified into six categories. If versed in the Buddhist doctrine, a novice had a *sakdina* grade of 300, a monk 600, and a monk of *phra khru* rank up to 2,400. If not so well versed, these grades were reduced to 200, 400 and 1,000, respectively.[30] De la Loubère speaks of a *sancrat* (*sangharat*, or *sangharaja* in Pali), head of the monastery of a certain rank, who alone "can make Talapoins [monks]." He also writes, "the King of Siam gives to the principal *Sancrats* a Name, an Umbrella, a Sedan, and some men to carry it. . . . The *Sancrat* of the Palace [temple?] is now called *Pra Viriat*."[31] Gervaise, a contemporary of de la Loubère, agrees with him that the order of a monk (*bhikkhu*) "can only be conferred by a *sancrat*." Gervaise maintains that the *sancrat* "are nominated by the king," from among those *bad-luang*, or priests, who are "from the best temple or most versed in knowledge of the law or most revered for the holiness of their life." The pagodas where the *sancrat* reside, he continues, "are distinguished from the rest by their beauty, their riches and their antiquity."[32] Earlier Huang-chung refers to *sêng-wang* in his *Hai-yü*, a sixteenth-century geography of Melaka and Ayutthaya. This Chinese term can be rendered verbatim into Pali as *sangharaja* and probably corresponds to the *sancrat* of the French writers. The Chinese author notes that in Siam monks are highly respected; the authority of the high-ranking monks "may be considered equal to that of the king." His status in society was so high that "a criminal condemned to death may be pardoned at his request."[33]

The extent of Siamese royal preoccupation with *sangha* affairs can be further seen in the Phraratcha Puccha ("The Royal Questions"), a collection of questions asked by three Ayutthayan kings of the late seventeenth and early eighteenth centuries of certain high-ranking monks on various topics, both doctrinal and ecclesiastic. Of special interest are those concerned with the administration of the *sangha*, which in theory has little to do with the secular king. King Phra Narai (r. 1656–88), for example, asked whether the ordination of a eunuch was appropriate. He also questioned whether monks should be allowed to pass critical comment on the conduct of the king.[34]

---

[30]"Tamnaeng Na Thahan Hua Müang 27," *Rüang Kotmai Tra Sam Duang*, p. 172.
[31]de la Loubère, 1986, p. 114.
[32]Gervaise, 1989, pp. 144–45.
[33]*Hai-yü*, bk. 1., in *Chung-kuo Shi-hsüeh Ts'ung-shu 35* (Taipei, 1984), p. 6.
[34]*Prachum Phraratcha Phuccha*, pt. 1. (cremation volume) (Bangkok, 1921), pp. 105–7, 75.

Royal Control of the Buddhist *Sangha* Strengthened

In the reign of King Rama I (r. 1782–1809) of the Chakri dynasty, a series of royal decrees was directly geared at controlling the affairs of the *sangha*.[35] Few documents from the Ayutthayan kingdom which directly indicate secular control of the *sangha* have survived, however, except one contained in the Phraratchakamnot Kau ("The Old Royal Decree"), dated 1737 and issued by King Boromakot (r. 1733–58), which prohibited a monk from interfering in the secular administration of justice in a case involving temple slaves turned bandits. Our reading of documents of the seventeenth century, however, suggests that numerous other royal decrees regarding *sangha* affairs must have been issued.[36] Concerning the privileges enjoyed by the monks, Gervaise writes: "Of all the privileges enjoyed by the monks that which exempts them from any taxes and public duties is easily the most considerable. It is this exemption which results in their being so numerous. The idleness which reigns in their monasteries is a potent attraction for this nation, which recognizes scarcely any pleasure greater than that of living without doing anything and at somebody else's expense."[37]

In a lightly populated country such as Siam in the Ayutthayan period, where the control of manpower was one of the most important tasks of any ruler, such a situation could not be ignored. Although courting disapproval from monks and concerned laymen, kings sometimes dared to intervene in the affairs of the *sangha*. Such was the case of King Phra Narai, whose intervention was at first indirect. The ecclesiastical examination he instituted ostensibly promoted Buddhist learning while aiming to eliminate unworthy elements from the *sangha*, otherwise outside his jurisdiction. De la Loubère writes: "To diminish the number of these privileged Persons, he [the king of Siam] causes them to be from time to time examined as to their knowledge, which respects the *Balie* language and its Books."[38]

According to Gervaise, the studying of the Balie (Pali) language was greatly respected in Ayutthaya and was thought to be essential to the monks. To become *bad-luang*, Gervaise writes, "they must at least be able to read and expound a little. This rule had been so neglected for

[35]*Rüang Kotmai Tra Sam Duang*, pp. 544–69.
[36]Ibid., pp. 602–4.
[37]Gervaise, 1989, p. 147.
[38]de la Loubère, 1986, p. 115.

Figure 6. King Narai leaving his palace on an elephant, his ministers prostrating them-selves before him, as drawn by a member of the French embassy. Photo: Bibliothèque Nationale, Paris, Estampes Od. 59.

many years that most monks could not even read the script until four years ago, when the king found a remedy for this neglect."[39]

King Phra Narai enforced this measure by expelling idle monks from the *sangha*. De la Loubère writes: "When we arrived in this Country, he had just reduc'd several Thousand to the Secular condition, because they had not been found learned enough."[40] Gervaise reports that a few days after the examination, "thousands of men still wearing their monk's robes could be seen working on the land, carrying bricks and suffering punishment for their ignorance."[41]

[39]Gervaise, 1989, p. 152. In Siam the Pali language used to be written in Khmer script, which ordinary people could not read.
[40]de la Loubère, 1986, p. 115.
[41]Gervaise, 1989, p. 152.

The examiner appointed by King Phra Narai was not a monk but a layman by the name of Oc Louang Souracac, "a young man of about Twenty eight or Thirty years old, the son of that Oc Pra Pipitcharatcha, who . . . commands the Elephants." That the disciplinary measures violated the time-honored custom of respect for the autonomy of the *sangha* by the secular power was demonstrated in the protest immediately lodged by the more disciplined *araññavasins*, ("Talapoins of the Woods"), who "had refused to submit to the Examination of a Secular, and consented to be examined only by one of their Superiors."[42]

At the end of the sixteenth century, King Naresuen not only regained political independence for his realm but also succeeded, by maximizing the fruits of prosperity derived from the royal monopoly of trade, in making the kingdom of Ayutthaya "the regional power of the first importance."[43] As his territory expanded, the need for ideological reinforcement of political authority was intensified. Throughout the sixteenth and seventeenth centuries, it has been noted, the Siamese kings seem to have been driven to strengthen their authority by elaborating their legitimizing symbols, on the one hand, and by domesticating religious institutions that provided them with a basis for legitimate rule, on the other. The institution of the *indrabhiṣeka* coronation, for example, represents a step toward the former. Magnificent images of the Hindu deities continued to be produced under royal sponsorship and demanded high respect at court ceremonies.[44] It has been pointed out, however, that Hinduism was accorded only a subordinate position in the Siamese belief system. The imported Angkorian concept of *dewaraja* (god-king) had little significance in Siam beyond enhancing royal dignity, since Hindu divinities had no place in the Buddhist faith of the populace.[45]

In Ayutthaya, Buddhism played by far the most important role in sustaining the established social order. Thus the Siamese king continuously used Buddhist symbols to enhance his political authority. Conspicuous expenditure for the construction of religious edifices and luxurious royal processions to centers of pilgrimage both served this purpose. At the same time, the king, fearing the Buddhist *sangha* was enjoying a degree of autonomy that might turn it into a haven for those

[42]de la Loubère, p. 115.

[43]Wyatt, 1982, p. 61.

[44]Thus we read in a royal chronicle that in 1601 "statues of Siva and Narayana were received, and on one and the same day homage was paid to the four statues [of the Brahmanic gods] by being carried in procession." Frankfurter, 1910, p. 62.

[45]Prince Dhani Nivat, "The old Siamese Conception of the Monarchy," in *Collected Articles by H. H. Prince Dhani Nivat Kromamun Bidayalabh Bhrdihyakorn* (Bangkok, 1969), pp. 100–101.

hoping to evade their corvée duties, eventually instituted an ecclesiastical examination under the pretext of screening the worthy monks from the layabouts.

The strengthening of secular intervention in the *sangha* which appears to have marked these centuries, along with the administrative development of the Ayutthayan kingdom, foreshadowed the total submission of the Buddhist *sangha* to the state represented by the promulgation of the Sangha Administration Law in the beginning of this century.

PART 4

Key Problems of the Seventeenth-Century Transition

One of the topics of great interest in the early modern world is the origin of the dichotomy between a Europe increasingly well endowed with capital and technology and the rest of the world, of which Southeast Asia is a particularly interesting case.

The three contributors to this section attack this problem from different perspectives. Pierre-Yves Manguin describes the large trading junks that dominated seaborne trade in the fifteenth and sixteenth centuries and analyzes the reasons for their disappearance. In the next two essays, the question whether the seventeenth century marked a critical retreat from commercialization by two states on the Southeast Asian mainland is considered. Victor Lieberman argues that in Burma it did not. Although seaborne trade became a less important factor in state revenues, the processes of commercialization and centralization continued relatively undisturbed. In Siam, according to Dhiravat na Pombejra, there was a dramatic decline in trade with Muslims and Europeans at the end of the seventeenth century, though Chinese trade partly filled the gap.

8

The Vanishing *Jong:*
Insular Southeast
Asian Fleets in Trade and War
(Fifteenth to Seventeenth Centuries)

Pierre-Yves Manguin

Research on the history of insular Southeast Asian trade networks has recently exposed the striking simultaneity of two trends that appear, at first sight, to be contradictory. Economic historians tell us that the significant economic boom experienced by sixteenth-century Old World states was largely generated by the growth of international exchange, and we also know that Southeast Asia as a whole, and its insular portion in particular, was part and parcel of these trade networks and experienced between the fifteenth and first half of the seventeenth centuries the same drastic economic growth.[1] Research carried out on more technical aspects of maritime history has also shown that these thriving insular Southeast Asian polities built and sailed during the fifteenth and early sixteenth centuries trading fleets of oceangoing vessels. These were among the main carriers of the eastern portion of this international trade. The mystery arises when all sources confirm that these ships of exceptional tonnage—inheritors of a Southeast Asian shipbuilding tradition by then some two thousand years old—had virtually disappeared by the end of the sixteenth century,

[1] For a recent, lengthy exposition on this Southeast Asian "age of commerce," see Anthony Reid, *Southeast Asia in the Age of Commerce, 1450–1680,* vol. 1: *The Lands below the Winds* (New Haven, Conn., 1988), and "An 'Age of Commerce' in Southeast Asian History," *MAS* 24, no..1 (1990), 1–30.

leaving behind only local fleets of much smaller coasters, precisely at a time when there was a greatly increased tonnage to carry about.

In this essay I try to reconcile these seemingly contradictory conditions. To do so, I first document the disappearance of the Southeast Asian component of Asian high-seas trading fleets and identify the replacement carriers. Then I describe and explain the concomitant development of war fleets and draw some tentative conclusions.

The Trading Fleets

When the Portuguese first arrived in Southeast Asian waters in 1509, they referred to a widely represented trading ship which they called *junco* (junk), a standard Portuguese transcription of Malay or Javanese *jong*. Malay classical texts such as the *Sejarah Melayu* often mention the existence of these trading *jong*. To the Portuguese sailors' surprise, they were more often than not larger than their own largest ships. The firsthand knowledge they gained of these vessels allowed them to produce excellent descriptions of their features, all of them typical of Southeast Asian technical traditions. Of concern to us here is their tonnage: it was considerable, at least by Portuguese standards of the time. The large Javanese fleet that sailed off Japara in 1512 to attack Melaka included some 60 *jong*, all of them over 200 tons burden.[2] There are sufficient indications in the texts to let us ascertain an average burden for these large *jong* of 350 to 500 tons deadweight; they would even have, exceptionally, reached a thousand tons and carried a thousand men aboard. During the first quarter of the sixteenth century, the main builders of these huge vessels were still to be found in harbor cities along the northern Javanese coast, on the southern coast of Borneo and in Pegu, all these areas being close to teak forests.[3] In the late fifteenth or early sixteenth century these *jong* carried cargoes belonging to rulers and merchants based in Melaka and in various other

---

[2]Tons, here and throughout, designate metric tons or deadweight tons.

[3]P.-Y. Manguin, "The Southeast Asian Ship: An Historical Approach," *JSEAS* 11, no. 2 (1980), 266–76. This essay, based on textual sources and ethnographic data only, was written before nautical archaeology brought about new data concerning shipbuilding techniques. Updates on archaeological data are found, together with the relevant bibliographical references, in J. Green and R. Harper, *The Maritime Archaeology of Shipwrecks and Ceramics in Southeast Asia*, Australian Institute for Maritime Archaeology Special Publication no. 4 (Albert Park, Australia, 1987), 1–37; P.-Y. Manguin, "The Trading Ships of Insular Southeast Asia: New Evidence from Indonesian Archaeological Sites," in *Proceedings, Pertemuan Ilmiah Arkeologi 5, Yogyakarta 1989*, Ikatan Ahli Arkeologi Indonesia (Jakarta, 1989), 1:200–220; and idem., "Trading Ships of the South China Sea: Shipbuilding Techniques and Their Role in the History of the Development of Asian Trade Networks," *JESHO* (in press).

harbor cities of Southeast Asia. They sailed chiefly to southern China, Maluku, and the Coromandel. But there are clear indications in Portuguese sources of late fifteenth- or early sixteenth-century Indian Ocean trips leading them as far west as the Maldives, Calicut, Oman, Aden, and the Red Sea, and the Portuguese transcribed still vivid memories of earlier voyages to Madagascar.[4]

The existence of these large ocean-going *jong* does not, of course, preclude that of a significant fleet of lesser coasters (under 100 tons) composed of small *jong* or other round bottoms and a multitude of multipurpose long vessels (*balang, lancang, kelulus, penjajap*) that could serve in war as well as in peace. In a period of prosperity, with no monopolies enforced, one expects to find both large traders specializing in long distances and weighty goods, sustained by communities of wealthy merchants gathered in large harbor cities, and a multitude of smaller boats plying interstitial networks, accumulating cargo for collection in main ports. But only the larger vessels attracted the attention of Portuguese witnesses: due to the absence of figures for the coasting fleet, it is unfortunately impossible to evaluate the total tonnage of the merchant fleet for the early sixteenth century.[5]

When the Dutch arrived in the region at the turn of the seventeenth century, they also came across local merchant vessels. But they only described vessels of a much smaller tonnage, as did contemporary Portuguese sources. The much reduced image they conveyed is that which was then taken as a basis for evaluation by early historians of Southeast Asian trade networks, including those—such as J. C. van Leur and M. A. P. Meilink-Roelofsz—who aimed at giving back to local shippers and traders their place in the economic history of the region. Drawing their information from Dutch sources of the first half of the seventeenth century, they described large fleets composed of vessels of 20 to a maximum of 200 tons, with a possible average of 100 tons. The only conspicuous exceptions were the *jong* belonging to Japara in the 1620s, some of which apparently still carried 200 tons and more. These

---

[4]Mentions of Southeast Asian shipping in the Indian Ocean are found in Geneviève Bouchon, "Les premiers voyages portugais à Pasai et à Pégou (1512–1520)," *Archipel* 18 (1979), 134 (Oman); Fernão Lopes de Castanheda, *História do descobrimento e conquista da Índia pelos Portugueses* (Coimbra, 1924–33), 2.21.256, 2.39.296 (Maldives and Red Sea); *The Book of Duarte Barbosa*, ed. M. L. Dames, 2 vols. (London, 1918), 1:56, 2:117 (Coromandel, Sri Lanka, Aden); Tomé Pires, *The Suma Oriental of Tomé Pires*, ed. and trans. Armando Cortesão, 2 vols. (London, 1944), 2:174, 182, 272 (Coromandel, Bengal, Aden); Gabriel Ferrand, "Les voyages des Javanais à Madagascar," *Journal Asiatique* (1910), 281–330 (Madagascar). On the Coromandel–Melaka trade, the most thorough study is now that of Sanjay Subrahmanyam, *The Political Economy of Commerce: Southern India, 1500–1650*, Cambridge South Asia Series (Cambridge, 1990).

[5]On the relationship between tonnages and the structure of trade, it is enlightening to refer to what Fernand Braudel has to say on the matter in his *La Méditerrannée*, 2 vols. (Paris, 1966), 1:271–86.

were used in the lucrative, monopolistic trade in rice carried out by the Javanese harbor city.[6]

The erroneous postulate of Dutch authors on the tonnage of pre–seventeenth-century ships stems from the limitations of the Portuguese sources they used. Hence also—chiefly in Meilink-Roelofsz's work—several inconsistencies and contradictions appeared when they tried to reconcile these data with the few earlier sources they had access to. Meilink-Roelofsz rejected statements on tonnages larger than those described in later Dutch sources and the mere possibility of oceanic navigation by Southeast Asians: she acknowledged the reputed Javanese shipbuilding of the early sixteenth century but stated that production must have been limited to "small, fast-sailing war proas and cargo ships of small tonnage"; the Javanese must have had navigational aids "to enable them to transport the produce of their fertile island over fairly long distances"; she also explained that Javanese junks were very solidly constructed but "cannot have been very suitable for navigating the Indian Ocean"; "foreigners" were called to the rescue when sources could not be rejected forthright. Portuguese monopolistic practices were nevertheless invoked to explain the disappearance of *jong* trade, despite the earlier denial of its magnitude.[7]

Basing his work on scattered figures gathered from the first half of the seventeenth century, van Leur deduced overall tonnages for foreign and local fleets trading at Batavia and extrapolated these data to calculate total tonnages for regional fleets. The paucity and inadequacy of the statistical sources he used do not allow much confidence in such figures, and there are no overall figures available for the early sixteenth century in any case to compare them with. Suffice it to note here that, with the exception of Japara, the picture that emerges for seventeenth-

[6]J. C. van Leur, *Indonesian Trade and Society: Essays in Asian Social and Economic History* (The Hague, 1955; 2d ed., 1967), pp. 98, 128, 195–96, 212–14, 349–50, n. 40; M. A. P. Meilink-Roelofsz, *Asian Trade and European Influence in the Indonesian Archipelago between 1500 and about 1630* (The Hague, 1962), p. 286. More recently, Gabriel Rantoandro drew more systematically on one such category of sources (the *Dagh Register Casteel Batavia*) and reached the same conclusion; see "Commerce et navigation dans les Mers de l'Insulinde d'après le Dagh-Register de Batavia (1624–1682)," *Archipel* 35 (1988), 51–87; Manuel Godinho de Erédia's early seventeenth-century description of Melaka carries portraits of smaller local ships; see *Malaca, l'Inde méridionale et le Cathay*, ed. L. Jansen, 2 vols. (Brussels, 1881–82). There are practically no Portuguese sources available from the 1540s to the late 1580s in Insular Southeast Asia. This gap does not facilitate our understanding of the changes occurring during the mid-sixteenth century.

[7]Meilink-Roelofsz, 1962, pp. 39, 65, 103–5, 114, 154. "A century of Portuguese monopoly policy apparently put an end to the Malaccan junk trade. . . . most of these junks must have been of foreign construction" (p. 65). In a later essay, Meilink-Roelofsz seems to be more aware of such contradictions, without going back on her earlier position; ("Trade and Islam in the Malay-Indonesian Archipelago prior to the Arrival of the Europeans," in *Islam and the Trade of Asia*, ed. D. S. Richards (Oxford, 1970), pp. 137–58).

century Malay and Javanese shipping is that of a sizable fleet of small-ish vessels involved exclusively in regional networks and maintained by merchants of the peddler category. From long-distance Asia-wide trade carried out in large *jong* to merely regional networks of small coasters, the change is considerable. It would take only a few more decades for the Dutch and the newly established Mataram sultanate jointly to contribute to the total disappearance of Javanese *pasisir* indigenous shipping, but this is another story.

Shifts in Asian Trade Networks

Early attempts at explaining changes in the sixteenth century were based on a crude awareness of the effects of Lusitanian presence in insular Southeast Asia. C. R. Boxer, V. Magalhães Godinho, L. F. Thomaz, and Sanjay Subrahmanyam have since then demonstrated that Portuguese attempts at imposing monopolies on Asian trade were far from successful, be it on Moluccan spices or on the pepper in the west of the Archipelago. Only a fraction of the Asian production of spices was ever consumed by the whole of Christendom in the fifteenth and sixteenth centuries, and a large share of that reached Europe through Asian channels. This is not to say that the official Portuguese commerce, carried out in the name of the crown from Melaka and a few outposts—not to mention the ever-growing private trade of the *casados* diaspora—had a negligible impact on local societies (if only in terms of reactions against the newcomers, as we see below). From the economic point of view, however, the Portuguese were but another component, another competitor on the local scene and in no way able to supplant their predecessors, be they Southeast Asians, Tamils, Gujaratis, or Chinese.[8]

[8]C. R. Boxer, "A Note on Portuguese Reactions to the Revival of the Red Sea Spice Trade and the Rise of Acheh, 1540–1600," *JSEAH* 10, no. 3 (1969), 415–28; V. Magalhães Godinho, *Os Descobrimentos e a Economia Portuguesa*, 2 vols. (Lisbon, 1963–65), 1:513; L.-F. Ferreira Reis Thomaz, "Maluco e Malaca," in *A viagem de Fernão de Magalhães a questó das Molucas*, ed. A. Teixeira da Mota, Centro de Estudos de Cartografia Antiga Memória no. 16 (Lisbon, 1975), pp. 27–48; idem., *Nina Chatu e o Comércio Português em Malaca* (Lisbon, 1976); idem., "Malaka et ses communautés marchandes au tournant du 16e siècle," in *Marchands et hommes d'affaires asiatiques dans l'Océan Indien et la Mer de Chine, 13e-20e siècles*, ed. D. Lombard and J. Aubin (Paris, 1988), pp. 31–48; Subrahmanyam, 1990. The role of the *casados* in insular Southeast Asia has yet to receive much attention. C. R. Boxer gives a first survey of the question; "Casados and Cabotagem in the Estado da India, 16th/17th Centuries," in *Actas do II Seminário International de História Indo-Portuguesa*, ed. Luís de Albuquerque and Inácio Guerreiro (Lisbon, 1985), pp. 119–35. Sanjay Subrahmanyam has started research on the subject, from the Indian side of the Bay of Bengal; "The Tail Wags the Dog: Or Some Aspects of the External Relations of the Estado da India, 1570–1600," forthcoming.

Therefore, to account for the downfall of the Southeast Asian component of Asian oceanic networks, rather than simply consider the Portuguese impact on insular Southeast Asia, I believe one should examine the global transformations that occurred in trade networks during the fifteenth and later centuries. The growth of Southeast Asian trade appears to have started in the fifteenth century and, possibly, to have peaked at the end of the century. The disruption brought about by aggressive Portuguese tactics in the western part of the Indian Ocean at the turn of the sixteenth century was short-lived and the consequent general slump in the spice trade was quickly overcome. Asian traders, as well as the Portuguese crown, soon recaptured more than their share of the profits.[9] In the Indonesian Archipelago, geopolitical changes occurring during the sixteenth century were in fact only an indirect consequence of the Portuguese takeover of Melaka. Indeed, a first explanation can be found in the defeat of the centripetal forces that had earlier worked in favor of the Malay harbor city, rather than in a monopolistic strategy carried out after its takeover by Western intruders. Driven as a wedge into the very heart of the converging network built up during the fifteenth century (a revival of the earlier centralizing process initiated by Sriwijaya around the Straits area), the Portuguese city cut it into two separate halves. In doing so, it set to work centrifugal forces and facilitated the multiplication of nodal points and entrepôts for local imports and exports. Such centrifugal tendencies in fact appear already to have been at work before the Portuguese entered the scene. The huge Javanese fleet of Patih Yunus sailed from Japara to attack Melaka in 1512. The attack was said to have been in preparation for many years and originally planned by the Javanese to take the Malay city.[10] In the second half of the century, as a consequence of these geopolitical shifts, two major trading polities appeared to the west and east of the Portuguese city (the growth of Makassar came later): Aceh became the main export center for the Muslim pepper trade to the Indian Ocean and the Red Sea; Banten dealt with the South China Sea market and pepper also dominated exchanges. By the end of the sixteenth century, pepper had become the major export of Southeast Asia. The growing demand for this staple commodity generated a considerable extension of cultivated areas and a shift toward cash crop agriculture. This in turn implied a change in the power structure of the

---

[9]Reid, 1990.

[10]João de Barros and Diogo do Couto, *Da Ásia* (Lisbon, 1777–78), 2.9.4; Castanheda, 1924–33, 3.100–102; R. A. Kern had already noted that Patih Yunus's fleet could not have originally been aimed at the Portuguese; "Pati Unus en Sunda," *BKI* 108 (1952), 125–26.

dominating pepper-producing polities, with increasing territoriality, centralization, and absolutism.

The global volume of goods traded to and from Southeast Asia, with pepper taking the lead, underwent a considerable boom during the second half of the sixteenth and first half of the seventeenth centuries.[11] The concomitant decrease in the tonnage of Southeast Asian ships can therefore only indicate that, during this same period, a share of this long-distance shipping must have changed hands. To the best of my knowledge, neither Aceh nor Banten owned large trading ships in the sixteenth century, and I have not come across references to maintaining or building such vessels in either place.[12] One question therefore needs to be answered: who took over the *jong*'s share of long-distance shipping of trade commodities to and from Southeast Asia?

Two Asian powers seem to have profited from this reorientation of trade networks. On the western side, Gujaratis soon dominated the Indian Ocean and Red Sea pepper and textile trade. They had long been active in Indian Ocean trade. It appears that, before Melaka was founded, they had gone all the way to eastern Java to sell their textiles for Moluccan spices. Later they sailed only as far as the Melaka entrepôt. They were driven out of their prominent position in the Malay city by the Portuguese, who favored the non-Muslim Tamil community. By the middle of the sixteenth century, they had regained their ground and an eminent position in Aceh: a large share of their pepper was purchased there and then transported in Gujarati bottoms to the Red Sea via the Maldives. It is worth noting here that Gujarati commerce in Aceh appears to have doubled in volume during the sixteenth century.[13] The growing trade between Masulipatnam and Aceh in the last quarter of the sixteenth century points to another facet of Aceh's commercial role: the replacement of Melaka as an entrepôt for the non-Portuguese Indian Ocean seaborne trade.[14] On the South China Sea side, trade at Banten was chiefly carried out with China, and Chinese junks and shippers were the new transporters. This happens to be the time when the Ming ban on trade was lifted (1567) and when Fujian

---

[11]Reid, 1990.

[12]Only later (after 1650) do we hear of a *wangkang* built in Banten by a local Chinese; Hoesein Djajadiningrat, *Critische Beschouwing van de Sadjarah Banten* (Haarlem, 1913), p. 62. During the decade preceding Banten's final demise under the VOC (1682), Sultan Tirtayasa appears to have successfully resuscitated a locally based fleet of high-seas traders; F. Colombijn, "Foreign Influence on the State of Banten, 1596–1682," *Indonesia Circle* 50 (1989), 25.

[13]Boxer, 1969; Geneviève Bouchon, "Un microcosme: Calicut au 16e siècle," in Lombard and Aubin, 1988, p. 54; Reid, 1990, p. 22.

[14]Subrahmanyam, 1990, p. 147.

merchants swept in, after more than a century of high-seas activities confined to illegality during which trade with the South Seas was never able to develop naturally.[15] In the early seventeenth century, Chinese merchants and advisers had acquired powerful positions at the Banten court which helped them foster their own trade ventures. By the turn of the seventeenth century, Aceh and Banten had therefore taken away a major share of Melaka's earlier role as a terminus for Indian Ocean and South China Sea shipping.

Both Chinese and Gujaratis made use of very large ships (500 to 1,000 tons) built along their own local shipbuilding traditions. These are therefore the oceangoing vessels that replaced the Southeast Asian component from high-seas shipping in the Indian Ocean and the South China Sea. Indeed, this is when the meaning of "junk" (and other European cognates), until then used as a transcription of Malay or Javanese *jong*, shifted for good toward that of "Chinese vessel." In Aceh, the large traders sailing off to the Red Sea were always referred to as *naos*—a term never applied to vessels of Southeast Asian build.[16]

In precisely the same manner as the Malay or Javanese *jong* on the same routes converging on pre–sixteenth-century Melaka, these huge Gujarati and Chinese vessels were well suited to the seasonal traffic of weighty commodities (pepper, textiles, ceramics) over long distances. But their ports of origin were no longer in Southeast Asia. The exception of Japara, noted above, was possible only because that harbor city managed to maintain for a while under Mataram—under the protection of a state monopoly—its trade in Javanese rice (another bulk com-

---

[15]Bobo Wiethoff, *Die Chinesische Seeverbotspolitik und der private Uberseehandel von 1368 bis 1567* (Hamburg, 1963); Leonard Blussé, "Chinese Trade to Batavia during the Days of the V.O.C.," *Archipel* 18 (1979), 195–214; Chang Teh-Ch'ang, "Maritime Trade at Canton during the Ming Dynasty," *Chinese Social and Political Science Review* 17 (1933–34), 264–82; Ng Chin-Keong, "Gentry-Merchants and Peasant-Peddlars: The Responses of the South Fukienese to the Off-shore Trading Opportunities, 1522–1566," *Nanyang University Journal* (1973), 173; Michel Cartier, "Le commerce de l'Océan Indien vu de Chine," in Lombard and Aubin, 1988, pp 125–45.

[16]*Naos do Gujarate* or *do Achem* are repeatedly mentioned and at times described at Aceh in Portuguese sources, as early as the 1510s; see Pires, 1944, 2:463; Boxer, 1969, p. 427. These belonged to a shipbuilding tradition different from that of Southeast Asia; P.-Y. Manguin, "Late Mediaeval Asian Shipbuilding in the Indian Ocean: A Reappraisal," *Moyen Orient & Océan Indien* 2, no. 2 (1985), 1–30. To state that the Chinese junks were built according to purely Chinese traditions is in fact inaccurate: recent finds in Southeast Asian marine archaeology suggest that some, if not most, of the ships used in the sixteenth and seventeenth centuries by southern Chinese traders belonged to a hybrid technical tradition, the "South China Sea tradition," which shared many Southeast Asian features; it is not yet clear if this hybridization took place around the period studied here or earlier; see P.-Y. Manguin, "Relationship and Cross-Influence between South-East Asian and Chinese Shipbuilding Traditions," *Final Report, SPAFA Workshop on Shipping and Trade Networks in Southeast Asia* (Bangkok, 1985), pp. 197–212, and idem., 1989. The merchants and shippers of such junks engaged in trade with Banten, however, were ethnic Chinese. Some vessels may have then already been built by or for them in Southeast Asia, to their own specifications, as also observed in the eighteenth and nineteenth centuries (see also note 12 above).

modity). Alone in Java it therefore managed to sustain at sea a local fleet of relatively large *jong* into the 1620s.[17]

The War Fleets

Historians have invoked the superiority of European armament and tactics to account for the failure of Asians to face up to the challenges of the sixteenth and seventeenth centuries. Destruction of insular Southeast Asian fleets has similarly been attributed to unsuccessful warfare with the Portuguese. Naval battles were no doubt numerous during the sixteenth century. But not all of them were fought against the Lusitanian enemy and, when they were, the initiative for war at sea often rested with the Southeast Asian powers, leaving the Portuguese largely on the defensive. With the exception of the early sixteenth century, most battles were fought against attacking Acehnese fleets; Portuguese attacks on Aceh were few, underpowered, and unsuccessful. More than a few battles were fought by Southeast Asians alongside the Portuguese against another local power. Many others resulted from regional feuds in which the Portuguese had little or no say, and these too contributed their share to the overall militarization of Southeast Asian waters (see the tables at the end of this chapter for a summary of sixteenth- and seventeenth-century descriptions of war fleets in insular Southeast Asia).

Such battles could at times be murderous, but most appear either to have constituted an essentially ritual display of might or to have been discontinued after the first noble blood was shed.[18] The history of the various polities sharing the Southeast Asian scene in the sixteenth century in fact shows that "defeats" at sea were far from removing them from the local scene. Fleets said to have been destroyed—such as those of Java—kept being reborn from their ashes (Japara carried out at least three major attacks on Melaka, with huge fleets, during the sixteenth century; see Table 2). Examples to illustrate this increase in the size and power of war fleets could be taken from many places in sixteenth-century Southeast Asia: Japara, Banten, Bintan, Johor, Ling-

[17]H. T. Colenbrander, *Jan Pietersz. Coen*, 5 vols. (The Hague, 1919), 1:419–20; H. J. de Graaf, *De Regering van Sultan Agung, Vorst van Mataram, 1613–1645*, VKI 23 (The Hague, 1958); van Leur, 1967, p. 372, n. 51.

[18]Anthony Reid, *Europe and Southeast Asia: The Military Balance*, James Cook University South East Asian Committee Occasional Paper, no. 16 (Townsville, Qld., 1982); Manguin, "Of Fortresses and Galleys: The 1568 Acehnese Siege of Melaka, Following a Contemporary Bird's-Eye View," in *Asian Studies in Honour of Prof. C. R. Boxer*, ed. G. Bouchon and P.-Y. Manguin, MAS 22, no. 3 (1988).

Figure 7. Tidore *kora-kora* surrounding two ships of the Dutch fleet, 1600. The king's galley is marked D. From *Tweede Schipvaart,* vol. 3, ed. J. Keuning (The Hague, 1942).

ga, Inderagiri, Pahang, Patani, or Aru all made more or less important fleets ready in various bellicose circumstances. Aceh, however, is the most revealing of all cases because of the sheer size and power of its fleets and the multiplication of attacks by sea on the Portuguese harbor city until it fell to the Dutch in 1641 (hence, also, an abundance of sources).

The first recorded war fleets sent to sea by the budding Sumatran harbor polity in the 1530s were still modest in number and size of vessels, and the manpower carried was accordingly smaller. These vessels seem to have been built along the lines of traditional long boats of insular Southeast Asia (Malay *lancang,* Javanese *kelulus,* etc.). In the 1560s and 1580s, however, Aceh was already capable of swiftly launching war fleets composed of three hundred or more long vessels, including a majority of mid-sized *fustas* and up to fifty large galleys, both models influenced by Mediterranean techniques learned from Portuguese renegades and Turkish shipwrights.[19] The largest of all was

---

[19]*Gorab/ghurab,* of Arabic origin, or *gali,* of Portuguese origin, are the words used in Malay texts to describe these new vessels (Portuguese sources have *fustas, galeras, galeotas,* depending on the size). On Turkish influences in insular Southeast Asia, see Anthony Reid, "Sixteenth Century Turkish Influence in Western Indonesia," *JSEAH* 10, no. 3 (1969), 395–414, and Boxer, 1969, and the references cited therein.

Figure 8. Godinho de Eredia's sketch of a seafight between the Portuguese and Acehnese fleets off Changi (Singapore) in 1577. The flagship of Mathias de Albuquerque is in the center. From Godinho de Eredia, *Historia dos servicos com martirio de Luis Monteiro Coutinho* (Biblioteca Nacional de Lisboa, Ms. 414).

built in the 1620s for Iskandar Muda: it was 100 meters in length, had three masts, and carried a crew of 700. According to the Portuguese who succeeded in capturing and taking this ship to Goa, its name was *Espanto do Mundo* ("Terror of the Universe") and was bigger than anything they had known.[20]

In marked coincidence with the vanishing of long-distance trading fleets of the Archipelago, there was therefore an ever increasing capacity to fight at sea. This circumstance served the expansionist policies of the sultans of Aceh or Banten in search of pepper output as much as— or probably a lot more than—it did their military crusades against the Lusitanian *kafir*.[21] The capital and energy spent on building, maintaining, and renewing these huge and profusely armed war fleets cannot but have laid considerable strain on the subjects of these two fast-growing powers. Indeed, the onus of providing the ruler with war vessels was traditionally borne by this clientele of *orang kaya* and outlying dependent *raja*, among which one would have earlier found those that outfitted and sailed the oceanic traders, no doubt to much greater personal benefit. This must have contributed to their inability to survive economically in the shipping sector of activity. It must also have made them more vulnerable and therefore lesser rivals for rulers who grew more and more autocratic. Farming out trade in Banten would have resulted in generating economic development that, at best, bolstered the revenues of the court or, at worst, bypassed rather than penetrated the existing local economy; the growing power of the Chinese at the court was largely acquired at the expense of the local nobility.[22] The accumulation of wealth at the Acehnese court under Iskandar Muda similarly contrasted with the traditional redistributive model of the Malay economy. The gradual elimination of *orang kaya* power in Aceh after the 1580s also corresponds with the growth of war fleets and a growing investment in arms and ammunition. The Hikayat Aceh, a panegyric of Iskandar Muda's reign, rather than dwelling on the role of

---

[20]The best Portuguese descriptions available in print are given by C. R. Boxer, "The Acehnese Attack on Malacca," in Bastin and Roolvink, 1964, pp. 105–21. See also Denys Lombard, *Le Sultanat d'Atjèh au temps d'Iskandar Muda, 1607–1636*, Publication de l'Ecole Française d'Extrême-Orient, no. 62 (Paris, 1967), p. 87.

[21]Sources describing military conquests of pepper-producing areas are not as abundant as those relating events involving the Portuguese. Most attacks by Aceh on pepper-growing areas of Sumatra and the Malay Peninsula could have been carried out only from the sea; Lombard (1967, pp. 91–94) describes Iskandar Muda's campaigns. The same is true for Banten in Lampung or its failed attack on Palembang in 1596; see Table 2 and H. J. de Graaf and Th. G. Th. Pigeaud, *De eerste Moslimse Vorstendommen op Java: Studiën over de staatkundige geschiedenis van de 15e en 16e eeuw, VKI 69* (The Hague, 1974), chaps. 8, 18.

[22]See J. Kathirithamby-Wells, "Banten: A West Indonesian Port and Polity," in *The Southeast Asian Port and Polity*, ed. J. Kathirithamby-Wells and J. Villiers (Singapore, 1990), pp. 107–126.

the *orang kaya* or *orang besar* makes constant reference to military chiefs.[23]

The preceding discussion suggests that it is incorrect to ascribe to the Portuguese presence in Southeast Asia the main responsibility for the disappearance of long-distance trading fleets, as a result of either over-emphasized monopolistic policies or repeated destruction at sea. Plausible explanations must take into consideration the global political and economic trends, from the Mediterranean all the way to the Middle Empire and over a longer period.

The local response to such a historical *conjoncture* brought a new type of political power, with a growing emphasis on territoriality, centralization, cash cropping economy, absolutism, and the rise of belligerence at sea (as well as on land when conditions permitted). It coincided chronologically with the disappearance of indigenous high-seas trading and shipping. The relationship between these two transformations appears to me to be inescapable, as is the interaction between war and trade. But considering the paucity of statistical sources available to describe in any detail the economic situation during the sixteenth century, I do not think it possible to delineate with any certainty the terms of this interaction. In other words, is this disengagement of local shippers from a lucrative activity in which they earlier competed on a par with Tamil, Gujarati, or Chinese merchants a consequence of the growing clout at sea of Chinese and Gujarati and other Indian Ocean long-distance trading fleets, which would have brought about as a corollary an adaptation of the local economy and power structure to the new environment? Or did the local rulers voluntarily adapt their economy to a growing demand for cash crops and willfully give up on their country's share of long-distance networks as a means to better enforce their growing autocratic power on their weakened clientele, thus leaving the maritime sector of their economy wide open to foreign entrepreneurship? No historical interpretation can be as clear-cut as the two rationalizations just offered. I would, however, tend to favor a process along the lines of the first alternative. As already noted, instability in the Straits area seems to have already been rife early in the sixteenth century, when the Javanese made their fleets ready to attack the sultan of Melaka. Also, it is clear that *jong* trading, at the time the Portuguese entered the scene, was less than it had been some decades earlier: local

[23]A. C. Milner, *Kerajaan: Malay Political Culture on the Eve of Colonial Rule* (Tucson, Ariz., 1982), particularly chap. 2, which deals with economic aspects; Lombard, 1967, p. 71; J. Kathirithamby-Wells, "Royal Authority and the Orang Kaya in the Western Archipelago, circa 1500–1800," *JSEAS* 17, no. 2 (1986), 264.

Table 1. Acehnese war fleets, 1512–1636

Date	Fleet size	Detail	Manpower
1512–13	30–40	*lancharas*	
1537	100	5 galleys, 100 *lancharas*	8,000
1539–40	160	vs. Aru: *navios de alto bordo, lancharas,* Javanese *calaluzes, galeotas*	
1547	70	*lancharas, fustas, galeotas*	5,000
1568	357	3 large *galeotas* from Malabar, 4 *galés bastardas,* 60 *fustas* and *galeotas,* 200 *lancharas,* 80 *balões,* 2 *champanas* for ammunition	15,000, 400 Turks
1569	200	20 galleys, 20 *juncos*	
1570	60	vs. Johor: 9 galleys and *galeotas,* plus *fustas* and *lancharas*	
1570–75		60 to 80 galleys available, plus small vessels	
1573	90	25 galleys (one very large), 34 large *fustas,* plus *lancharas* and smaller boats	7,000
1577	150	40 royal galleys, 110 *fustas* and *lancharas*	10,000
1571–79	360+	10 *kapal,* 120 large *ghorab,* 230 *fustas,* plus *sumbuk, pilang, dendang, banting*	

Manuscript sources: Manuel Godinho de Erédia, *Serviço com martyrio de Luís Monteiro Coutinho* (MS Biblioteca Nacional de Lisboa, FG 414); ANTT, *Corpo Cronológico,* 1.41.29, Jorge Cabral a El Rei, 5 July 1528; 1.66.37, Pero de Faria a El Rei, 25 Nov. 1529; *Livro das Monções* 35, fols. 297v–298r, 300r–304v, 310r–314v; *Chancelaria Privada de Dom João,* 3.5.126v.

Printed sources: João de Barros and Diogo do Couto, 1777–78, *Décadas,* 2.6.1, 2.9.2–3, 7, 3.3.2, 3.8.6, 4.9.14, 6.5.1, 6.9.5–9, 8.21–22, 30, 34, 9.17, 9.27, 10.3.2, 10.8.13–15; Fernão Lopes de Castanheda, 1924–33, 3.100–102, 242–50; 3.135.327; 3.151.361; 4.45.455; 4.48.461; 6.100.303–4; 7.22.37; Pires, 1944, 2:395; Jorge de Lemos, *História dos cercos que em tempo de António Monis Barreto Governador que foi dos estados da Índia, os Achens e Jaos puseram á fortaleza de Malaca* (Lisbon, 1585); Fernão Mendes Pinto, *Peregrinação,* 6 vols. (Porto, 1944–45), 1:101, 121; 6:142; G. M. A. W. Lodewijcksz, *Premier livre de l'histoire de la navigation aux Indes Orientales, par les Hollandais* (Amsterdam, 1598), fol. 35r; Manoel Xavier, *Vitórias do Governador Nuno Alvares Botelho* (Lisbon, 1633), chap. 5; fol 7v. See also C. R. Boxer, "The Acehnese Attack on Malacca in 1629, as Described in Contemporary Portuguese Sources," in *Malayan and Indonesian Studies,* ed. J. Bastin and R. Roolvink (Oxford, 1964), pp. 114–18, 140, 243;

vessels were still very large, but the remotest destinations had been abandoned, leaving only southern India and China open to their enterprise outside Southeast Asia. A sizable proportion of Melaka-based merchants sailing these large *jong* in the 1510s were of nonindigenous Southeast Asian communities; prominent among them were the Tamils involved in the Moluccan spice trade, in which they competed head on with Javanese merchants and seem to have taken the lead. The Gujarati merchants and their *naos* had by then almost established a monopoly over Melakan trade with the western shores of the Indian Ocean, a

Table 1. (Continued)

Date	Fleet size	Detail	Manpower
1581–82	150	7 *naos de alto bordo* (*galeões*), 11 *galés bastardas*, plus *lancharas, bantis, calaluzes*	15,000
1584	300	40 galleys, plus *fustas, lancharas, bantins*	
1586	300	10 *naos*, 50 galleys, 150 *fustas*, plus *lancharas, bantins*	
c. 1600	±100	[available fleet]	40,000
c. 1615	350	60 galleys	
1618–20		vs. Pahang, Perak, Kedah	17,000
pre-1621		100 large galleys available at Aceh, Daya, and Pedir, one-third of them larger than Christian ones	
1629	236	38 galleys "much larger than ours," plus *panchelões, pangaios, bantins*	20,000
1635	70	Some royal galleys and a few more ordinary galleys	
1636		40 large galleys	
1636		19 *galés grandes de gaveas*	

Augustin de Beaulieu, *Relation de l'état présent du commerce des Hollandais et des Portugais dans les Indes Orientales*, in Melchisédec Thévenot, *Relation des divers voyages curieux*, 3 vols. (Paris, 1666), 2:106; Teuku Iskandar, ed., *De Hikajat Atjeh*, VKI 26 (The Hague, 1958), p. 175; *Documenta Indica*, ed. Ioseph Wicki S. I., 12 vols. (Rome, 1948–84), 2:205–20, 10:19–39; *Documentação para a história das missões do Padroado português do Oriente: Insulíndia*, ed. A. Basilio de Sá, 5 vols. (Lisbon, 1954–58), 1:181–91, 2:55; *Lettera di Giovanni da Empoli a Leonardo su padre . . . e fragmenti di altre lettere del medesimo*, intro. Iacopo Graberg da Hemso, *Archivio Storico Italiano*, vol. 3 (1846), appendix, p. 73. *Voyages and Work of John Davis, the Navigator* (London, 1880), p. 150; E. H. Blair and J. A. Robertson, *The Philippine Islands, 1493–1898*, 55 vols. (Cleveland, 1903–9), 4:125–26, 134, 151, 167, 184; 17:255; *Cartas de Affonso de Albuquerque, seguidas de documentos que as elucidam*, ed. A. de Bulhão Pato and H. Lopes de Mendonça, 7 vols. (Lisbon, 1884–1935), 3:121; B. Schrieke, *Indonesian Sociological Studies*, 2 vols. (The Hague, 1955–59), 2:141; Hubert Jacobs, "The First Locally Demonstrable Christianity in Celebes, 1544," *Studia* 17 (1966), 293; I. A. MacGregor, "A Sea Fight near Singapore in the 1570's," *JMBRAS* 29 no. 3 (1956), 5–21; Manguin, 1988, p. 619.

forewarning of their role at Aceh later in the sixteenth century.[24] There are thus good reasons to believe that the Southeast Asian withdrawal from high-seas shipping in the second half of the sixteenth century was only the epilogue of a long-term, pan-Asian process.

This in turn raises far broader questions, with answers beyond the scope of this essay. To what extent were Southeast Asian polities able to develop and maintain an Asia-wide trade network, or just to stand their own ground, when two neighboring and mighty world-systems such as India and China—not to mention the West—were in a phase of

[24]Pires, 1944, 2:367, 496; Thomaz, 1975, 1976, 1988.

Table 2. Malay Archipelago war fleets (excluding Aceh), 1500–1626

Date	Fleet size	Detail	Manpower
1500	200	Melaka vs. Siam: *lancharas, calaluzes*	
1512	300	Japara vs. Melaka: 60 *juncos* plus *lancharas, calaluzes*	
1512	50	Javanese ("Pate Quetir," from Melaka): *lancharas, calaluzes, balões*	
1513	70	Lingga and Bintan vs. Kampar: 1 large *lanchara* as big as a *galé*	2,500
1514	32	Bintan: *lancharas*	
1514	80	Lingga: *lancharas*	6,000
1515	24	Bintan vs. Kampar and Melaka: 24 *lancharas*, including 6 large ones called *gurab*	
1517	60	Bintan vs. Melaka: *lancharas*	
1518	85	Bintan vs. Melaka: *lancharas*	500
1519	60	Bintan: *lancharas* and *calaluzes*	
1520	100	Bintan: *lancharas* and *calaluzes*	
1523	80	Bintan: 50 *lancharas* plus smaller boats	
1525	160	Bintan and Inderagiri vs. Lingga: *lancharas*	8,000
1526	33	Pahang: *lancharas*	2,000
1528	150	Aru: *lancharas*	
1539–40?	215	Johor vs. Aceh: 15 *juncos*, 200 *lancharas, calaluzes, joangas*	
1544	20	Makassar: *paros* of 70 to 80 rowers	1,600
1547	300	Johor, Perak, and Pahang vs. Patani: galleys, *lancharas, bantins*	8,000
1551	300	Johor and Japara vs. Melaka: 1 galley, 80 *lancharas (fustas)*, etc.	3,000 Malays and 10,000 Javanese
1574	300+	Japara vs. Melaka: 80 *juncos* of up to 400 tons, *calaluzes*	15,000
1578	200	Brunei vs. Spain: 100 galleys (of +24 benches) and *galeotas* (18 benches), 100 small vessels	7,000–8,000
1587	120	Johor	5,000–6,000
1595	200	Banten vs. Palembang	
1624	2,000	Mataram: *gurab*, small "proas," etc.	1,500
1626	160	Johor vs. Aceh	
1626	100	Patani vs. Aceh	9,000

Sources: See Table 1.

overseas economic expansion? Could they resist being turned into a periphery of Chinese or Indian trade networks? Was Southeast Asia able to thrive economically only on the alternative, empirical markets periodically proposed by Asian history? The second part of the first millennium would have been such a period when world trade needed Southeast Asian products and China was not yet a maritime power, therefore allowing Sriwijaya to prosper. The commercial expansion of the Song largely contributed to the downfall of the Malay trade-oriented polity.[25] Melaka-based Southeast Asian shipping would have similarly thrived on the Ming ban, after the harbor city's rise was prodded by early fifteenth-century Chinese overseas expeditions. Similar patterns should be identifiable on the Indian Ocean side of Southeast Asia. In times of overseas economic expansion of either the eastern or western neighbors of Southeast Asia (or of both), only the enduring local peddling networks would have kept region-wide economies alive, with only marginal or temporary setbacks brought about by the constraints of world market forces.[26]

[25]O. W. Wolters, in his *Early Indonesian Commerce* (Ithaca, N.Y., 1967), has been an exponent of this "opportunity seizing" approach.

[26]The questions raised in these last few paragraphs were posed by H.-D. Evers in "Traditional Trading Networks in Southeast Asia," *Archipel* 35 (1988), 89–100. His starting point is quite different, though: after observing the resilience of Indonesian small-scale trade networks right into the modern world, he concludes that Van Leur's "peddling trade" theory remained valid.

9

Was the Seventeenth Century a Watershed in Burmese History?

Victor Lieberman

In 1599 the city of Pegu, which was located near the coast and had served as Burma's imperial capital during most of the sixteenth century, fell to an assault by invaders and provincial rebels. The city was burned, and the so-called First Toungoo empire disintegrated. A younger generation of princes succeeded in restoring a truncated version of the empire, but between 1599 and 1635 they transferred the capital from the maritime region, hitherto the locus of an energetic foreign trade, to Ava, some four hundred miles up the Irrawaddy. In this comparatively remote zone the Burmese throne remained for the next two and a half centuries, until its extinction by the British.

Two historiographic approaches have portrayed these events as a turning point in Burmese development. In the early twentieth century, British colonial scholars argued that the shift of capital from the coast to the interior deprived the Burmese of vital commercial-cum-cultural stimuli and thus condemned the country to centuries of parochialism and stagnation. Thus D. G. E. Hall, the doyen of British historians of Southeast Asia, observed in 1928:

> The removal of the Burmese capital from Pegu to Ava in 1635 was, without doubt, one of the cardinal events of Burmese history. No matter what arguments there were in favour of the step, the fact remains that it signalised the triumph of the more intransigent elements in Burmese character and governmental policy—elements which contributed their full share in the first place towards the failure

Research for this article was assisted by grants from the National Endowment for the Humanities, the Social Science Research Council, and the Economic History Association.

of early European efforts to trade with Burma, and ultimately towards the collapse of two dynasties and the political ruin of the country.[1]

Britain's foremost specialist in the Burmese chronicles, G. E. Harvey, agreed that the move away from the coast isolated, and thus weakened, the monarchy. He contrasted Burma's development with that of Siam, "which had its capital in a seaport, developed a more enlightened government than the Burmese kingship, and is independent today."[2] The historical contribution of a beneficent British colonialism in reopening Burma to international trade thus became self-evident.

More recently, from a very different historiographic perspective, Anthony Reid also has argued for the fundamental importance of the seventeenth century in Southeast Asian and, by extension, Burmese development. Reid took as his point of departure the much-discussed "general crisis" of seventeenth-century Europe and lesser known but analogous dislocations in East Asia during the same period. In a series of imaginative, carefully constructed, seminal essays, he suggested that a variety of factors—including a drop in world silver production and a period of unusually cold weather that reduced agricultural output in several parts of Eurasia—combined in the 1630s and 1640s to inhibit international trade and to depress prices in Southeast Asian markets no less than in Europe. The growing squeeze on profits intensified the determination of the Dutch to destroy their commercial rivals in Southeast Asia and to establish a monopoly on the most valuable long-distance commodities. Unable to withstand European economic and military pressures and further weakened perhaps by local climatic deterioration, Southeast Asian societies in the seventeenth century therefore reversed those intertwined trends toward commercial florescence and political centralization that had characterized the preceding period of prosperity from c. 1450 to 1630. Indigenous cities contracted, cosmopolitan urban and religious cultures languished, cash crops yielded to subsistence agriculture, and once-powerful archipelagic states entered a long-term political decline that would culminate in full European colonial control.[3]

---

[1]D. G. E. Hall, *Early English Intercourse with Burma, 1587–1743* (1928; 2d ed., London, 1968), p. 11.

[2]G. E. Harvey, *History of Burma* (London, 1925; rpt., 1967), pp. 248–49; see also p. 193.

[3]Anthony Reid, "The Origins of Southeast Asian Poverty," in *Scholarship and Society in Southeast Asia*, ed. W. E. Wilmott (Christchurch, N.Z., 1979), pp. 33–49; *Europe and Southeast Asia: The Military Balance* (Townsville, Australia, 1982); Takeshi Ito and Reid, "From Harbour Autocracies to 'Feudal' Diffusion in Seventeenth Century Indonesia: The Case of Aceh," in *Feudalism: Comparative Studies*, ed. Edmund Leach et al. (Sydney, 1985), pp. 197–213; Reid "An

Such tendencies, in Reid's view, were no less pronounced on the mainland than in island Southeast Asia. Indeed, in an effort to fend off the Europeans and to insulate themselves from the vagaries of a declining market, the mainland states, including Burma, are said to have turned away from international commerce more completely than their insular counterparts.[4] Yet without trade revenues, these bureaucratic regimes could not be maintained effectively. Burma, Vietnam, and Siam therefore suffered recurrent crises and a "relative isolation and stasis"[5] that was not reversed until temporary and frequently unsuccessful efforts at state reform in the mid-nineteenth century. In short, the seventeenth century stands forth as a watershed between an age of commercially driven expansion and an era of stagnation, if not parochialism and regression, in economic, institutional, and even cultural forms.

This essay seeks to test that periodization. While accepting the essential characterization of archipelagic Southeast Asia, I find the emphasis on the seventeenth-century watershed basically inapplicable to Burma. This period clearly modified the balance between maritime and agrarian sectors in the political economy; it permanently reduced Mon influence within the empire and perhaps also slowed the gunpowder revolution in Burma. The seventeenth century did not, however, alter what I consider to have been more basic and sustained developments. Territorial expansion and administrative centralization, to cite two outstanding trends, continued after 1635 well into the nineteenth century. The dynastic collapse of the Restored Toungoo state in 1752 should be seen more as a symptom of temporary institutional weakness and perhaps even of commercial expansion than as an indication of secular political or military decline. Religious orthodoxy and ethnic homogenization also continued to gain ground to the eve of the British conquest, so that in fact the early Konbaung state presided over a more cohesive political and cultural order than had any of its predecessors.

These patterns of integration drew strength from the persistent vitality of Burma's maritime trade after 1635; from improvements, both extensive and intensive, in agricultural production; from the sustained monetization and commercialization of the economy; and from the

---

'Age of Commerce' in Southeast Asian History," *MAS* 24, no. 1 (1990), 1–30; idem., "The Seventeenth Century Crisis in Southeast Asia," *MAS* 24, no. 4 (1990), 639–59.

[4]Reid, 1990 ("Seventeenth Century Crisis"), p. 645.

[5]Reid, 1979, p. 43. The quote refers only to Burma and Siam, but Vietnam receives a similar characterization in Reid, 1990 ("Seventeenth Century Crisis"), p. 645. See also Reid, "The Islamization of Southeast Asia," in *Historia*, ed. Muhammad Abu Bakar et al. (Kuala Lumpur, 1984), p. 30.

inflexible demands of indigenous interstate competition. To all these processes, Europeans remained quite marginal. No European power, least of all the Dutch, mounted an effective military or commercial challenge to Burma before 1824, and the decision to transfer the capital from Pegu to Ava in the early 1600s was determined overwhelmingly by domestic geopolitical and cultural circumstances, not by maritime pressures. Burma (and, I suspect, the rest of the mainland) thus stands in relatively sharp contrast to island Southeast Asia, and the concept of seventeenth-century decommercialization seems to me an inadequate historiographic bridge between the two regions.

Maritime Resources and Regional Dominance

Any analysis of the seventeenth century obviously hinges on our assessment of the preceding era. What were the dominant trends in Burmese political economy prior to the collapse of the First Toungoo dynasty in 1599?

The significance of the First Toungoo empire derives from two principal features. Most fundamental, it reunified the Irrawaddy basin in the mid-sixteenth century after almost 270 years of fragmentation; in effect, only under this dynasty did a stable tradition of political unity arise. Originally, the core of modern Burma had known a limited degree of integration under the classical empire of Pagan. Following Pagan's collapse in 1287, however, the lowlands had dissolved into a medley of warring principalities. Successive efforts at reconquest had aborted. Then, between 1539 and 1558, with astounding celerity the First Toungoo kings subdued the entire Irrawaddy basin, together with a vast area of Tai-speaking kingdoms stretching into modern Laos and Thailand over which Pagan had never claimed nominal suzerainty.

The other noteworthy aspect of the First Toungoo dynasty is that it derived its principal strength from the maritime zone of Lower Burma rather than from the dry zone of the interior. Notwithstanding the fact that the coast enjoyed superior rainfall, the lighter soils of the north, the reduced incidence of malaria, and the availability of excellent irrigation facilities combined to produce overall populations in the dry zone that were normally as much as three times as large as those in Lower Burma.[6] Demographic easily translated into military superiority. The classical empire of Pagan, the post-Pagan empire of Ava (which exer-

---

[6]Victor Lieberman, *Burmese Administrative Cycles: Anarchy and Conquest, c. 1580–1760* (Princeton, N.J., 1984), pp. 16–23. The coastal zone is here defined as the area south of the 19th parallel.

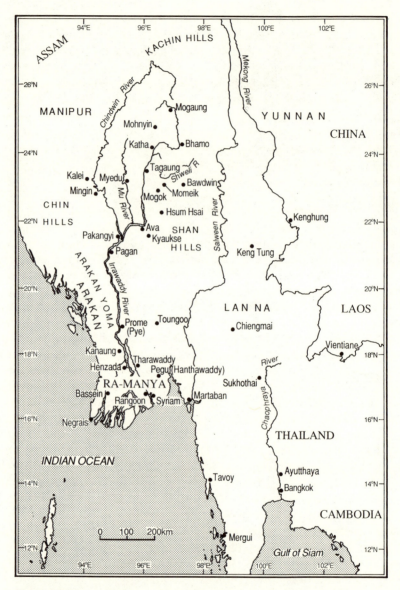

Map 6. The Irrawaddy basin and adjacent regions

cised a loose and fluctuating authority over two-thirds of the basin
between about 1365 and 1510), and all post-1600 empires were based in
the north; until the British converted Rangoon into the national capital,
the First Toungoo empire, with its capital at Pegu, was therefore highly
anomalous.

The peculiar achievements of the First Toungoo dynasty should be seen as the culmination of long-term trends in Upper and Lower Burma that were mutually reinforcing but of essentially separate origin.[7] In the dry zone the unchecked accumulation of tax-exempt religious lands during the fourteenth and fifteenth centuries gradually undermined Ava's financial base. Much like their late Pagan predecessors, for both ideological and political reasons Ava's kings found themselves unable to halt the constant donation of secular lands to monastic sects, hence unable to tap effectively what was actually an increase in overall cultivation. Exploiting the resultant debility of Burman military authority and perhaps also responding to novel demographic pressures in the highlands, successive groups of semi-pagan Tai-speaking Shans invaded the northern lowlands. The Shans disrupted local settlements, displaced Burman leaders, and thus further weakened central power.

Meanwhile the coast prospered. The relative superiority of commercial wealth over land in the south, and the fact that the south lay outside the core area intensively patronized by generations of pious Pagan donors, inhibited the growth of tax-exempt religious lands comparable to those of the classical heartland. At the same time, mountain barriers and distance from the main Shan concentrations rendered the south relatively immune from Shan incursions. Most important, the coast benefited far more directly than the interior from the sustained expansion of international trade. The period c. 1450–1620 saw a resumption of population growth and an intensification of market demand in Europe, China, Japan, and various sectors of the Indian Ocean littoral; in response, Southeast Asian commercial networks, including those of Lower Burma, grew rapidly in scale and complexity. The florescence of Lower Burma in the late fifteenth and sixteenth centuries therefore corresponded to the enhanced prosperity of Ayutthaya and Phnom Penh, and of such famed archipelagic centers as Melaka, Aceh, Banten, northern Java, Brunei, Makassar, and Maluku.[8]

Maritime contacts conferred several advantages on the Lower Burma state. Most obvious, they provided wealth that could be used to enhance the majesty of the capital, to increase patronage, and to hire mercenaries. It was these attractions that led the Burman leaders of the

[7]On factors shaping the sixteenth-century political economy, see Victor Lieberman, "Europeans, Trade, and the Unification of Burma, c. 1540–1620," *Oriens Extremus* 27, no. 2 (1980), 203–26.

[8]On the growth of trade, see Anthony Reid, "The Structure of Cities in Southeast Asia: Fifteenth to Seventeenth Centuries," *JSEAS* 11, no. 2 (1980), 235–50; David Chandler, *A History of Cambodia* (Boulder, Colo., 1983), pp. 77–80; David Wyatt, *Thailand: A Short History* (New Haven, Conn., 1982), chaps. 4, 5; M. A. P. Meilink-Roelofsz, *Asian Trade and European Influence in the Indonesian Archipelago between 1500 and about 1630* (The Hague, 1962), chaps. 1, 2, 6; Ashin Das Gupta and M. N. Pearson, eds., *India and the Indian Ocean 1500–1800* (Delhi, 1987), chaps. 3, 4; Lloyd E. Eastman, *Family, Fields, and Ancestors* (New York, 1988), pp. 123–28.

First Toungoo dynasty to transfer their capital from the interior (Toungoo, in the Sittang valley) to Pegu in 1540 and to exploit systematically maritime trade.

Moreover, especially from the second quarter of the sixteenth century the ports provided unique access to Portuguese, and of somewhat lesser value, Muslim firearms. Although small cast-iron guns apparently had been used at Pegu for some time,[9] Portuguese matchlocks and bronze muzzle-loading cannon were more powerful, accurate, and reliable than anything hitherto available; they quickly became indispensable for siege warfare and, to a lesser extent, for field battles. Frequently the guns were serviced by Portuguese or Muslim mercenaries, who came to form elite guard units. To be sure, some weapons also found their way into the interior: in an inscription of 1540–41 the lord of Pakangyi in Upper Burma boasted that he had many matchlocks comparable to the "celestial thunderbolt weapons" of the god Sakka.[10] Nonetheless, in the absence of any significant local manufacture, firearms—as well as foreign gunners—remained far more readily available at the ports than in the dry zone. As contemporary chronicles recorded in graphic detail, Portuguese cannon contributed substantially to the rapid First Toungoo conquest of Upper Burma and the Tai highlands in the 1540s and 1550s.[11]

Despite, or because of, its rapid expansion, the First Toungoo empire proved extremely short-lived. Lacking either a riverine artery by which to communicate with Laos and Thailand or elementary administrative institutions outside the Lower Burma core, the empire remained an improbable assemblage of autonomous principalities held in obedience by personal ties to the High King and by the threat of chastisement. Ayutthaya's revolt from 1584 to 1593 precipitated throughout the Tai world and the Irrawaddy basin a series of rebellions that Pegu proved helpless to suppress. The manpower of the coastal region was consumed in futile punitive expeditions until finally the capital fell as described at the outset of this paper.

Upper Burma's traditional economic and geographic advantages now reasserted themselves, while earlier constraints on northern power dissolved. Between 1599 and 1635 those princes who restored the Toungoo empire therefore returned their capital from Pegu to the dry

---

[9]Meilink-Roelofsz, 1962, p. 123, attributing them to Chinese influence.

[10]*Inscriptions Collected in Upper Burma*, 2 vols. (Rangoon, 1900, 1903), 2:160–61, lines 11–12. This is inscription 1065 numbered according to Charles Duroiselle, comp., *A List of Inscriptions Found in Burma. Part 1* (Rangoon, 1921).

[11]See the sixteenth-century chronicle *Nidana Ramadhipati-katha*, ed. Phra Candakanto (Pak Lat, Siam, 1912), pp. 84–95, 151. For the global context, see Geoffrey Parker, *The Military Revolution* (Cambridge, 1988), chaps. 3, 4.

zone city of Ava. Throughout the Restored Toungoo (1597–1752) and early Konbaung (1752–1824) eras, these same factors continued to dictate a northern locale for the monarchy.

Perhaps the central attraction was Upper Burma's agricultural-cum-demographic superiority, which was substantially enhanced following the devastation of Pegu in the 1590s. As the experience of Pagan as well as of the First Toungoo empire had shown, northern kings could control the mercantile wealth and limited population of the south, concentrated in a few key districts, far more easily than coastal rulers could monitor the dispersed population of the interior. It is true, as noted, that during the fourteenth and fifteenth centuries powerful monastic organizations had impeded royal mobilization of the interior population; but after c. 1530, Shan persecutions of the monkhood combined with unsettled conditions to transfer extensive acreages to secular landowners, who became subject to royal taxation following the return of the capital to the north. At the same time, the Shans themselves ceased to threaten Upper Burma as a result of ambitious Toungoo pacification projects, facilitated by the new firearms, as well as of increased military pressure from Ming and later Qing China. Finally, if we are to explain adequately the return to Ava, we should recall that Restored Toungoo and Konbaung kings were emotionally attached to the Burman culture of the interior over and against the predominantly Mon culture of the coastal region. This attachment can only have gained strength after more or less explicitly Mon rebellions in the 1590s and again in 1634–35 had threatened Burman rule.[12]

Quite possibly, as Hall and others have long contended, the return to the interior diminished maritime influences at court and within the wider society of the capital region. If Mon culture lacked the heavy mercantile orientation of, say, the Bugis, Mons obviously depended on foreign trade far more heavily than did Burmans from the interior. Significant numbers of Mons during the sixteenth century collected forest produce, grew crops, and manufactured pottery for export; or worked in Pegu's shipyards. Mons (and perhaps some Burmans living near the coast) also regularly journeyed as sailors and traders to ports as distant as Goa, Melaka, Banten, and Aceh.[13] The First Toungoo dynasty's self-conscious determination to include prominent Mons in

---

[12]Victor Lieberman, "The Transfer of the Burmese Capital from Pegu to Ava," *JRAS* 1980, no. 1, 64–83.

[13]Tomé Pires, *The Suma Oriental of Tomé Pires*, ed. Armando Cortesão, 2 vols. (London, 1944), 1:99–103; Manuel de Faria y Sousa, *The Portuguese Asia*, 3 vols. (1695; rpt., Westmead, England, 1971), 1:180–81; Harvey, 1967, pp. 341–42; D. G. E. Hall, *A History of South-East Asia*, 4th ed. (London, 1981), p. 402; S. Adhyatman and Abu Ridho, *Martavans in Indonesia* (Jakarta, 1984), p. 64.

its inner councils probably afforded some representation to these maritime connections. In any case, by virtue of its physical location and
dependence on maritime revenues, the sixteenth-century monarchy
was thrown into regular contact with merchants from around the Indian Ocean. After the return to Ava, however, the number of Mons
enjoying prominent appointments at court declined steadily.[14] At the
same time, entries in the Burmese royal chronicles to embassies from
such traditional maritime trading partners as Golconda, Aceh, Bengal,
and Delhi became less frequent, while references to Shan and overland
Chinese merchants increased.[15] By themselves, chronicle references of
this sort hardly prove a decline in the level of maritime trade, but they
may reflect accurately the reduced importance after c. 1640 of maritime
contacts in the political calculus and general outlook of the court.

This reorientation was associated with certain modifications in the
structure of Burmese coastal trade. Rice exports, which during the
sixteenth century apparently flowed without royal interference from
Lower Burma to such centers as Melaka and Aceh, became subject to
greater royal restriction. We have sufficient evidence to dismiss Harvey's blanket assertion that rice exports after 1600 were "forbidden by
the benighted kings of Ava."[16] Yet it is true that between c. 1630 and
1885 Burma's rulers, now ensconced in the interior and concerned with
the threat of rice shortages among what was probably a growing population in the dry zone, began to divert a sizable portion of Lower
Burma's surplus for shipment to the north, while periodically forbidding export of cereals that remained in coastal granaries.[17] Furthermore, after the mid-seventeenth century Mons (and southern Burmans)
reduced their involvement in overseas trading ventures. Although
ships and crews from Lower Burma still visited the western Archipelago and India, after c. 1650 the large-scale movement of Peguan
ships to Malaya and northern Sumatra which attracted comment during the sixteenth century was far less evident. Conceivably this re-

[14]See appointments at *Hman-nan maha-ya-zawin-daw-gyi* [henceforth *HNY*], 3 vols. (Mandalay, 1908), 3:229–408; Thi-ri-u-zana, *Law-ka-byu-ha kyan* [henceforth *LBHK*], ed. U Hpo Lat
(Rangoon, 1968), pp. 200–215.

[15]U Kala, *Maha-ya-zawin-gyi*, 3 vols. (Rangoon, 1926, 1932, 1961), 2:387; 3:67–68, 180–83, 240–
41; *HNY*, pp. 33–40, 308, 361–62, 376–77.

[16]Harvey, 1967, p. 175. On post-1630 rice exports, see Khin Maung Nyunt, "Burma's Rice
Trade in the 17th Century," *The Guardian* 17, no. 4 (1970), 12–20; George V. Smith, *The Dutch in
Seventeenth-Century Thailand* (DeKalb, Ill., 1977), p. 83; *The Royal Orders of Burma, A.D. 1598–
1885*, 10 vols. [henceforth *ROB*], ed. Than Tun (Kyoto, 1983–90), 4:650 (implying an interrup-
tion of normal rice exports); 6:488.

[17]*Reprint from Dalrymple's Oriental Repertory of Portions Relating to Burma*, 2 vols. (Rangoon,
1926), 1:130–31, 174–75; 2:375, 377; *ROB*, 6:488; Michael Symes, *An Account of an Embassy to the
Kingdom of Ava* (1800; rpt., Westmead, England, 1969), pp. 233, 259, 325; Henry Gouger, *Personal
Narrative of Two Years' Imprisonment in Burma* (London, 1860), pp. 19–20.

flected the disruption of Mon seafaring traditions after recurrent disorders at the coast—and perhaps also, as we see below, keener competition from Indian and private European traders. Possibly too—in the absence of statistics, again one can only speculate—the decline in Asian bullion supplies that Reid and William Atwell describe during the late 1630s and 1640s temporarily depressed Burmese trade, compounding the difficulties of Mon merchants.[18]

Yet, if maritime concerns figured less prominently in royal deliberations after 1635 and if rice exports and indigenous seafaring declined, there is no reason to believe that the court lost interest in maritime income in a general sense, or that Burma retreated to an isolationist policy, as is usually alleged. Neither necessity nor self-interest inclined the court in such a direction, and any attempt to conflate Burma's seventeenth-century adjustment with that of the Archipelago entails certain dangers.

The cardinal difference between archipelagic and Burmese experience arose from the role of Europeans. In their determination to monopolize the spices of Banda and Maluku, the Dutch destroyed Ternate, Tidore, and Goa as major military powers and depopulated Hoamoal. In Java as well, the Dutch helped to eviscerate indigenous maritime trade, seized control of export and entrepôt functions, and thus broke the self-sufficiency of both Banten and Mataram. Even in Perak and western Sumatra, Dutch competition for tin and pepper during the seventeenth century contributed to the erosion of Aceh's once-formidable authority.[19] But until 1824 Burma never faced a credible European military or commercial challenge, and the Dutch in particular showed scant interest.[20] This was partly because Burma's land forces were far stronger than those of the typical archipelagic state, partly because its geography made the application of European naval power more problematic, and most especially because Burma never offered the same initial attractions as areas heavily involved in the spice and pepper trade. Small-scale European interventions—by Portuguese adventurers at Syriam in 1600–13, by the French at Syriam in 1751–56, and by the English at Negrais in 1753–59—were easily routed and in each case actually bolstered the military position of the Burmese throne.

[18]Reid, 1990 ("Seventeenth Century Crisis"), pp. 646–49; William S. Atwell, "Some Observations on the 'Seventeenth-Century Crisis' in China and Japan," *JAS* 45, no. 2 (1986), 229.

[19]On Dutch inroads, see M. C. Ricklefs, *A History of Modern Indonesia* (London, 1981), esp. chaps. 6–8; Ito and Reid, "Feudal Diffusion," 199, 205, 207; Barbara Watson Andaya and Leonard Y. Andaya, *A History of Malaysia* (London, 1982), pp. 61–62, 68–72.

[20]D. G. E. Hall, "The Daghregister of Batavia and Dutch Trade with Burma in the Seventeenth Century," *JBRS* 29 (1939), 139–56.

Figure 9. Reception of the English embassy led by Michael Symes at the Burmese palace of Amarapura, 1795. Depicted here is the audience hall, with the throne elevated five feet above the floor. From Michael Symes, *An Account of an Embassy to the Kingdom of Ava in the Year 1795* (Edinburgh, 1827).

As a result of this very different relation to European power, the Burmese court never faced any significant restriction on its ability to draw profits from trade reaching its coasts. The return to Upper Burma in the early seventeenth century, as I have just sought to demonstrate, responded primarily to local geopolitical and cultural factors, not external pressure. As we know from contemporary poems and chronicle accounts, the basic decision to make Ava the imperial capital had been made by 1615, well before Dutch intervention transformed the Archipelago and while Japanese and New World silver production was still in full spate.[21] The subsequent contraction of commerce in the mid- and late 1630s may have had a marginal impact on royal evaluations of coastal profitability, but the Mon revolt of 1634–35 and the conclusion of frontier negotiations with Ayutthaya in 1635 were surely more important determinants of the final transfer of the royal entourage from Pegu to the new palace at Ava in early 1635.[22] In short, it is difficult to connect the return to Ava to a putative seventeenth-century crisis of Southeast Asian trade.

Even if we take a longer view and examine not merely the return to Ava in 1635 but changing policies toward coastal resources after that date, European activities still seem peripheral. Admittedly, intensifying Dutch competition may have contributed indirectly to the decline of Burman and Mon seafaring, insofar as Dutch restrictions in the Archipelago induced Indian traders to shift their activities toward more open areas like Burma, Thailand, and the upper peninsula.[23] The ensuing threat to local shippers would only have intensified with the growth of private English trade in the late seventeenth and eighteenth centuries. Yet two considerations suggest that the decline of Mon shipping did not fundamentally impair Burmese imperial finances: (a) by hiring foreign captains to sail ships with Mon and Burman crews and by renting foreign ships, the Burmese crown well into the nineteenth century could still sponsor a significant number of demonstrably profitable trading expeditions to places as distant as the Coromandel coast, Sumatra, and Vietnam;[24] (b) the crown's principal maritime profits even

[21]U Kala, 3:167–77, 187, 189; Min-zei-ya-yan-dameik-hso yadu-hnin shin than-hko-hso yadu (Mandalay, 1920), pp. 3–5, 10–11.

[22]U Kala, 3:199, 209–12, 217–32; Rangoon University Library MS 45235 [henceforth RUL 45235], Than Tun typescript, Edicts 7–15, pp. 5–15. See discussion in Lieberman, 1980, pp. 64–83.

[23]Sinnappah Arasaratnam, Merchants, Companies, and Commerce on the Coromandel Coast, 1650–1740 (Delhi, 1986), pp. 206–7, 347–52; Das Gupta and Pearson, 1987, pp. 126, 151; Tapan Raychaudhuri, Jan Company in Coromandel, 1605–1690 (The Hague, 1962), pp. 119–29.

[24]B. R. Pearn, A History of Rangoon (1939; rpt., Westmead, England, 1971), pp. 70, 74–75; ROB, 5:805; 6:488, 670, 681; Toyo Bunko Microfilm no. 93, pt. 4, NL 747, p. 9; India Office Records, London, Records of Fort St. George. Diary and Consultation Books, 1711–1733, containing almost annual references to "ships belonging to the king of Pegu" visiting Madras. ROB, 6:681, cites royal profits of 167 percent.

in the First Toungoo era derived not from royal shipping ventures but from customs duties on foreign merchants, merchant gifts, and a variety of import and export monopolies. These not only continued but, by most indications, expanded long after 1635.

English, Dutch, and Burmese records all suggest that the total volume of trade at Burmese ports, far from entering a secular decline, increased over the period 1600–1830. Possibly, as noted, trade did fall off during the early and mid-seventeenth century. Starting about 1660 and more especially about 1680, however, Burmese trade benefited both from European investments on the Coromandel coast and from the aforementioned shift of Indian trade to the western mainland and the Archipelago. In other words, rather than precipitate a uniform regional downturn, Dutch curbs on Asian trade in the Archipelago contributed to a compensatory increase in those parts of the mainland, including coastal Burma, which remained, in D. K. Bassett's words, "a politically independent, free trade zone of maritime South East Asia."[25] Burmese customs stood to profit from any such increase in traffic. The second half of the eighteenth and the early nineteenth centuries saw a further acceleration of trade between Lower Burma and India, as Indian, Armenian, Persian, and private European merchants sought to open new textile markets and to satisfy the growing Indian Ocean demand for Burmese timber. In 1709 a total of 20 sail are said to have visited Lower Burma each year, but by 1811–22 the annual number of large square-rigged vessels visiting Rangoon alone was reliably reported to have ranged between 35 and 56; Bassein and secondary ports would have further swelled the total. This traffic was modest compared to that at Saigon or Bangkok, but it probably equaled or exceeded Peguan trade during its height in the sixteenth century. In the late Restored Toungoo and Konbaung eras, a growing portion of Burmese exports seems to have consisted of bulk goods—such as metals, cotton and especially timber—rather than luxuries. At the same time, low labor costs and high-quality local teak made the shipyards of Lower Burma among the most important in Asia.[26]

Rather than turn their backs on these sources of income, post-1600

[25]See sources in note 23, above. Quote is from unpublished paper by D. K. Bassett, "Local Trade Networks and British 'Country' Trade in the Thai and Malay Worlds, c. 1680–1770," p. 1. Nor would Dutch inroads into the pepper market in the western Archipelago or Dutch control over clove, nutmeg, and mace in the east have seriously impaired Lower Burma's trade insofar as these goods (especially eastern spices) do not appear to have been a major component in the mix of domestic and emporium items available at late sixteenth-century Pegu. See "Extracts of Master Caesar Frederike," in *Hakluytus Posthumus or Purchas His Pilgrimes,* vol. 10 (Glasgow, 1905), p. 133; "Voyage of Master Ralph Fitch," ibid., 10:191–92.

[26]On the volume of maritime trade c. 1660–1830, see Alexander Hamilton, *A New Account of the East Indies,* 2 vols. (Edinburgh, 1727), 2:41; Lieberman, 1984, pp. 156–57; India Office Records, London, Bengal Secret Consultations, June 20, 1805. On the structure and composi-

kings were impelled by pressures of interstate warfare and domestic politics to exploit maritime revenues systematically and creatively. Restored Toungoo officials and their Konbaung successors therefore offered a variety of privileges and concessions to individual merchants and groups of merchants, sent Burmese embassies to foreign ports, created numerous import and export monopolies, and organized overseas trading expeditions. To monitor activities at the ports—and to shortcircuit potential rebellions in Lower Burma—Restored Toungoo kings reduced the authority of provincial governors while establishing alternate lines of communication between the capital and each provincial center. Through such channels, refined in the Konbaung era, the Upper Burma court was able to supervise in some detail the level of maritime customs duties, the treatment of foreign traders, and the behavior of royal factors and officials.[27]

Gaetano Mantegazza, a Catholic missionary who resided in Burma from 1772 to 1784, claimed (without specifying cash or in-kind income): "Le principal revenu du Roi est la douane de Rangon. . . . Ce revenu, quand il y vient beaucoup de vaisseaux, surpasse, tous ensemble, les autres revenus du royaume."[28] On the other hand, Burmese and English records from 1784 to 1797 show that, while the crown's cash (chiefly silver) income from Rangoon, Tavoy, and Mergui was indeed two to nine times greater than cash income from Upper Burma's richest agricultural basin of Kyaukse, total in-kind *and* cash revenues from Kyaukse in good years were comparable to cash revenues from the above three ports.[29] If we remember that the Upper Burma monarchy controlled extensive agricultural districts in addition to Kyaukse, Mantegazza's maritime emphasis seems somewhat exaggerated. Given the First Toungoo dynasty's more modest agricultural base, one suspects that maritime revenues constituted a larger portion of overall royal income—though not a larger absolute figure—prior to 1600 than during the next two centuries.

Nonetheless, it seems fair to conclude that, whereas in Mataram,

tion of trade, also see Pearn, 1939, pp. 65–79; Symes, 1969, p. 457; *ROB*, 5:947; John Crawfurd, *Journal of an Embassy from the Governor General of India to the Court of Ava*, 2 vols. (London, 1834), 2:195–99; Hall, 1968, chaps. 8, 10.

[27]See sources in notes 24–26, above; *ROB*, 5:802, 816, 1031; 6:473; Lieberman, 1984, pp. 59–60, 113–27; Symes, 1969, pp. 160, 459.

[28]"The principal revenue of the King is the Rangoon customs. . . . When many vessals come there, this revenue exceeds all the other revenues of the kingdom together." Renzo Carmignani, ed., *La Birmania: Relazione Inedita del 1784 del Missionario Barnabita G. M. Mantegazza* (Italian preface, French text) (Rome, 1950), p. 103. The other revenues are identified as products of the mines, rice-in-kind, and regular and extraordinary presents.

[29]This assumes a conversion ratio of five baskets of rice to 1 *kyat* of silver. U Tin, *Myan-ma-min ok-chok-pon sa-dan* [henceforth *MMOS*], 5 vols. (Rangoon, 1932), 2:157; India Office Records, Bengal Political Consultations, 2 March 1798, Cox to Shore, 27 Nov. 1797.

Banten, and certain other archipelagic states subject to Dutch hegemony royal revenues from the ports declined sharply after c. 1680, in Burma they retained their vitality. Such income, particularly in cash, proved indispensable for a variety of architectural, patronage, and most especially military projects; and in this respect, Burma was not unique among mainland states. One can argue that the ambitions of Bodawhpaya (r. 1782–1819) against Thailand governed his enthusiastic, if somewhat episodic, policies on maritime trade; and that Thailand's escape from Burmese hegemony between c. 1770 and 1811 reflected in large measure the fact that Thai maritime trade in this period grew yet more rapidly than did Burma's.[30]

Because military and commercial considerations were intertwined, it is hardly surprising that Restored Toungoo and early Konbaung courts determined to retain control over the firearms of the coast as well as over its revenues. Even more obviously than with trade, arms policy was heavily influenced by the logic of intensifying interstate warfare.

The Portuguese and Muslim mercenaries of the sixteenth century had proven extraordinarily useful, but they had also been politically fickle, expensive, and available only on a short-term basis. Post-1613 kings therefore sought to organize their own musketeers and artillerymen, bound to the throne like other military servicemen through royal land grants on a hereditary basis. These units were drawn in part from Portuguese and Muslim prisoners, but increasingly as well from Shan deportees and Burman levies. Conceivably the concentration of gunners, many of them relatively inexperienced, in the interior, far from the technological stimulus of the coast, dampened the pace of military change. Western arms innovations reached Upper Burma imperfectly and relatively late, while indigenous arms production remained rudimentary.

Military technique, however, was not static. By the late Restored Toungoo and early Konbaung periods, flintlock muskets had come into general use in lieu of less reliable matchlocks; the percentage of frontline troops equipped with handguns had expanded over the early seventeenth century; and new tactics successfully integrated musketeers, artillerymen, cavalry, and spearmen.[31] Such innovations were

---

[30]On Burmese-Thai warfare in this period and on Bodawhpaya's revenue projects, see William Koenig, *The Burmese Polity, 1752–1819* (Ann Arbor, Mich., 1990), pp. 19–36; and *ROB*, 5:805, 1031; 6:473, 670. On maritime contributions to Thailand's rejuvenation, see Hong Lysa, *Thailand in the Nineteenth Century* (Singapore, 1984), chaps. 2–4.

[31]On improvements in firearm quality, numbers, and deployment, see *ROB*, 1:230; 4:388–92, 557, 574–75; Frank Trager and William Koenig, *Burmese Sit-tans, 1764–1826* (Tucson, Ariz., 1979), p. 73; Father Sangermano, *A Description of the Burmese Empire* (rpt., New York, 1969), pp. 97–98; Toyo Bunko Burmese Microfilm no. 78, pt. 8, NL 1605, *gaw v.*; Harvey, 1967, pp. 255–57, 340–41; Major Snodgrass, *Narrative of the Burmese War* (London, 1827), pp. 94–95.

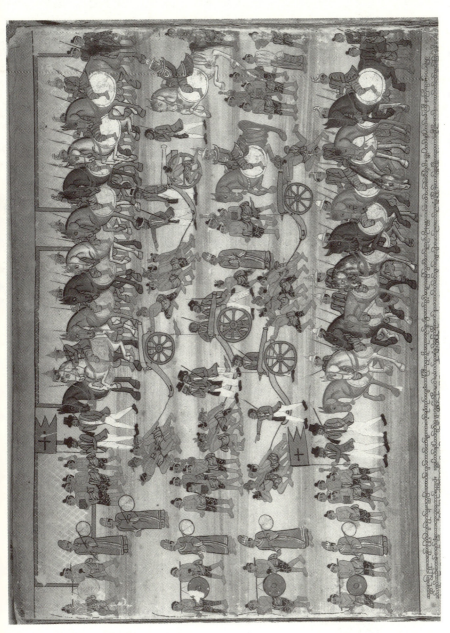

Figure 10. Military procession to the court of Ava in 1865, as represented in a nineteenth-century Burmese illustrated manuscript (*parabaik*). The Portuguese artillerymen stand out by their dress. From Or. 12013, British Library, London.

the sine qua non for extending imperial control into the Shan states, Manipur, Arakan, and Assam and for improving or defending Burma's position in bitter campaigns between 1759 and 1811 against comparatively well-equipped (by Asian standards) Thai and Chinese armies. Without significant domestic firearms manufacture, Burmese forces necessarily relied on maritime sources—English, French, and Muslim. Thus Konbaung agents purchased guns and ammunition overseas, confiscated cannon from hostile traders, systematically levied customs tolls in these goods, and, under Bodawhpaya, organized an elaborate quota arrangement whereby Burmese and foreign traders plying the Irrawaddy were obliged to provide specified quantities of flintlocks, lead, and powder.[32]

In sum, the twin pillars of First Toungoo ascendancy, maritime revenues and firearms, continued to sustain imperial authority long after 1600, notwithstanding the return of the capital to Upper Burma. To abandon control over coastal resources was never a viable option. According to these parameters at least, there was no seventeenth-century watershed.

Agricultural Growth and Domestic Commercial Activity

Thus far I have focused exclusively on maritime influences, for it is in those terms that the historiography of the seventeenth century has always been framed. Yet restricting our vantage point to that available from the deck of a European ship risks obscuring the fact that the Burmese economy as a whole remained overwhelmingly agricultural. Restored Toungoo and Konbaung kings retained their capital in the north precisely because they sought to supervise directly the agrarian heartland. In essence they transcended the limits of the First Toungoo dynasty by joining more effectively the resources of the coast with those of the interior. As I have argued elsewhere, agricultural production and domestic commerce, particularly in the dry zone, underwent significant expansion throughout the precolonial period. Far from declining after 1600, these developments, in combination with maritime

---

[32]See, in addition to previous note, Carmignani, 1950, p. 103; *ROB*, 4:590, 669; 5:788–1042; 6:323–653; Symes, 1969, pp. 5–6, 319–22; *Kon-baung-zet maha-ya-zawin-daw-gyi* [henceforth *KBZ*], ed. U Tin, 3 vols. (Rangoon, 1967, 1968), 1:111, 292–300. The suggestion that in and of itself the court's early seventeenth-century withdrawal to Upper Burma slowed military innovation is provisional. To test such a hypothesis, one might compare changes in Burmese firearms and deployment c. 1600–1830 with military changes in Thailand, where the capital remained more directly exposed to maritime influences.

trade, contributed to the long-term consolidation of imperial institutions and orthodox culture.[33]

My analysis of over five hundred Burmese lithic inscriptions from between 1350 and 1550 indicates that dry zone lands totaling on the order of 300,000 to 400,000 acres were brought under tillage, of which a large proportion were ricelands. After the return of the capital to Ava in the seventeenth century, these lands, many originally controlled by the monkhood, became subject to reasonably effective royal census and taxation. From 1600 to 1830, another 400,000 to 500,000 largely virgin acres in Upper Burma were converted on a sustained basis to agriculture, again including a large portion of rice fields. Together these increases represented at least a 50 percent growth in Upper Burma's total cultivated acreage (rice and dry crops) over the putative figure for 1350. In Lower Burma as well, despite severe dislocations in the 1590s, 1660s, and 1750s, cultivation expanded during the Konbaung period, so that by 1830 a minimum of 650,000 acres were under rice.

The extension of cultivation drew strength from a variety of factors. Particularly during the Restored Toungoo and early Konbaung periods, more effective controls over the Shan hills and more successful domestic pacification created conditions suitable for an extension of settlement. As studies of Europe and other Southeast Asian areas have emphasized, dislocations attending warfare were usually one of the most severe inhibitors of agricultural and demographic expansion. At the same time, the existing population of both Upper and Lower Burma was frequently augmented from peripheral zones east and west of the valley. In part this was a matter of upland peoples—Shans, Karens, Chins, Kachins—seeking more fertile or secure lowland environments. But, more basically, central authorities forcibly deported rebellious vassal peoples in order both to strengthen the empire's military core and to weaken refractory vassal states. I estimate that by 1830, after a period of particularly intense Konbaung transfers, perhaps a fifth of the population of Upper Burma were descended from deportees or were themselves deportees. Finally, the vitality of foreign and domestic (see below) commerce provided individual cultivators—and more especially nobles in control of debt-bonded and tenant labor—with market incentives to open new rice fields as well as lands specializing in vegetables, cotton, and fruit.

While acreage expanded, new crop types contributed to more effi-

[33]For documentation of the claims in this section, see sources cited in Victor Lieberman, "Secular Trends in Burmese Economic History, c. 1350–1830, and Their Implications for State Formation," *MAS* 25, no. 1 (1991), 1–31.

cient land use and higher yields in certain districts. The late thirteenth and fourteenth centuries saw the introduction or rapid dissemination of tea cultivation in the Shan uplands and, more important, of cotton in the dry zone, where it provided a new source of income for villages on marginal lands. During the Restored Toungoo and Konbaung periods, cotton came to supply one of Burma's key domestic trades and its most profitable export to Yunnan. Moreover, starting in the fourteenth century and continuing into the Konbaung era, longer-maturing varieties of rice—chiefly strains of *kauk-gyi* ("long [season] rice")—gained popularity at the expense of less productive summer rices and winter rice. Continuously refined to suit specialized soil, climatic, and insect conditions, improved strains combined with better systems of irrigation and drainage to produce what may have been quite significant increases in yield.[34]

In combination, the lateral extension of cultivation and improved land use facilitated, as well as reflected, a secular growth in population. Again our data, consisting of censuses, military lists, and local histories, are less detailed than one would wish. Yet in combination these materials strongly suggest that the population of the Irrawaddy basin as a whole was at least 50 percent, and probably closer to a 100 percent, larger in 1830 than in 1350. Most of the increase seems to have been concentrated during the Restored Toungoo and Konbaung periods.

The growth in population and productivity in turn stimulated domestic commerce and interregional exchange. More people meant increased aggregate demand for salt, dried fish and fish paste, iron goods, pottery, cheap textiles, carts, and other such items produced in specialist centers and disseminated throughout the countryside through a network of village and provincial markets. Insofar as rural productivity grew, per capita expenditures also must have increased, either by primary producers themselves or by various elites who derived wealth from taxation and rents. In response to stronger demand, local and provincial markets were upgraded to supply more satellite markets and to provide more complex services. By itself, the growth of urban populations and specialized occupational groups (salt boilers, fish-paste makers, potters, miners, boatmen) further strengthened commercial demand, because these communities relied on markets for food and materials more regularly than did the average peasant cultivator.

Like earlier regimes, the state during the Restored Toungoo and

---

[34]See the discussion at ibid., pp. 10–11. Note, however, that claims, based on translations by Than Tun, for increases in specific *kauk-gyi* yields have been effectively questioned by Michael Aung-Thwin, *Irrigation in the Heartland of Burma* (De Kalb, Ill., 1990), pp. 38–51.

Konbaung periods assisted internal commerce through a variety of interventions. These could be direct and more or less self-conscious, as when the court attempted to regulate key markets, to standardize weights and measures, to reduce tolls, or to ensure bullion supplies. Interventions could also be largely inadvertent, though nonetheless significant, as when the political reunification of Upper and Lower Burma removed impediments to trade and diverted rice from overseas to interior markets, or when pacification campaigns and deportations increased the density of settlement and substantially assisted agricultural production. So too state-directed urbanization, though essentially political in inspiration, helped to convert increased rural output into market demand.

Alongside such domestic influences on commerce, the aforementioned growth of maritime contacts, and to a lesser extent the intensification of overland trade with Yunnan, also conditioned exchange patterns within the Burmese empire. Although our materials are inadequate to quantify the relative contributions of foreign and domestic stimuli, and although these contributions no doubt varied with time and locale, international trade clearly had a major impact on economic specialization throughout the period under study. (I leave aside, for the time being, the indirect economic contribution of guns via improved pacification.) Indian Ocean and Chinese demand, for example, stimulated a variety of Burmese enterprises producing partially or even primarily for export: ceramic production, shipbuilding, teak extraction, the mining of gems and certain metals, and the commercial cultivation of indigo, rice, and cotton. By providing cash advances to primary producers of such goods and by furnishing Indian textiles and other imported goods that could attract peasants to provincial markets, foreign merchants pioneered or reinforced commercial circuits throughout the interior. As these exchange networks strengthened, goods intended purely for domestic consumption—foodstuffs, salt, oils, silk and cotton textiles, various handicrafts—could all be distributed more easily, so the impact of foreign trade radiated throughout the countryside. Furthermore, in assessing the contribution of foreign trade, one should recall that Burma's supplies of specie depended heavily on alien inputs. In the north, Chinese miners worked the famous mines of Bawdwin, while at the coast imported copper and later silver lubricated virtually all large-scale commercial exchanges.

Evidence that economic specialization and monetization continued, indeed intensified, after 1600 is not difficult to find. Between c. 1610 and 1783 the number of local markets grew from approximately 145 to over 200, while the physical size and population of most towns on which we have information—including Prome, Henzada, Kanaung, Ava, and Rangoon—increased.[35] Long-distance domestic trade in tea, raw and finished cotton, and perhaps earth-oil all apparently originated in the fourteenth or fifteenth century, but by the nineteenth century they had become staples of interregional exchange. So too, only after the early seventeenth-century unification did Upper Burma begin to depend heavily on southern supplies of rice and salted fish. The seasonal movement of thousands of rice boats from the delta to Upper Burma is graphically described in early nineteenth-century sources. Early Konbaung accounts also refer to an unprecedented array of riverine towns specializing in handicrafts and foodstuffs and to a growth of roadways and riverine conveyances. Moreover, the eighteenth and early nineteenth centuries saw a proliferation in commercial contracts (*thet-kayit*). Dealing with land sales, mortgages, and loans, these contracts are a further indication that landlords, tenants, and owner-occupiers had access to cash and engaged in reasonably widespread commercial production.

But perhaps the most convincing and objective evidence of growing commercialization relates to the use of coinage in rural transactions. Lithic inscriptions from Upper Burma show that in 64 percent of all extant land sales between 1350 and 1512 the properties were exchanged for in-kind goods (animals, textiles, beer, metal trays) or for a combination of lump-coinage and in-kind goods. By contrast, commercial contracts from Upper Burma dated between 1750 and 1830 show that 97 percent of the lands were paid for exclusively in silver lump-coinage. Moreover, whereas the early inscriptions reflected the activities of elites with easy access to specie supplies in the capital, Konbaung era contracts were overwhelmingly from rural areas.[36] One can only conclude that the Burmese rural economy in the Konbaung period was considerably more monetized than in the fourteenth or fifteenth century. The hypothesis that the seventeenth century inaugurated an era of decommercialization in Burma thus seems quite untenable.

It is no surprise that these changes in the domestic economy promised important benefits to imperial centralization. Along with guns and maritime revenues, the expansion of domestic resources between c. 1500 and 1830 reinforced the military-political imbalance between the Irrawaddy lowlands, which formed the heart of the Restored Toungoo

---

[35]Lieberman, 1991, p. 18, n. 47 refers to 188 "cities and district towns" in 1783. This figure excludes, however, a significant number of Shan towns, whereas the early seventeenth-century figure includes Shan areas. The 1783 census was substantially reproduced in the 1802/3 census.

[36]Ibid., pp. 19–21.

and Konbaung states, on the one hand, and more peripheral imperial zones such as the Shan highlands, Manipur, and the upper Chindwin valley, on the other. Even if the rural economies of the core and periphery had grown at the same rate, the former area would have constantly increased its overall superiority in manpower and rice, because it started at a higher level. Yet, in fact, royal policy consistently sought to transfer manpower from outlying areas to irrigated districts in the Upper Burma heartland. In an era of as yet limited military specialization, the latter region thus tended to acquire a cumulative advantage.

At the same time, the growth of markets, especially within the lowlands, enhanced the empire's long-term ability to extract and mobilize resources. The bulkiness of in-kind agricultural levies impeded collection and transmission, particularly in outlying areas, and helps explain the traditional appeal of maritime revenues. As domestic markets developed and cultivators found cash easier to obtain, the commutation of agricultural taxes became more feasible. Notwithstanding the crown's determination to retain some rice levies to safeguard against famine, many agricultural, household, and domestic commercial taxes showed a long-term movement from kind to cash: according to my analysis of inquest records, cash taxes constituted only 21 percent of recorded local levies between 1350 and 1550, but 42 percent from 1600 to 1752 and almost 70 percent from 1752 to 1804.[37] In addition to improving the collection of such traditional taxes, Bodawhpaya began to sell to Burmese and foreign traders commercial monopolies for specific consumer goods. Bodawhpaya's court also had virtual fleets trading along the Irrawaddy as well as overseas on behalf of the crown and individual princes.

Along with maritime revenues, domestic cash income was used to strengthen royal control over patronage, to hire labor, to compensate elite military groups, and to purchase the firearms and supplies needed for repeated military offensives against Thailand and other states. Monetization also gradually transformed patterns of religious patronage. In lieu of the system of perpetual landed donations that had prevailed in Upper Burma during Pagan and post-Pagan times, the Toungoo and Konbaung courts began to patronize the monkhood out of current income. This represented less a threat to the throne's economic security than the cumulative alienation of limited riceland and, along with new institutional controls over the monkhood and curbs on nonroyal donations, eliminated a fundamental weakness in the pre-1600 political economy.

[37]Ibid., p. 24.

Finally, commercial integration aided central authority by eroding local loyalties. During the fourteenth and fifteenth centuries the sustained decline of royal administration and the large-scale entry of Shans into Upper Burma had encouraged a localization of religious and political identities, symbolized, for example, by the proliferation of monastic sects and the florescence of politicoreligious cults associated with particular principalities. By breaching the self-sufficiency of these communities, however, growing interregional exchange gave local merchants and producers a stronger interest in the maintenance of imperial peace. It also magnified the physical movement of peddlers, seasonal laborers, monks, pilgrims, and agricultural migrants throughout the basin and between the basin and the Shan uplands. In combination with more effective political patronage and autonomous cultural movements (see below), economic integration helped to diffuse lowland culture to outlying areas and thus to promote a degree of cultural uniformity that privileged lowland norms over those of the periphery.

Imperial Centralization and Expansion

In short, demographic and commercial growth joined with maritime inputs to create an environment favorable to administrative centralization. Lest we reduce administrative history to a mere function of economic change, however, several considerations bear emphasis. First, the timing for such reform normally was governed by narrow political and military pressures rather than by broad economic trends. Reforms typically responded to short-term crises, that is, foreign invasion or domestic revolts. Thus, not only did administrative innovation tend to be convulsive and episodic, but, insofar as these innovations enhanced the state's extractive capacity, there was no necessary short-term correlation between the throne's income and overall trends in the economy.

Furthermore, as becomes more apparent in the ensuing discussion, over the long term a variety of noneconomic factors also favored centralization. Improvements in firearms, changes in Buddhist sensibility, the gradual assimilation of Shan migrants, the spread of lay literacy, and, perhaps most important, cumulative refinements in administrative technique all served to elevate royal authority. These other factors, of course, interacted with economic change in various ways, but each also had its own dynamic. Finally, while economic change modified the context of state formation, the reverse was equally true: to magnify their military power, Toungoo and Konbaung rulers systematically and repeatedly encouraged certain types of trade, agricultural development, and new settlement.

When discussing administrative change in Burma, we should remember that it occurred in a context of patron-client chains and patrimonial privileges that defied European or even Confucian norms of bureaucracy. Through 1824—indeed 1885—succession disputes and princely revolts bedeviled the court, while jurisdictions were omnicompetent and superficial. In many respects, the provinces remained subject to minimal royal interference. Nonetheless, when judged against First Toungoo standards, Restored Toungoo and early Konbaung government undoubtedly became more stable and effective. Moreover, despite the collapse of the First Toungoo domain, the Burmese empire again expanded notably during the early Konbaung period. Therefore, as was true of maritime trade, military technology, and domestic economic growth, in the sphere of territorial integration and political control pre-1600 trends continued long after that date.

As we have seen, the First Toungoo ambition to control Laos and Thailand proved totally unrealistic, and in the aftermath of Pegu's collapse Restored Toungoo kings introduced several changes in imperial structure. To what extent they were driven by contemporary trial and error and to what extent they had carefully analyzed First Toungoo weaknesses is impossible to say from surviving records, but the impact of their modifications is clear enough. They abandoned claims to dominion throughout the Tai world and accepted a zone of control reaching no farther east than Kenghung and Chiengmai. Thereby they constructed a more integral and stable domain, with a primary axis in the Irrawaddy basin and with peripheral zones that did not extend in any direction to that point where Burma's supply lines were more vulnerable than those of her nearest lowland rival. At the same time, as I have emphasized, they removed the capital to Upper Burma, the traditional center of political gravity.

Most ingenious, both to ensure effective control over the resources of Lower Burma and to reduce the general problem of princely dissidence, the Restored Toungoo throne undertook a series of provincial reforms.[38] The First Toungoo empire had welded together several long-independent kingdoms whose essential sovereignty persisted in the minds not only of their own people but also of the High Kings at Pegu. Accordingly, during the sixteenth century the princely heads of major principalities, even within the Irrawaddy basin, had served in effect as

---

[38]On reforms, see RUL 45235, pp. 15–17, 39–40, 66–67, 70–79; U Kala, 3:105, 275, 287, 384; LBHK, pp. 42, 59, 194, 311; HNY, pp. 275, 293–95, 301, 304, 317, 380–84; KBZ, p. 71; Hpaya-byu Hsaya-daw, Tha-thana bahu-thu-ta paka-thani (Rangoon, 1928), pp. 171–73.

subkings, with their own courts, military forces, and royal insignia. Restored Toungoo kings now moved lowland principalities farther along the road from full independence to genuine subordination. They increased the status differential between themselves and provincial rulers by reducing the latters' ceremonial insignia and appointing more junior men; henceforth, senior princes were normally obliged to reside at the capital under close supervision. The crown also took direct control over provincial deputies, developed more effective links with local headmen in the provinces, and magnified Ava's military superiority over the provinces by expanding the *ahmu-dan* service system around the capital. Starting in 1635, unprecedentedly comprehensive censuses, requiring a high degree of scribal expertise, strengthened central access to provincial manpower and tax collections. Furthermore, after c. 1635 the Upper Burma monkhood periodically became subject to more effective financial and personnel controls. As a result of these strategic and administrative initiatives, aided over the long term by demographic and economic changes already discussed, the Restored Toungoo dynasty survived two and a half times longer than its predecessor and experienced far less frequent and less severe provincial challenges.

The fall of the Restored Toungoo dynasty in the mid-eighteenth century is sometimes interpreted as part of a secular decline in administrative vigor, but in fact the early Konbaung regime quickly matched and then excelled Restored Toungoo levels of control. The Restored Toungoo collapse in 1752 reflected the intersection of two phenomena: (a) institutional weaknesses at the capital, leading to intensified factionalism and succession disputes; (b) the uneven impact that growing trade, and also perhaps accelerating price inflation, had on the income of various sectors of the elite. Those officials who lacked direct access to commercial income apparently sought to compensate for their relative impoverishment through extraordinary impositions on royal servicemen, a situation that weakened the entire military system and aggravated tension between factions pledged to rival princes at the capital.[39] Insofar as the growth of international trade, urbanization, and the consolidation of new commercial groups may have helped to weaken political institutions and contributed to the enfeeblement or collapse of Ayutthaya, the Vietnamese states, and Mughal India during roughly this same period, Restored Toungoo disintegration may prove to have

[39]Lieberman, 1984, pp. 156–88. In my original analysis I fail to explore adequately the degree to which price inflation and commercialization impaired peasant autonomy not only indirectly, via compensatory elite abuse, but also directly, through peasant-initiated indebtedness to moneylenders and landlords.

been part of a general eighteenth-century crisis of southern Asian societies that was partly rooted in economic growth.[40]

In contrast to the Mughal empire—but in common with Thailand and Vietnam—Burma succeeded in the late eighteenth and early nineteenth centuries in reviving and at the same time modifying central institutions. After reconcentrating the population into traditional tax-paying and service groups, Alaunghpaya's sons, particularly Bodawhpaya, attempted to exploit new sources of revenue: as noted, they sold commercial monopolies, expanded tax farms, organized new royal trading ventures, attempted to introduce an official coinage, and countenanced a further movement from in-kind to cash payments.[41] In these ways—with how much self-conscious insight into their predecessors' weaknesses, again we cannot say—early Konbaung leaders sought to adjust to what I have argued was an increasingly monetized, commercialized economy. So too, in order to eliminate rigidities in military recruitment and perhaps also to take advantage of both population growth and the court's enhanced scribal capacity, the early Konbaung court replaced the antiquated system of fixed regional levies with variable quotas set for each campaign by the *Hlut-daw* council. Similarly, it may have instituted the program of cash payments to on-duty servicemen (*nauk-dauk*) that was a prominent feature of nineteenth-century military organization.[42] Finally, the early Konbaung court replaced certain hereditary provincial leaders (*myo-thu-gyis*) with appointed governors (*myo-wuns*), who presumably were more dependent on the throne. This policy extended to cis-Salween Shan states, which were increasingly integrated into the taxation, supervisory, and military systems of the lowlands.[43]

With these new departures went a basic conservatism. As William Koenig has convincingly shown, the early Konbaung court reconstituted basic Toungoo political institutions and suffered from a recrudescence of many of the same problems—cumulative loss of royal

---

[40]On commercial growth and its potentially destabilizing effects in the great Muslim empires, see C. A. Bayly, *Imperial Meridian* (London, 1989), pp. 16–61; Muzaffar Alam, *The Crisis of Empire in Mughal North India* (Delhi, 1986); M. Athar Ali, "The Passing of Empire: The Mughal Case," *MAS* 9, no. 3 (1975), 385–96; André Wink, *Land and Sovereignty in India* (Cambridge, 1986). Lieberman, 1984, pp. 290–91; and Nguyen Thanh-Nha, *Tableau économique du Viet Nam aux XVIIe et XVIIIe siècles* (Paris, 1970), offer more speculative views on Thailand and Vietnam.

[41]Lieberman, 1991, pp. 24–25, plus *ROB*, 5:570; 6:488, 506, 802; Ko U, *Myan-ma dinga-mya* (Rangoon, 1974), pp. 67–90; *MMOS*, 3:139.

[42]On military organizational changes, see Koenig, 1990, p. 117; Sangermano, 1969, p. 98; Trager and Koenig, 1979, p. 298; R. R. Langham-Carter, "The Burmese Army," *JBRS* 27, no. 3 (1937), 254–76.

[43]On gubernatorial changes, see *ROB*, 4:54; 5:525, 564, 660, 873; 6:685, 688, 724, 808, 816, 880; Sao Saimong Mangrai, *The Shan States and the British Annexation* (Ithaca, N.Y., 1965), chap. 3; Trager and Koenig, 1979, pp. 363–70.

servicemen, ill-restrained factionalism—as had weakened the Restored Toungoo state. Self-destructive princely rivalries remained the bane of Burmese politics. After 1770, Burma began to lose ground to its arch rival, Thailand, which proved more innovative commercially and also eventually developed a more stable succession pattern than did Burma. Despite their remarkable sack of Ayutthaya in 1767, Burmese forces were forced out of Chiengmai by 1776 and thereafter failed in repeated campaigns to repenetrate the Thai inner provinces.[44]

Nonetheless, the military record of the early Konbaung era as a whole remained impressive. Stymied in the east, Burmese forces turned westward, in 1784 annexing Arakan for the first time, devastating and subduing Manipur from 1759 to 1824, and dominating distant Assam after 1816. In the face of bitter Tai and Chinese competition, they also retained control over Mergui and Tai areas as far as Kenghung.[45] Except for the ephemeral First Toungoo realm, the Konbaung empire in 1824, on the eve of the British intrusion, was the largest in Burmese history. Notwithstanding its basically galactic structure, it was also the most effectively integrated state for at least 540 years.

In sum, in terms of administration and territorial control no less than in economic terms, the post-1600 era saw a consolidation and refinement of key sixteenth-century trends.

Theravada Orthodoxy and Cultural Integration

I turn finally to a consideration of long-term cultural-cum-ethnic integration, which both facilitated and reflected political integration.

During the two and a half centuries that preceded the First Toungoo unification, there was no preeminent center whose customs were accepted as normative by elites throughout the Irrawaddy basin and surrounding highlands. No doubt the memory of Pagan exerted a wide, if diffuse, influence. It is also true that local courts, held together by patron-client ties and legitimated in terms of Buddhist universalism, normally had a polyethnic clientele. Yet, particularly in periods of transition, ethnicity could serve as a badge of political allegiance, and each of the main principalities was normally associated with a particular ethnic group whose language, dress, and rituals dominated court life. Shans controlled the highland states ringing the northern basin and in the early sixteenth century exercised increasing influence over the Avan court, notwithstanding the fact that the great majority of cultiva-

---

[44]Koenig, 1990, chaps. 4 and 7, and pp. 14–22, 30–36.
[45]Ibid., pp. 17–30.

tors in the northern dry zone undoubtedly spoke Burmese and continued to regard themselves as Burmans. In the southeast corridor, Burman emigration had given Toungoo a solidly Burman character; this principality, home of the unifying dynasty, would serve as a rallying point for Burman authority. Finally, in the southern lowlands below Toungoo and Prome lay the historic coastal kingdom of Ra-manya, whose culture at both elite and popular levels was quintessentially Mon. According to the early seventeenth-century(?) epic *Hanthawaddy hsin-byu-shin ayei-daw-bon*, in Lower Burma "there are as many Talaings [Mons] as there are hairs on a bullock, but we Burmans are as few as the horns."[46]

Political and ethnic diversity was in turn associated with a plethora of syncretic and localized religious traditions. Although most Shans before 1550 probably regarded themselves as Buddhist in some sense, contemporary Burman inscriptions habitually identified Shan raiders as infidels (*meisa-ditthi*).[47] Claiming that pagodas were no more than treasure chambers, in 1540 the Shan ruler of Ava slaughtered 360 Upper Burma monks and ransacked sacred edifices. Yet Burman monks themselves, notwithstanding their orthodox self-image and superior textual erudition, followed certain rituals—including the ritual killing of animals and the consumption of beer (*thei*) and liquor (*ayek*)—which revealed strong pre-Buddhist influence and which later generations would sharply modify or reject.[48] Not surprising perhaps, the Burman lay population propitiated household *nat* spirits with alcohol and with pig and ox sacrifices and in general appear to have accorded animist rituals greater prominence than their nineteenth-century descendants.[49] Popular observance in Ra-manya may well have been comparable to that in the interior, although the coast's maritime orientation—as suggested in the late fifteenth-century "purification" program of King Dama-zei-di—gave it greater exposure to reformist influences emanating from Sri Lanka.[50]

After unifying the basin and surrounding uplands, the First Toungoo

---

[46]*Hanthawaddy hsin-byu-shin ayei-daw-bon* (Rangoon, 1918), p. 8, referring to the sixteenth century. On ethnicity and political identity, see H. L. Shorto, "A Mon Genealogy of Kings," in *Historians of South East Asia*, ed. D. G. E. Hall (London, 1962), pp. 63–72.

[47]For example, *Original Inscriptions Collected by King Bodawpaya in Upper Burma and Now Placed near the Patodawgyi Pagoda, Amarapura* (Rangoon, 1913), p. 277 (A.D. 1369, Duroiselle 655), lines 1–5; *Inscriptions Collected in Upper Burma*, 1:67 (A.D. 1393, Duroiselle 761), lines 9–10.

[48]References to such practices were exceedingly common. See, for example, inscriptions numbered according to Duroiselle, 1921, 643, 656, 665, 671, 693, 704, 714, 718, 732, 752, 769, 779, 793, 833, 847, 883, 902, 998, and the general discussion in Than Tun, "Maha-kathapa gaing," *JBRS* 42, no. 2 (1959), 81–98.

[49]See, for example, *Inscriptions of Pagan, Pinya, and Ava* (Rangoon, 1892), p. 75 (A.D. 1416, Duroiselle 853), lines 27–29; ibid., p. 350 (A.D. 1431, Duroiselle 897), lines 7–9.

[50]On Dama-zei-di's reforms, see *The Kalyani Inscriptions Erected by King Dhammaceti at Pegu in 1476 A.D., Text and Translation* (Rangoon, 1892).

rulers, from their new capital of Pegu, sought to promote practices in accord with what they deemed the orthodox teachings of textually accomplished Burman and Mon monks. Such impulses had also inspired Pagan, Ra-manyan, and even some Avan rulers before them. As in these earlier instances, standardization—or more accurately, perhaps, the temporary reconciliation and adjudication—of conflicting religious traditions offered the crown, in addition to sincerely sought rewards of good karma, a variety of practical benefits: "purification" encouraged local leaders to regard the capital as a transcendent source of moral authority; it justified central interference in the political as well as ceremonial life of provincial communities; it simplified administration by providing a common vocabulary and reference. Like Dama-zei-di and other reformers, First Toungoo kings instinctively favored textually based, externally validated (often via Sri Lanka) sources of authority over local traditions, not least perhaps because the court frequently could control the interpretation of texts and channels of religious communication with the exterior. (Similar dynamics may help to explain the contemporary move to textual orthodoxy in Islamic and Neo-Confucian Southeast Asia.)

The major difference between First Toungoo and previous reformers, however, was that Toungoo kings alone had the power to initiate—and, in many cases, to impose, at least temporarily—their projects at key centers throughout the basin and Shan uplands. In the reign of Bayin-naung (r. 1551–81) began not only the military pacification of the Shan interior but also the sustained incorporation of Shan religious life within the Mon and Burman orbit. Thus Bayin-naung outlawed human sacrifices associated with Shan royal burials, built pagodas and monasteries in Shan centers, distributed copies of the scriptures, and in some principalities obliged Shan rulers and local monks alike to follow the instruction of lowland preceptors. In the same spirit, he attempted to outlaw animist sacrifices in Upper Burma and to unify religious calendars, weights, and measures throughout the realm.[51]

Following the return of the capital to Upper Burma in the early seventeenth century, Restored Toungoo and then Konbaung kings pursued a similar policy of cultural and especially religious integration. They established a reasonably elaborate hierarchy and examination system to supervise the monkhood in leading provincial centers.[52] They attempted to suppress certain magical practices and the consumption of intoxicants. To bring texts and monastic rituals in line with

[51]On Bayin-naung's reforms, see U Kala, 2:293–94, 307, 312–13; *Shei-haung mon kyauk-sa baung-gyok*, ed. U Chit Thein (Rangoon, 1965), pp. 105–8.
[52]Koenig, 1990, pp. 126–30; Lieberman, 1984, pp. 109–12.

capital practices, they also dispatched missionary monks to outlying areas. For example, in 1784 Bodawhpaya established what was in effect a missionary training school from which monks were rotated to the Shan hills, Arakan, and other newly conquered regions.[53]

A significant new emphasis in cultural policy arose from the fact that post-1600 rulers accorded Mon traditions far less prominence than their First Toungoo predecessors. Being Burmans from the interior, the First Toungoo kings had been regarded with a certain suspicion by their predominantly Mon subjects in the delta; perhaps for that reason, First Toungoo rulers had felt obliged to patronize Mon cultural traditions alongside the more congenial Burman modes of speech, ritual, and costume (thus, for example, Bayin-naung's predecessor Tabin-shwei-hti is said to have cut his hair in Mon fashion and to have allowed Mon princesses to retain their customary dress).[54] Conceivably a hybrid Burman-Mon culture was evolving at court in the mid- and late sixteenth century, although, as the anti-Burman revolts of the 1590s suggested, this amalgam faced inherent instabilities. In any case, after the return to the interior, Mon influence at court rapidly decreased, and the models Restored Toungoo and early Konbaung kings sought to propagate became more exclusively Burman. This was true not only of religious rituals and definitions of orthodoxy but more particularly of the court punctilio, coinage, commercial weights and measures, calendars, orthography, and spelling endorsed in repeated royal decrees.

Yet in truth the precolonial state was too weak to legislate, to force cultural change outside a few privileged locales. Probably of greater homogenizing significance than coercion were various mechanisms, both intentional and unplanned, which encouraged outlying elites to adhere voluntarily to capital norms. Such inducements had also operated during the First Toungoo period, but during the seventeenth and eighteenth centuries, as imperial institutions stabilized and the court became more able to disburse rewards and punishments in outlying centers, incentives became more persuasive. These inducements were basically twofold: (a) identification with capital usages could enhance one's prestige within provincial society; (b) outward adherence to Burman cultural norms (including bilingualism) could improve one's prospects for imperial patronage in the Restored Toungoo and Konbaung system.[55]

[53]ROB, 4:316, 352–53, 614; Toyo Bunko Microfilm 79, no. 1 (NL 1605), ne v.

[54]U Kala, 2:214–16; Harvey, 1967, p. 160.

[55]See, for example, Sao Saimong Mangrai, The Padaeng Chronicle and the Jengtung State Chronicle Translated (Ann Arbor, Mich., 1981), pp. 252–55; U Kala, 3:280–86; J. George Scott and J. P. Hardiman, comps., Gazeteer of Upper Burma and the Shan States [henceforth GUBSS] (Rangoon, 1900–1901), 2.1:406.

Figure 11. Ceremonial dress of Burmese court officials, 1795; right, senior royal secretary (*sa-yei-daw-gyi*); center, a minister of the interior (*atwin-wun*); left, the latter's wife. From Michael Symes, *An Account of an Embassy to the Kingdom of Ava in the Year 1795* (Edinburgh, 1827).

Provincial and vassal leaders had ample opportunity to imbibe Avan traditions through the annual *kadaw* homage festivals, through obligatory residence at court as hostages or pages, through intermarriage with court figures, and through contact with Burman officials and soldiers stationed in provincial cities. Ambitious Shan as well as provincial leaders therefore proceeded to mimic in varying degrees Avan religious observance, dress, ceremonial, literature, architecture, and administrative and literary motifs.[56] In turn these norms provided a standard for subordinate elites, so that Upper Burman norms diffused not only outward but downward within each provincial hierarchy. Through such direct and indirect influences, the Upper Burma state after 1600 thus carried forward, albeit with a more pronounced Burman orientation, the work of cultural standardization promoted by the First Toungoo court.

Finally between c. 1500 and 1800 important mechanisms of cultural

[56]Mangrai, 1981, pp. 4–6, 34–37, 204–5; idem., 1965, p. 33; U Kala, 2:307, 312; *LBHK*, esp. pts. 4, 9; *MMOS*, 4:120; *ROB*, 5:396–97; Leslie Milne, *Shans at Home* (London, 1910), pp. 213–14; *GUBSS*, 1.1:198–212, 280–88, 320, 326, 2.1:399; Lieberman, 1984, pp. 133–34.

integration affected the peasant population as much as elites and did not necessarily depend on imperial mediation. Insofar as surviving documents are overwhelmingly official records, these changes are more difficult to reconstruct than court-directed activities; yet as a whole they may have been more influential in eroding regional identities. I refer, for example, to proselytism by semiautonomous groups of Burman and Mon monks who circulated throughout the Irrawaddy lowlands and the Tai interior, spreading lowland norms of ordination, ritual, and Pali grammar, recasting the Buddhist self-image of isolated communities, and in the process strengthening the psychological connections between basin and uplands. Thus, starting as early as the fourteenth century, Forest Dwellers and other monastic sects propagated Sinhalese-style Buddhism along the routes leading from Martaban, Pegu, and Ayutthaya to such interior centers as Mogaung, Sukhothai, Chiengmai, and Keng Tung.[57]

Similarly, sustained emigration by Upper Burma peasants seeking new lands on the fringes of the dry zone and in Lower Burma helped to disseminate dry zone language and social customs. Such settlements— sometimes under royal direction, but more generally on an individual family basis—facilitated intermarriage and contributed to the increasing tendency among some minority communities to identify as Burmans. The aforementioned growth of interregional commerce played a similar role in diffusing Burman traditions, as presumably did the periodic integration of local units on military campaigns and large-scale corvées. None of this is to claim that cultural change was either uncontested or unidirectional, that Mon culture, for example, had no impact on Burman self-expression; only that the political and heavy demographic superiority of Burmans within the lowlands gave them a preponderant influence over whatever interchange or standardization occurred.

Increased literacy was yet another phenomenon only partially dependent on state direction which encouraged local communities to identify with capital norms. Why people should have become more literate we can only speculate: growing per capita income, Shan assimilation, and increased security in the Upper Burma countryside after c. 1550 may have combined to multiply monastic schools and students, while novel censuses probably encouraged record-keeping skills among the gentry. Expanded literacy, especially among laymen, between c. 1500 and 1830 was reflected in the florescence of legal and especially

---

[57]Mangrai, 1981, pp. xiv, 102–12; see also Wyatt, 1982, pp. 31, 59–63, 76. Sect leaders also undertook proselytizing missions in response to royal invitations.

historical literature written by laymen as well as monks; in the sharply reduced cost of *Tipitaka* transcriptions; in the expansion of lay, rather than monastic, scribes; in the proliferation of local commercial contracts; and in the change from antique square orthography, derived from stone inscriptions, to circular orthography, based on increasingly common palm-leaf manuscripts.[58] By the mid-nineteenth century, not only did male literacy in lowland Burma stand at the extraordinary level of almost 50 percent,[59] but legal codes patronized by the court (e.g., the *Manu-kye*), royal chronicles, and religious texts enjoyed wide circulation. Insofar as these sources were incorporated into the world-view of local communities, and insofar as they portrayed Upper Burman religious and court practice as normative ideals, they must have strengthened identification with the capital.

Thus I am arguing that political centralization and cultural homogenization, though to some extent of separate origins, became mutually reinforcing; and that these movements, far from halting in the late sixteenth or early seventeenth century, continued throughout the period under consideration.

The cultural integration of the Burmese empire between c. 1500 and 1830 may be measured in several ways. In terms of ethnicity, the Irrawaddy basin and its immediate upland perimeter became more uniformly Burman; that is, certain areas which in the fifteenth century had been overwhelmingly Mon, Shan, or Shan-Kadu had, by the mid-nineteenth century, populations in which a plurality or majority identified themselves as Burmans. This was partly a matter of population displacement but partly too the result of intermarriage and voluntary changes in self-identification on the part of increasingly bilingual resident populations. Shan areas experiencing change of this sort included the districts of Kalei and Mingin in the upper Chindwin valley; Myedu, Bhamo, Mogok, Tagaung, Momeik (Mong Mit), and Katha in the north; and Hsum Hsai (Thonze) in the northeast.[60] Mon areas that by 1850 had become predominantly Burman included Tharawaddy, much of

[58]On these changes in literary, scribal, and orthographic expression, see Victor Lieberman, "How Reliable Is U Kala's Burmese Chronicle?" *JSEAS* 17, no. 2 (1986), 250–55; *ROB*, 1:363–64; 4:358, 414, 482–92; 5:874; Ryuji Okudaira, "The Role of Kaingza Manuyaza, an Eminent Jurist of the 17th Century, in the Development of the Burmese Legal History," *JAAS* 27 (1984), 180–86; *Inscriptions Copied from the Stones Collected by King Bodawpaya and Placed near the Arakan Pagoda, Mandalay*, 2 vols. (Rangoon, 1897), 1:336 (Duroiselle 1045); U Pei Maung Tin, *Myan-ma sa-pei thamaing* (Rangoon, 1955), esp. chaps. 3–6; Than Tun, *Hkit-haung myan-ma ya-zawin* (Rangoon, 1964), p. 182.

[59]J. George Scott, *Burma: A Handbook of Practical Information* (London, 1906), pp. 161–63. Scott's figures were for 1891 and 1901, but the system of rural education they portray was in place throughout the Konbaung era. "It is strange," he notes, "that the proportion of literates should be highest in the rural districts, and particularly in Upper Burma."

[60]*GUBSS*, 1.1:198–208, 281; 2.1:48, 233, 280, 326; 2.3:14–15. This homogenizing trend was not negated by large-scale deportations to Upper Burma from outlying areas insofar as de-

Toungoo, the urban districts of Bassein and Rangoon, and most of the Irrawaddy stretching from Prome to Henzada.[61] With Mons increasingly confined to the south and southeastern littoral, the Mon kingdom of Ra-manya was becoming an ill-preserved memory. As repeated Mon revolts between c. 1590 and 1826 testified, such assimilation was neither universal nor always voluntary. But it carried to a logical conclusion the Burman cultural assault on the delta and Shan highlands which started with the First Toungoo explosion. (One suspects that differences in dialect and custom between provincial Burman traditions also decreased, but the issue has yet to be researched.)

Even in those areas that retained an overwhelmingly Tai ethnic identity, however, Tai rulers and monks adopted specific Avan features. Thus, as noted, court ceremonies, dating systems, scripts, literature, weights and measures, patterns of taxation, royal and religious architecture all became Burmanized in varying degrees. The pattern was most pronounced in those cis-Salween Shan states most exposed to Burman military pressure, but distant Keng Tung and Chiengmai also imbibed certain Burman elements that distinguished them from Tai principalities more subject to China or Ayutthaya.[62]

At the same time, Buddhist orthodoxy as defined by the court continued to grow at the expense of animist, Hindu, and local syncretic elements. Although this was most obviously true in the Shan region, where human sacrifices and other pre-Buddhist practices yielded to lowland pressure, in the basin as well signs of more orthodox sensibilities were numerous and varied. By the Restored Toungoo era, if not earlier, the old Upper Burma custom of publicizing land transfers with lavish consumption of alcohol and freshly killed meat had died out. Instead, Buddhist sensibilities demanded that pickled tea be consumed to solemnize legal agreements. Whereas kings and monks in the fifteenth century had publicly drunk alcohol, Konbaung kings now sternly forbade any consumption of intoxicants; a voluntary teetotal movement also seems to have spread among Buddhist laypeople from an early date.[63] By the same token, although the *nat* cult remained an

---

portee families not only gradually assimilated to Burman norms but sometimes served as a bridge for cultural transmission to their home regions.

[61]Michael Adas, *The Burma Delta* (Madison, Wis., 1974), pp. 16–19, 57, 232.

[62]See sources in note 56, above.

[63]See sources in notes 48, 49, above, plus Than Tun, "Social Life in Burma in the 16th Century," *Tonan Ajia Kenkyu* 21, no. 3 (1983), 272; ROB, 1:70, 4:220; *Original Inscriptions*, p. 283 (Duroiselle 682), line 44; *Inscriptions Copied from the Stones*, 1:462 (Duroiselle 780), lines 17–18; Sangermano, 1969, pp. 159–60: Symes, 1969, pp. 51, 65–66, 174; Harvey, 1967, p. 278. Anthony Reid has observed that the spread of Islam and Buddhism in the early modern era reduced meat and liquor consumption often associated with animist rites throughout Southeast Asia; see *Southeast Asia in the Age of Commerce, 1450–1680* (New Haven, Conn., 1988), 34–40.

important element of Burmese supernaturalism, revels and animal sacrifices formerly associated with *nat* propitiation became socially marginalized.[64]

In the same spirit a variety of legal, historical, and genealogical trea-
tises that derived from Hindu or non-Buddhist traditions were rewrit-
ten at the Restored Toungoo and early Konbaung courts so as to provide the monarchy with a more explicitly Buddhist charter. Thus, for
example, the great Konbaung history *Hman-nan-maha-ya-zawin-daw-
gyi*, building on U Kala's early eighteenth-century national chronicle,
changed the official progenitor of the Burmese ruling house from a sun
spirit to Gotama Buddha.[65] Whereas the First Toungoo dynasty had
sought to popularize the partly Buddhicized, partly Hindu thirteenth-
century *Wareru Dhammathat*, the two most famous subsequent legal
compilations—the *Kaing-za Maha-ya-za-that-gyi* (c. 1629–48) and the
Manu-kye (c. 1758)—both showed a strong tendency to support Burman customary law with explicitly Buddhist scriptural justifications.[66]
Significant too, I suspect, was the tendency for squabbling monastic
sects to legitimate their behavior by citing textual authority rather than
local tradition.[67]

I readily concede the possibility that significant cultural, economic,
and even political changes occurred in the early and mid-seventeenth
century. Along with rice exports and Mon-Burman seafaring, maritime
income as a proportion of total royal income and royal sensitivity to
maritime issues in general apparently diminished after c. 1640. The
pace of military change also may have slowed, while Mon influence in
imperial councils declined.

But in a wider sense the period c. 1640–1830 maintained and per-
fected certain sixteenth-century experiments. The basic achievement of
the First Toungoo dynasty, in my view, was to unify politically the
basin and highland perimeter for the first time in almost three centuries. By the eve of the first Anglo-Burmese war, this area was more

[64]Previous note, plus *ROB*, 3:229. On the relation of the *nat* cult to Burmese Buddhism, see
Melford Spiro, *Burmese Supernaturalism* (Englewood Cliffs, N.J., 1967).

[65]Koenig, 1990, pp. 86–87. Note, however, that claims of Sakyan ancestry for Burmese rulers
had pre-Konbaung precedents; see *Inscriptions Copied from the Stones*, 1:335 (A.D. 1501,
Duroiselle 1045), lines 10–12.

[66]E. Forchhammer, *The Jardine Prize: An Essay on the Sources and Development of Burmese Law*
(Rangoon, 1885); Okudaira, 1984, pp. 180–86; J. S. Furnivall, "Manu in Burma: Some Burmese
Dhammathats," *JBRS* 30, no. 2 (1940), 362–70; Kaing-za Manu-yaza, *Maha-ya-za-that-gyi*
(Rangoon, 1870).

[67]See Maha-dama-thin-gyan, *Tha-thana-lin-ga-ya sa-dan* (Rangoon, 1897), p. 186. Note too
Bodawhpaya's criticism of religious laxity under Restored Toungoo kings and his attempts to
launch yet another textually based purification of popular custom; *ROB*, 4:471–75, 6:352–93.

effectively united than ever before. Long-term administrative integration drew strength from, and at the same time helped shape, the emergence of a more productive, specialized, regionally interdependent, and monetized economy in which foreign trade remained a vital element. In a cultural sense as well, the early Konbaung period carried forward halting First Toungoo steps to assimilate the Shans and to disseminate cosmopolitan, orthodox, and textually based norms at the expense of local traditions. If we recognize that the First Toungoo conquest of Lower Burma imposed an unprecedented degree of Burman cultural authority over the Mon country, the post-1600 decline of Mon ethnicity also could be interpreted, not as a reversal, but as a continuation of sixteenth-century trends.

10

Ayutthaya at the End of the Seventeenth Century: Was There a Shift to Isolation?

Dhiravat na Pombejra

After the long wars with Burma in the sixteenth century, the kingdom of Ayutthaya began to revive its economy during the early seventeenth century. Siam's sphere of commercial and diplomatic activities expanded. The Siamese kings, always the principal traders in their own realm, established a royal monopoly system in an attempt to control Siamese trade with foreigners and to facilitate crown trading overseas. These seventeenth-century kings also had junks and ships fitted out in their name and dispatched to ports as far apart as Mocha and Manila, Batavia and Bandar Abbas. The so-called forest produce of Siam (sappanwood, eaglewood, deerskins, and other goods) was exported to several parts of Asia, and tin from the southern provinces of the kingdom was bought up by "Moor" (Indian and Persian Muslim), Chinese, Dutch, French, and other traders. Embassies were exchanged with European as well as Asian potentates. The city of Ayutthaya was recognized as being a leading entrepôt and the most significant port in the mainland states of Southeast Asia. For the period c. 1600–88, then, the case of Ayutthaya fully supports the hypothesis that there was an "age of commerce" in Southeast Asia.[1]

Of all the seventeenth-century kings of Ayutthaya, King Narai (r. 1656–88) was the most enterprising and energetic in his dealings with foreigners. Not only did he encourage all foreign nations to come to

---

[1] Anthony Reid, *Southeast Asia in the Age of Commerce 1450–1680*, vol. 1: *The Lands below the Winds* (New Haven, Conn., 1988), pp. 234–35.

Figure 12. Jesuits showing King Narai a solar eclipse in April 1688. Photo: Bibliothèque Nationale, Paris, Estampes Od. 59d.

trade in Ayutthaya, but he also sent out his own vessels to trade at various ports in western, southern, southeastern, and eastern Asia. King Narai was also intellectually curious and tried to learn more about other cultures, notably Persian[2] and French. He welcomed the French missionaries so courteously, and plied them with so many questions about Christianity and France, that King Louis XIV and others began to nurture real hopes of converting the king to the Catholic faith. Two of King Narai's greatest court favorites were a Persian, Aqa Muhammad, and a Greek, Constantine Phaulkon. Indeed, during this reign hundreds of Europeans (British, French, Portuguese) were in the Siamese royal service, some as officials, others as ship captains, merchants, or mercenaries, and yet others as experts in fields as diverse as medicine and military fortification. Toward the end of his reign, King Narai and his adviser, Phaulkon, adopted a pro-French policy that led to some suspicion and discontent at court, especially when, in late 1687,

[2]Ibn Muhammad Ibrahim, *The Ship of Sulaiman*, trans. J. O'Kane (London, 1972), pp. 98–99.

the French were allowed to garrison key fortresses at Bangkok and Mergui.[3]

The 1688 "Revolution" in Siam

The anti-French and anti-Catholic mood of some important elements in the Siamese court coincided with the onset of King Narai's final bout of illness in early 1688. What should have been a straightforward succession conflict became a series of events with anti-French and anti-Catholic overtones. King Narai had no son, and his two surviving brothers were politically powerless. The way was thus clear for an ambitious aspirant to seize the crown. The master of the royal elephants, Okphra Phetracha, did just that. In a coup d'état during April 1688 he seized control of the royal palace in Lopburi (where King Narai held court for most of the year) and thus gained custody of the king. He then proceeded to eliminate all potential rivals, including Phaulkon and the dying king's two brothers. When King Narai died on 11 July 1688, Okphra Phetracha was able to accede to the throne unopposed. The new king, the founder of Ayutthaya's last dynasty (the Ban Phlu Luang dynasty), forced the French garrisons to withdraw by the end of 1688. The 1688 "revolution" was therefore a court conflict above all, one among the many succession crises in Ayutthayan history. The major issue at stake all along had been the royal succession, not the French presence in Bangkok. Attempts to interpret 1688 as an anti-foreign uprising or a Franco-Siamese conflict have not been very convincing. Okphra Phetracha certainly exploited the issues of a French threat and a Roman Catholic peril to Buddhism in drumming up support from among the officials, the *sangha* (Buddhist monkhood), and the Lopburi populace, but it was the succession that he and his son Okluang Sorasak were primarily concerned about.[4]

The 1688 uprising was not a social or structural revolution but a political conflict that led to a change of dynasty. The next question to be analyzed is whether it marked a turning point in Siamese history, whether Siam under the new king became isolationist in outlook and policy.

---

[3]For details see, E. W. Hutchinson, *Adventurers in Siam in the Seventeenth Century* (London, 1940), pp. 155–78.

[4]W. A. R. Wood, *A History of Siam* (London, 1926), pp. 211–14, and Hutchinson, 1940, pp. 165–77, emphasize the Franco-Siamese conflict; Busakorn Lailert, "The Ban Phlu Luang Dynasty, 1688–1767: A Study of the Thai Monarchy during the Closing Years of the Ayutha Period," Ph.D. diss., University of London, 1972, pp. 24–25, emphasizes the issue of the royal succession.

To E .W. Hutchinson, the death of Phaulkon marked the end of "the era of opportunity for adventure and trade enjoyed by foreigners in Siam during the seventeenth century. From 1689 until the middle of the nineteenth century Siam regarded Europeans with a suspicion which was the result of King Narai's disastrous foreign policy, as manipulated with unscrupulous daring by Phaulkon."[5] If by foreigners Hutchinson really means Europeans, then this assessment is reasonable. But he goes too far when he maintains that an antiforeign outlook produced in the Siamese of the post-1688 era "a spirit of blind and arrogant self-sufficiency" and repeats John Crawfurd's disparaging remarks on Siam in the nineteenth century being no more advanced than it had been in Simon de la Loubère's time.[6] To presume that continued cultural contact with the West would have led to Siam's advancement is to argue from the dubious premise that Western civilization is intrinsically superior. According to this line of argument, Ayutthaya shut itself off from all Western influences after the events of 1688. As I show below, this was not strictly true.

David Wyatt's *Short History* of Thailand takes a more moderate line. Wyatt says that the coup makers of 1688 were motivated not only by "xenophobic sentiments" but also by the feeling that Ayutthaya "had stepped too far into the deep, murky, dangerous waters of great-power politics. They may have felt more comfortable in a world in which commerce and international relations were conducted on a simpler, smaller scale. They did not want to reject the outside world, but they did want to deal with it on a more manageable and perhaps traditional level."[7] Wyatt does not cover the commerce and international relations of the post-1688 era in any detail, nor does Busakorn Lailert Karnchanacharee in her thesis on the Ban Phlu Luang dynasty, but both historians show an awareness of the crucial roles played by Chinese and "Moor" traders and officials in Siam during the 1688–1767 period.[8]

The 1688 succession crisis and the usurpation of King Phetracha, then, may be seen either as the beginning of a period of self-imposed isolation for Ayutthaya or as the point from which the Siamese shifted from close contacts with the West back to a more traditional, or manageable, way of dealing with foreign nations. The primary sources for this period (notably the VOC, French missionary, Chinese, and Japanese sources) indicate clearly that there was no policy of self-imposed isolation along the lines of the Tokugawa seclusion policy in Japan. To

---

[5]Hutchinson, 1940, p. 179.
[6]Hutchinson, 1940, pp. 192–193.
[7]David K. Wyatt, *Thailand: A Short History* (London, 1984), pp. 117–18.
[8]Busakorn, 1972, pp. 24–25, 35; Wyatt, 1984, pp. 126–32.

understand the post-1688 situation better, it is necessary to take a closer look at Siam's foreign relations and participation in international commerce at the end of the seventeenth century. For convenience, I focus on the reign of King Phetracha himself (r. 1688–1703) and only touch on events and development in other reigns.

King Phetracha and the Royal Trading System

A topic somewhat neglected in all discussions of post-1688 Siam concerns royal trade or, more specifically, the revenues and benefits to be gained from participation in international trade. Viewed as a long-term development, the participation of the Siamese royal family and elite in international commerce was an irreversible trend that had begun long before 1688 and reached a high point during the seventeenth century. By participating in overseas trade, Siamese kings obtained luxury goods, up-to-date firearms, precious metals, as well as money and merchandise for use in further trade with foreigners. The material magnificence of the court, the grand scale of the monarchs' merit making, and the upkeep of princely or high officials' retinues: all these depended on more than just effective control of manpower or a self-sufficient agrarian economy. As Joost Schouten remarked in 1636, the king's revenues were mostly derived from foreign trade, customs duties, "Tributes and Presents from Subject-Princes, and Governours of Cities and Provinces," and the "inland trade," to which must be added other forms of taxation. According to Schouten, "most of these monies are expended in building and repairing of Temples, in rewarding of merits, and defraying the publick charges of the kingdom; the residue being brought into the Treasury, which is esteemed rich and great."[9] A close study of Dutch records dating from King Phetracha's reign reveals that the Siamese court was mainly interested in receiving steady supplies of silver, copper, cash, Indian and Persian textiles, and Chinese goods such as silk. To initiate a policy of national isolation would have been contrary to the court's interests.

The post-1688 kings of Siam also had a well-established system of royal storehouses and royal monopoly to rely on. By compelling foreign traders to buy certain types of merchandise from the royal storehouses, the kings could control the prices of these commodities and derive the kind of profit that comes from having no competitors. In

---

[9]François Caron and Joost Schouten, *A True Description of the Mighty Kingdoms of Japan and Siam*, trans. Roger Manley, intro. and annot. John Villiers (Bangkok, 1986), pp. 130–31.

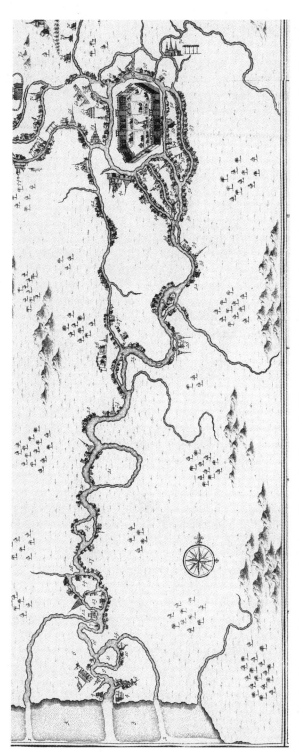

Figure 13. Ayutthaya and its river, as drawn by a Dutch artist. Dutch facilities are marked with flags: the warehouse near the mouth of the river (5), and the Dutch residence (53). From François Valentijn, *Oud en Nieuw Oost-Indien* (Dordrecht, 1724–26).

1694, the Siamese court confirmed the following to be crown monopoly goods, not to be bought except from the king's factors and storehouses: lead, tin, copper, gunpowder, sappanwood, areca, eaglewood, deerskins, elephant teeth, and rhinoceros horns. All foreigners wanting these goods had to approach the king through the *phrakhlang* minister.[10] The VOC was allowed to retain its export monopolies on deerskins and Ligor tin which it had been granted by kings Prasatthong and Narai, respectively. The above list is similar to the data on royal monopoly goods in La Loubère's work, though La Loubère includes sulphur and arms and does not mention lead, copper, sappanwood, eaglewood, or rhinoceros horn.[11]

The kingdom of Ayutthaya, then, required goods that could be obtained only through overseas trade. It also possessed a royal trading system that enabled it to play a part in international commerce. King Phetracha and other kings of the Ban Phlu Luang dynasty made full use of the fleet of crown ships and junks, the royal storehouses, and the royal monopoly system that had been built up over several decades during the seventeenth century.

Conflicts and Crises

Although King Phetracha's intention was to carry on trading with China, Japan, India, and the Dutch, events in Siam itself did not always facilitate the conduct of commerce. The rebellions, wars, and natural disasters that afflicted the Ayutthaya kingdom during his reign caused some inconvenience and uncertainty among foreign traders.

As an official who usurped the throne by eliminating two princes with legitimate claims to the succession, King Phetracha was often faced with internal unrest as well as conflicts with tributary states. During his fourteen-year reign there were at least two internal revolts and one war against a tributary state. The Siamese royal chronicles mention four rebellions, two at Khorat in the northeast, one in the central plains, and one at Ligor in the south.[12] The VOC records do not mention the second Khorat rebellion or the Ligor rebellion, but they contain fragmented data about a war between Ayutthaya and Patani in

---

[10]VOC 1536, "Translaet ordre voor den Hollandsen Capitain," fols. 112–113. The *phrakhlang* ministry or department was responsible for foreign relations and commerce.

[11]Simon de la Loubère, *The Kingdom of Siam* (rpt., Kuala Lumpur, 1969), pp. 94–95.

[12]"Phongsawadan Krung Si Ayutthaya chabap Phan Chanthanumat," in *Prachum Phongsawadan*, part. 64 (cremation volume, Bangkok, 1936), pp. 385–89. *Phraratchaphongsawadan Krungkao* (Dr. Bradley version, cremation volume, Bangkok, 1958), pp. 297–300, 301–4, 305–12, 315–18.

1691–92 as well as a conflict between Ayutthaya and Kedah in 1693. The Patani army inflicted a heavy defeat on the Ayutthaya forces, killing 6,000 Siamese troops. Trouble with Kedah began when the sultan of Kedah, emboldened by Patani's example, refused to send the *bunga mas* tribute to King Phetracha and even imprisoned the Ayutthaya envoys to Kedah.[13] Both conflicts seem to have remained at a stalemate for the rest of King Phetracha's reign.

Natural phenomena and epidemics could also affect foreign trade. In 1693 an epidemic in the northern provinces of Siam (Sukhothai, Phitsanulok, Kamphaengphet, and even as far east as Khorat) caused countless animals to die, thus hindering the trade in animal skins. The Dutch complained about this epidemic but thanked God that it did not kill any human beings.[14] But in 1696 a drought followed by "pestilentie" caused "thousands of men" to die in this same region. No one was able to collect forest produce such as deerskins, namrack, or sappanwood, leading to a shortage of these goods in Ayutthaya. Overseas trade did not come to a standstill, however, because at around this time King Phetracha and his son, the *phra maha uparat* (Prince Sorasak), compelled the Dutch to sell 1,000 pieces of buffalo hides and 5,500 pieces of deerskins to them so that they could assemble a suitable cargo for their Japan-bound junks.[15]

It would not be fair to dwell too much on these troubles and disasters, because they did not stop foreigners from coming to trade in Siam or the Siamese from trading abroad. One major reason foreigners were able to maintain contact with Siam was that within the court of Ayutthaya there were officials who were experienced in dealing with foreign traders—and who were in some cases traders themselves. Many of these officials were foreigners.

Foreigners at the Court of Ayutthaya

The employment of foreigners in royal service was not a new phenomenon. The Siamese port department (*krom tha*) during the Ayutthaya period was divided into two main sections, one under the supervision of a Chinese official (*chodük ratchasethi*) and the other under a

---

[13]*Generale Missiven van Gouverneurs-Generaal en raden aan Heren XVII der V.O.C.*, ed. W. Ph. Coolhaas, 9 vols. (The Hague, 1960–88), 31 Jan. 1692, 5:464; 9 Feb. 1693, 5:588; 6 Feb. 1694, 5:660.

[14]VOC 1536, van Son to governor-general, 27 Nov. 1693, fol. 94v.

[15]VOC 1580, van Son to governor-general, 27 Nov. 1696, fols. 171–72; *General Missiven* letter of 19 Feb. 1697, 5:829.

Muslim official (*čhula ratchamontri*).[16] Chinese and Muslim traders and seafarers had always been useful to the Ayutthaya kings. Portuguese, Cham, Malay, and Japanese mercenaries were also employed by the Siamese kings. The common feature linking all these foreigners was their special know-how. King Narai, being exceptionally interested in trade and diplomacy, employed Westerners as well as Asians. The Greek Constantine Phaulkon, the Englishman Samuel White ("Siamese White"), and the Frenchman the Chevalier de Forbin, were the major examples, but there were several others, such as the Frenchmen René Charbonneau (governor of Phuket) and Beauregard (governor of Mergui).[17] The events of 1688 put an end to this brief period of European participation in Siamese administration and internal politics.

The 1680s had demonstrated to the Siamese elite that it was potentially dangerous to employ so many Westerners in royal service. The Siamese kings from Phetracha onward did not trust Westerners enough to use them in administrative capacities. A Portuguese mestizo, "Jan Domingos de Matto," served King Sanphet VIII (Phráčhao Süa, r. 1703–9) as an envoy to the English East India Company in Madras, charged with the task of persuading the English company to return to trade in Siam. He was given the name and title of Okluang Ritthirawi.[18] King Phetracha himself did not employ any Westerners apart from a former VOC surgeon, Daniel Brochebourde, and his son Moses. Both surgeons were given Siamese ranks and titles, Moses Brochebourde succeeding his father as the king's surgeon in 1697 with the title of Opra Petosat (Okphra Phaetosot?).[19] In the reign of King Boromakot (1733–58) a grandson of Phaulkon, also named Constantine, is mentioned in both French and Dutch sources. French missionary sources call him Racha Mantri and say that he was both supervisor of the Christians at Ayutthaya and an overseer of the royal storehouses. Phaulkon's widow, Marie Guimar, served in the royal kitchens between 1717 and 1724.[20] That seems to be all that can be unearthed from the archives concerning Westerners in royal service after 1688.

The intellectual curiosity and receptiveness apparent in the Siamese court's earlier dealings with the West seem to have diminished greatly

[16]*Rüang Kotmai Trasamduang*, "Phra aiyakan tamnaeng na phonlarüan" (Bangkok, 1978), pp. 117–18.

[17]Hutchinson, 1940, pp. 48, 161; Nidhi Aeusrivongse, *Kanmuang Thai samai Phra Narai* (Bangkok, 1984), pp. 71–79, ascribes Narai's employment of foreigners to the king's distrust of Siamese officials and courtiers.

[18]VOC 1719, Cleur to governor-general, 22 Oct. 1706, fol. 1837.

[19]VOC 1609, Siam *dagregister* extracts, 18 Jan. 1698, fols. 4–7; VOC 1596, van Son to governor-general, 8 Dec. 1697, fol. 59.

[20]Hutchinson, 1940, pp. 194–96; VOC 2332, van den Heuvel to governor-general, 25 Jan. 1736, fol. 3574.

after 1688. Siamese kings no longer asked the Europeans to send technicians, soldiers, or craftsmen to work for them in Ayutthaya as King Prasatthong (r. 1629–56) and King Narai had done. The European era in the Ayutthayan court had indeed ended with Phaulkon's demise.

Other groups of foreigners, however, came back into prominence. The Jesuit Claude de Bèze related that during 1688 Phetracha had won the "Moors" over "by liberal treatment."[21] The "Moors" had ample reason to dislike Phaulkon and his Western friends, who had taken over their role in the king of Siam's India trade. The first pieces of evidence concerning the "Moors" in Ayutthaya during the post-1688 period are in the VOC archives and Engelbert Kaempfer's *Description of the Kingdom of Siam* (1690). Kaempfer refers to the presence of several "Moor" officials in the king of Siam's service and mentions in particular an Opera Tsijat (Okphra Siyot or perhaps Okphra Čhula) and an Oja Tewijata. Opera Tsijat, an Indian, was the king's *syahbandar* and head of the "Moor" community in Ayutthaya. Oja Tewijata, or Oya Thephiata, was even more powerful. According to VOC archival records, he was a Pathan whose real name was Hossen Chan (Hosain Khan?) and—as the king's bosom friend—a particularly influential man whose favor the Dutch sought. He was a skilled horseman, like King Phetracha and his son, Prince Sorasak, and his official position was equerry of the royal elephants. Hossen Chan was also involved in trade and bought spelter from the VOC in 1689–90, possibly for reexport to India. Dutch records dating from the later part of King Phetracha's reign do not mention Hossen Chan again.[22] Indeed, as the eighteenth century wore on, ever more Chinese officials rose to prominence at the Siamese court, overshadowing the "Moors."

In 1690, Kaempfer recounted that a learned Chinese held the position and title of *okya yomarat* (chief justice). King Phetracha must have received some support from the Chinese community in 1688, because on ascending the throne he gave the Chinese some property and employed several Chinese in the *phrakhlang* ministry. Toward the end of his reign, a Chinese court favorite rose to a position of great influence. In a letter of 31 January 1702, the VOC chief agent, Gideon Tant, wrote to the governor-general that the king's Chinese favorite, Okya Sombatthiban, had established a total dominance over foreign commerce in Ayutthaya. Not only had he monopolized the gumlac trade, but his

[21]Claude de Bèze, *Mémoir*, trans. with commentary by E. W. Hutchinson as *1688 Revolution in Siam* (Hong Kong, 1968), p. 111.

[22]VOC 1498, Wagensvelt to governor-general, 13 Jan. 1692, fol. 282v.; VOC 1485, van den Hoorn to governor-general, 5 Feb. 1690, fol. 119v.; VOC 1503, van Son to governor-general, 13 Dec. 1692, fols. 520–21; Engelbert Kaempfer, *A Description of the Kingdom of Siam, 1690*, trans. J. G. Scheuchzer (1727; rpt., Bangkok, 1987), pp. 28, 38.

political power was such that the requests of all foreign traders (the VOC included) had first to be submitted for his approval. Even the minister himself, Okya Phrakhlang, did not dare act on behalf of any foreign trader without Okya Sombatthiban's prior approbation.[23] By January 1703, Okya Sombatthiban had been promoted to assume the title and ministerial position of Okya Phrakhlang, but he remained in this capacity for only a short time. In February 1703, King Phetracha died and his eldest son, Prince Sorasak, succeeded to the throne as Sanphet VIII. The new king, better known as Phračhao Süa ("King Tiger"), had his half-brother Čhao Phra Khwan and his supporters killed in April 1703. The Chinese Okya Sombatthiban/Phrakhlang was among those executed.[24]

Phračhao Süa, too, had his Chinese favorites: another Okya Sombatthiban, an Okya Lauja, and an Okluang Phibun.[25] As the Chinese private junk trade with Ayutthaya reached a high point during King Thaisa's reign (1709–33), another Chinese became Okya Phrakhlang. Many Chinese immigrated into Siam, and Chinese officials and merchants continued to serve the kings of Siam right until the fall of Ayutthaya. The great general Phya Tak (Sin) who reunified Siam after 1767 was himself half-Chinese and had good connections with Chinese traders who helped revive the Siamese economy during the late eighteenth century.[26]

To sum up, the court of King Phetracha and his successors retained some of the cosmopolitanism of earlier years. Europeans no longer served as courtiers or administrators, but the "Moors" and Chinese returned to their dual prominence in the *phrakhlang* ministry. Malays and various mestizos (Japanese, Portuguese) also continued to work for the Ban Phlu Luang kings.[27] Given the Siamese kings' continued participation in international trade, such cosmopolitanism was not surprising.

Siamese Crown Shipping

Data obtained from primary sources concerning Siamese royal trade overseas during King Phetracha's reign are too sketchy to support any

---

[23]Kaempfer, 1987; VOC 1663, Tant to governor-general, 31 Jan. 1702, fols. 10, 24.

[24]VOC 1691, Cleur to governor of Malacca, 9 Feb. 1704, fols. 57–60.

[25]VOC 1691, Cleur's "Relaas," fols. 61–72; VOC 1743, Cleur's "Berigt" of 2 June 1707, fols. 83–84.

[26]Wyatt, 1984, pp. 140–41.

[27]VOC 1636, Tant to governor-general, 17 Jan. 1700, fol. ll, mentions a Japanese mestizo who held the position of *okya phonlathep*; Kaempfer, 1987, p. 39, mentions a Malay of *phya/phraya* rank.

statistical analysis, but they nevertheless give a fairly clear overall impression of this trade. Dutch records mention Siamese crown shipping regularly, largely because the king of Siam was the most considerable merchant in Ayutthaya and thus a key rival of the VOC. A notable feature of Siamese overseas trade during the seventeenth and early eighteenth centuries was the participation of several members of the royal family. During King Phetracha's reign Prince Sorasak also sent several ships to trade abroad, mainly to Japan and China but also to the Coromandel coast and Tonkin.[28]

VOC documents suggest that King Phetracha and Prince Sorasak sent out more ships to trade abroad during the years 1692–97 than during the last years of the reign. For example, the king sent four junks to Japan and one to China in 1692, and Prince Sorasak also had a junk fitted out for trade with China. But between December 1701 and October 1702, King Phetracha did not send any crown vessels abroad at all, and Prince Sorasak sent one junk to Japan and had a consignment of goods on a Batavia-bound Portuguese country trader's vessel.[29] There may have been several reasons for this temporary decline in Siamese crown trade overseas. One is that the crown's capacity to participate in international trade was declining because of a constant lack of silver. Another may have been that there was considerable internal unrest in Siam around the turn of the century, the Khorat rebellion lasting from 1699 to 1701.[30] It is also possible that foreign shipping during the 1698–1702 period brought in sufficient merchandise to satisfy the demands of the Siamese court.

The Japanese *ka'i-hentai* sources (shipping reports collected at Nagasaki) are detailed as far as Japan-bound Siamese and Chinese ships are concerned. The data from these invaluable documents tally (more or less) with the VOC sources on the number of junks sent by the Siamese king to Japan for the 1689–1703 period.[31] What makes the Dutch sources especially valuable is the amount of information they contain on Siamese crown shipping to other destinations.

According to the VOC records, King Phetracha and Prince Sorasak sent ships to China (in 1692, 1694, 1696, 1697), Manila (1693, 1694),

[28]Data from VOC records in the *Overgekomen Brieven en Papieren* series, for example from "Siam" documents in VOC 1541 (fols. 1087v–1088), VOC 1580 (fols. 32–33, 54–58), VOC 1596 (fol. 54), VOC 1676 (fols. 73–76, 76–77, 92–95).

[29]VOC 1503, van Son to governor-general, 13 Dec. 1692, fols. 530–31. See also sources mentioned in note 28.

[30]On the Khorat rebellion: VOC 1623, Tant to governor-general, 24 Nov. 1699, fol. 3, and 20 Dec. 1699, fol. 61. On shortage of silver: VOC 1580, van Son to governor-general, 25 Nov. 1695, fols. 12–15; VOC 1637, Tant to governor-general, 28 Dec. 1700, fols. 55–56.

[31]Sarasin Viraphol, *Tribute and Profit: Sino-Siamese Trade, 1652–1853* (Cambridge, Mass., 1977), pp. 260–61; Yoneo Ishii, "Seventeenth Century Japanese Documents about Siam," in *Collected Articles in Memory of H. R. H. Prince Wan Waithayakorn* (Bangkok, 1976), pp. 170–71.

Tonkin (1694), the Coromandel coast (1695, 1697, 1702), Surat (1703), and Batavia/Java (1702, 1703).[32] King Phetracha's court was interested in a few foreign commodities, either for use in Siam or for resale, and evidence shows that—like his predecessor, King Narai—he was willing to use crown ships to obtain these commodities at their source as well as to pick and choose from what foreign traders brought to Ayutthaya.

Sino-Siamese and Sino-Siamese-Japanese Triangular Trade

The subject of Sino-Siamese trade and tributary relations has been well researched, especially by Sarasin Viraphol, Jennifer Cushman, and Suebsaeng Promboon, and need not be explained here in any detail.[33] To sum up, during the late seventeenth and first half of the eighteenth centuries there was a thriving commerce between Siam and China, in spite of temporary restrictions imposed by the Ch'ing government such as the revival of the maritime ban in December 1716. Indeed, Chinese shipping of one kind or another dominated the Southeast Asian–South China Sea region. When the *hai-chin* (maritime ban) on Chinese overseas trade was lifted in 1684, there began a steady upsurge in the Sino-Siamese junk trade and a corresponding increase in Chinese immigration into Siam. The forms the Sino-Siamese trade relationship now took consisted of the traditional Sino-Siamese tributary trade, the Sino-Siamese private junk trade, and the Sino-Siamese-Japanese triangular trade (including participation by Siamese royal junks).[34]

Siamese tributary missions to China stopped temporarily during the 1689–1707 period. No missions were dispatched during King Phetracha's reign and only one during Phračhao Süa's reign (in 1708).[35] For the Siamese court, this temporary lull in Sino-Siamese diplomacy was offset by the number of Chinese junks coming to Ayutthaya and by crown junks participating in the Sino-Siamese-Japanese trade. During King Phetracha's reign, the number of Chinese junks coming to Ayutthaya far outnumbered other nations' vessels. In 1697, for instance, at

[32]Data from *Overgekomen Brieven en Papieren* series; see note 28.
[33]Sarasin Viraphol, 1977; Jennifer Wayne Cushman, "Fields from the Sea: Chinese Junk Trade with Siam during the Late Eighteenth and Early Nineteenth Centuries," Ph. D. diss., Cornell University, 1976; Suebsaeng Promboon, *Khwam samphan nai rabob bannakan rawang thai kab chin*, trans. Kanchanee La-ongsri, ed. Charnvit Kasetsiri (Bangkok, 1982).
[34]Sarasin, 1977, pp. 47, 59–60.
[35]Suebsaeng, 1982, p. 68.

least ten Chinese junks were reported to have come to Ayutthaya—
and this in a year of supposedly stagnant foreign trade in Siam. In a
good year such as 1695, as many as twenty Chinese junks traded at
Ayutthaya. During that year all the tin available in Ayutthaya was sold
to the Chinese.[36] The upturn in the Sino-Siamese-Japanese triangular
trade meant that the competition to assemble cargoes of goods that
could be sold in Japan became keenly contested in Ayutthaya between
the Chinese and the Dutch (who also traded at Nagasaki), with the
Siamese crown having a monopoly of most goods. These goods included sappanwood and tin. Deerskins were a VOC export monopoly,
but such was the royal trading system in Siam that the king and his son
were able to compel the Dutch to sell them deerskins whenever the
need arose. In 1697, King Phetracha sent two junks to Japan and
bought 10,000 animal skins from the VOC to form part of his cargo. In
1699, the king and Prince Sorasak sent one junk each to Japan, laden
with sappanwood, tin, sugar, namrack, silk, and 8,000 animal skins.[37]
The Siamese junks going to Japan often stopped at a Chinese port on
the way back to Siam, selling Japanese copper and other goods and
then buying a new cargo to take to Ayutthaya.[38] It was therefore already apparent, from the 1680s onward, that Chinese trade with Siam
would become more extensive and lucrative than before. It is no surprise that King Phetracha and Prince Sorasak seized this opportunity to
increase their revenues through participation in international trade.

Indian Textiles, Siamese Elephants, and Horses

Siam's trade with India during the years 1688–1703 appears to have
declined from the high point reached during the reigns of King Prasatthong and King Narai, when several Muslim traders from India, Persia,
Arabia, and even Turkey came to Siam, some of them becoming high-
ranking servants of the Siamese crown.[39] But Ayutthaya and Mergui,
Siam's key port on the Bay of Bengal, still traded with India, ships from
the subcontinent calling at Mergui regularly. Since Indian textiles were
considered to be essential imports by the Siamese court, serious efforts

[36]VOC 1596, van Son to governor-general, 8 Dec. 1697, fols. 53–54; VOC 1580, van Son to
governor-general, 25 Nov. 1695, fols. 17–18.
[37]VOC 1596, van Son to governor-general, 8 Dec. 1697, fol. 38; VOC 1623, shipping list, fols.
110–13.
[38]Sarasin, 1977, chap. 4.
[39]Ibn Muhammad Ibrahim, 1972, pp. 94–106; Dhiravat na Pombejra, "A Political History of
Siam under the Prasatthong Dynasty, 1629–1688," Ph. D. diss., University of London, 1984,
pp. 81–82, 325–32.

were made to ensure availability of these goods. In 1697 the king had a new ship and two more sloops built at Mergui for use in trade with the Coromandel, the most important source of the textiles wanted by the court. King Phetracha and Prince Sorasak sent Siamese elephants to be sold in India, along with ivory, tin, spelter, and Japanese copper. The trading was done on behalf of the king and prince largely by "Moor" servants of the Siamese court, as had been the case during King Narai's reign.[40]

A notable feature of Siamese royal trade to India was the revival of the trade in elephants and elephant teeth. King Phetracha sent elephants to be sold on the Coromandel coast in 1695, and in that same year Prince Sorasak also sent a ship to trade there laden with twenty elephants.[41] In addition to Coromandel, Surat, and Bengal piece goods, the king also wanted Indian (Persian?) horses. He and Prince Sorasak ordered horses from India, Java, the Philippine Islands, and China. The Siamese court's interest in fine horses had in fact begun during King Narai's reign, when horses were bought from Java. During the eighteenth century Javanese horses became the foreign horses most sought after by the Siamese kings, presumably for use in their cavalry force. Toward the end of his reign King Phetracha sent a barque to Java (via Batavia) laden with gifts for the *susuhunan* (ruler) of Mataram. These gifts included two elephants, Chinese inlaid mother-of-pearl boxes, tin, and Japanese copper. The true objective of this expedition was probably to facilitate arrangements for buying Javanese horses. The Siamese court also depended on Dutch good will, because its horsebuyers often traveled on VOC Batavia-bound vessels.[42]

Although there was no definite break in the trading relationship between Siam and various ports in India during the 1688–1703 period, the Siamese-"Moor"/Indian trade was less dynamic than during the pre-1688 period. During 1697, the VOC was urged by the Siamese court to bring more Indian textiles to Siam because there was a shortage. The VOC *opperhoofd* van Son explained that this shortage of Indian cloth was a result of the Siamese court's mistreatment of foreign traders, who had therefore been deterred from calling at Siamese ports.[43] If there were complaints against the Siamese authorities, then there were

[40]VOC 1596, van Son to governor-general, 8 Dec. 1697, fol. 54; VOC 1676, Phrakhlang's *tra*, 21 Nov. 1702, fols. 73–74, and Okya Phiphat's order, 29 Nov. 1702, fols. 76–77.

[41]VOC 1580, van Son to governor-general, 25 Nov. 1695, fols. 32–35.

[42]VOC 1676, Tant to governor-general, 1 Feb. 1703, fols. 92–95; *Ruang Kotmai Trasamduang*, pp. 131–33 (on Siamese cavalry).

[43]VOC 1596, van Son to governor-general, 8 Dec. 1697, fol. 53.

also complaints directed against the Indian authorities. In 1695 or 1696, the *chaophraya phrakhlang* wrote to Mustapha Kulikhan in Masulipatnam to complain that the Siamese king's factors had received unfair treatment from the Masulipatnam authorities, having had to pay tolls even though the emperor Aurangzeb had issued a decree allowing the Siamese king's men to trade in India without having to pay any. Furthermore, the minister claimed, the Siamese had been faithful to the terms of this reciprocal arrangement, not levying any tolls on the Mughal emperor's subjects trading in Siam.[44] The Siamese crown factors may not have levied tolls, but they were said to have bought textiles from a Surat "Moor" ship at very low prices in 1701.[45] The "Moors" may have been hampered too by the turbulent conditions in India during the 1690s.

King Phetracha and the VOC: Mutual Disappointment

King Phetracha's eagerness to renew the 1664 Treaty and Alliance of Peace with the VOC in late 1688 gave the Dutch hope for trouble-free, profitable commerce in Ayutthaya. This hope was to be consistently disappointed, not only during King Phetracha's reign but throughout the rest of the Ayutthaya period. The renewal of the 1664 treaty on 14 November 1688 confirmed that the VOC was to retain its deerskin export monopoly in Siam, its "perfect freedom to carry on trade" in all Siamese ports, and its liberty to trade with "all persons, no matter what rank they occupy." In November 1688 an additional clause was added to this treaty, a confirmation of the VOC's export monopoly on Ligor tin, granted to it by King Narai in 1671.[46]

The Dutch had frequent disputes with the court and the crown's factors concerning matters such as the pricing of commodities, the Siamese king's debt to the company, and the inability of the VOC to obtain much tin from Ligor in spite of having a monopoly. Some of the VOC's merchants in Ayutthaya were also unable to get along with Siamese officials (for instance Pieter van den Hoorn, *opperhoofd* be-

---

[44]VOC 1580, Phrakhlang to Mustapha Kulikhan, fol. 117; VOC 1517, Phrakhlang to governor-general, fols. 446–47.

[45]VOC 1663, Tant to governor-general, 31 Jan. 1702, fols. 31–32.

[46]George Vinal Smith, *The Dutch in Seventeenth-Century Thailand* (De Kalb, Ill., 1977), pp. 41, 138; Jan J. Boeles, "Note on the Treaty between Siam and the Netherlands of 1688 A.D. in Thai," in *Proceedings of the International Conference on Thai Studies*, vol. 3 (Bangkok, 1984).

tween 1688 and 1691, and Thomas van Son, *opperhoofd* between 1692 and 1697). The VOC, on whom the Siamese court hoped to rely for supplies of silver currency and Indian textiles, overpriced their textiles (insisting on at least a 50 percent profit) and once exchanged some silver with Chinese traders in Ayutthaya rather than with the royal treasury, incurring Siamese wrath.[47]

If the Dutch became more disenchanted with the Siamese court, then the Siamese were also disappointed with the Dutch. The Dutch were unable to supply Ayutthaya with as much silver currency (Spanish reals of eight) as the Siamese demanded, at a time when the court was desperately short of silver. Also, the VOC itself was on the decline generally. In Siam it could not cope with Chinese competition, especially the Sino-Siamese-Japanese trade. The Dutch complained of stagnant trade in Siam, but during King Phetracha's reign over fifty Chinese junks came to Ayutthaya, and Ayutthaya sent thirty *tosen* junks to trade at Nagasaki, with Ligor and Songkhla also sending junks to trade in Japan.[48] Such data prove that there was no stagnation of foreign trade overall, and that it was largely from the VOC's point of view that trade had been a grave disappointment.

Things did not improve after the death of King Phetracha. In 1705 the VOC withdrew temporarily from Siam after disputes with the Siamese court over the pricing of goods, royal monopoly practices, and the VOC Ligor office's inability to obtain enough tin. The VOC's trade in Siam sputtered on for a few more decades, the company closing down its Ayutthaya and Ligor offices again in 1741 after a dispute with King Boromakot. The Ligor office remained closed for the rest of the Ayutthaya period, but it appears that around late 1742 the Ayutthaya office was reopened. The VOC's eighteenth-century records contain reports about whether to continue trading in Siam. The office was not making a profit (but then most other VOC offices were also suffering losses), the Siamese officials were uncooperative, and there was some private trading on the part of VOC employees in Ayutthaya. But, despite all these problems, the VOC kept its Ayutthaya office open, partly because Siamese sappanwood was still valuable to the company, partly because Siamese rice was useful in times of emergency, and also because the Dutch feared that other European powers might step in should they decide to leave. When in late 1765 the last VOC resident left Ayutthaya, the Burmese were already at the gates of the city.[49]

[47]Smith, 1977, pp. 45, 147; *Generale Missiven*, 30 Nov. 1697, 5:842.
[48]Sarasin, 1977, pp. 55, 260–61, 266–67.
[49]Han ten Brummelhuis, *Merchant, Courtier, and Diplomat: A History of the Contacts between the Netherlands and Thailand* (Lochem, The Netherlands, 1987), pp. 45, 49–50.

Other Westerners in Ayutthaya

If the Chinese and the Dutch were gratified by the immediate effects of 1688, the French must have felt the opposite. The French, with their garrisons in Bangkok and Mergui and their association with Phaulkon, were the natural targets of the Phetracha party. Having withdrawn their garrisons in late 1688, they did not try to return to Siam immediately afterward. Bangkok garrison commander General Desfarges occupied Phuket temporarily during 1689 but failed to effect a reconciliation with the Siamese court.[50] Fortunately for Ayutthaya, the French were too busy fighting the War of the League of Augsburg (1688–97) and later the War of the Spanish Succession (1701–13/14) to have the time or resources to spare for reprisal against the Siamese. When the French were once again free to expand their trading empire in the East, they concentrated on India rather than Southeast Asia.

One Frenchman who persisted in trying to reestablish a French trading and political presence in Ayutthaya was the Jesuit Guy Tachard. Father Tachard made two fruitless attempts, in 1690 and 1697–99, to persuade King Phetracha and his *phrakhlang* minister (the former Siamese ambassador to France, Kosa Pan) to allow the French Compagnie des Indes to return to Siam. A letter of 1699 from King Phetracha to King Louis XIV was courteous but hardly warm or welcoming. In 1700, Bishop Quémener came to Ayutthaya via Mergui with a request to the *phrakhlang* asking for an audience with the king. Quémener's task was to reestablish ties between King Louis XIV and the king of Siam and to ask that the French company be allowed to set up a factory at Mergui. The Siamese court maintained its aloofness, rejecting the French request concerning Mergui.[51]

Those Frenchmen who stayed on in Siam after 1688 were the missionaries of the Société des Missions Etrangères and assorted ex-employees of King Narai such as René Charbonneau, former governor of Phuket. The missionaries suffered considerably during the immediate aftermath of the 1688 coup, a period Adrien Launay called the years of persecution. Bishop Laneau and his fellow missionaries were imprisoned until April 1691, when they were released and allowed to carry on their work in Siam, teaching and proselytizing. In 1706 their seminary at Ayutthaya contained Siamese, Cochinchinese, Tonkinese, Chinese, Bengali, Portuguese-Mon, Japanese-Mon, and other mestizo students. The missionaries also worked in the Mergui and Chantabun

[50]Hutchinson, 1940, pp. 180, 182–83.
[51]Hutchinson, 1940, pp. 184–89; Adrien Launay, *Histoire de la mission de Siam, 1662–1811: Documents historiques*, 2 vols. (Paris, 1920), 2:20, 29, 33–41.

Figure 14. French soldiers assisting Siamese forces in Narai's reign, as depicted in a Thai painting of the period. From Paknam, *Farang rai sinlapa Thai* [Westerners in Thai Art] (Bangkok, 1986).

areas, but it appears that the number of converts remained disappointingly low. King Phetracha was not intrinsically anti-Catholic, as otherwise he would have chased the French missionaries out of Siam when he had the opportunity to do so in 1688. His actions were those of a shrewd politician, not a religious bigot. During King Narai's reign the French missionaries had been given land, building materials, and access to the king, but after 1691 they were merely tolerated. Some of them, like the saintly Laneau (Bishop of Metellopolis), were respected, but the missionaries were certainly not pampered or favored by any of the Ban Phlu Luang kings.[52]

In 1688 the English East India Company was still officially at war with Siam. In 1689 the council at Fort St. George in Madras debated whether to send ships to attack Mergui but decided against it, resolving instead to demand from King Phetracha payment of the company's claims against King Narai. King Phetracha repudiated all responsibility for the debts contracted while Phaulkon was in charge of Siam's foreign affairs.[53] There was little the company could do about the matter short of sending ships to attack or blockade Siam. The company's return to Siam during King Narai's reign had been a fiasco, and the Court of Committees in London did not rate Siam very highly: "Syam never did nor never will bring the Company two-pence advantage, but many thousands of pounds loss. It serves the Dutch well with Deer Skins for their Japan trade and with Provisions and Timber for Batavia, and may serve you and particular Merchants for sale of some Choromandel Commodities, and therefore spend none of our Money about it."[54]

The Englishmen who came to trade in Siam during the 1688–1703 period (and indeed right up to 1767) were country traders based in India. They brought cargoes of Indian textiles to Ayutthaya, some of which was from the East India Company's stock. In 1692 two English ships (possibly those of William Keeling and Lemuel Blackmore) came to Ayutthaya with a cargo of textiles, and in 1694 the Englishman Samuel Baron came to Ligor from Madras. The English country traders bought tin, copper, and spelter from Siam for resale in India. During the eighteenth century English country traders, such as members of the Madras-based Powney family, continued to frequent Siam.[55]

The Portuguese village or *campo* in Ayutthaya was a mestizo community that had been living in Siam for several generations. These mestizos were united by their common faith (or at least a nominal allegiance to Roman Catholicism). In 1688 some Portuguese (along with Spaniards and Armenian Christians) were caught up in the upheavals and arrested by Siamese officials who were hoping for rich ransoms, but they were soon released. The Portuguese were allowed their usual freedom to worship and to trade, and presumably some continued to

---

[52]Launay, 1920, 1:219–22, 247–49, 268–70.

[53]*Records of the Relations between Siam and Foreign Countries in the Seventeenth Century*, 5 vols. (Bangkok, 1921), 5:48–49 (Court of Committees to Fort St. George, 27 Aug. 1688), 5:95–96 (Consultation, Fort St. George, 7 March 1689); Hutchinson, 1940, pp. 189–90.

[54]*Records*, 1921, 5:113 (Court of Committees to Fort St. George, 18 Feb. 1691).

[55]VOC 1541, van Son to governor-general, 15 Dec. 1694, fol. 1092v; *Records*, 5:130 (Fort St. George to EIC, 12 June 1693).

serve the Siamese king as mercenaries. Priests of the Dominican, Augustinian, and Jesuit orders continued their work within the Portuguese village at Ayutthaya. Portuguese country traders based in Ayutthaya also carried on a regular trade, their ships plying between Ayutthaya and Batavia or Manila. Batavia-based mestizos and Melaka burghers also participated in this trade. In common with Portuguese communities elsewhere in Asia, the Portuguese in Ayutthaya maintained contact with the larger colonial settlements at Macao and Goa, though the records do not mention much Macao or Goa shipping to Ayutthaya.[56] More research needs to be done on Portuguese (and Spanish) contacts with post-1688 Ayutthaya before a clearer picture can emerge.

Siam, Cambodia, and Lanchang

I have paid little attention to Siam's neighbors in mainland Southeast Asia, partly because Ayutthaya's relations with Burma, Cambodia, and Lanchang do not give any useful indications as to whether Ayutthaya had become isolationist or not. But a cursory look at Siamese relations with Cambodia and Lanchang during King Phetracha's reign does give some idea of how Ayutthaya viewed itself in the regional context.

During the eighteenth century Siam and Vietnam both sought to establish hegemony over Cambodia. The internal politics of Cambodia were extremely unstable, and the perennial court conflicts in this kingdom led to differing factions seeking outside aid—from Ayutthaya, from the Nguyen kings of Vietnam, and from other groups. The Ayutthayan kings had always claimed suzerainty over Cambodia, at least from the late sixteenth century, but were unable to compel the Cambodian kings to send regular tribute to Ayutthaya. Kings Thaisa and Boromakot were both concerned enough by events in eighteenth-century Cambodia to send armies to fight there in 1720 and in 1749–50, both campaigns involving a struggle against Cambodian kings who had Vietnamese support.[57] During King Phetracha's reign, c. 1695, a white elephant was found in Cambodia. The Siamese king sent an embassy to Cambodia to ask for this elephant, but the Cambodian ruler refused to hand over the sacred animal. The Cambodian king then sent an embassy to Ayutthaya, bringing fifty praus as presents for King

---

[56]Adrien Launay, *Histoire de la Mission de Siam* (Paris, 1920), pp. 75–77; VOC 1609, fols. 47–49; VOC 1648, fols. 135–39; VOC 1663, fols. 58–61; VOC 1676, fols. 86–89 (shipping lists): "Siam" documents; Kaempfer, 1987, pp. 51–52.

[57]Wyatt, 1984, pp. 126, 129–30.

Phetracha, but the latter (who would have preferred the white elephant) refused to accept these boats and sent them back to Cambodia. Forty Cambodians who came with this mission were also put in prison, from which they escaped in 1698, an incident that led to fears about an imminent war.[58] These fears were not realized, but Siam's attitude toward Cambodia at the end of the seventeenth century was indicative of an assumed superiority (that of suzerain over vassal), an attitude that was to last well into the nineteenth century.

Nothing is recorded in Siamese, French, or Dutch sources about Siamese relations with Burma during the years 1688–1703, a period when Ava was in the throes of administrative decay.[59] The Siamese were not strong or interested enough to exploit Burmese weakness, and by the late 1750s it was Ava that had become the more dynamic and expansionist kingdom. Ayutthaya's contacts with the Lao kingdom of Lanchang during the 1688–1703 period are also largely unrecorded. Dutch records, however, mention that in April 1702 Prince Sorasak married a Lao princess, "daughter of the king of Lanchang."[60] It is not known which "king of Lanchang" the Dutch were referring to because the Lanchang kingdom had, after 1698, begun to disintegrate.

It is no longer possible to argue that Ayutthaya adopted an isolationist approach to foreign trade or foreign affairs after 1688. There was a narrower range of contacts with foreign nations, with fewer European traders in Siam and fewer Siamese embassies sent abroad. But the Siamese never stopped engaging in overseas trade. That the volume of trade seems to have varied from year to year, depending on internal as well as external factors, does not indicate any isolationism on the part of the Siamese. As for the post-1688 reaction against employing Westerners at court or in the royal trade system, it was not so much xenophobic as cautious, an expression of the elite's wish to return to the pre-Narai status quo.

Did developments after 1688 constitute a decline? The question of Ayutthaya's decline is a vexed one. It is tempting to rely too much on hindsight and explain that Ayutthaya's final defeat and destruction in 1767 was the result of a general decline. There were indeed several conflicts among the princes and high officials during the 1688–1767 period, state control over manpower resources was not as efficient as it should have been, and the last Ayutthaya king was not an able

[58]VOC 1609, Siam *dagregister* extracts, 18 Jan. 1698, fols. 5–7.

[59]Victor B. Lieberman, *Burmese Administrative Cycles* (Princeton, N.J., 1984), chaps.3–4, esp. pp. 224–28.

[60]VOC 1676, Tant to governor-general, 29 Jan. 1703, fols. 60–61.

ruler. These factors, along with that of Burma's resurgence under Al-aunghpaya, were important reasons for the kingdom's defeat, but they are not in themselves indicative of a decline in Ayutthayan civilization. The issues of administrative decline and cultural decline have to be analyzed separately. If the analytical framework of the administrative cycle[61] is used, then the Ayutthaya kingdom was indeed declining as an administrative unit, with weaknesses in the system being exploited to the full by princes, high officials, and other groups within the state.

The interpretation of post-1688 Siam as being in an age of general decline, however, may be contradicted by evidence concerning culture, religion, material prosperity, and trade. Quite apart from evidence of Sino-Siamese trade and other royal trade overseas, there are also accounts that emphasize Siam's prosperity, such as the account of the Sinhalese envoys to Ayutthaya in 1751. Indeed, the "golden age" of Ayutthayan history is sometimes identified as being the reign of King Boromakot (1733–58). During his long reign, splendid *wat* (temples) were built, expanded, or restored. Siamese Buddhism was considered doctrinally pure and the Sinhalese court at Kandy actually asked Siamese priests to go to Ceylon to ordain and teach Sinhalese monks. Literature also flourished under royal patronage: King Boromakot's own son, Čhaofa Thammathibet, was one of the greatest Siamese lyric poets.[62]

Isolation and decline, then, are two concepts that do not explain late Ayutthayan history adequately. The reality must have been more complex, as even this tentative study of King Phetracha's reign shows. What is now needed is more research, using Dutch, Portuguese, and French missionary sources, so that a detailed analysis of post-1688 Ayutthaya in the wider context of Southeast Asian history may be attempted.

[61]Lieberman, 1984, pp. 3–14, 271–92; Busakorn, 1972, pp. 166–82.

[62]Busakorn, 1972, p. 105; Rong Syamananda, *A History of Thailand* (Bangkok, 1977), pp. 87–88; K. W. Goonewardena, "Ayutthia in the Twilight Years and Its Triangular Relations with the V.O.C. and Sri Lanka," *Sri Lanka Journal of the Humanities* 6, nos. 1-2 (1980), 1, 36–37, 45–47.

Glossary

Abbreviations: (A) Arabic, (D) Dutch, (J) Javanese, (M) Malay, (P) Portuguese, (Pa) Pali, (S) Spanish, (Sk) Sanskrit, (T) Ternatan, (Th) Thai

adat (A/M)	custom
arak (M)	distilled (rice) wine
bad-luang (Th)	priest
bahar/bahara (M)	measure of weight, equivalent to 3 *pikul*. Variable, but approximately 180 kilograms for pepper
beli-belian (M)	mutual sale
bendahara (M)	principal official in Malay kingdoms
bobato (T)	"regulators"; chiefs
bovenlander (D)	uplander
bunga mas (M)	golden flower, the form in which tribute was sent to Siam
cakravartin (Sk)	world ruler
candi (J/M)	Hindu-Buddhist shrine
casado (P)	married Portuguese settled in the East
cash (Anglo-Indian)	Copper or lead-tin alloy coin of low denomination, especially Chinese. From Portuguese *caixes* (see Javanese *picis*)
casis (P)	see *kadi*

celates (P)	people of the Straits of Malacca (Malay *selat*); *orang laut*
cruzado (P)	Portuguese gold coin
dato (M)	elder, chief; also chiefly title
derhaka (M)	disloyalty
dewaraja (Sk)	god-king
dusun (M)	hill garden, orchard
extirpatie (D)	extirpation, notably of plants
fiqh (A)	(Islamic) jurisprudence
hajj (A)	pilgrimage to Mecca
hamba (M)	dependent or slave
hilir (M)	flowing down; downstream
hukum (A/M)	decree, law; in Ternate, a magistrate
hulu (M)	head; upriver
jenang (M)	royal representative; overseer
jihad (A)	holy war
jinn (A)	spirits, created by God out of flame
jong (J/M)	junk; large trading vessel
kadi (A/M)	judge in Islamic law
kafir (A/M)	infidel; unbeliever
kati (M)	Malay equivalent of Chinese pound (*chin*). One-hundredth of a *pikul*, or approx. 0.6 kilograms. English catty.
khunnang (Th)	nobility
kolano (T)	lord; chief of settlement
kora-kora (T)	fast galley with outriggers
kris (M/J)	dagger
kupang (M)	small gold coin, usually one quarter of a *mas*
laksamana (M)	admiral; court official
last (D)	Dutch weight for bulk cargo, about 1.5 metric tons.
mas (M)	gold; gold coin issued by Aceh, Makassar, and some Malay states
mendelika (M)	provincial governors

merantau (M)	travel in search of fortune
mestizo (S)	person of mixed race
müang (Th)	land, principality; the town, with or without its dependent villages, ruled by a lord (*chao*).
muhsan (A)	legally responsible married male
mukim (A/M)	Islamic parish; in Aceh, a territorial division
nakhoda (M)	shipowner or his representative on the ship; supercargo
nao (P)	large freight-carrying ship
nat (B)	household spirit
negeri (M)	settlement, city, state
opperhoofd (D)	head of (VOC) office
orang besar (M)	chief, notable
orang hulu (M)	highlanders
orang kaya (M)	aristocrats, generally with wealth from trade
orang laut (M)	sea nomads (see *celates*)
panglima (M)	war leader; royal representative
pasisir (J)	northern coast of Javanese-speaking area
penghulu (M)	headman; superintendent
peso (P)	weight; port duty in Melaka
pétak (M)	partition, notably of a ship's hold
phrayamahanakhon (Th)	provinces governed by princes
piagem (J)	written authority
picis (J/M)	vulgar coin of lead, lead/tin, or copper, with hole in center to facilitate stringing (see *cash*)
pikul (M)	weight a man can carry on shoulder-pole; about 62.5 kilograms.
prakhlang (Th)	minister of finance, and his *krom* (service group)
raja (Sk/M)	king
raja muda (M)	junior king; heir apparent
raka' (A)	ritual movements in prayer
rantau (Minangkabau)	frontier areas
real (S)	*peso de ocho*, or piece of eight; standard Spanish coin of 25.5 grams silver

sakdina (Th)	dignity marks
sancrat	*see* sangharaja
sangha (Pa)	Buddhist monkhood
sangharaja (Pa)	patriarch of the *sangha*
saudagar raja (M)	king's merchant
sawah (J/M)	flooded rice field
shahada (A)	Islamic confession of faith ("There is no God but God, and Muhammad is His Prophet")
Shari'a (A/M)	Islamic law
syahbandar (M)	harbormaster
syeich (A/M)	honorific; head of a mystical order (*tariqa*)
tahil (M)	Malay equivalent of Chinese ounce (*liang*), one-sixteenth of a *kati*
tasbih (A)	Islamic rosary
temenggong (M)	senior official, often with police powers
thammasat (Th)	Buddhist legal canon (Pali: *dhammasattham*)
Tipitaka (Pa)	The Pali canon of Buddhism
tombo (P)	cadastral survey
tosen (Japanese)	Chinese junks (trading to Nagasaki)
tukang (M)	craftsman; on a ship, deck officer
ulama (A/M)	Islamic scholars (plural in Arabic, but here used also for singular)
ulèëbalang (Aceh)	war leader (see Malay *hulubalang*), though evolving into territorial chief
VOC (D)	Dutch East India Company (Vereenigde Oost-Indische Compagnie)
wali (A)	saint; in Java, the semilegendary apostles of Islam
wat (Th)	Buddhist temple
wong ratchathani (Th)	capital province
zina (A/M)	fornication

Contributors

BARBARA WATSON ANDAYA is a Lecturer in History of the University of Auckland, New Zealand. Her publications include *Perak, the Abode of Grace: A Study of an Eighteenth Century Malay State* (Kuala Lumpur, 1979), and "The Cloth Trade in Jambi and Palembang Society during the Seventeenth and Eighteenth Centuries," *Indonesia* 48 (1989). She coauthored with Leonard Andaya *A History of Malaysia* (London, 1982).

LEONARD Y. ANDAYA teaches in the Department of History at the University of Auckland. His most recent book, *The World of Maluku: A History of Eastern Indonesia in the Sixteenth, Seventeenth, and Eighteenth Centuries*, is in press. His earlier publications include *The Kingdom of Johor, 1641–1728* (Kuala Lumpur, 1975) and *The Heritage of Arung Palakka: A History of South Sulawesi (Celebes) in the Seventeenth Century* (The Hague, 1981) as well as *A History of Malaysia* written with Barbara Watson Andaya.

YONEO ISHII is Professor of Southeast Asian History in the Faculty of Foreign Studies and the Institute of Asian Cultures of Sophia University (Tokyo). Former director of the Centre for Southeast Asian Studies at Kyoto University, he is the author of *Sangha, State, and Society: Thai Buddhism in History* (Honolulu, 1986) and the editor of *Thailand: A Rice-Growing Society* (Honolulu, 1978). He coedited *The Computer Concordance to the Law of the Three Seals*, 5 vols. (Bangkok, 1990).

JEYAMALAR KATHIRITHAMBY-WELLS is Professor of Asian History at the University of Malaya. Her publications include *The British West Sumatran Presidency (1760–85): Problems of Early Colonial Enterprise* (Kuala Lumpur, 1976). She coedited with John Villiers *The Southeast Asian Port and Polity: Rise and Demise* (Singapore, 1990).

277

VICTOR LIEBERMAN is Professor of Southeast Asian History at the University of Michigan. His publications include *Burmese Administrative Cycles: Anarchy and Conquest, c. 1580–1760* (Princeton, N.J., 1984) and *Eurasian Variants: A Comparative History of Early Modern Southeast Asia* (forthcoming).

PIERRE-YVES MANGUIN is presently chargé de recherche at the Ecole Française d'Extrême Orient and chargé de conférences at the Ecole Pratique des Hautes Etudes (IVe section). He specializes in maritime history and archeology of insular Southeast Asia. He is the author of *Les Portugais sur les côtes du Viet-Nam et du Campa* (Paris, 1972) and *Les Nguyen, Macau et le Portugal* (Paris, 1984).

DHIRAVAT NA POMBEJRA teaches in the Department of History at Chulalongkorn University (Bangkok). He is coauthor of *The Dutch East Indies Company in Japan, Siam, and Indonesia* (Amsterdam, 1982) and author of articles including "Crown Trade and Court Politics in Ayutthaya during the Reign of King Narai (1656–88)" in *The Southeast Asian Port and Polity: Rise and Demise* (Singapore, 1990).

ANTHONY REID is Professor of Southeast Asian History in the Research School of Pacific Studies of the Australian National University (Canberra). His most recent book is the two-volume *Southeast Asia in the Age of Commerce, 1450–1680* (New Haven, Conn., 1988 and forthcoming). He has edited *Slavery, Bondage, and Dependency in Southeast Asia* (New York, 1983) and coedited *Pre-Colonial State Systems in Southeast Asia* (Kuala Lumpur, 1975) and *Perceptions of the Past in Southeast Asia* (Singapore, 1979).

KEITH W. TAYLOR is Professor of Asian Studies at Cornell University and author of *The Birth of Vietnam* (Berkeley, Calif., 1983).

LUIS FILIPE FERREIRA REIS THOMAZ is Professor of Overseas History at the Universidade Nova de Lisboa. His publications include *De Malaca a Pegu: Viagens de um feitor Português (1512–1515)* (Lisbon, 1966) and "Les Portugais dans les mers de l'Archipel au XVIe siècle," *Archipel* 18 (1979).

Index

279

Library of Congress Cataloging-in-Publication Data

Southeast Asia in the early modern era : trade, power, and belief /
   edited by Anthony Reid.
      p.   cm.—(Asia, east by south)
   Includes bibliographical references and index.
   ISBN 0-8014-2848-3.—ISBN 0-8014-8093-0
   1. Asia, Southeastern—History.   I. Reid, Anthony, 1939–
II. Series.
DS526.4.S68   1993
959—dc20   92-54969